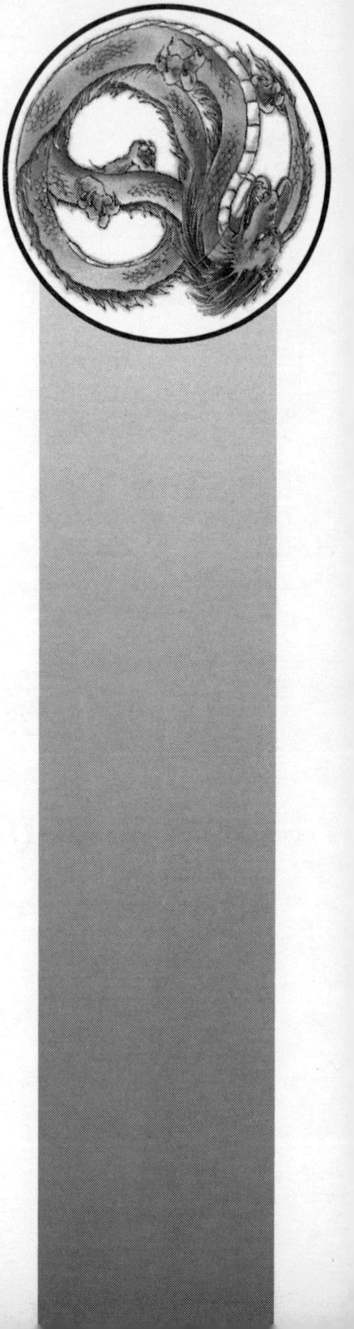

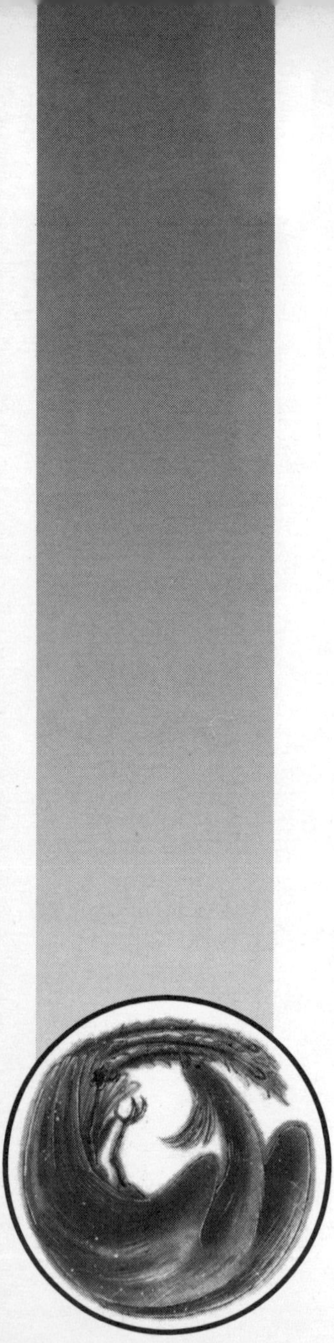

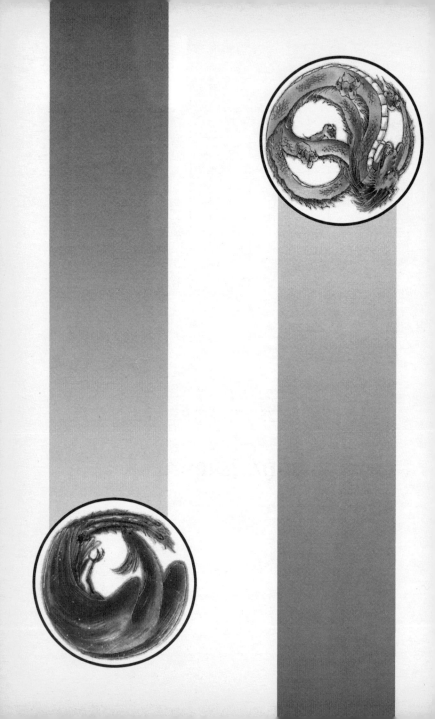

fushigi yûgi™

The Mysterious Play
VOL. 1: PRIESTESS

FUSHIGI YÛGI
THE MYSTERIOUS PLAY, VOL. 1: PRIESTESS
Gollancz Manga Edition

STORY AND ART BY YUU WATASE

English Adaptation/Yuji Oniki
Translation Assist./Kaori Kawakubo Inoue
Touch-Up & Lettering/Andy Ristaino
Cover, Graphics & Design/Hidemi Sahara
Editor/William Flanagan and Elizabeth Kawasaki
UK Cover Adaptation/Sue Michenwicz

First published by Shogakukan Inc. in Japan as "Fushigi Yugi"
English publication rights in United Kingdom arranged by Shogakukan Inc.
through VIZ Media, LLC, U.S.A and Tuttle-Mori Agency, Inc., Japan and Ed Victor Ltd., U.K.

This edition published in Great Britain in 2005 by Gollancz Manga,
an imprint of the Orion Publishing Group, Orion House, 5 Upper St Martin's Lane,
London WC2H 9EA, and a licensee of VIZ Media LLC.

1 3 5 7 9 10 8 6 4 2

A CIP catalogue record for this book is available from the British Library

ISBN 0 575 07740 9

Printed and bound at Mackays of Chatham, PLC

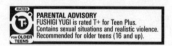

RATED T+ FOR OLDER TEENS
PARENTAL ADVISORY
FUSHIGI YUGI is rated T+ for Teen Plus.
Contains sexual situations and realistic violence.
Recommended for older teens (16 and up).

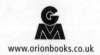

www.orionbooks.co.uk

fushigi yûgi ™

The Mysterious Play
VOL. 1: PRIESTESS

Story & Art By
YUU WATASE

CONTENTS

MODERN JAPAN AND A CHINA THAT NEVER WAS

The story of FUSHIGI YÛGI ("The Mysterious Play") takes place in two different worlds—present-day Japan and a version of ancient China that can be found in the romantic Chinese epics.

The main character of our story, Miaka, is a junior-high-school student who, like every other Japanese student her age, must pass a difficult test to enter the school of her choice. The better a reputation the school has, the harder the entrance exam. For that purpose, students in their third and final year of junior high become very serious about their studies and not only engulf themselves in their school work, but also go to evening "cram schools" where they take even more classes directed at passing their examinations.

The fantasy world of the book, THE UNIVERSE OF THE FOUR GODS, is based on classics of Chinese literature such as THE ROMANCE OF THE THREE KINGDOMS and many other tales of adventure and magic written nearly two-thousand years ago. It is an age where warring states vie for control of the most advanced civilization in the ancient world, and young emperors have inherited regimes that have been passed down from their forefathers in an unbroken line spanning thousands of years. It is a world of beauty and danger, and to enter, you have but to turn the page....

THE UNIVERSE OF THE FOUR GODS is based on ancient China, but Japanese pronunciation of Chinese names differs slightly from their Chinese equivalents. Here is a short glossary of the Japanese pronunciation of the Chinese names in this graphic novel:

Chinese	Japanese	Person or Place	Meaning
Xong Gui-Siu	Sô Kishuku	Tamahome's name	Demon Constellation
Hong-Nan	Konan	Southern Kingdom	Crimson South
Gong Wu	Kyûbu	A clue	Palace Strength
Tai Yi-Jun	Tai Itsukun	An oracle	Preeminent Person
Kang-Lin	Kôrin	A lady of Hong-Nan	Peaceful Jewel
Daichi-San	Daikyokuzan	A mountain	Greatest Mountain

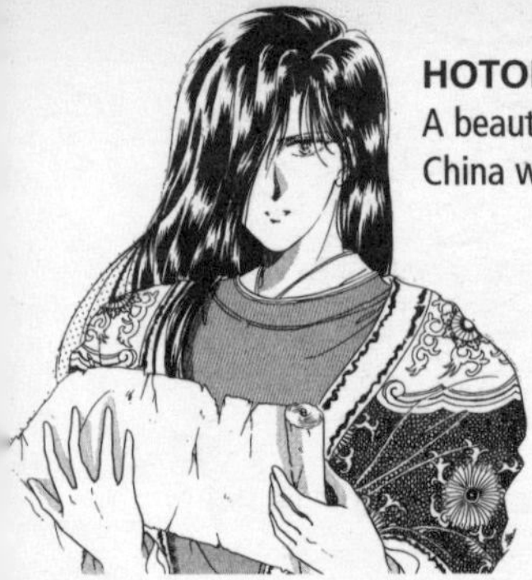

HOTOHORI
A beautiful noble of ancient China who lives in the palace

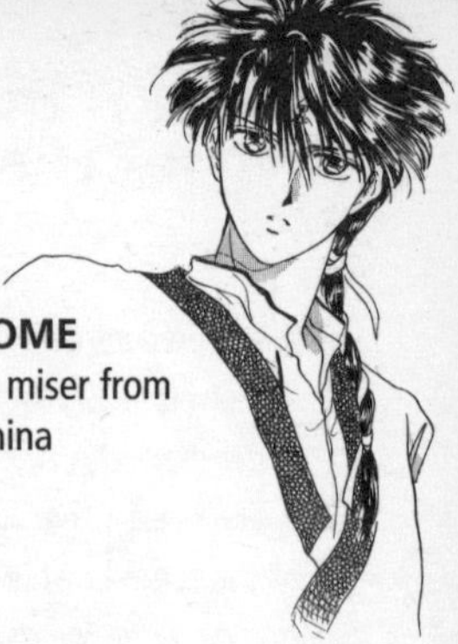

TAMAHOME
A dashing miser from ancient China

YUI
Miaka's best friend and a very intelligent girl who is certain to get into Jonan High School easily

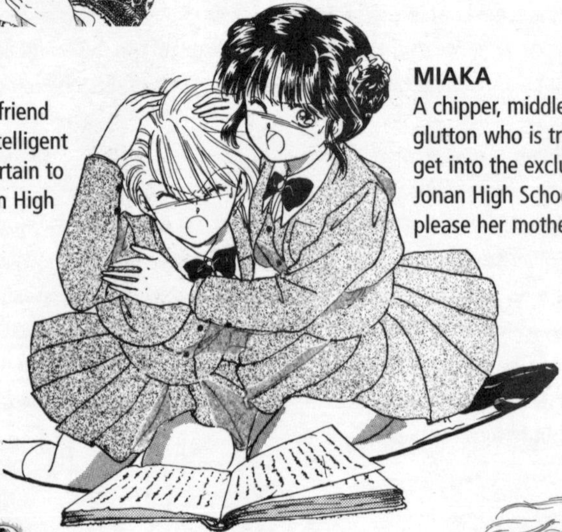

MIAKA
A chipper, middle-school glutton who is trying to get into the exclusive Jonan High School to please her mother

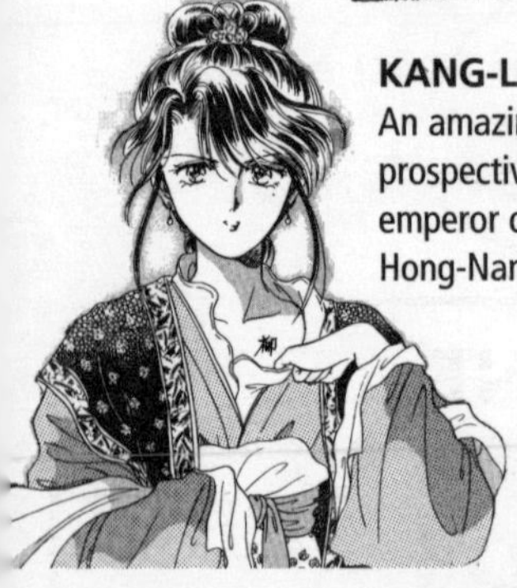

KANG-LIN
An amazingly strong prospective bride for the emperor of the country of Hong-Nan in ancient China

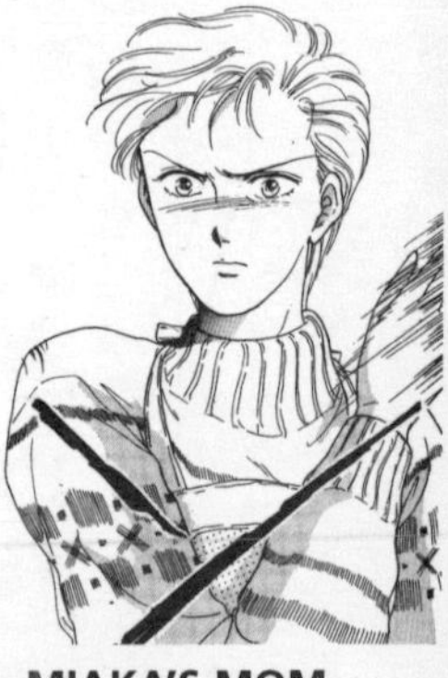

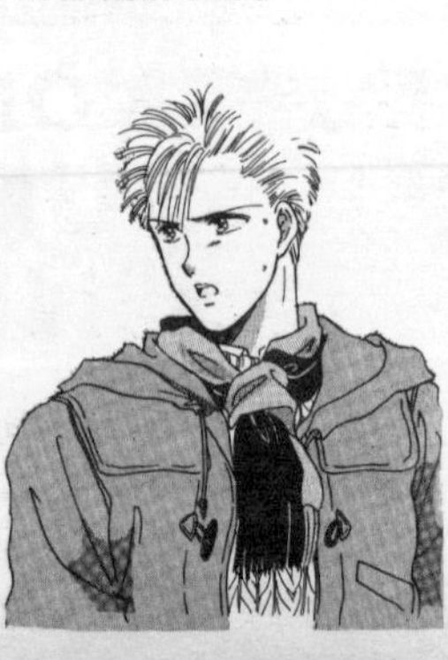

MIAKA'S MOM
A divorced, single mother who is trying to see that her children receive the best education available

KEISUKE
Miaka's kind, college-student brother

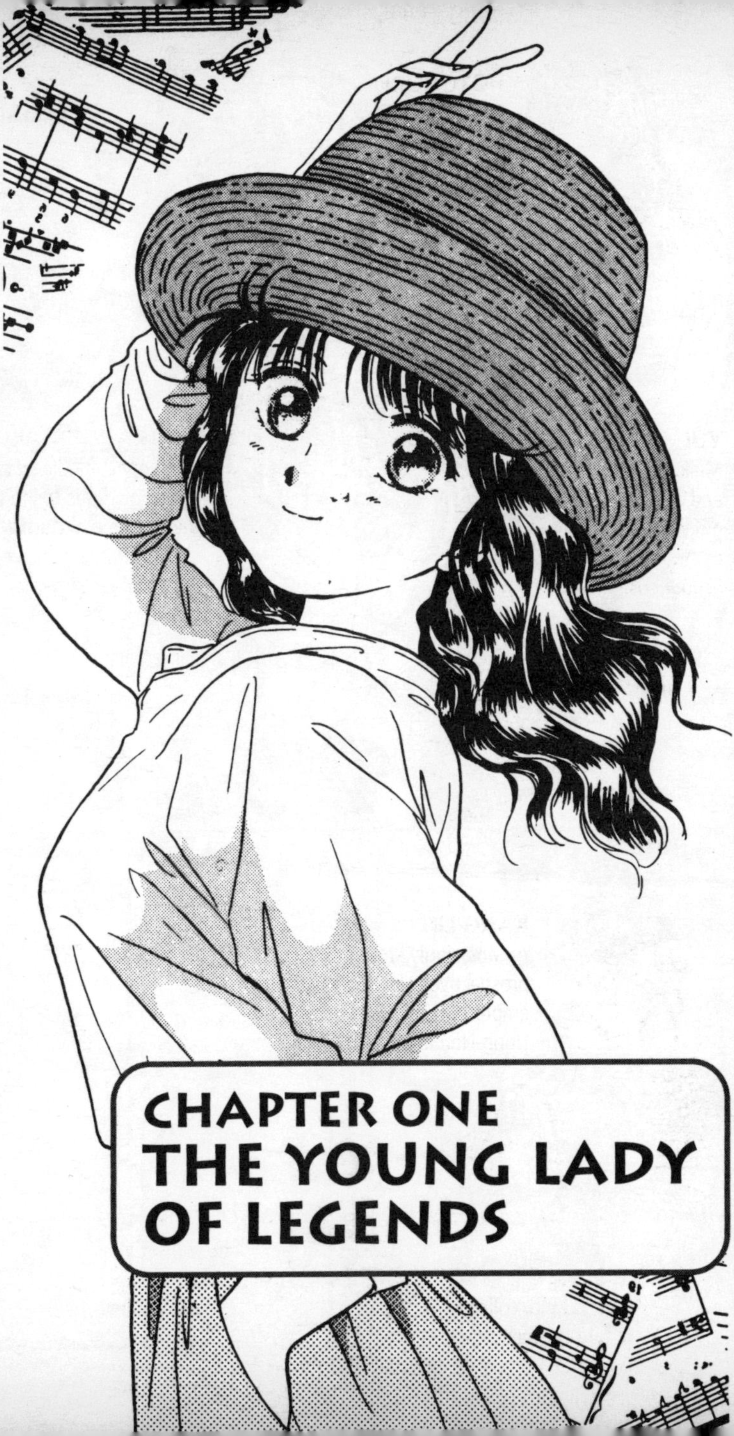
CHAPTER ONE
THE YOUNG LADY OF LEGENDS

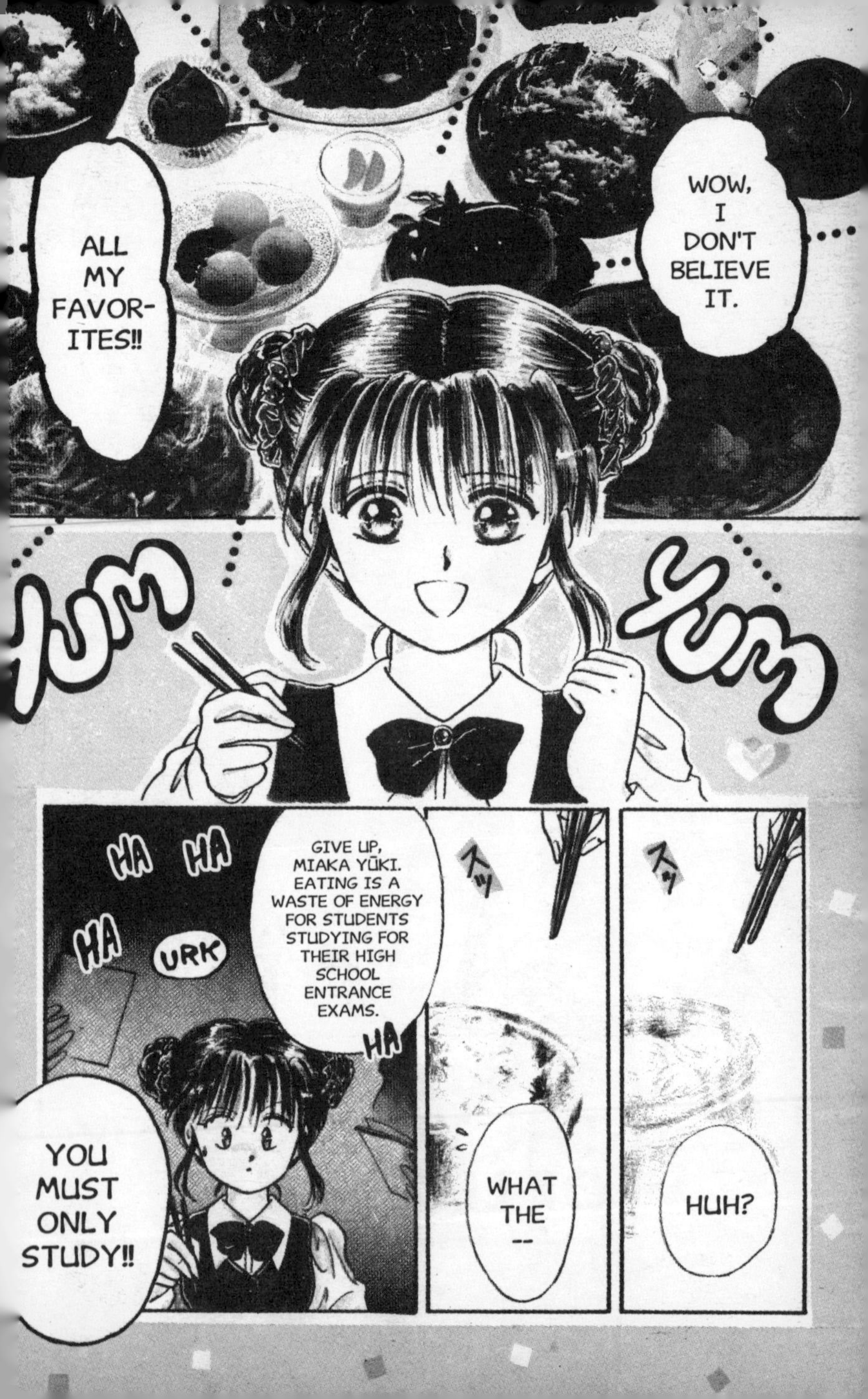
WOW, I DON'T BELIEVE IT.
ALL MY FAVOR-ITES!!
YUM
YUM
スッ
HUH?
スッ
WHAT THE --
HA HA
HA
URK
GIVE UP, MIAKA YŪKI. EATING IS A WASTE OF ENERGY FOR STUDENTS STUDYING FOR THEIR HIGH SCHOOL ENTRANCE EXAMS.
HA
YOU MUST ONLY STUDY!!

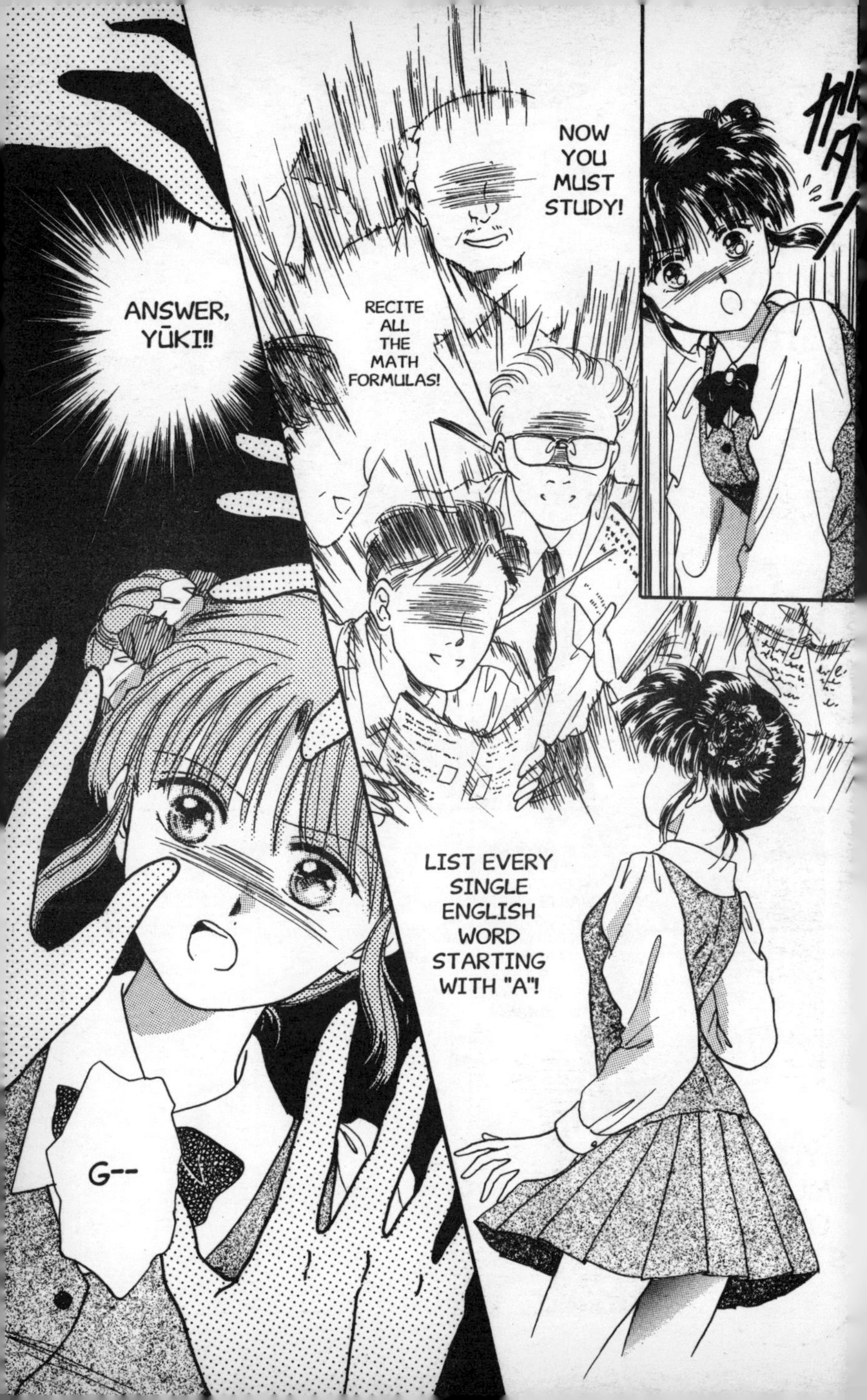
NOW YOU MUST STUDY!
RECITE ALL THE MATH FORMULAS!
ANSWER, YŪKI!!
LIST EVERY SINGLE ENGLISH WORD STARTING WITH "A"!
G--

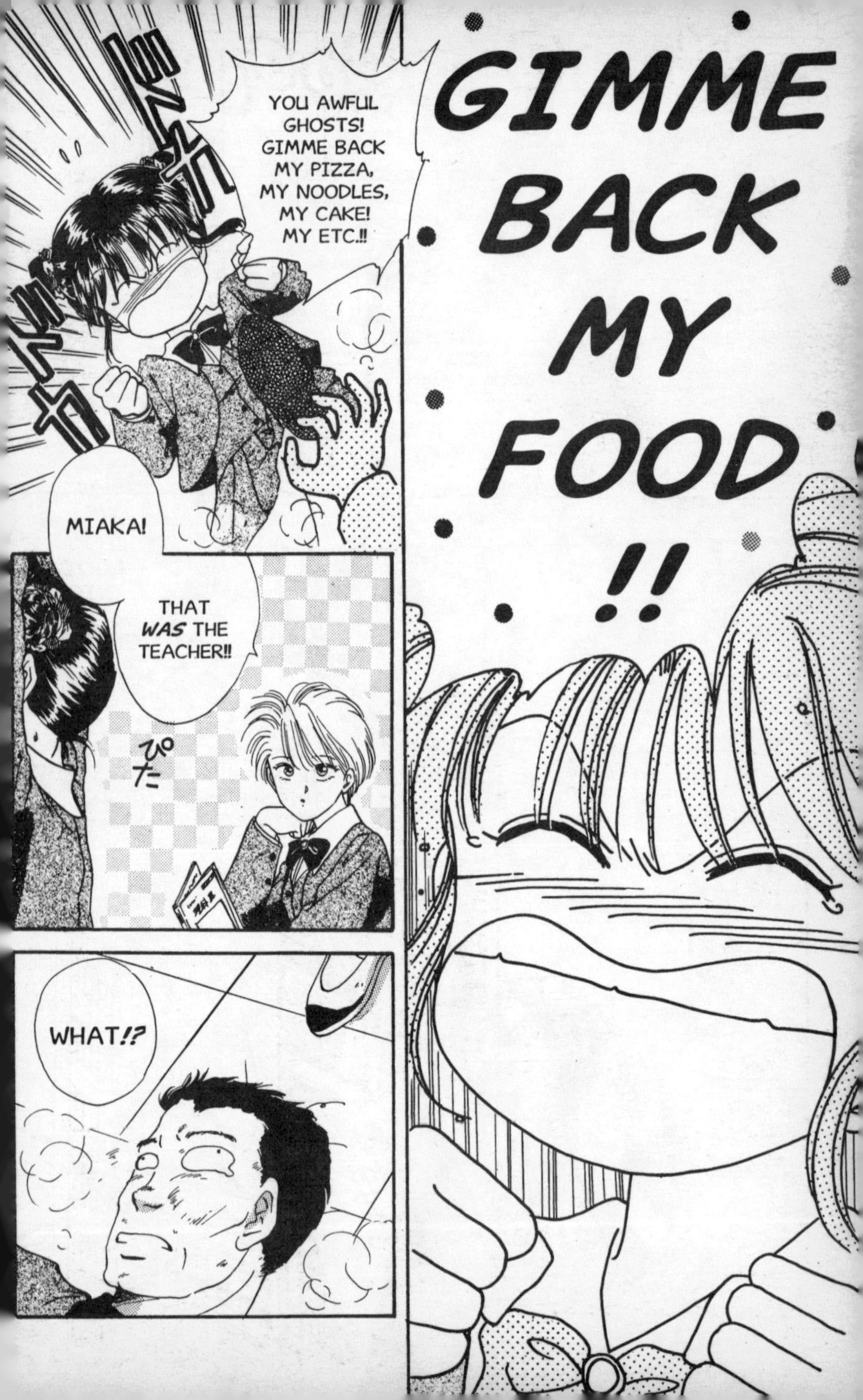
GIMME BACK MY FOOD!!
YOU AWFUL GHOSTS! GIMME BACK MY PIZZA, MY NOODLES, MY CAKE! MY ETC.!!
MIAKA!
THAT *WAS* THE TEACHER!!
ぴた
WHAT!?

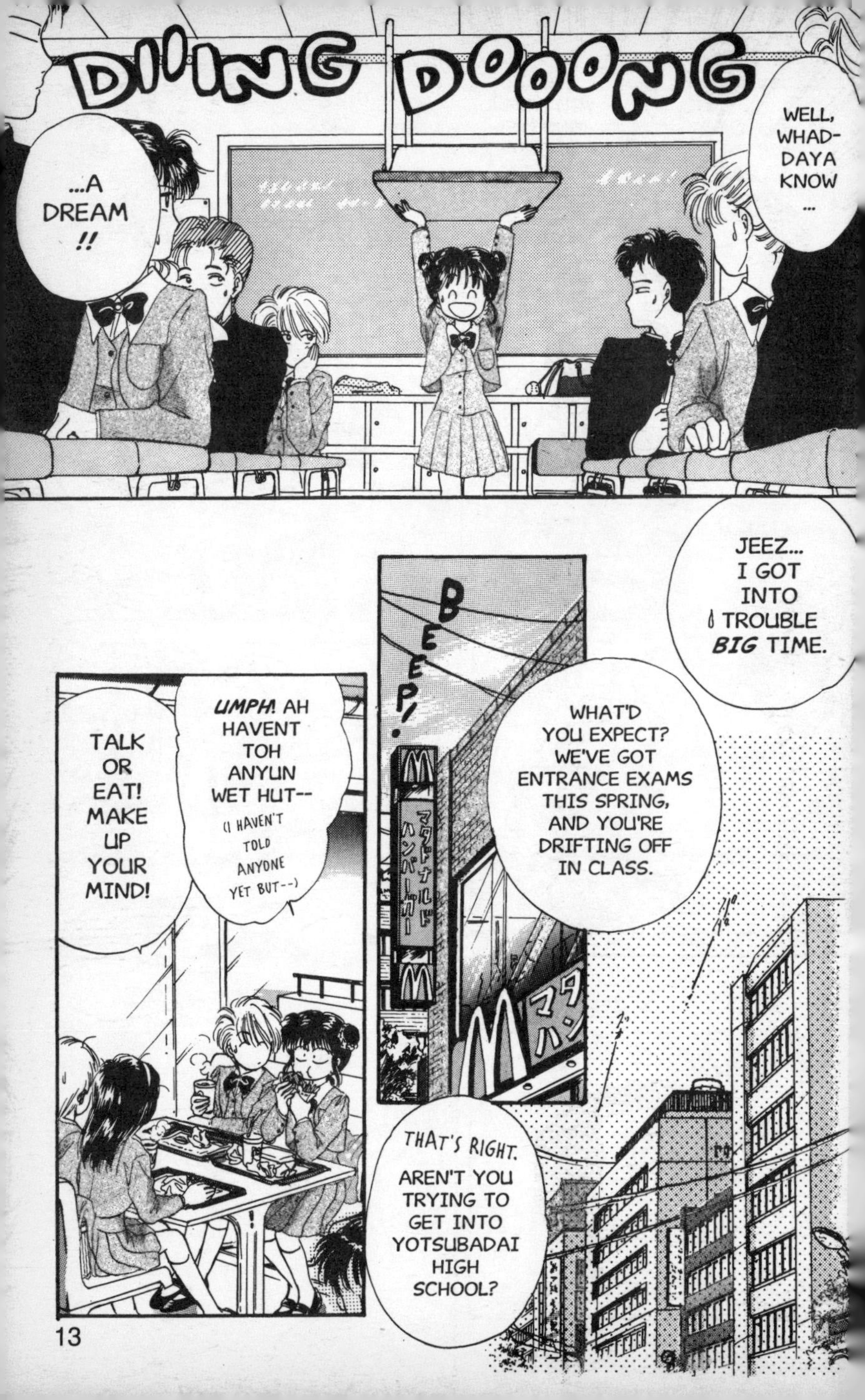
DIIING DOOOONG
WELL, WHADDAYA KNOW ...
...A DREAM !!
JEEZ... I GOT INTO TROUBLE *BIG* TIME.
BEEP!
WHAT'D YOU EXPECT? WE'VE GOT ENTRANCE EXAMS THIS SPRING, AND YOU'RE DRIFTING OFF IN CLASS.
THAT'S RIGHT. AREN'T YOU TRYING TO GET INTO YOTSUBADAI HIGH SCHOOL?
UMPH! AH HAVENT TOH ANYUN WET HUT-- (I HAVEN'T TOLD ANYONE YET BUT--)
TALK OR EAT! MAKE UP YOUR MIND!

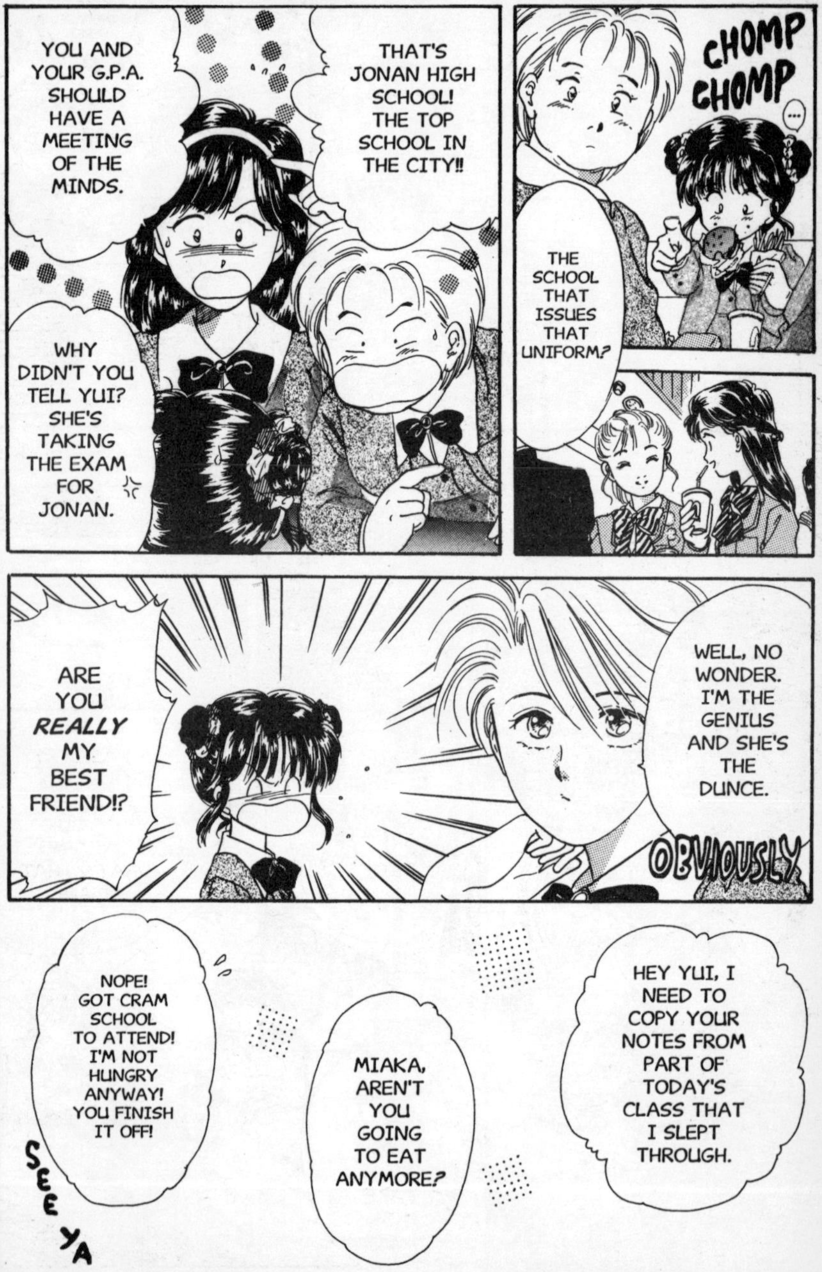
CHOMP CHOMP
...
THE SCHOOL THAT ISSUES THAT UNIFORM?
THAT'S JONAN HIGH SCHOOL! THE TOP SCHOOL IN THE CITY!!
YOU AND YOUR G.P.A. SHOULD HAVE A MEETING OF THE MINDS.
WHY DIDN'T YOU TELL YUI? SHE'S TAKING THE EXAM FOR JONAN.
WELL, NO WONDER. I'M THE GENIUS AND SHE'S THE DUNCE.
OBVIOUSLY
ARE YOU *REALLY* MY BEST FRIEND!?
HEY YUI, I NEED TO COPY YOUR NOTES FROM PART OF TODAY'S CLASS THAT I SLEPT THROUGH.
MIAKA, AREN'T YOU GOING TO EAT ANYMORE?
NOPE! GOT CRAM SCHOOL TO ATTEND! I'M NOT HUNGRY ANYWAY! YOU FINISH IT OFF!
SEE YA

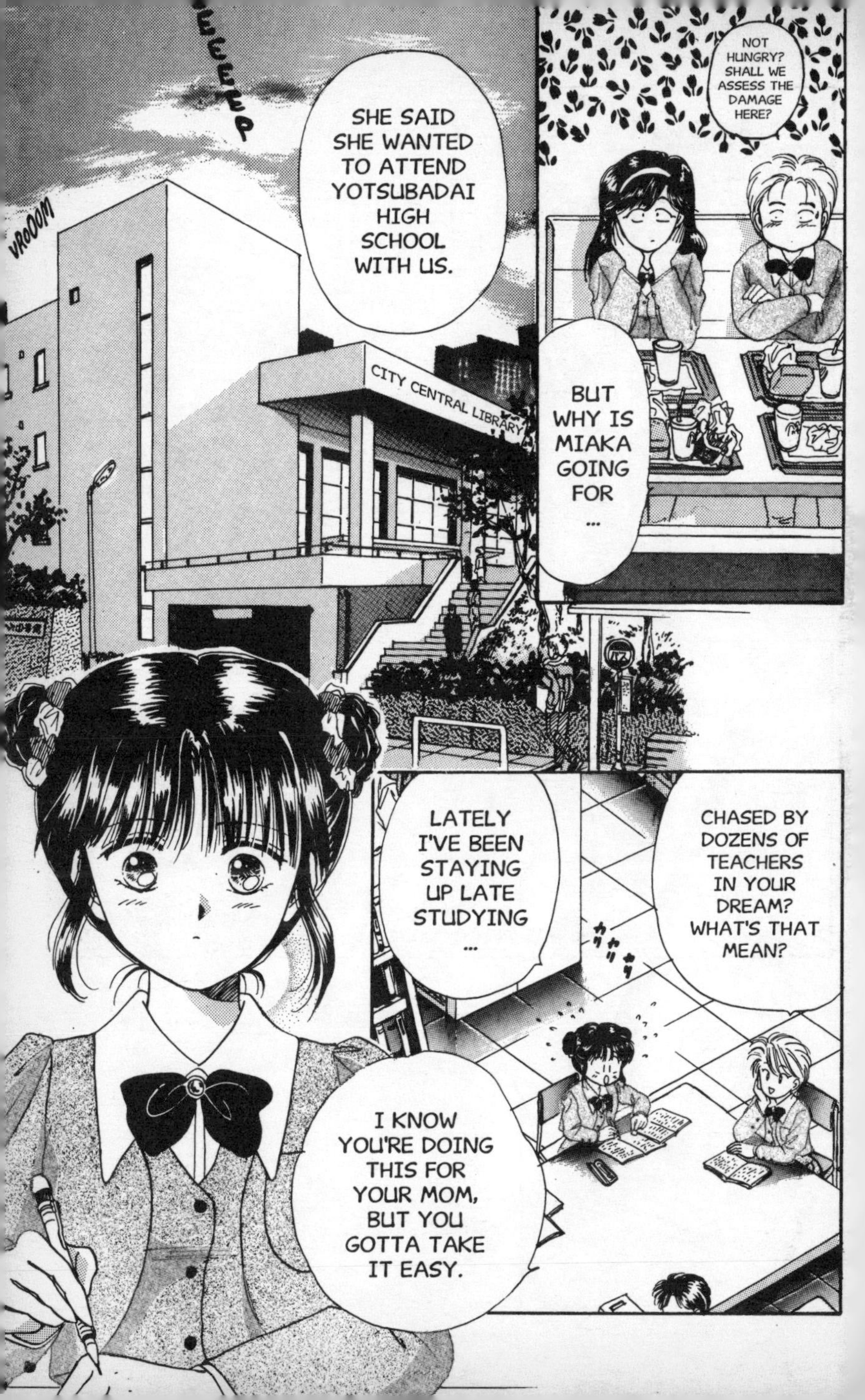
NOT HUNGRY? SHALL WE ASSESS THE DAMAGE HERE?
BUT WHY IS MIAKA GOING FOR ...
SHE SAID SHE WANTED TO ATTEND YOTSUBADAI HIGH SCHOOL WITH US.
EEEEEP
VROOOM
CITY CENTRAL LIBRARY
CHASED BY DOZENS OF TEACHERS IN YOUR DREAM? WHAT'S THAT MEAN?
LATELY I'VE BEEN STAYING UP LATE STUDYING ...
I KNOW YOU'RE DOING THIS FOR YOUR MOM, BUT YOU GOTTA TAKE IT EASY.

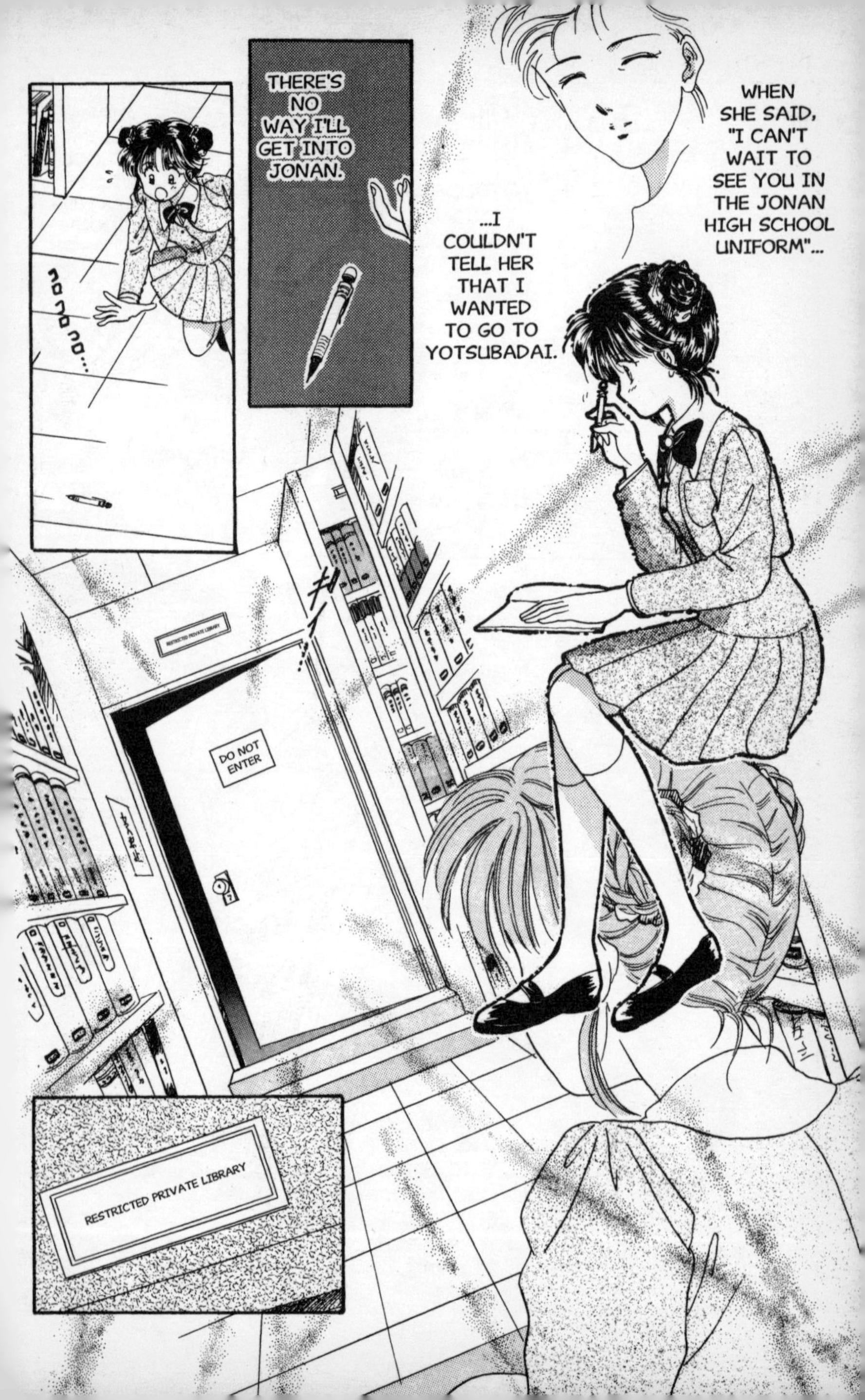
WHEN SHE SAID, "I CAN'T WAIT TO SEE YOU IN THE JONAN HIGH SCHOOL UNIFORM"...
...I COULDN'T TELL HER THAT I WANTED TO GO TO YOTSUBADAI.
THERE'S NO WAY I'LL GET INTO JONAN.
RESTRICTED PRIVATE LIBRARY
DO NOT ENTER
RESTRICTED PRIVATE LIBRARY

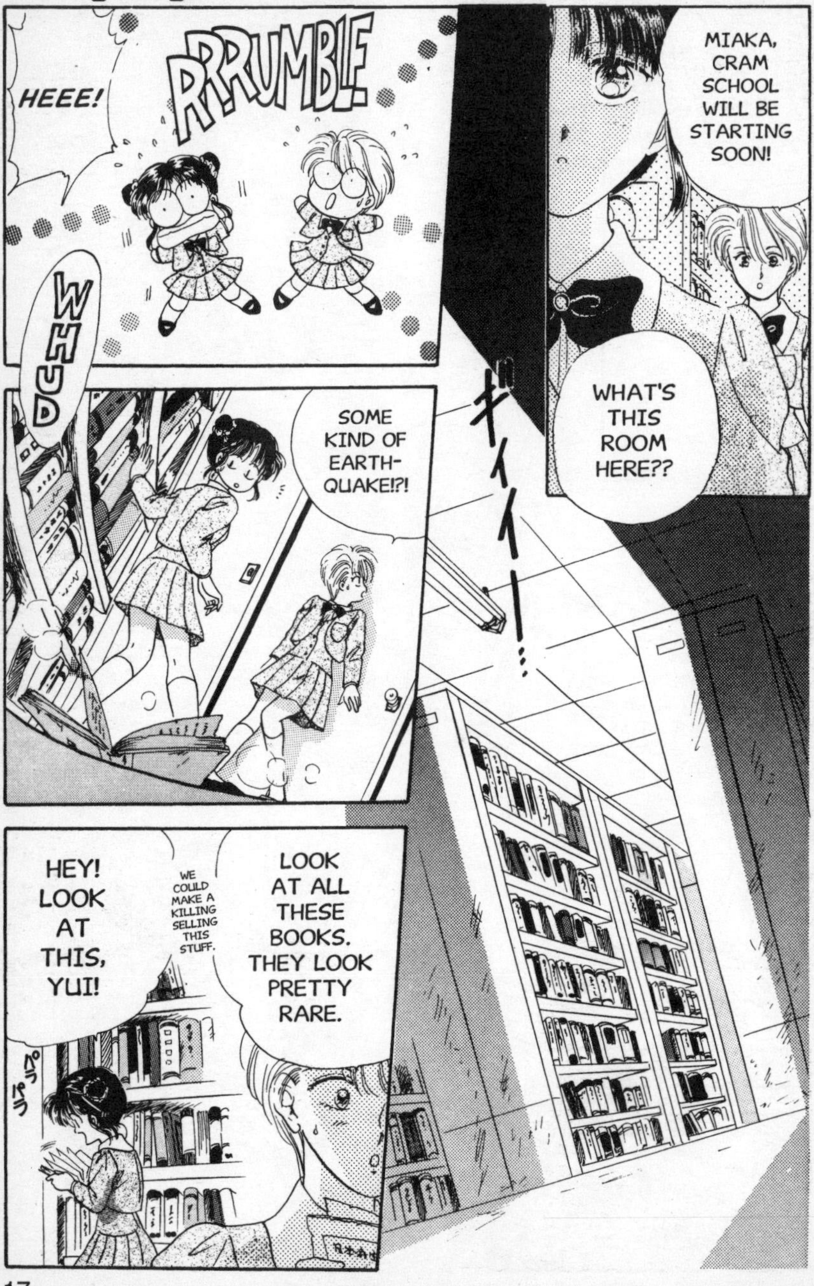
MIAKA, CRAM SCHOOL WILL BE STARTING SOON!
WHAT'S THIS ROOM HERE??
RRRUMBLE
HEEE!
WHUD
SOME KIND OF EARTH-QUAKE!?!
LOOK AT ALL THESE BOOKS. THEY LOOK PRETTY RARE.
WE COULD MAKE A KILLING SELLING THIS STUFF.
HEY! LOOK AT THIS, YUI!

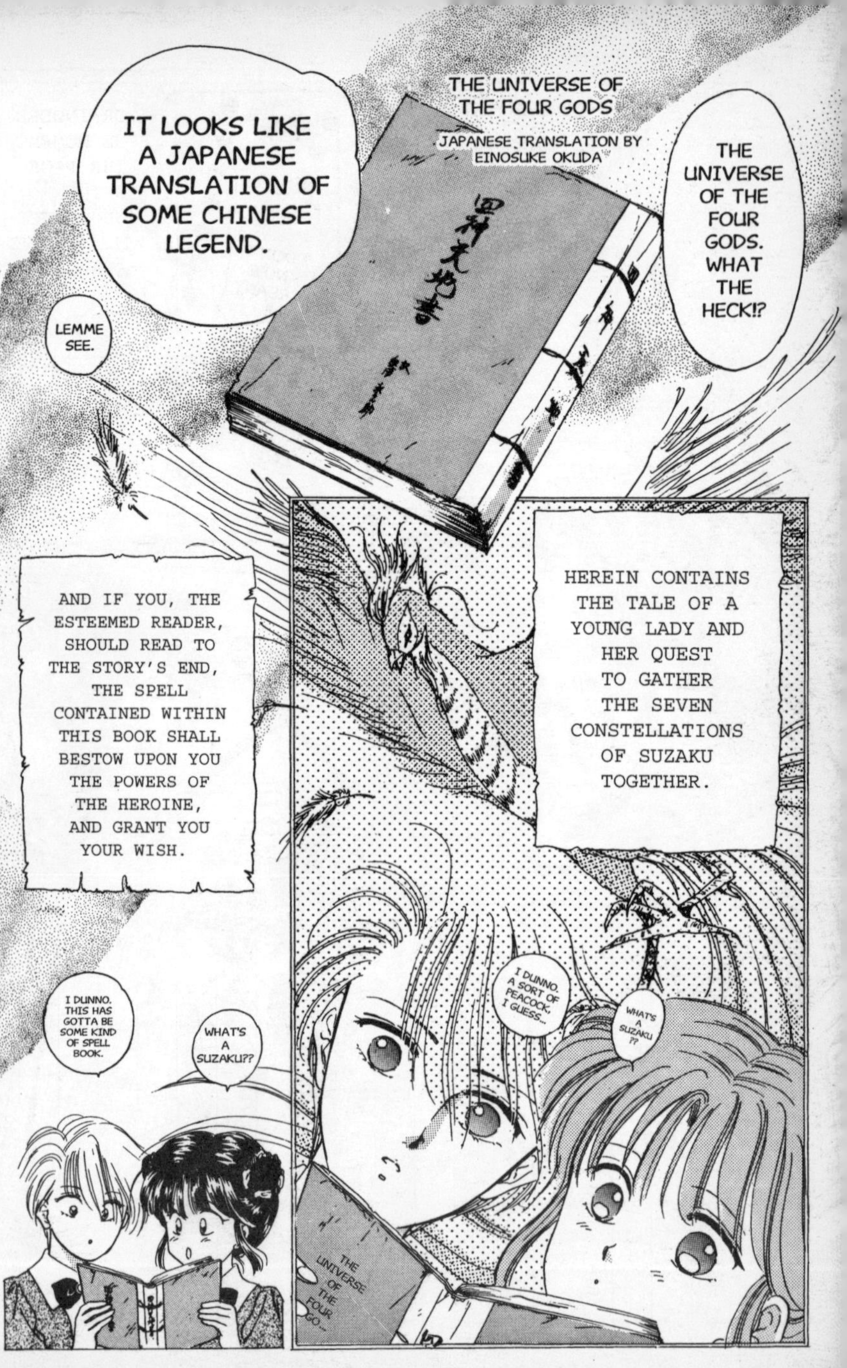

IT LOOKS LIKE A JAPANESE TRANSLATION OF SOME CHINESE LEGEND.
THE UNIVERSE OF THE FOUR GODS
JAPANESE TRANSLATION BY EINOSUKE OKUDA
THE UNIVERSE OF THE FOUR GODS. WHAT THE HECK!?
LEMME SEE.
HEREIN CONTAINS THE TALE OF A YOUNG LADY AND HER QUEST TO GATHER THE SEVEN CONSTELLATIONS OF SUZAKU TOGETHER.
AND IF YOU, THE ESTEEMED READER, SHOULD READ TO THE STORY'S END, THE SPELL CONTAINED WITHIN THIS BOOK SHALL BESTOW UPON YOU THE POWERS OF THE HEROINE, AND GRANT YOU YOUR WISH.
WHAT'S A SUZAKU??
I DUNNO. A SORT OF PEACOCK, I GUESS...
WHAT'S A SUZAKU??
I DUNNO. THIS HAS GOTTA BE SOME KIND OF SPELL BOOK.
THE UNIVERSE OF THE FOUR GO...

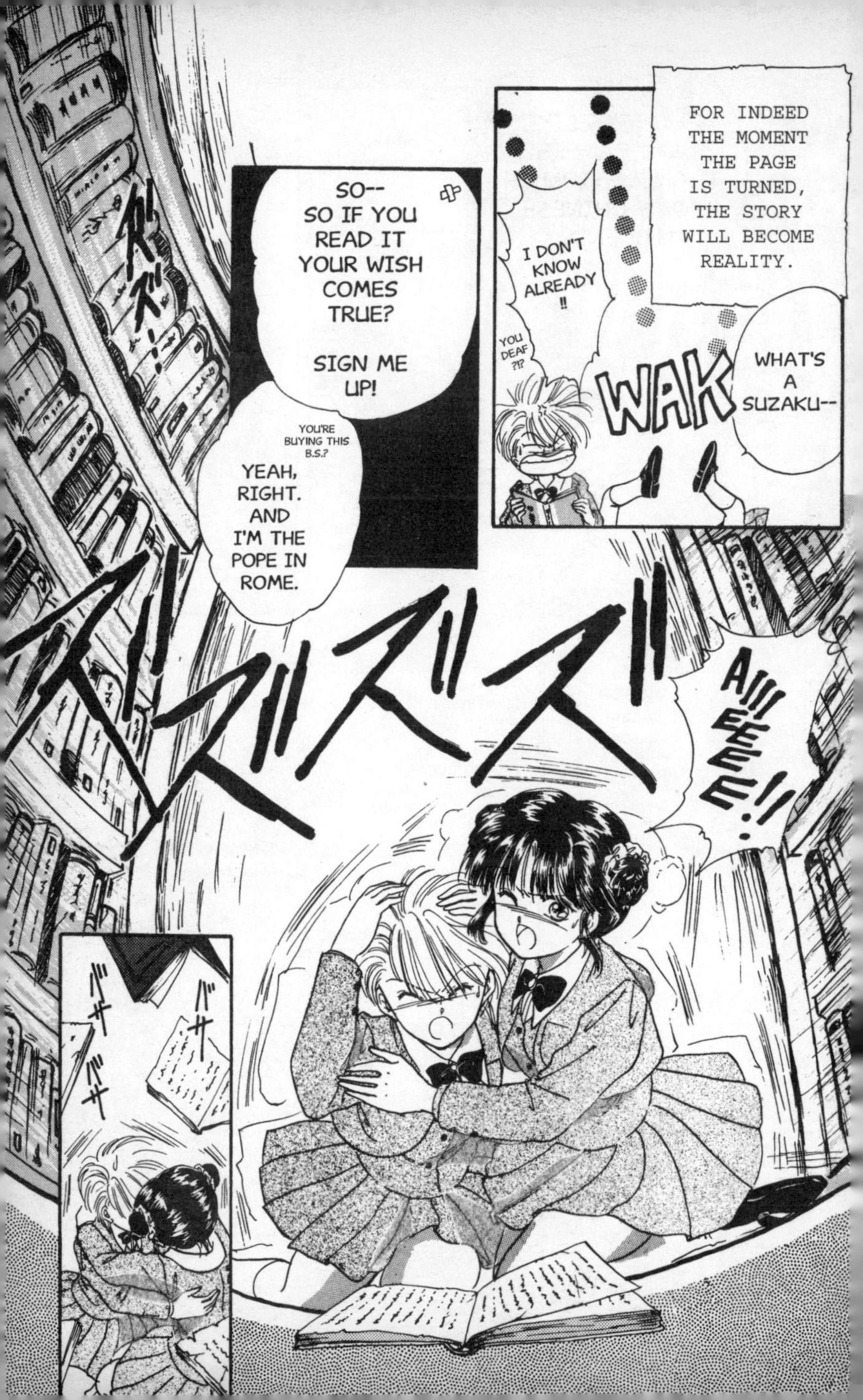
FOR INDEED THE MOMENT THE PAGE IS TURNED, THE STORY WILL BECOME REALITY.
WHAT'S A SUZAKU--
WAK
I DON'T KNOW ALREADY !!
YOU DEAF ?!?
SO-- SO IF YOU READ IT YOUR WISH COMES TRUE? SIGN ME UP!
YEAH, RIGHT. AND I'M THE POPE IN ROME.
YOU'RE BUYING THIS B.S.?
AIIIEEEE!!

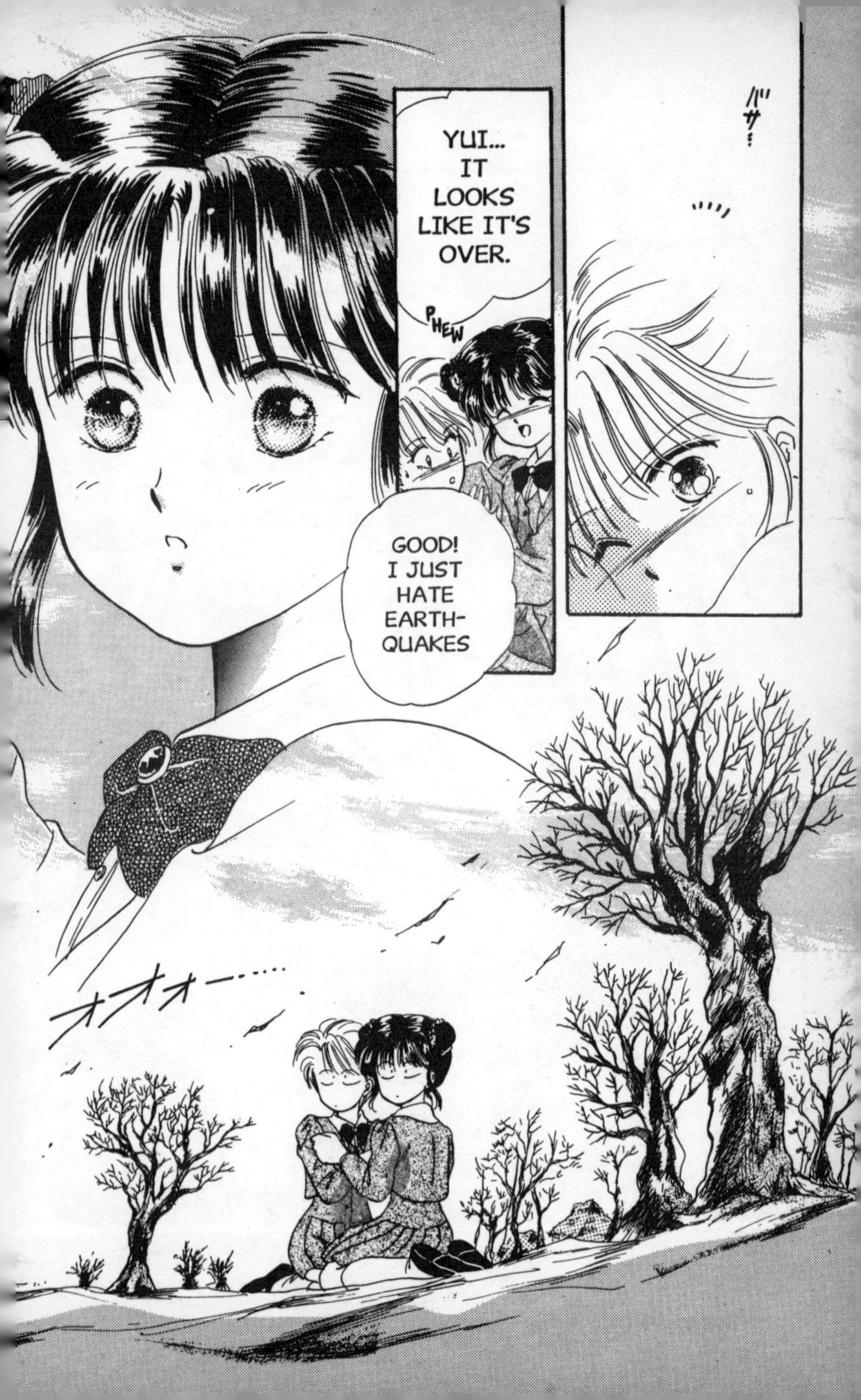
バサ
YUI... IT LOOKS LIKE IT'S OVER.
PHEW
GOOD! I JUST HATE EARTH-QUAKES
オオオー

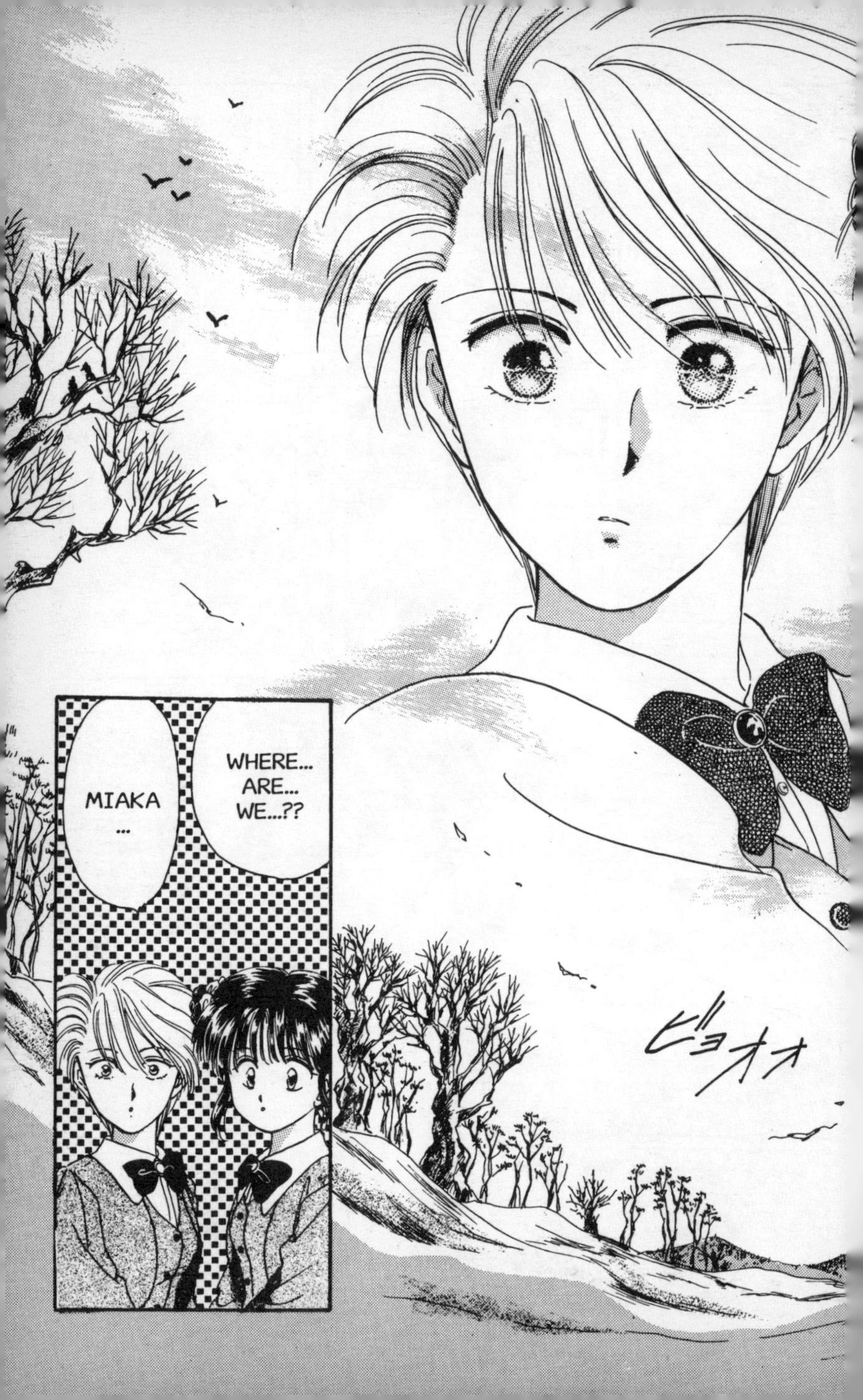
WHERE... ARE... WE...??
MIAKA ...
ビョオオ

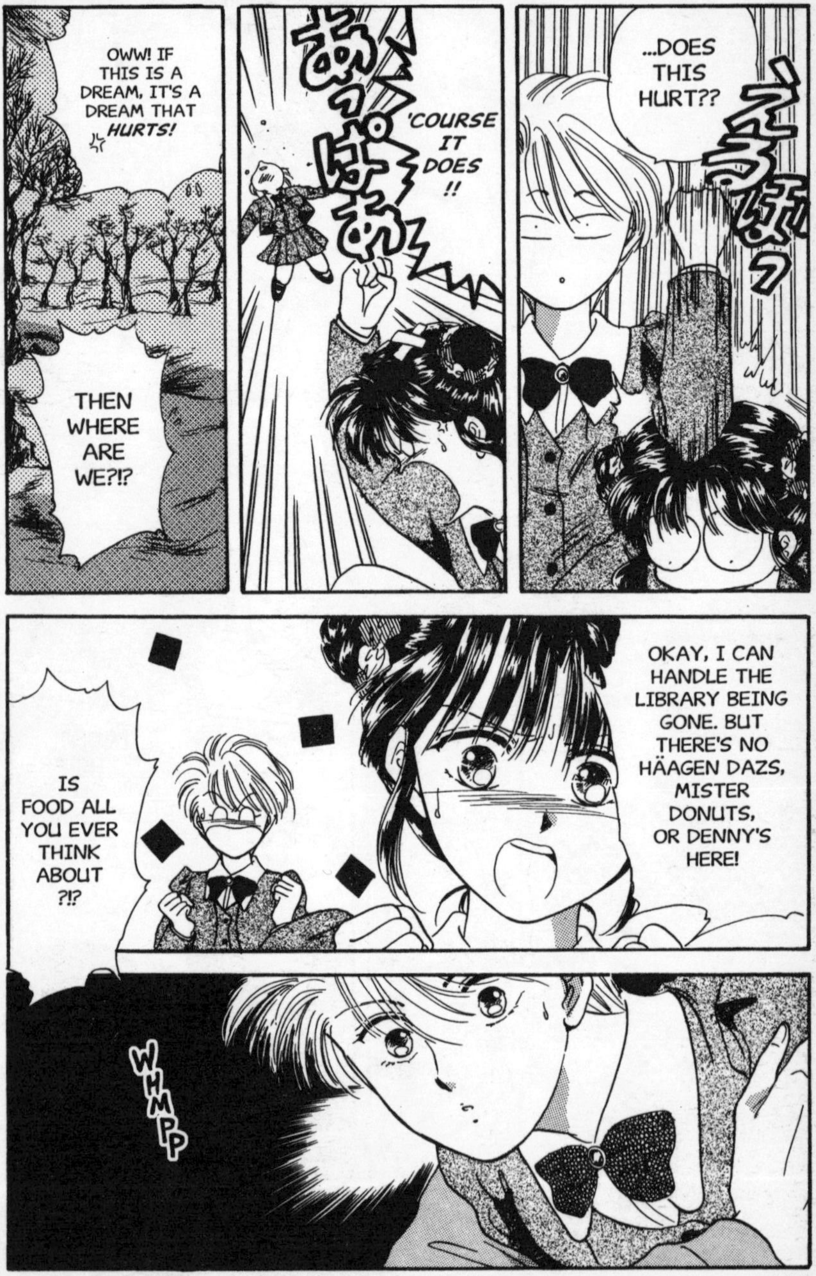
...DOES THIS HURT??
'COURSE IT DOES!!
OWW! IF THIS IS A DREAM, IT'S A DREAM THAT HURTS!
THEN WHERE ARE WE?!?
OKAY, I CAN HANDLE THE LIBRARY BEING GONE. BUT THERE'S NO HÄAGEN DAZS, MISTER DONUTS, OR DENNY'S HERE!
IS FOOD ALL YOU EVER THINK ABOUT?!?
WHMPP

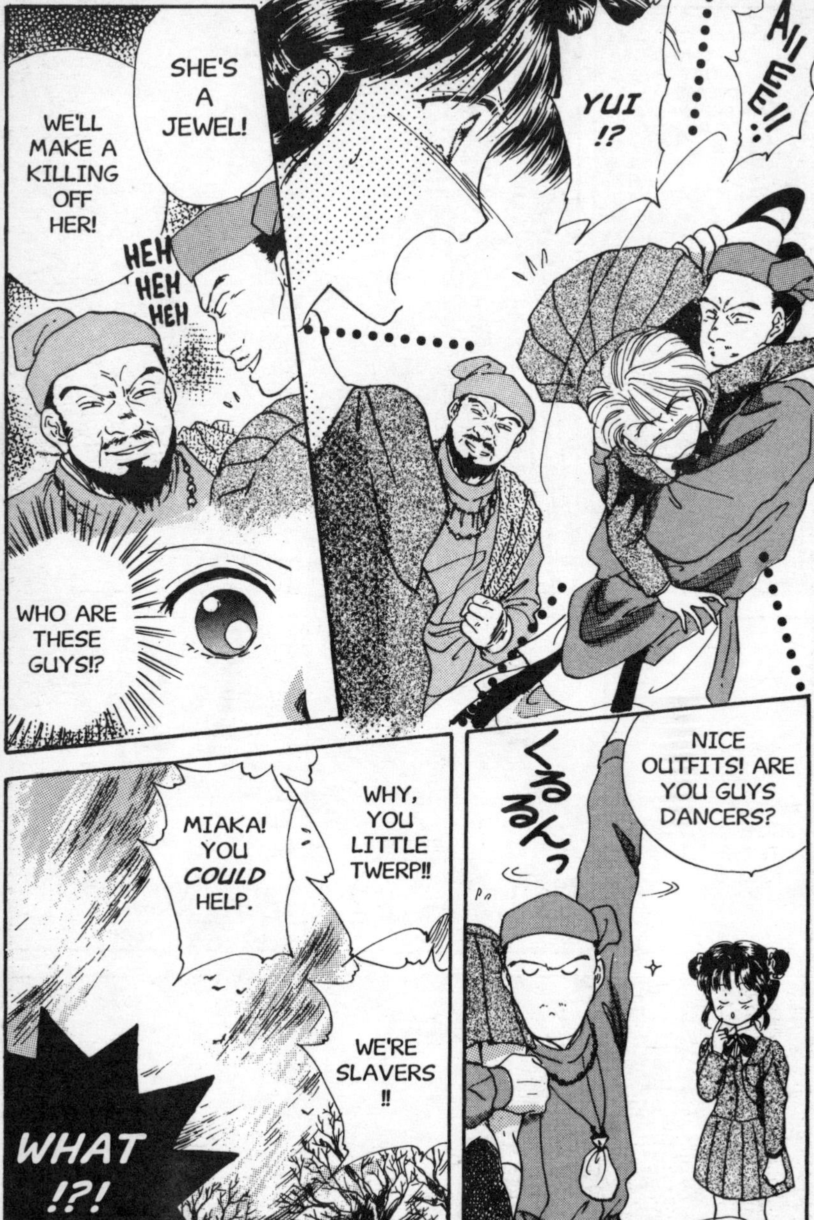
AIIEE!!
YUI !?
SHE'S A JEWEL!
WE'LL MAKE A KILLING OFF HER!
HEH HEH HEH
WHO ARE THESE GUYS!?
くるるんっ
NICE OUTFITS! ARE YOU GUYS DANCERS?
WHY, YOU LITTLE TWERP!!
WE'RE SLAVERS !!
WHAT !?!
MIAKA! YOU *COULD* HELP.

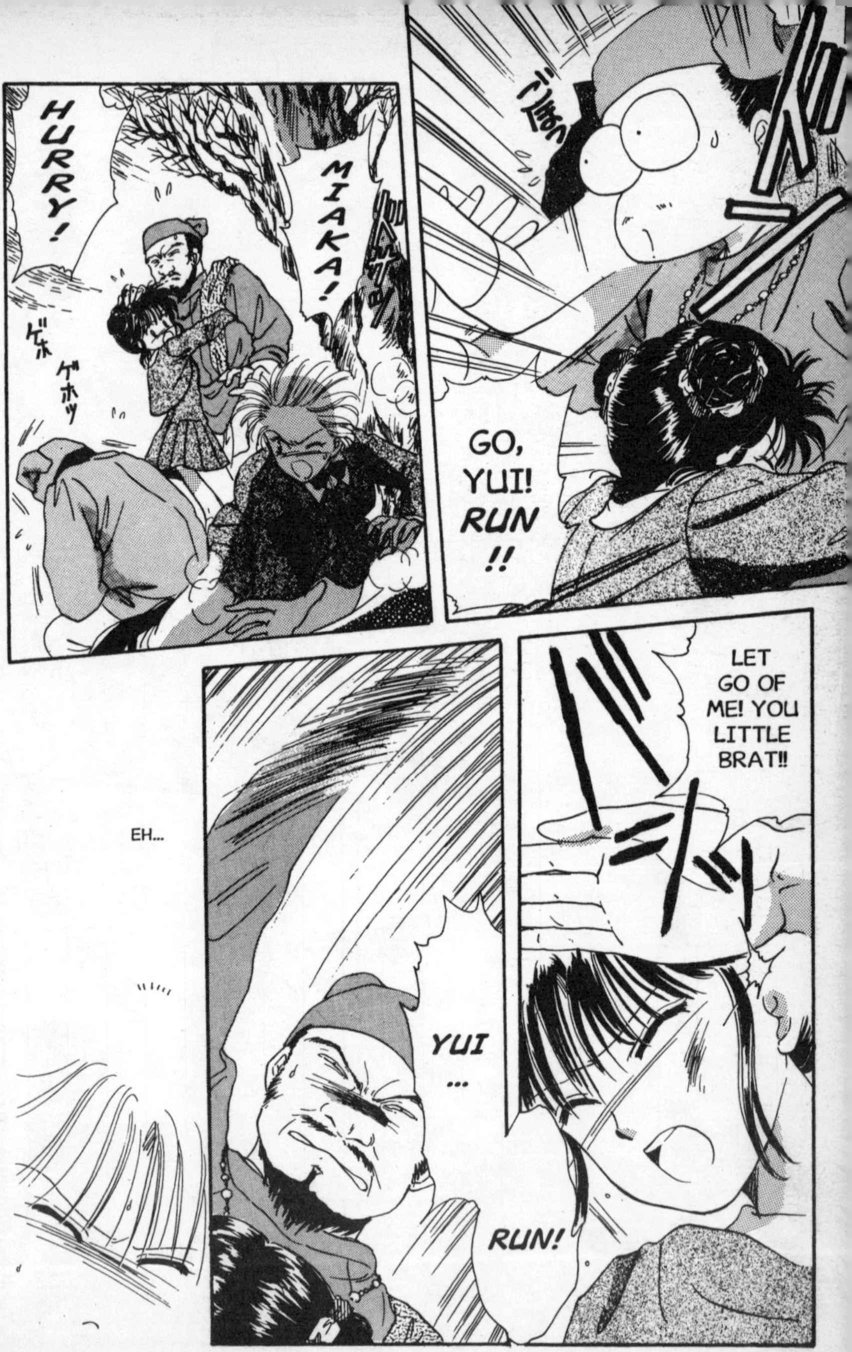
ごほっ
GO, YUI! RUN!!
MIAKA!
HURRY!
ゲホ ゲホッ
LET GO OF ME! YOU LITTLE BRAT!!
YUI...
RUN!
EH...

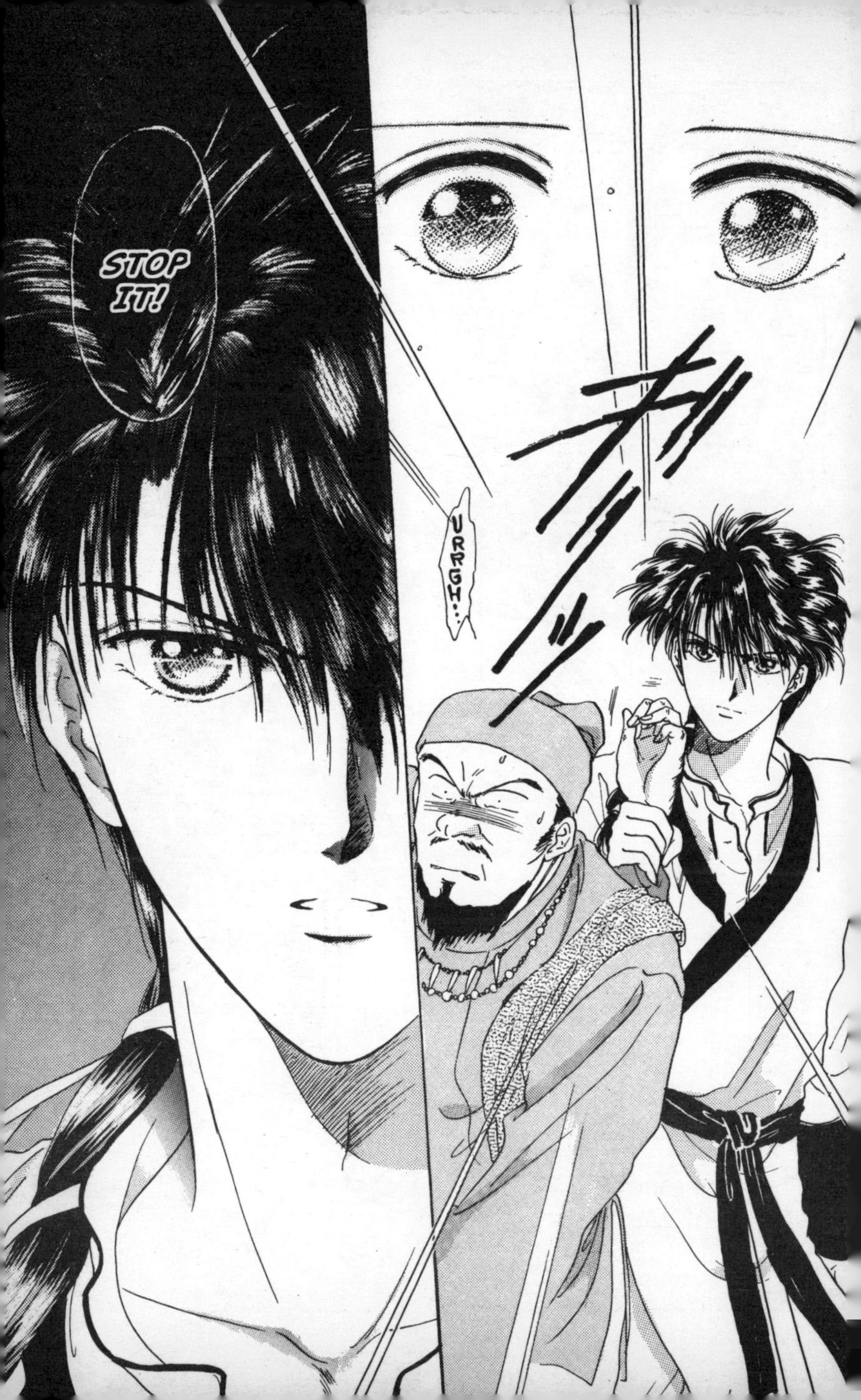
STOP IT!
URRGH...

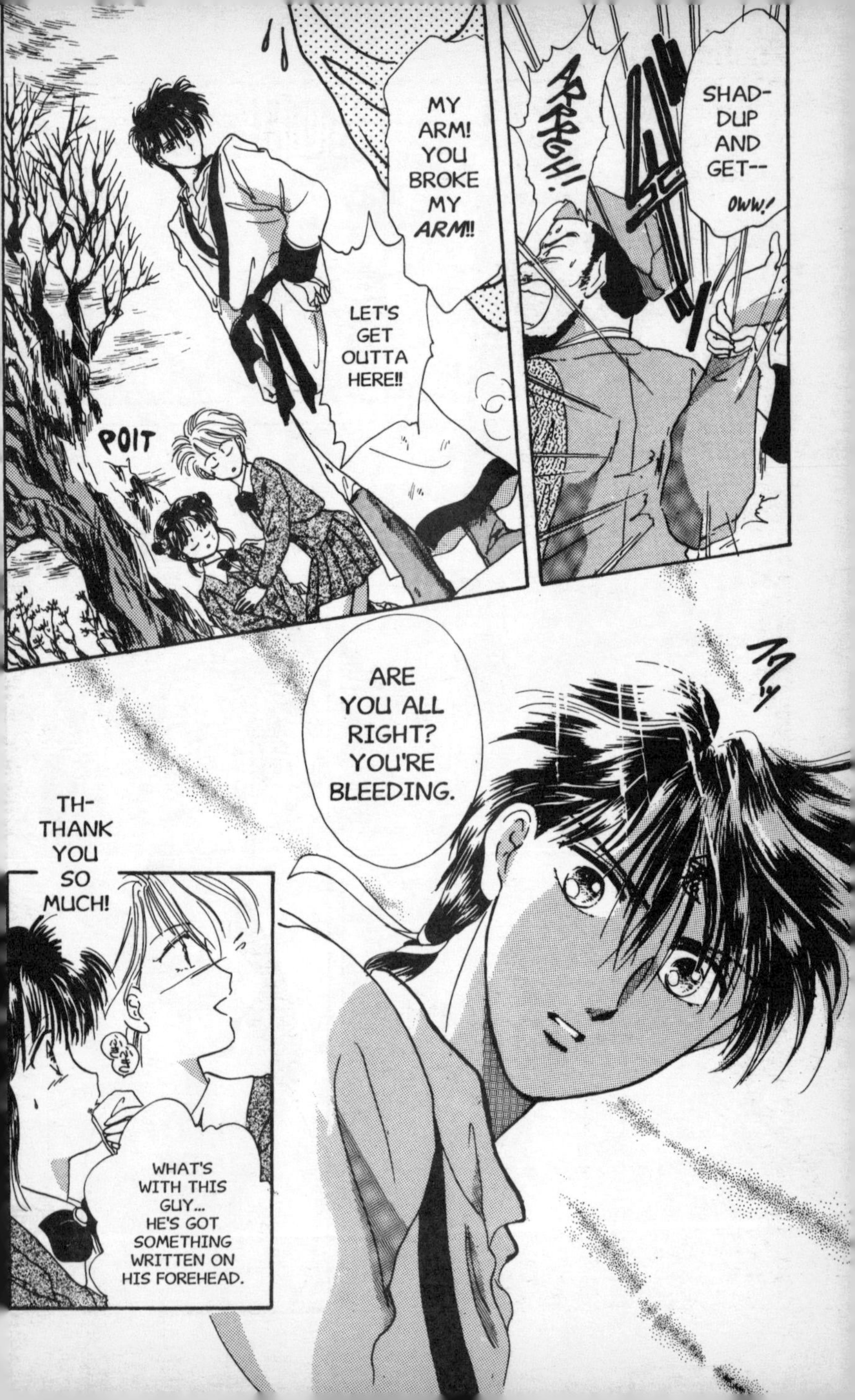
SHAD-DUP AND GET--
OWW!
ARRGGH!!
MY ARM! YOU BROKE MY ARM!!
LET'S GET OUTTA HERE!!
POIT
ARE YOU ALL RIGHT? YOU'RE BLEEDING.
TH-THANK YOU SO MUCH!
WHAT'S WITH THIS GUY... HE'S GOT SOMETHING WRITTEN ON HIS FOREHEAD.

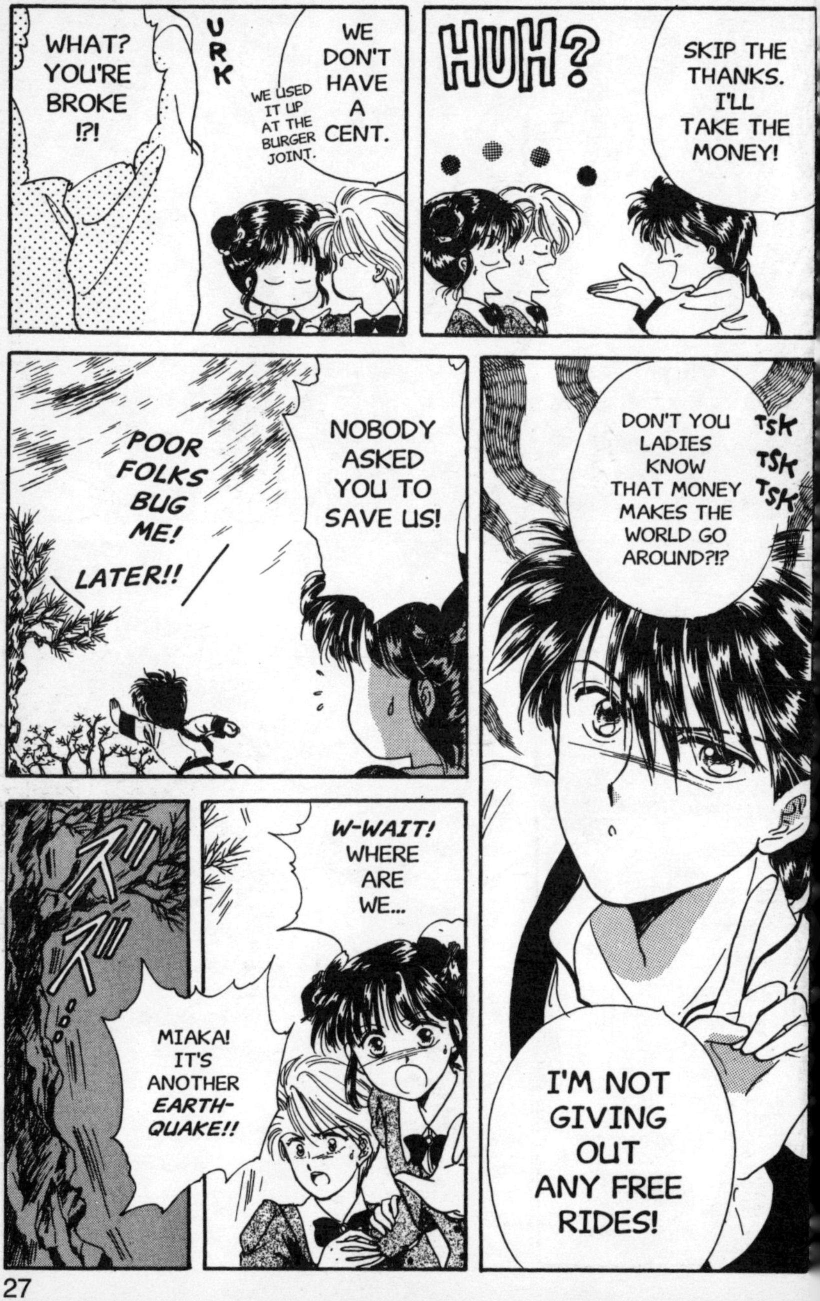
WHAT? YOU'RE BROKE !?!
URK
WE DON'T HAVE A CENT.
WE USED IT UP AT THE BURGER JOINT.
HUH?
SKIP THE THANKS. I'LL TAKE THE MONEY!
DON'T YOU LADIES KNOW THAT MONEY MAKES THE WORLD GO AROUND?!?
TSK TSK TSK
I'M NOT GIVING OUT ANY FREE RIDES!
NOBODY ASKED YOU TO SAVE US!
POOR FOLKS BUG ME!
LATER!!
W-WAIT! WHERE ARE WE...
MIAKA! IT'S ANOTHER EARTH-QUAKE!!

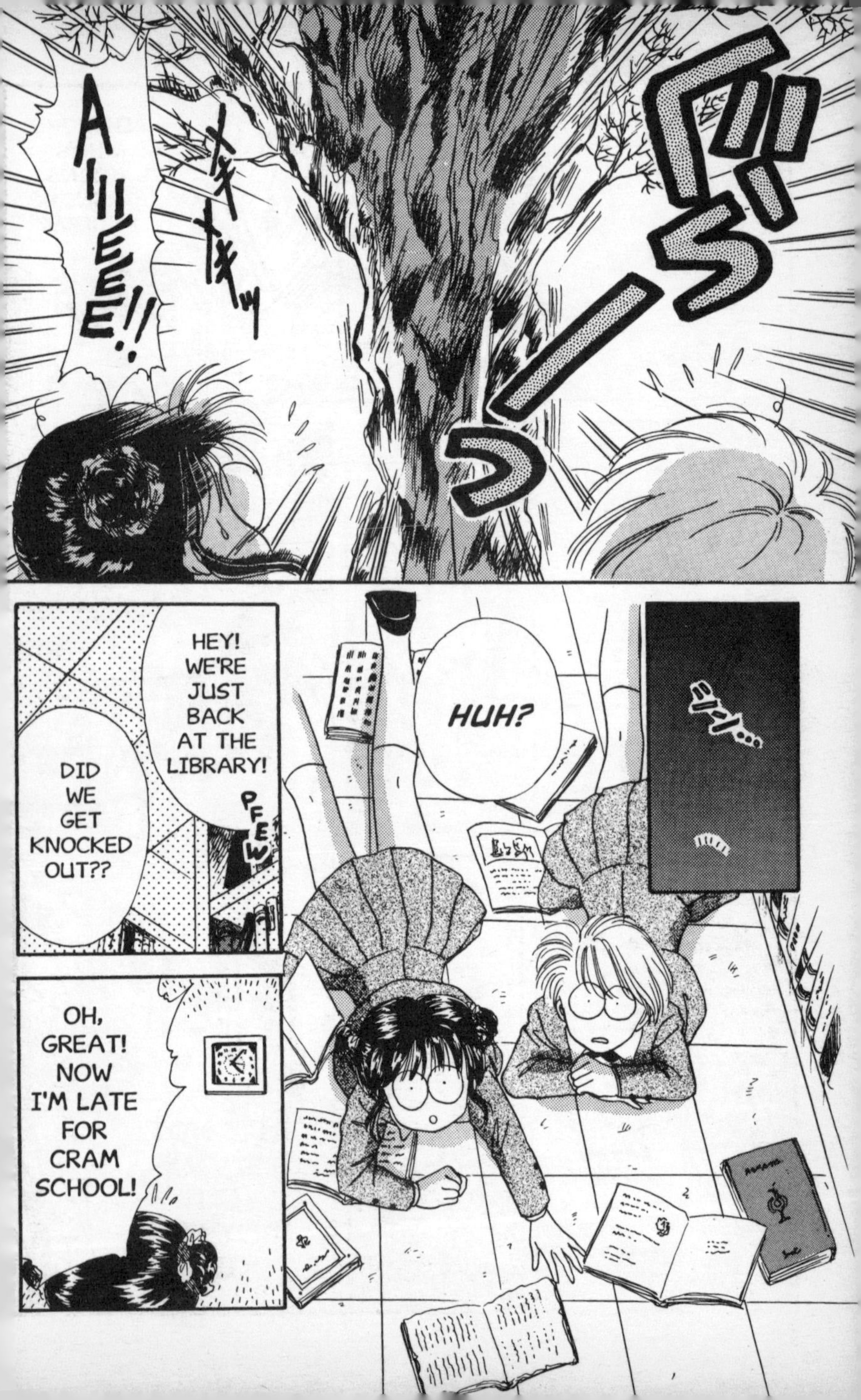

AIIIEEEE!!
HUH?
HEY! WE'RE JUST BACK AT THE LIBRARY!
DID WE GET KNOCKED OUT??
PFEW
OH, GREAT! NOW I'M LATE FOR CRAM SCHOOL!

Hello. It's me, Watase, and I'll be using this space to chat a little. I know, I know. You're complaining about my bad handwriting, sorry but I just scribble stuff down.
(Bad handwriting approximated for the English edition - ed.)
I don't like writing by hand. But since my writing is difficult enough to read I've decided to take some pains to write more legibly.
Yeah right.

Now let's see, "Fushigi Yûgi"... when I was eighteen, before I got published, I looked up this incredibly thick "Buddhist Philosophy Encyclopedia" and was delighted to find how the character for "Oni" was read as "Tamahome." I discovered that "when the light of the Tamahome star in Suzaku's seven southern star constellations (out of a total of 28 constellations) fades, it is a sign of a bad harvest." As I came across this information, I came up with the idea for this story. I thought up the characters of Tamahome 鬼宿, and Hotohori 星宿, but Miaka still wasn't part of the picture. (I wanted to use the character for star rather than constellation which would make Tamahome 鬼星 (pronounced Kisei) but that would have made Hotohori 星星 (pronounced Seisei) so I decided against it). I submitted the "FY" story idea along with my "Shishunki Miman Okotowari" (No Interest in Prepubescence) idea. "Shishunki" was accepted instead of "FY."

Although I've done my share of research on China for this story, it's still not a Chinese story. "FY" departs significantly from some basic historical facts. So please don't read it as if it were Chinese history. Who would? (For example, the emperor calls himself "Chin" so I decided against him using his real name.) I just want to let you know that I haven't been delinquent in my research. I read through 10 books before I began working on this serial. If there are any discrepancies, they're being made with my knowledge.

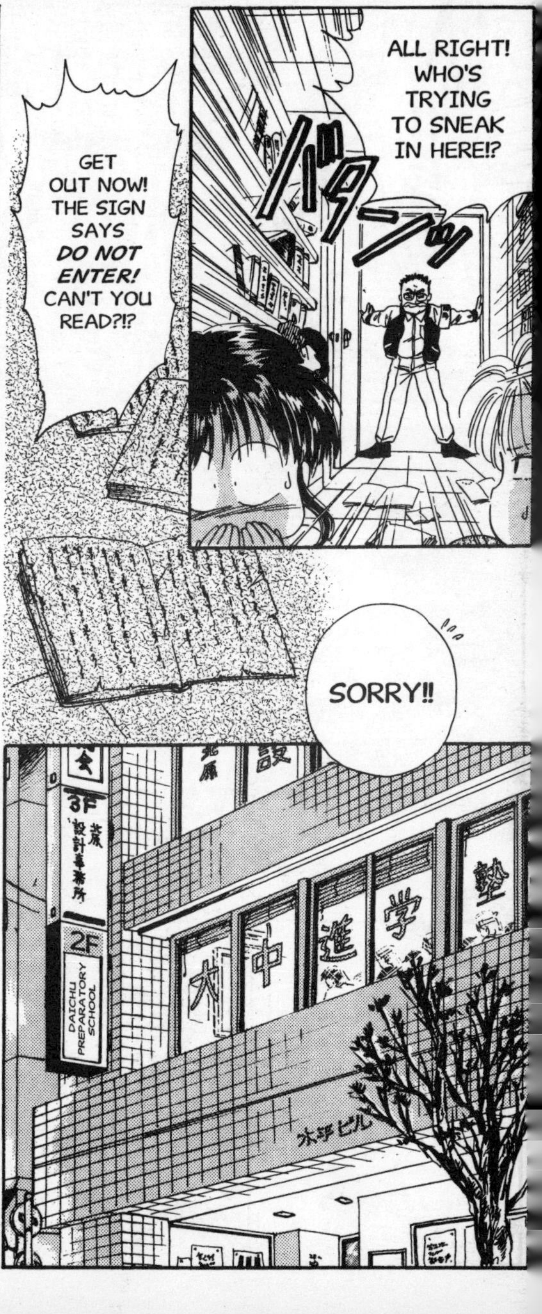
ALL RIGHT! WHO'S TRYING TO SNEAK IN HERE!?
GET OUT NOW! THE SIGN SAYS *DO NOT ENTER!* CAN'T YOU READ?!?
SORRY!!
3F
2F
DAICHU PREPARATORY SCHOOL
大中進学塾

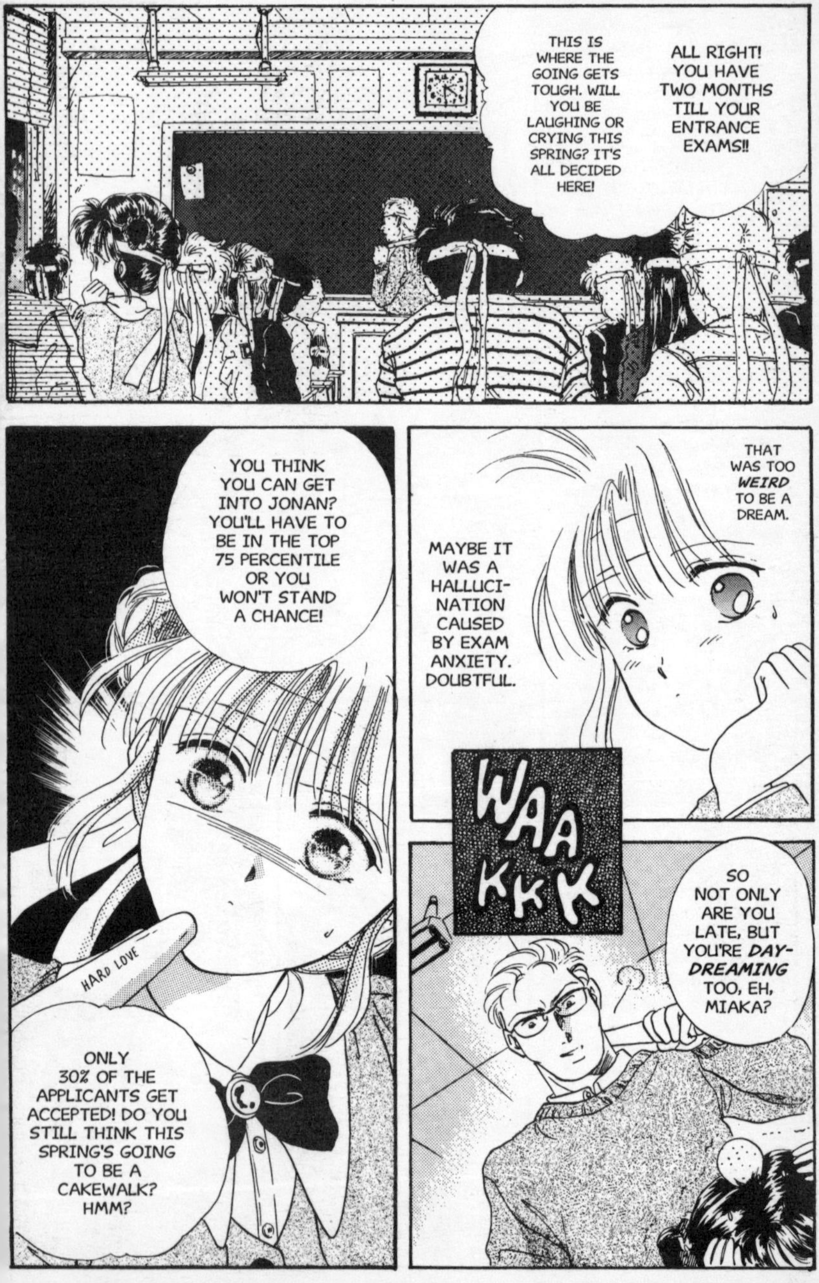
ALL RIGHT! YOU HAVE TWO MONTHS TILL YOUR ENTRANCE EXAMS!!
THIS IS WHERE THE GOING GETS TOUGH. WILL YOU BE LAUGHING OR CRYING THIS SPRING? IT'S ALL DECIDED HERE!
YOU THINK YOU CAN GET INTO JONAN? YOU'LL HAVE TO BE IN THE TOP 75 PERCENTILE OR YOU WON'T STAND A CHANCE!
HARD LOVE
ONLY 30% OF THE APPLICANTS GET ACCEPTED! DO YOU STILL THINK THIS SPRING'S GOING TO BE A CAKEWALK? HMM?
THAT WAS TOO *WEIRD* TO BE A DREAM.
MAYBE IT WAS A HALLUCI-NATION CAUSED BY EXAM ANXIETY. DOUBTFUL.
WAAKKK
SO NOT ONLY ARE YOU LATE, BUT YOU'RE *DAY-DREAMING* TOO, EH, MIAKA?

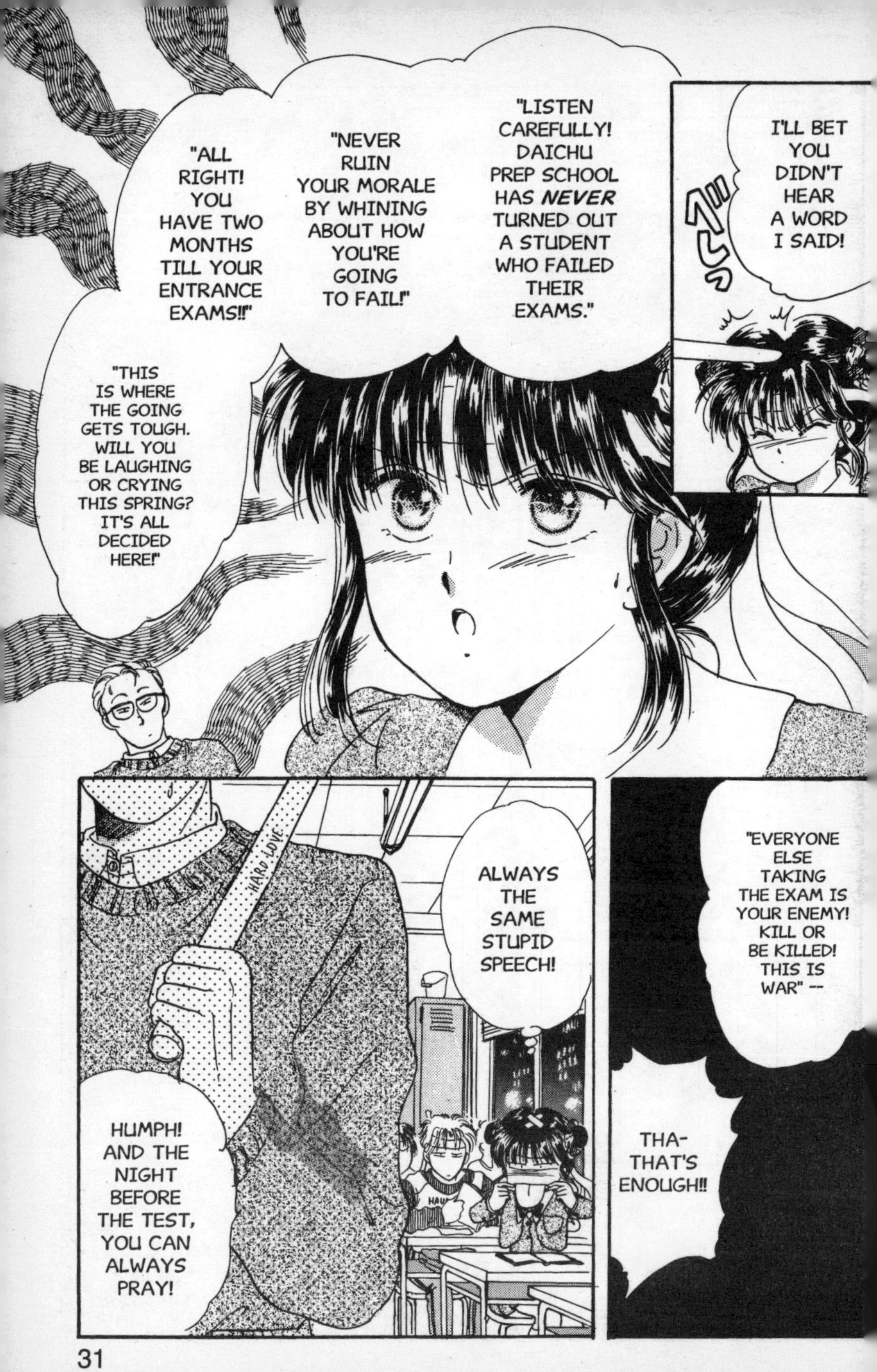
"ALL RIGHT! YOU HAVE TWO MONTHS TILL YOUR ENTRANCE EXAMS!!"
"NEVER RUIN YOUR MORALE BY WHINING ABOUT HOW YOU'RE GOING TO FAIL!"
"LISTEN CAREFULLY! DAICHU PREP SCHOOL HAS *NEVER* TURNED OUT A STUDENT WHO FAILED THEIR EXAMS."
"THIS IS WHERE THE GOING GETS TOUGH. WILL YOU BE LAUGHING OR CRYING THIS SPRING? IT'S ALL DECIDED HERE!"
I'LL BET YOU DIDN'T HEAR A WORD I SAID!
HARD LOVE
ALWAYS THE SAME STUPID SPEECH!
HUMPH! AND THE NIGHT BEFORE THE TEST, YOU CAN ALWAYS PRAY!
"EVERYONE ELSE TAKING THE EXAM IS YOUR ENEMY! KILL OR BE KILLED! THIS IS WAR" --
THA-THAT'S ENOUGH!!

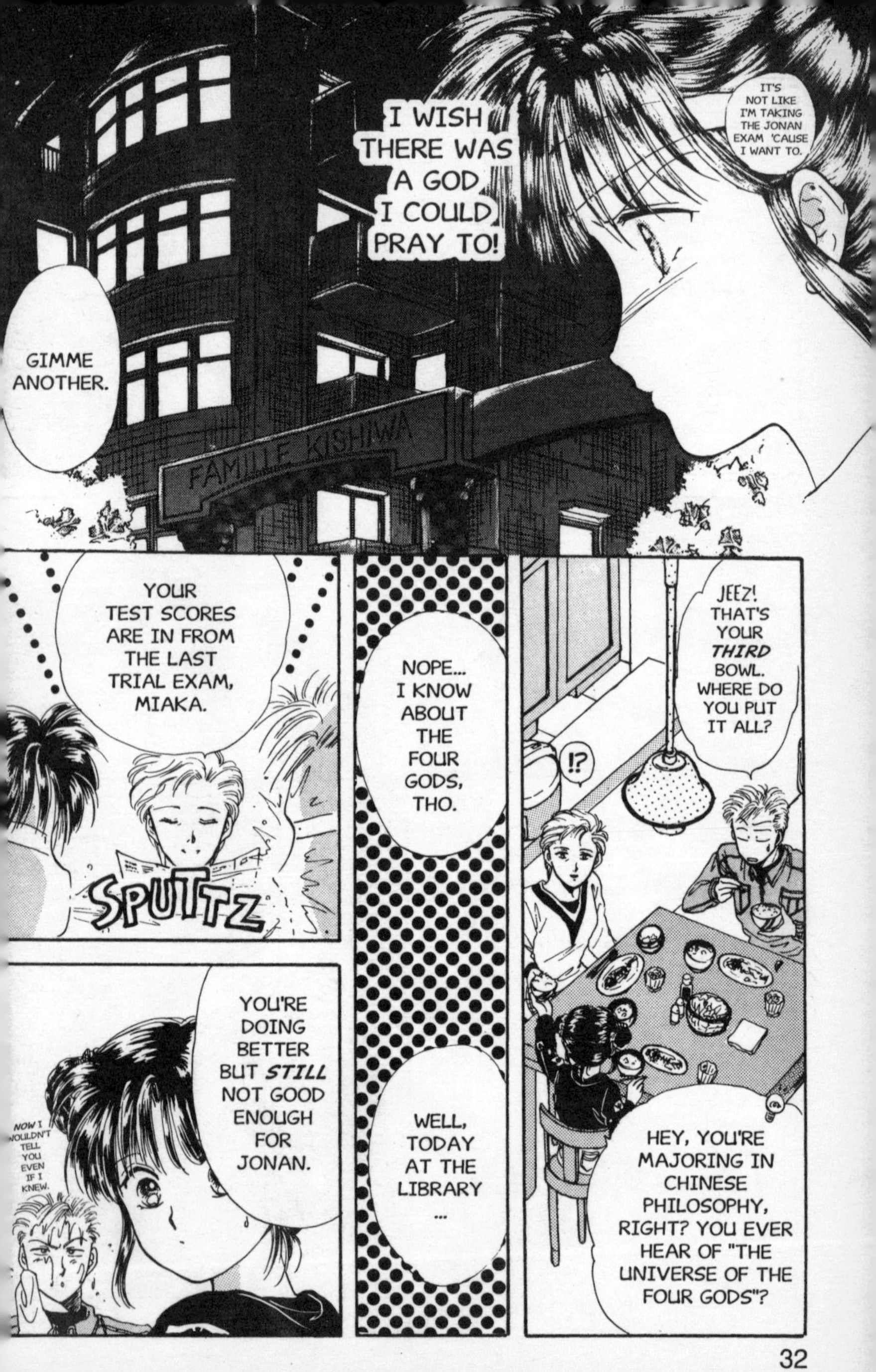
IT'S NOT LIKE I'M TAKING THE JONAN EXAM 'CAUSE I WANT TO.
I WISH THERE WAS A GOD I COULD PRAY TO!
GIMME ANOTHER.
FAMILLE KISHIWA
JEEZ! THAT'S YOUR *THIRD* BOWL. WHERE DO YOU PUT IT ALL?
!?
HEY, YOU'RE MAJORING IN CHINESE PHILOSOPHY, RIGHT? YOU EVER HEAR OF "THE UNIVERSE OF THE FOUR GODS"?
NOPE... I KNOW ABOUT THE FOUR GODS, THO.
WELL, TODAY AT THE LIBRARY ...
YOUR TEST SCORES ARE IN FROM THE LAST TRIAL EXAM, MIAKA.
SPUTTZ
YOU'RE DOING BETTER BUT *STILL* NOT GOOD ENOUGH FOR JONAN.
NOW I WOULDN'T TELL YOU EVEN IF I KNEW.

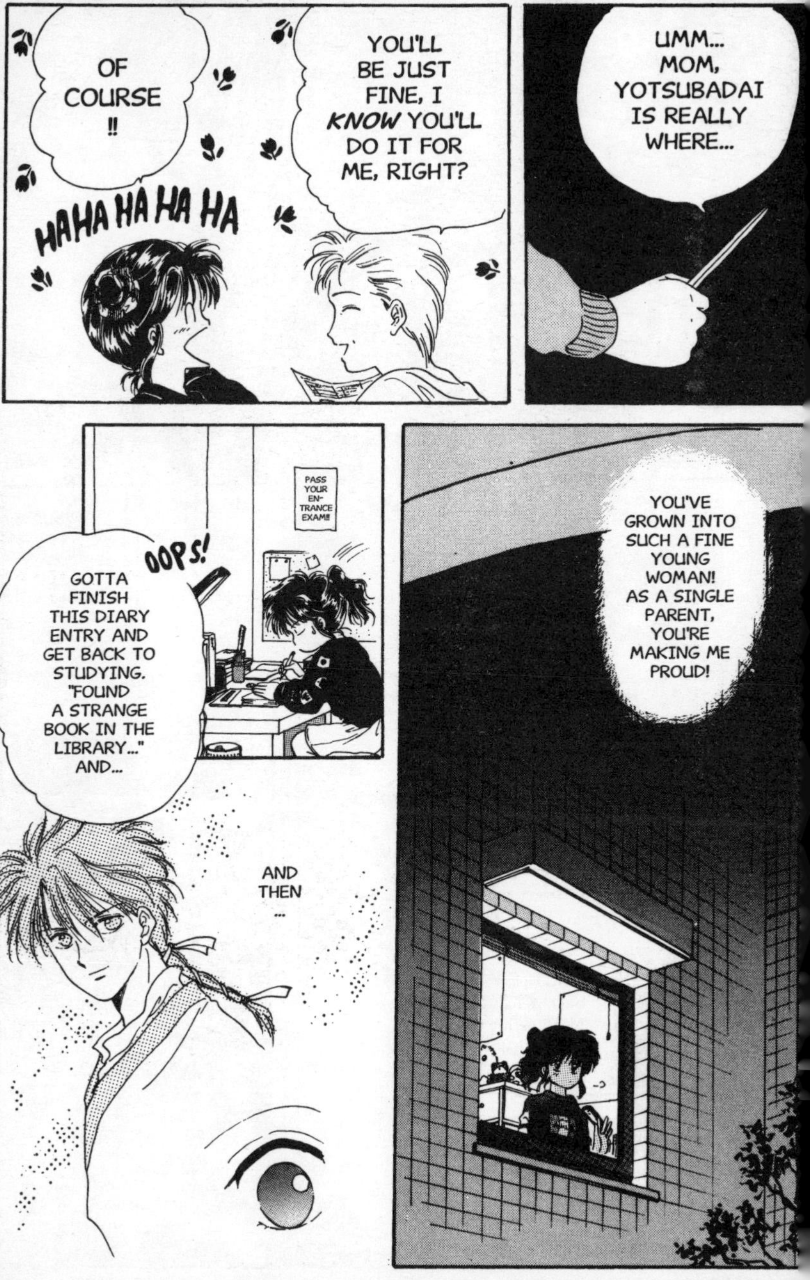
UMM... MOM, YOTSUBADAI IS REALLY WHERE...
YOU'LL BE JUST FINE, I *KNOW* YOU'LL DO IT FOR ME, RIGHT?
OF COURSE !!
HAHA HA HA HA
YOU'VE GROWN INTO SUCH A FINE YOUNG WOMAN! AS A SINGLE PARENT, YOU'RE MAKING ME PROUD!
PASS YOUR EN-TRANCE EXAM!!
OOPS!
GOTTA FINISH THIS DIARY ENTRY AND GET BACK TO STUDYING. "FOUND A STRANGE BOOK IN THE LIBRARY..." AND...
AND THEN ...

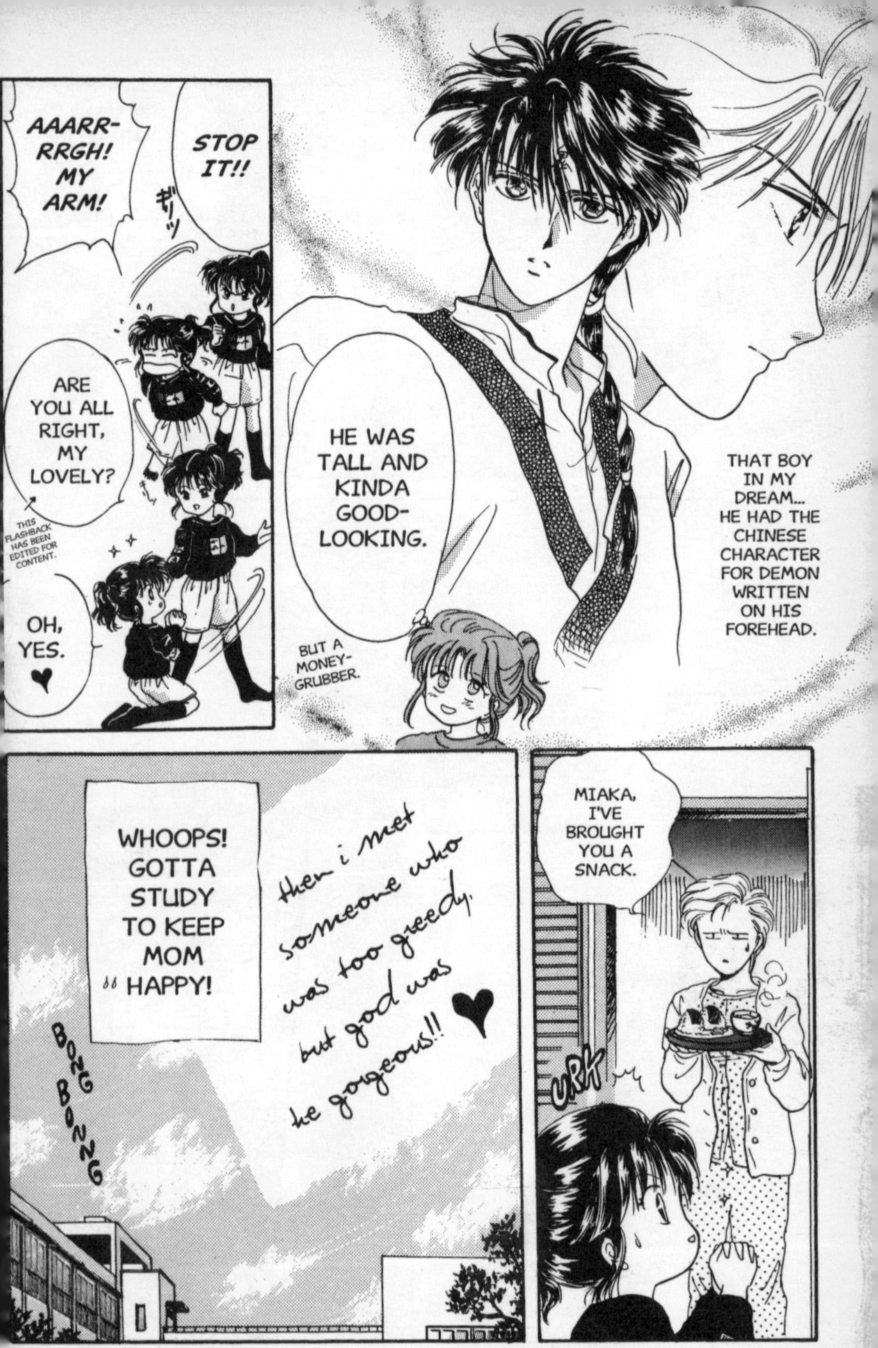

THAT BOY IN MY DREAM... HE HAD THE CHINESE CHARACTER FOR DEMON WRITTEN ON HIS FOREHEAD.
HE WAS TALL AND KINDA GOOD-LOOKING.
BUT A MONEY-GRUBBER.
STOP IT!!
ギリッ
AAARR-RRGH! MY ARM!
ARE YOU ALL RIGHT, MY LOVELY?
THIS FLASHBACK HAS BEEN EDITED FOR CONTENT.
OH, YES.
MIAKA, I'VE BROUGHT YOU A SNACK.
URK
WHOOPS! GOTTA STUDY TO KEEP MOM HAPPY!
then i met someone who was too greedy, but god was he gorgeous!!
BONG BONNG

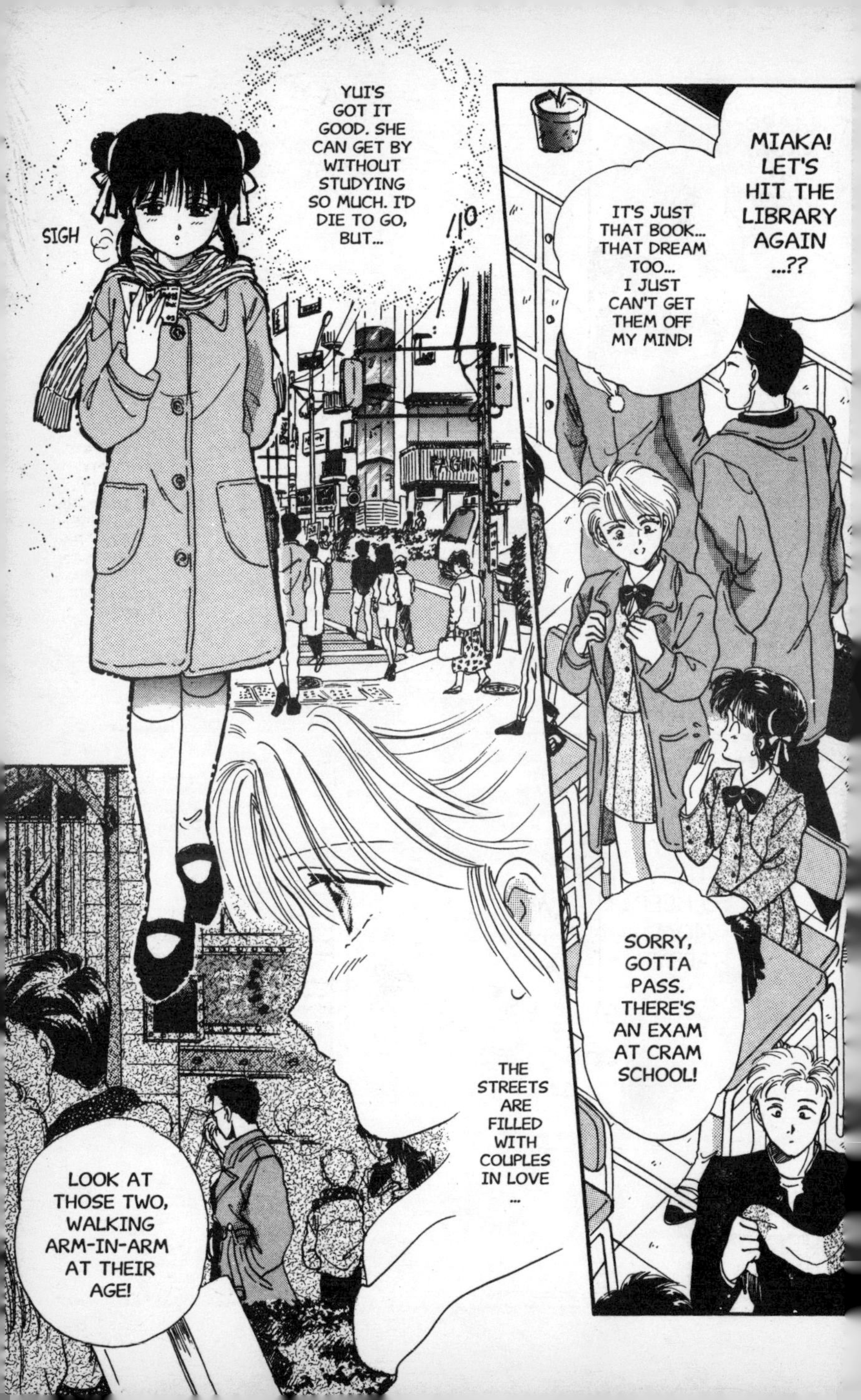
SIGH
YUI'S GOT IT GOOD. SHE CAN GET BY WITHOUT STUDYING SO MUCH. I'D DIE TO GO, BUT...
MIAKA! LET'S HIT THE LIBRARY AGAIN ...??
SORRY, GOTTA PASS. THERE'S AN EXAM AT CRAM SCHOOL!
IT'S JUST THAT BOOK... THAT DREAM TOO... I JUST CAN'T GET THEM OFF MY MIND!
THE STREETS ARE FILLED WITH COUPLES IN LOVE ...
LOOK AT THOSE TWO, WALKING ARM-IN-ARM AT THEIR AGE!

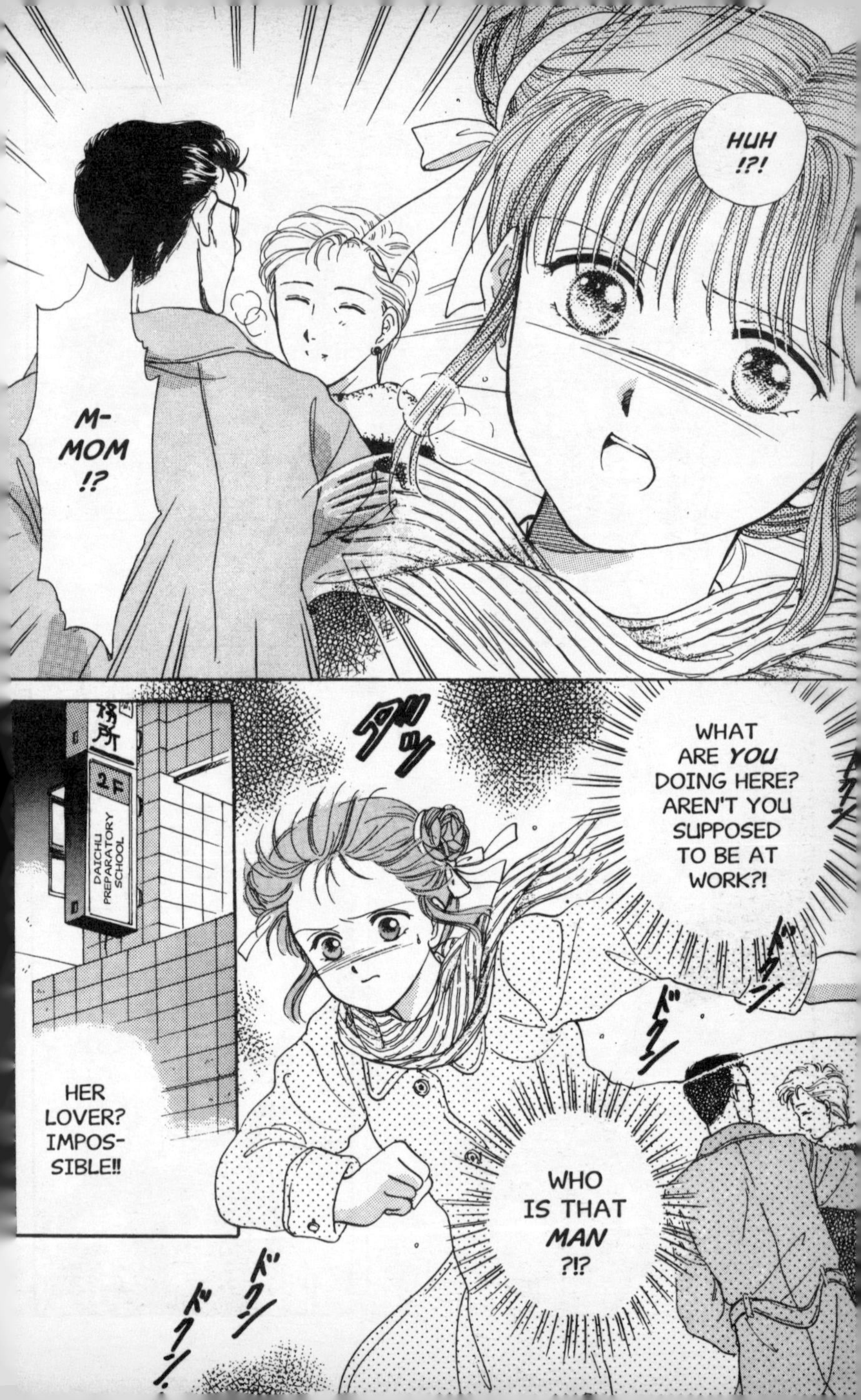
HUH !?!
M-MOM !?
WHAT ARE *YOU* DOING HERE? AREN'T YOU SUPPOSED TO BE AT WORK?!
2F
DAICHU PREPARATORY SCHOOL
WHO IS THAT *MAN* ?!?
HER LOVER? IMPOSSIBLE!!

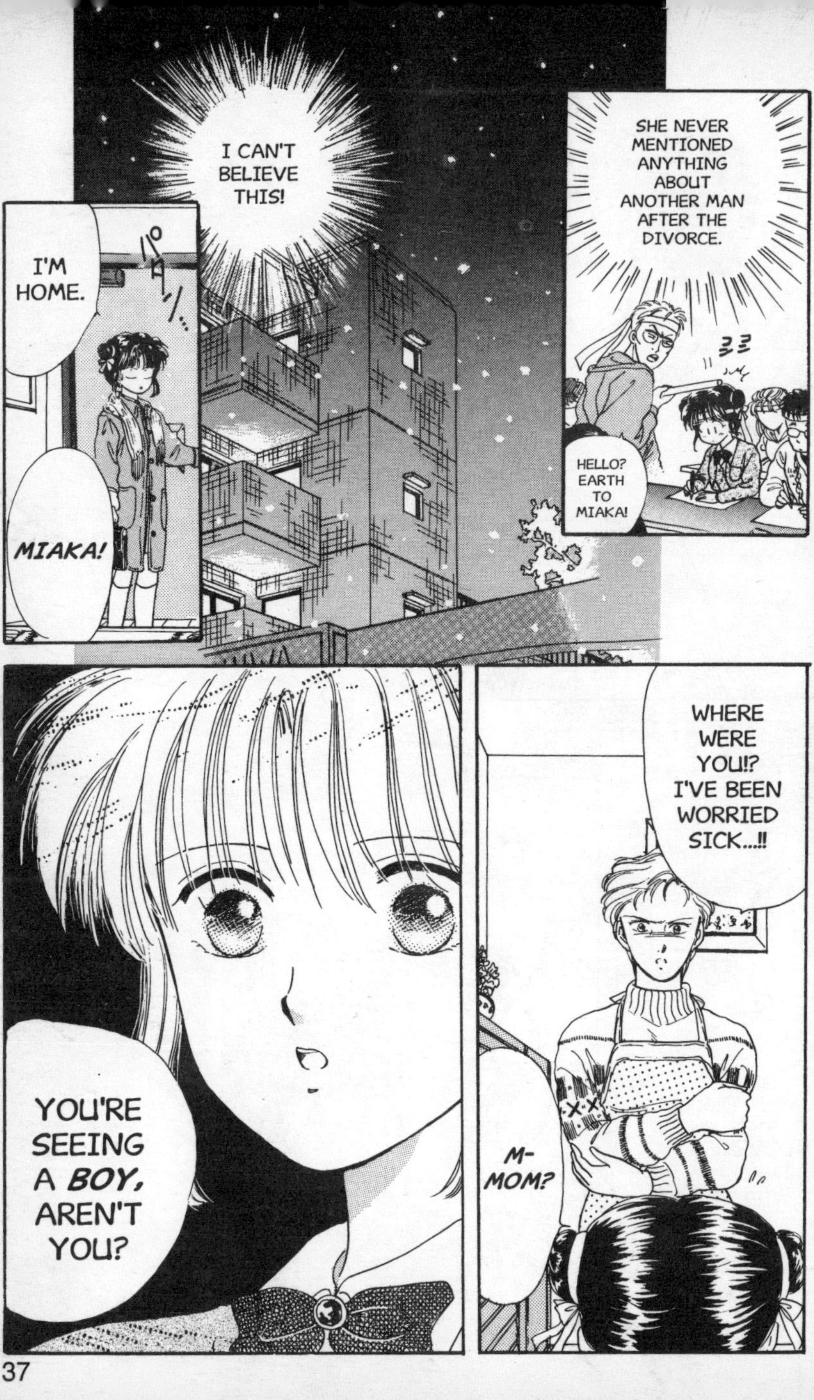
SHE NEVER MENTIONED ANYTHING ABOUT ANOTHER MAN AFTER THE DIVORCE.
HELLO? EARTH TO MIAKA!
I CAN'T BELIEVE THIS!
I'M HOME.
MIAKA!
WHERE WERE YOU!? I'VE BEEN WORRIED SICK...!!
M-MOM?
YOU'RE SEEING A BOY, AREN'T YOU?

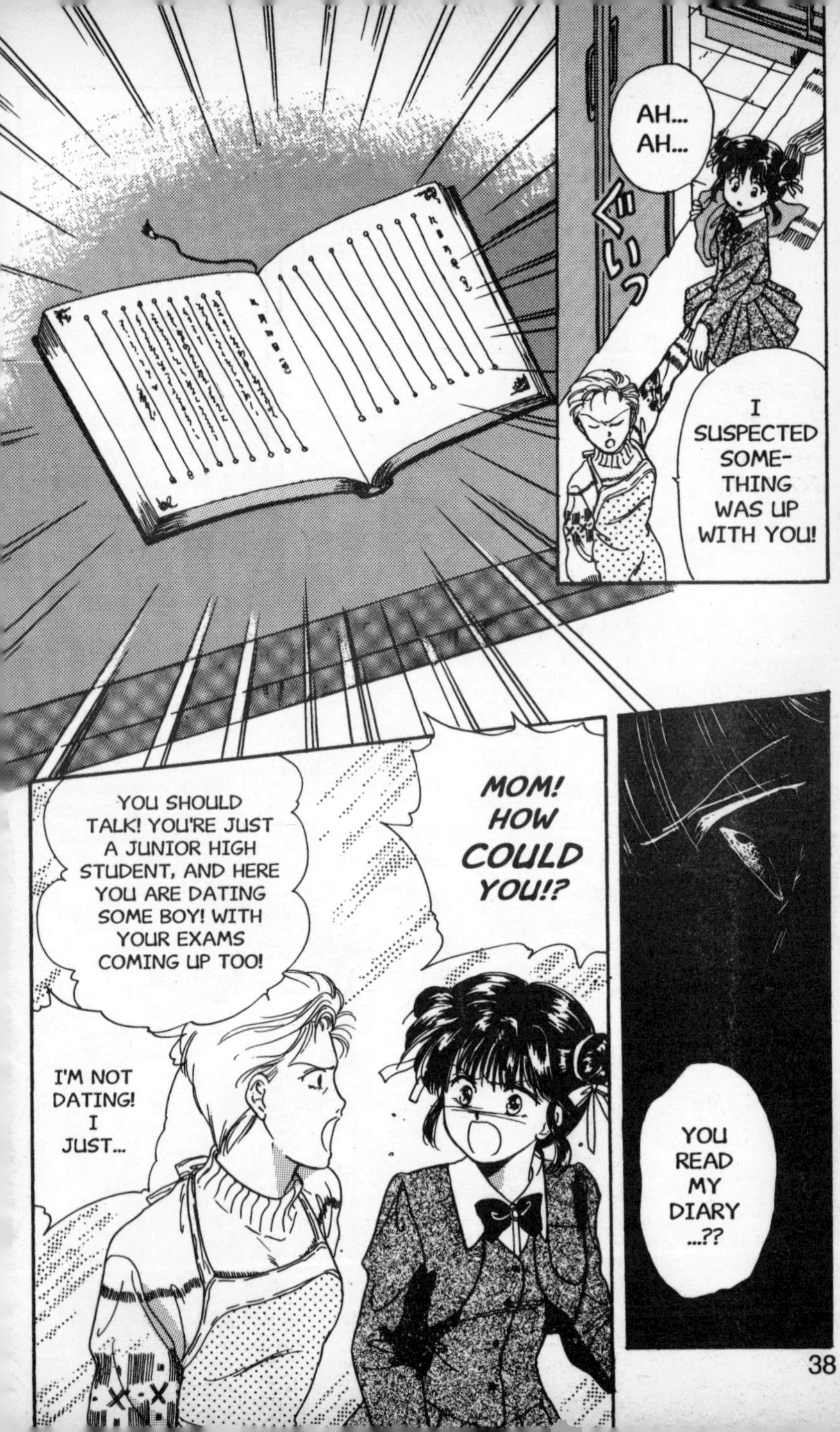
AH... AH...
I SUSPECTED SOMETHING WAS UP WITH YOU!
YOU READ MY DIARY ...??
MOM! HOW COULD YOU!?
YOU SHOULD TALK! YOU'RE JUST A JUNIOR HIGH STUDENT, AND HERE YOU ARE DATING SOME BOY! WITH YOUR EXAMS COMING UP TOO!
I'M NOT DATING! I JUST...

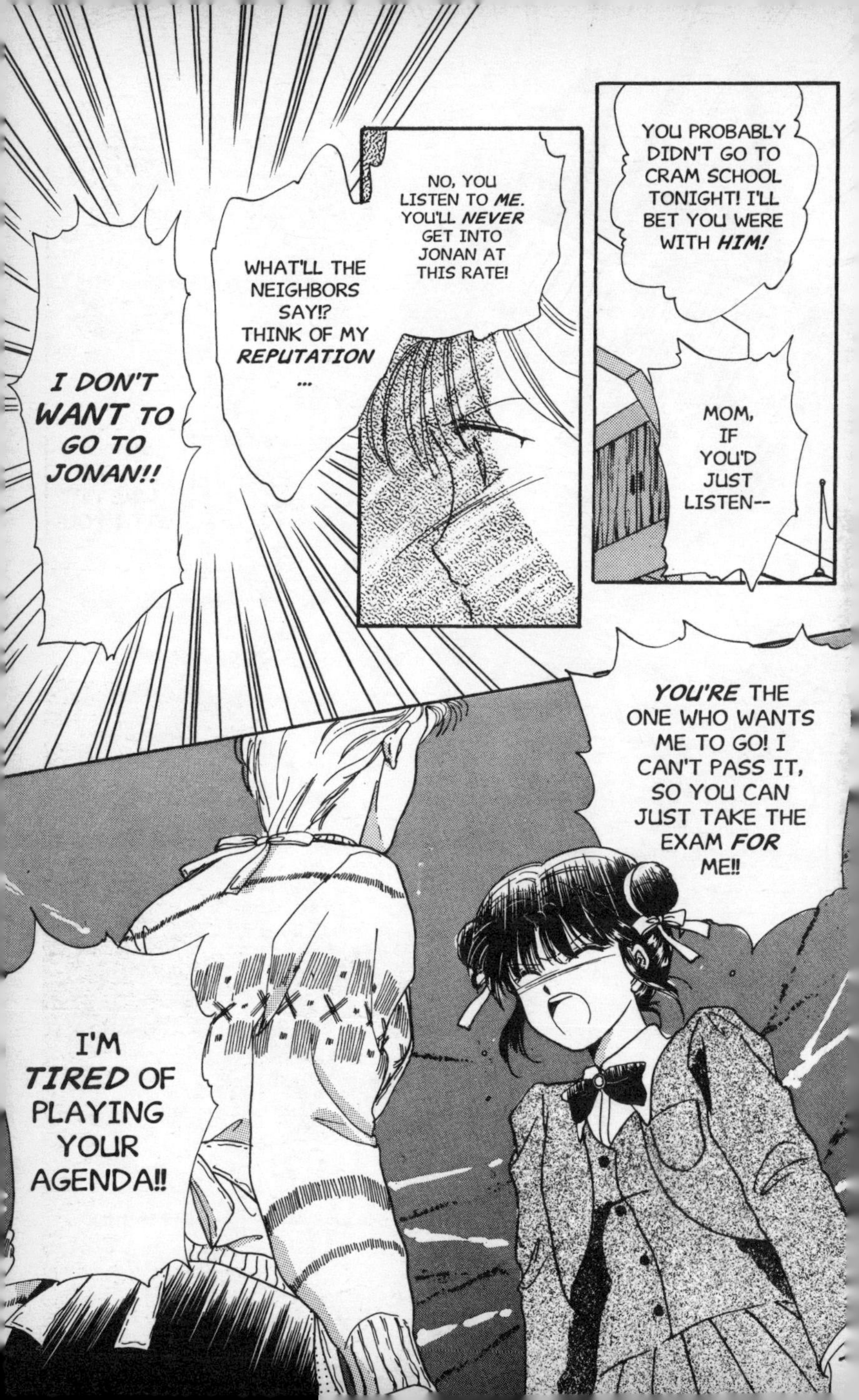
YOU PROBABLY DIDN'T GO TO CRAM SCHOOL TONIGHT! I'LL BET YOU WERE WITH *HIM!*
MOM, IF YOU'D JUST LISTEN--
NO, YOU LISTEN TO *ME*. YOU'LL *NEVER* GET INTO JONAN AT THIS RATE!
WHAT'LL THE NEIGHBORS SAY!? THINK OF MY *REPUTATION* ...
I DON'T WANT TO *GO TO JONAN!!*
YOU'RE THE ONE WHO WANTS ME TO GO! I CAN'T PASS IT, SO YOU CAN JUST TAKE THE EXAM *FOR* ME!!
I'M *TIRED* OF PLAYING YOUR AGENDA!!

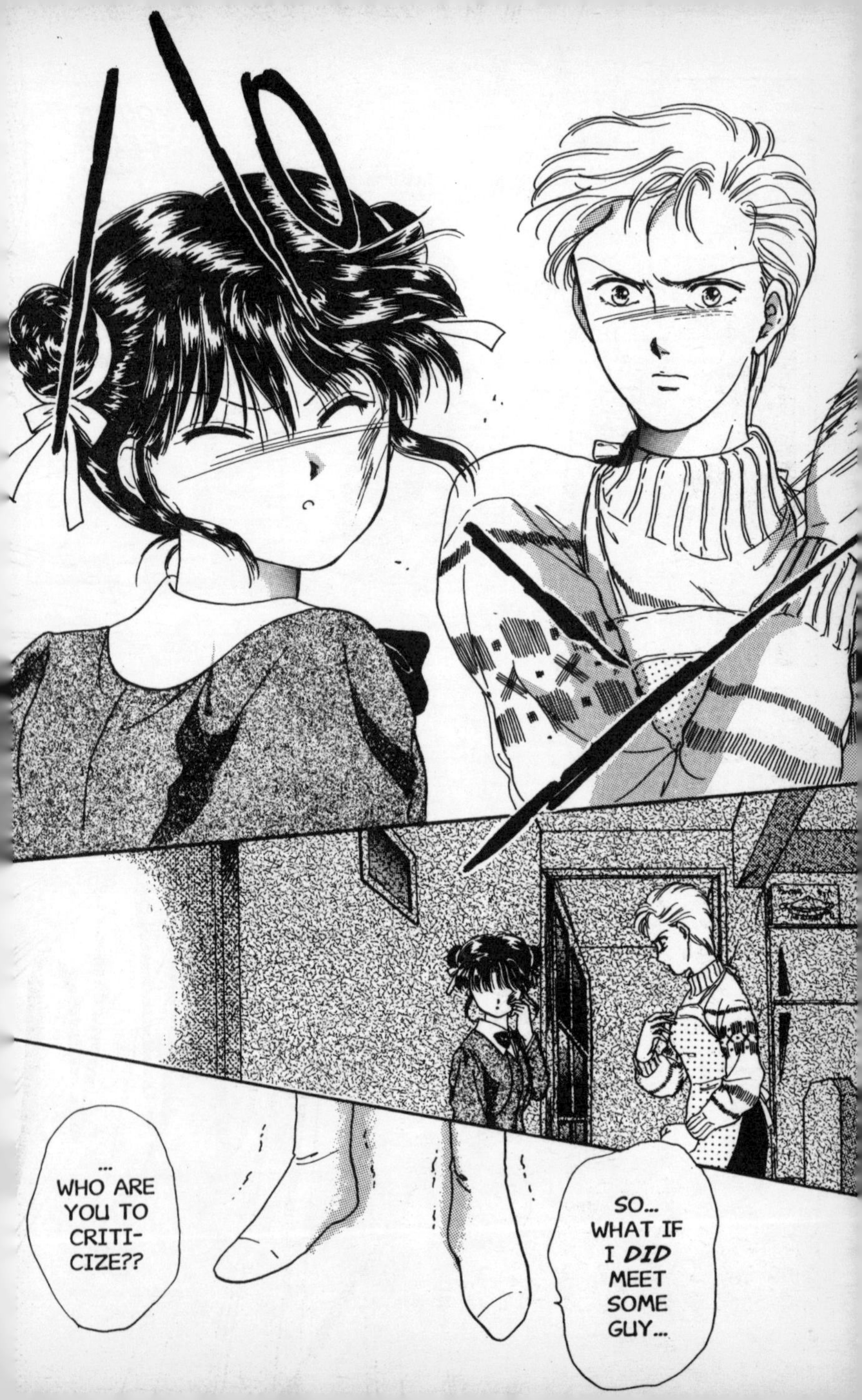
SO... WHAT IF I *DID* MEET SOME GUY...
... WHO ARE YOU TO CRITI- CIZE??

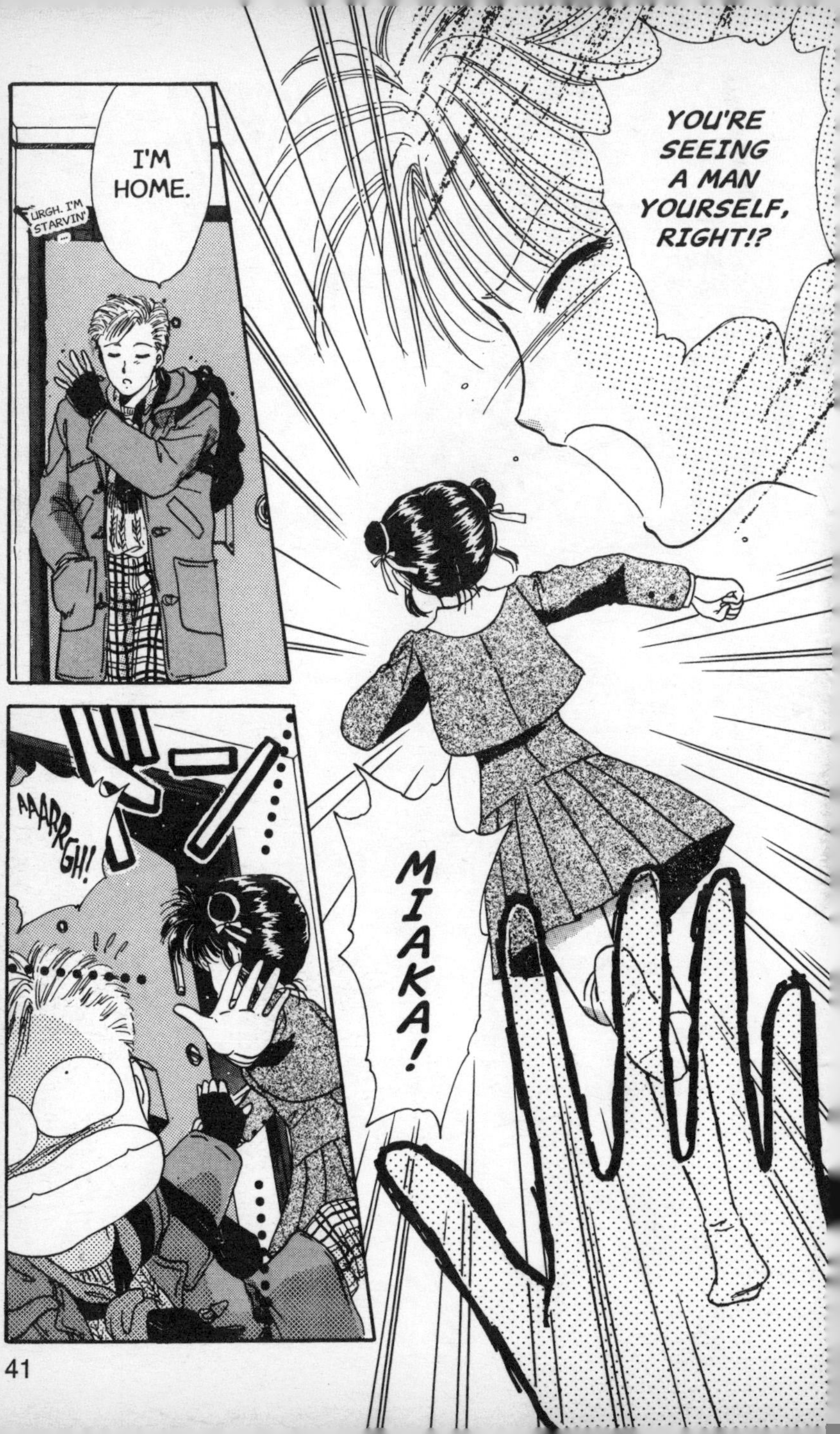
YOU'RE SEEING A MAN YOURSELF, RIGHT!?
I'M HOME.
URGH. I'M STARVIN'
...
MIAKA!
AAARRRGH!

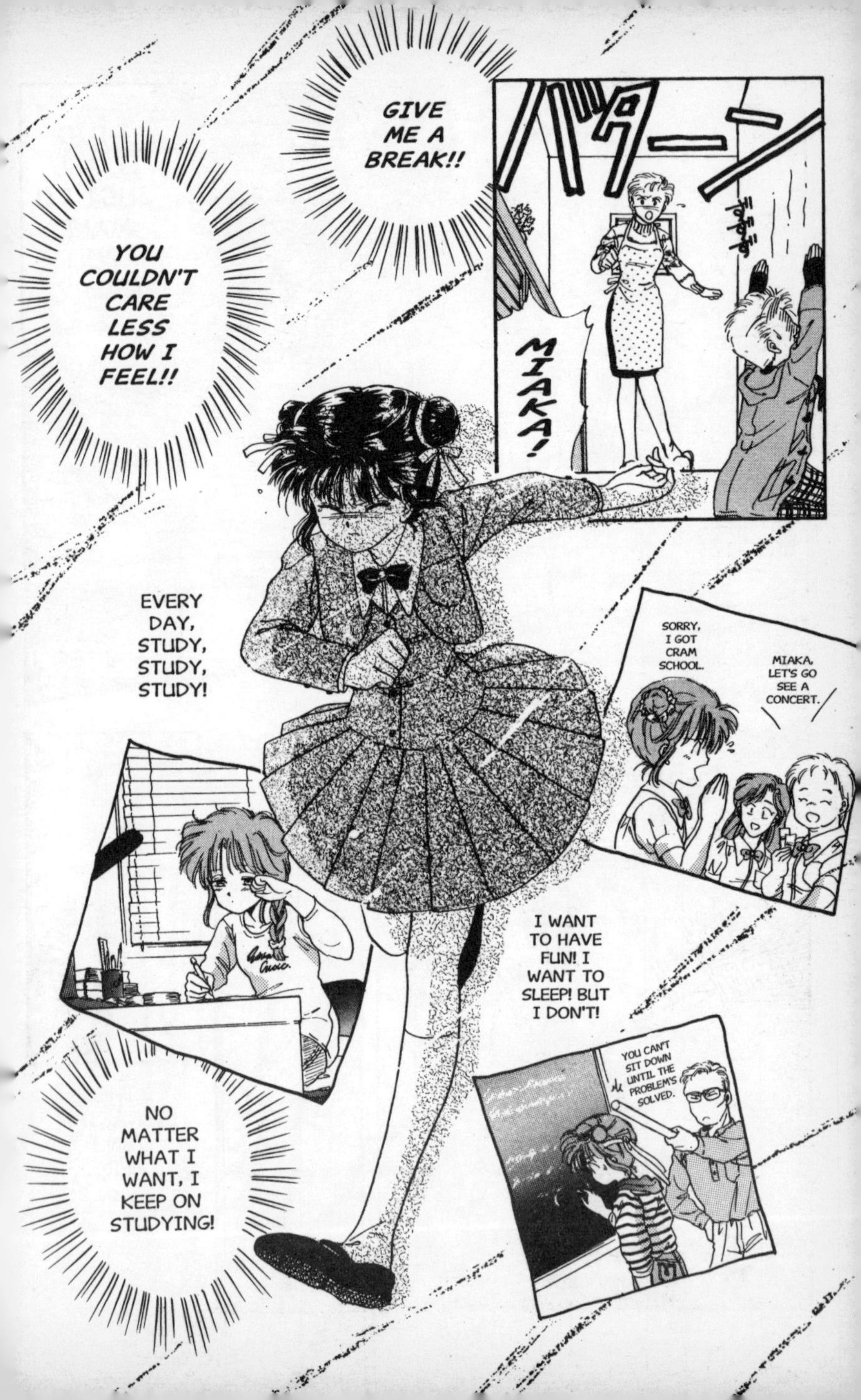

MIAKA!
GIVE ME A BREAK!!
YOU COULDN'T CARE LESS HOW I FEEL!!
EVERY DAY, STUDY, STUDY, STUDY!
MIAKA, LET'S GO SEE A CONCERT.
SORRY, I GOT CRAM SCHOOL.
I WANT TO HAVE FUN! I WANT TO SLEEP! BUT I DON'T!
YOU CAN'T SIT DOWN UNTIL THE PROBLEM'S SOLVED.
NO MATTER WHAT I WANT, I KEEP ON STUDYING!

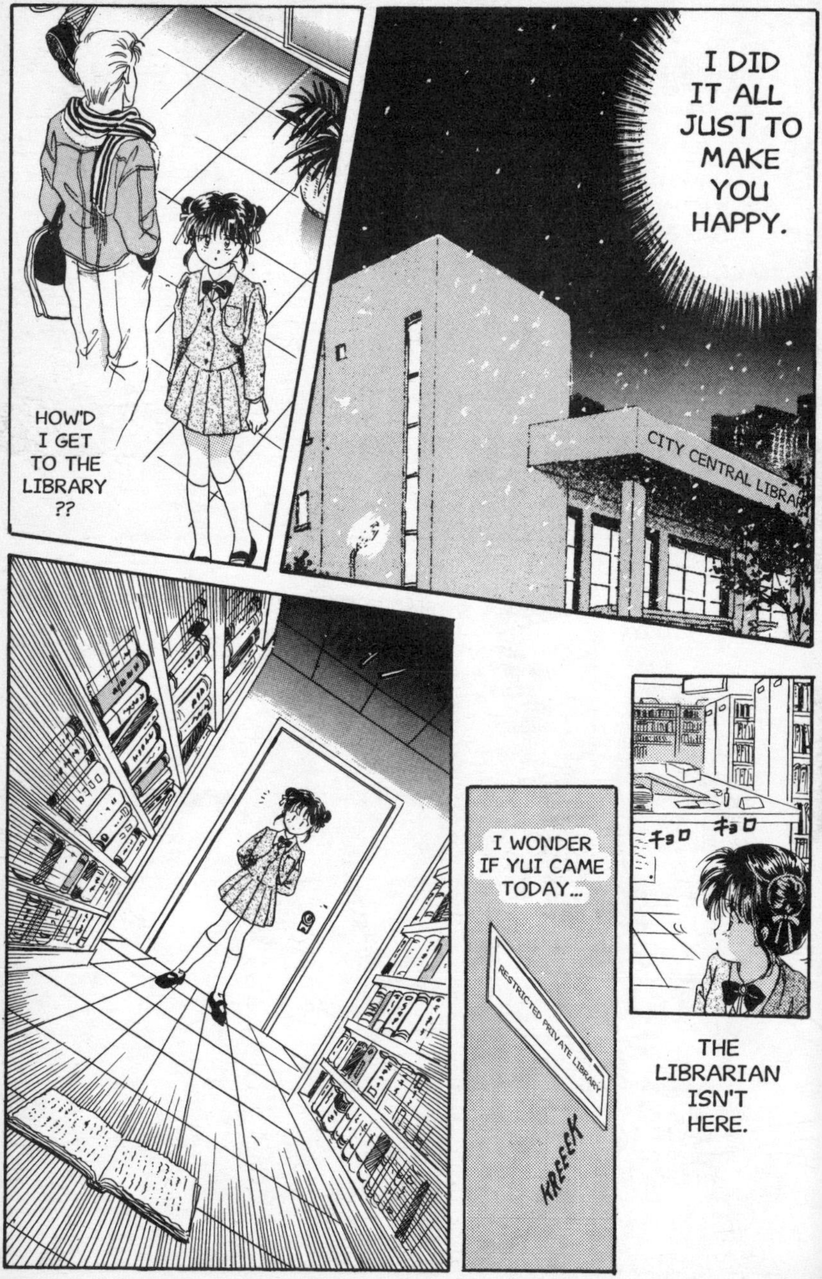
I DID IT ALL JUST TO MAKE YOU HAPPY.
CITY CENTRAL LIBRAR
HOW'D I GET TO THE LIBRARY ??
キョロ キョロ
THE LIBRARIAN ISN'T HERE.
I WONDER IF YUI CAME TODAY...
RESTRICTED PRIVATE LIBRARY
KREEEK

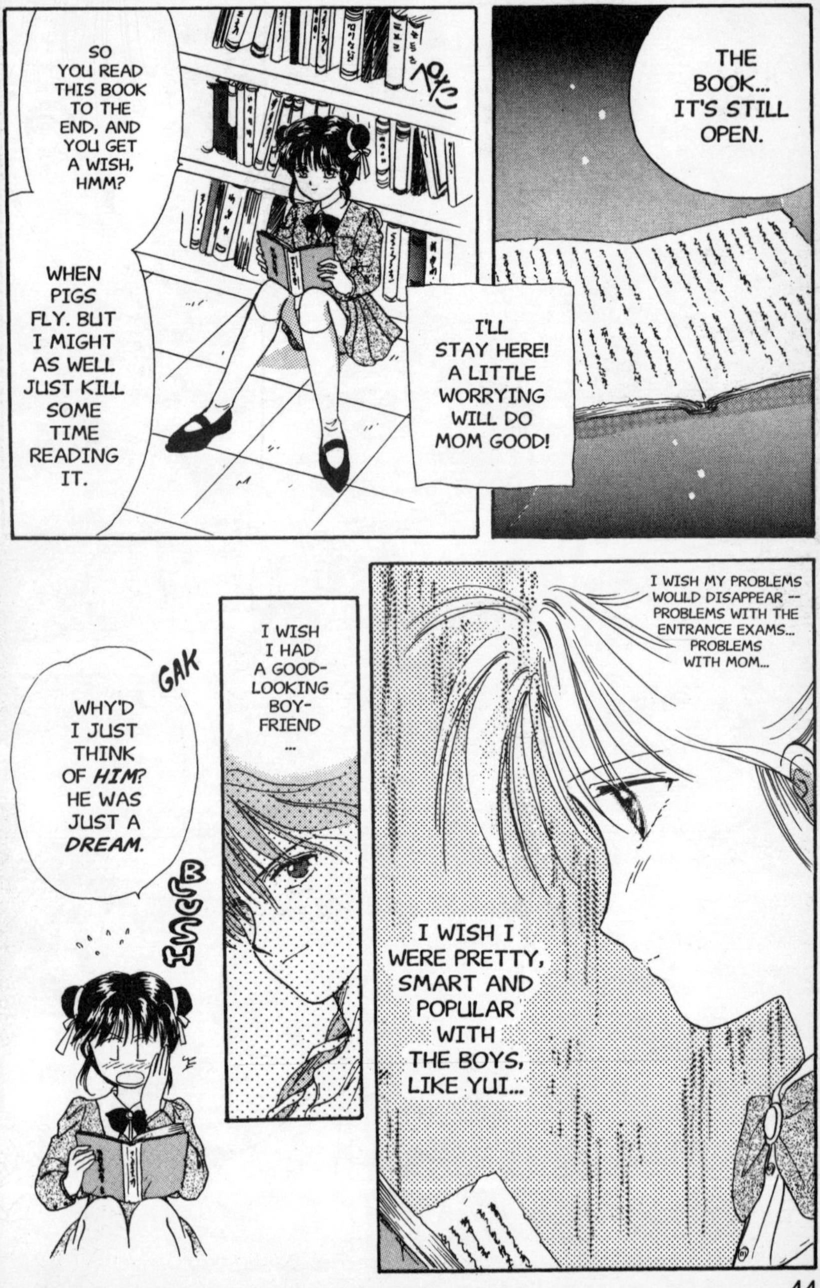

THE BOOK... IT'S STILL OPEN.
I'LL STAY HERE! A LITTLE WORRYING WILL DO MOM GOOD!
SO YOU READ THIS BOOK TO THE END, AND YOU GET A WISH, HMM?
WHEN PIGS FLY. BUT I MIGHT AS WELL JUST KILL SOME TIME READING IT.
I WISH MY PROBLEMS WOULD DISAPPEAR -- PROBLEMS WITH THE ENTRANCE EXAMS... PROBLEMS WITH MOM...
I WISH I WERE PRETTY, SMART AND POPULAR WITH THE BOYS, LIKE YUI...
I WISH I HAD A GOOD-LOOKING BOY-FRIEND ...
GAK
WHY'D I JUST THINK OF *HIM*? HE WAS JUST A *DREAM*.
BLUSH

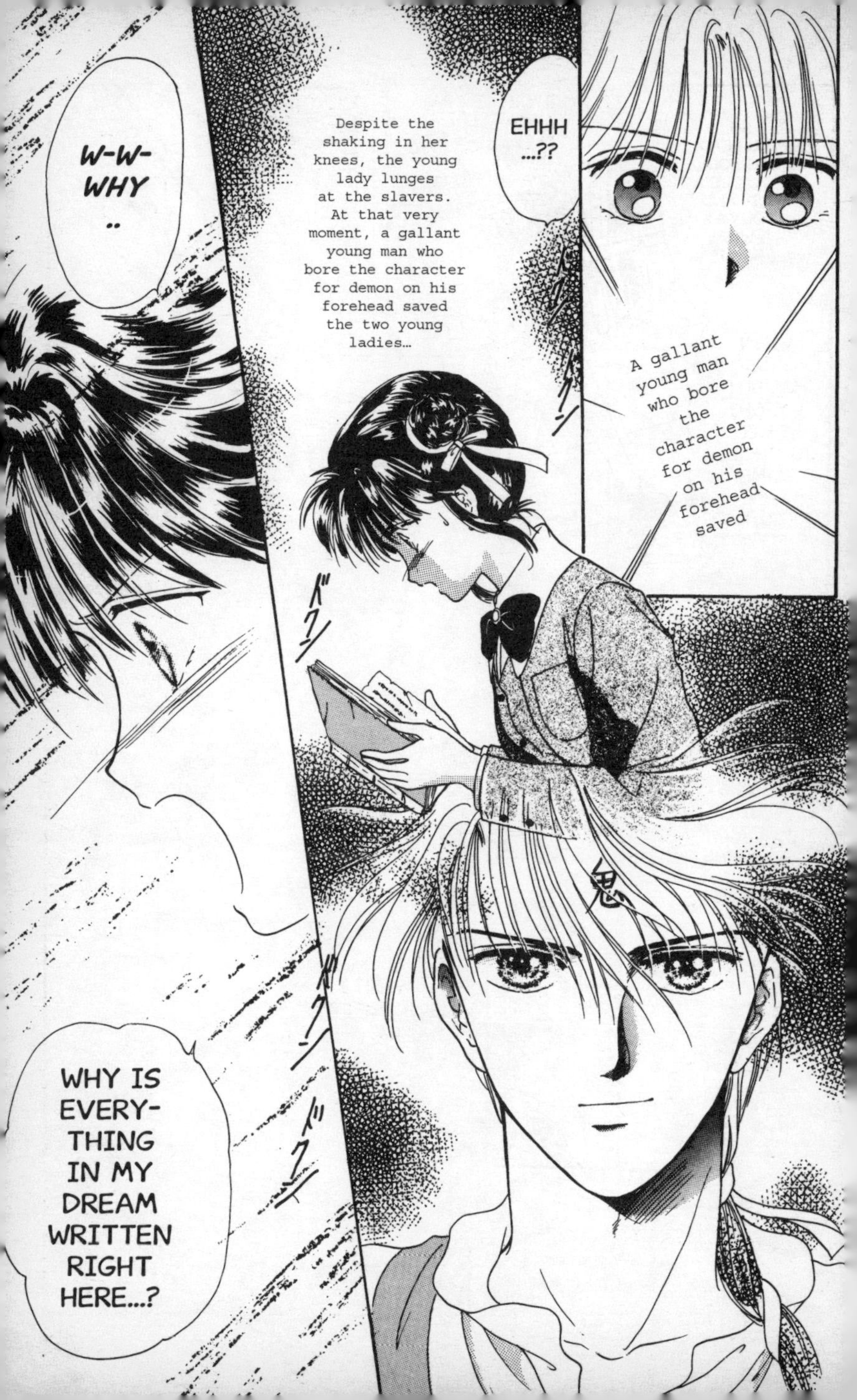
EHHH ...??
A gallant young man who bore the character for demon on his forehead saved
Despite the shaking in her knees, the young lady lunges at the slavers. At that very moment, a gallant young man who bore the character for demon on his forehead saved the two young ladies...
W-W-WHY ..
WHY IS EVERY-THING IN MY DREAM WRITTEN RIGHT HERE...?

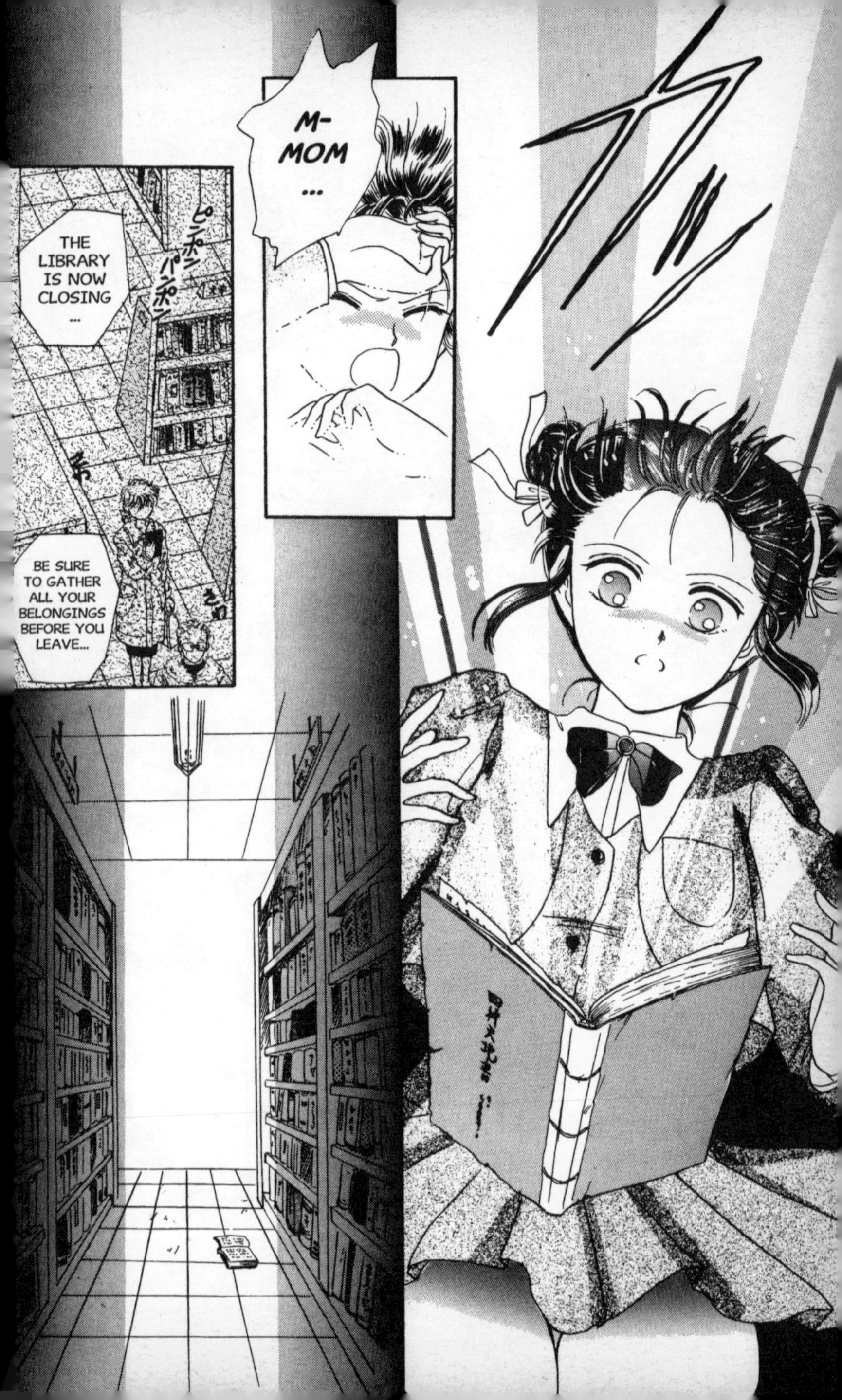
M-MOM ...
THE LIBRARY IS NOW CLOSING ...
BE SURE TO GATHER ALL YOUR BELONGINGS BEFORE YOU LEAVE...

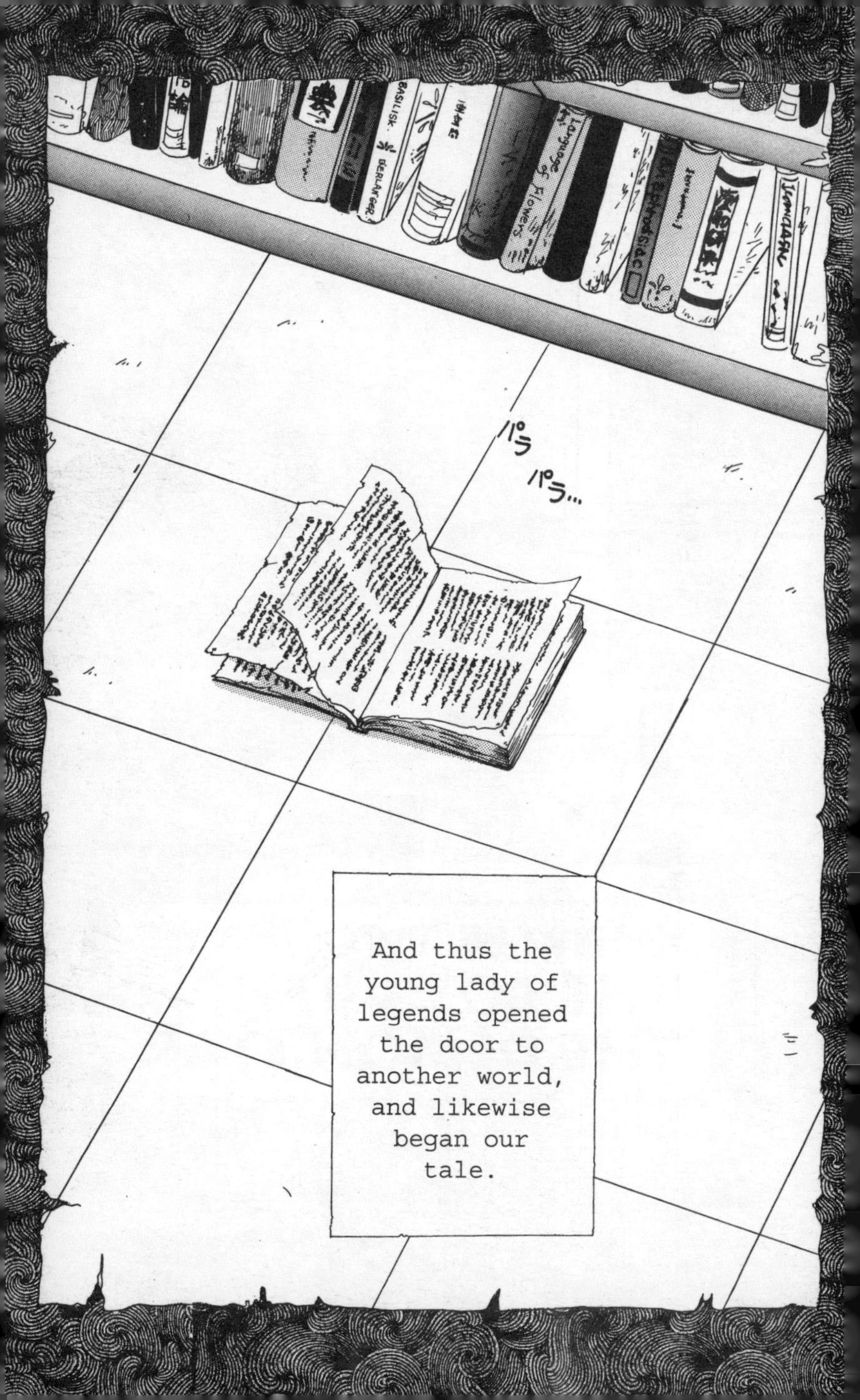
パラ
パラ...
And thus the young lady of legends opened the door to another world, and likewise began our tale.

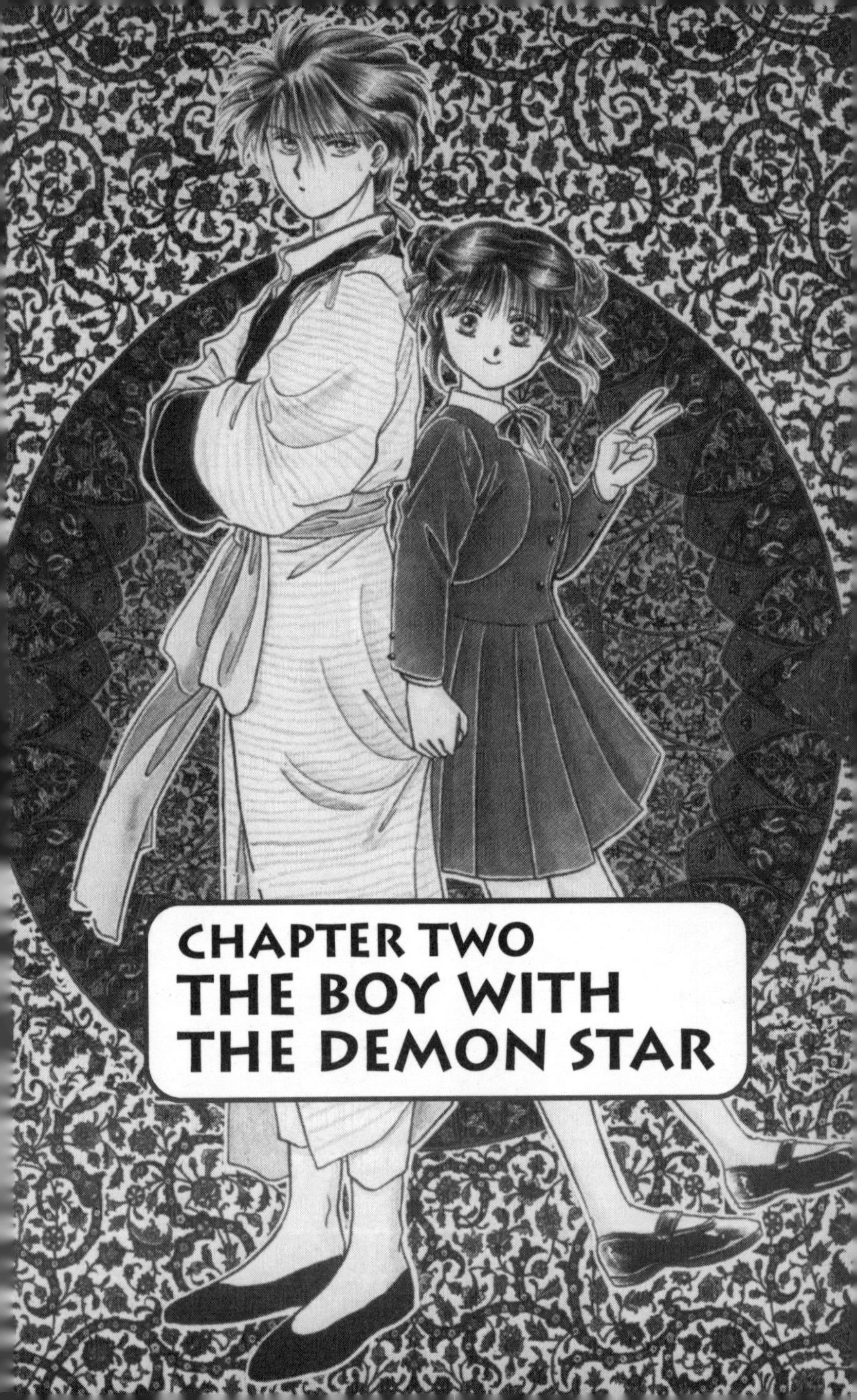
CHAPTER TWO
THE BOY WITH
THE DEMON STAR

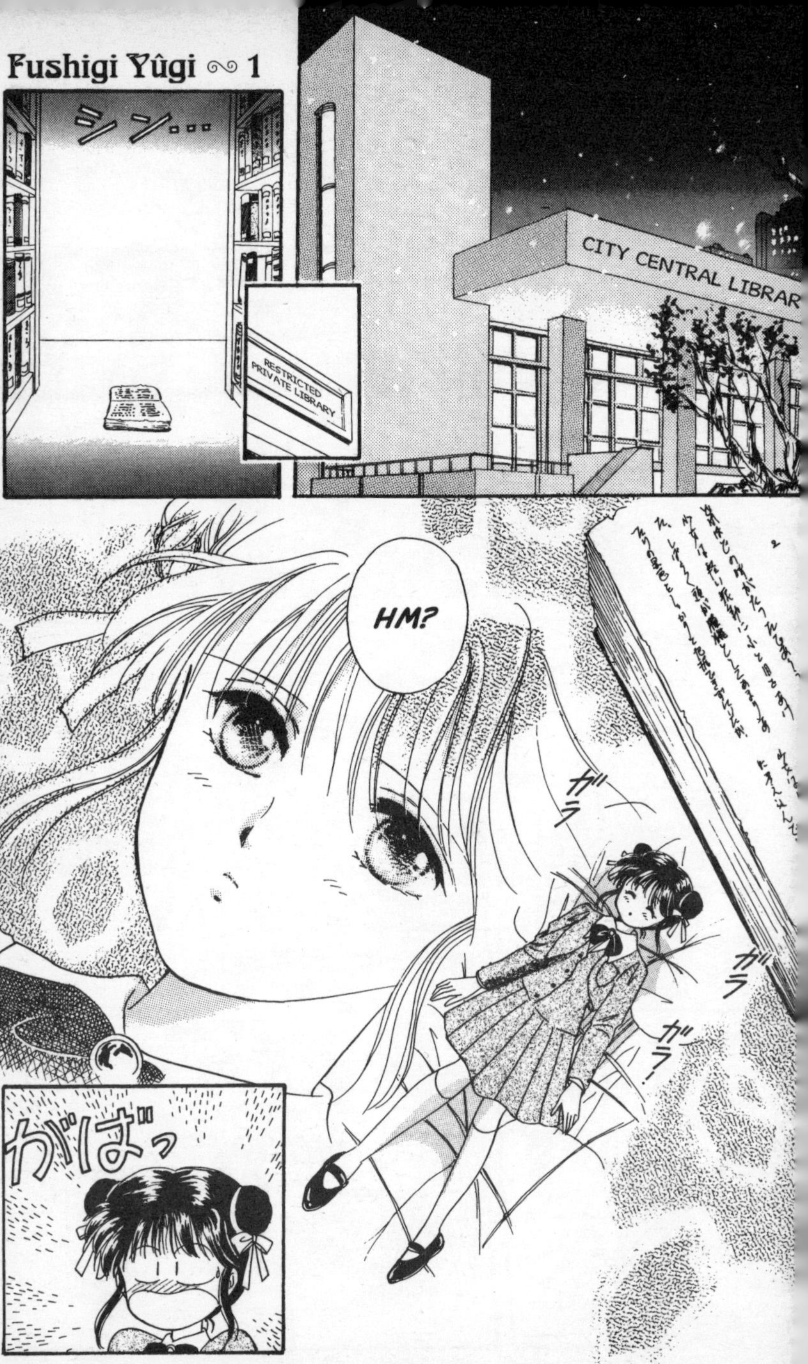
CITY CENTRAL LIBRAR
RESTRICTED
PRIVATE LIBRARY
シン…
HM?
ガラ
ガラ
ガラ!
がばっ

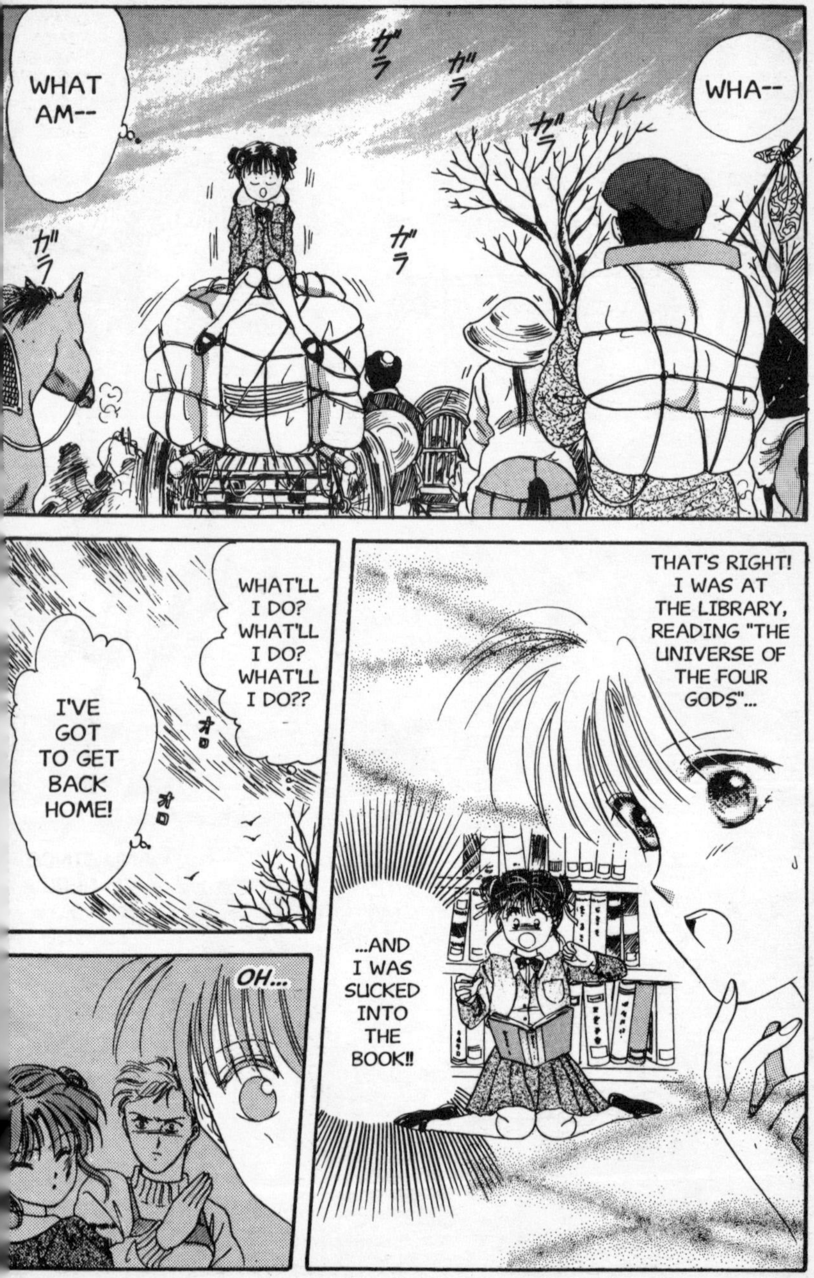
ガラ
ガラ
ガラ
ガラ
ガラ
WHA--
WHAT AM--
THAT'S RIGHT! I WAS AT THE LIBRARY, READING "THE UNIVERSE OF THE FOUR GODS"...
...AND I WAS SUCKED INTO THE BOOK!!
WHAT'LL I DO? WHAT'LL I DO? WHAT'LL I DO??
オロ
オロ
I'VE GOT TO GET BACK HOME!
OH...

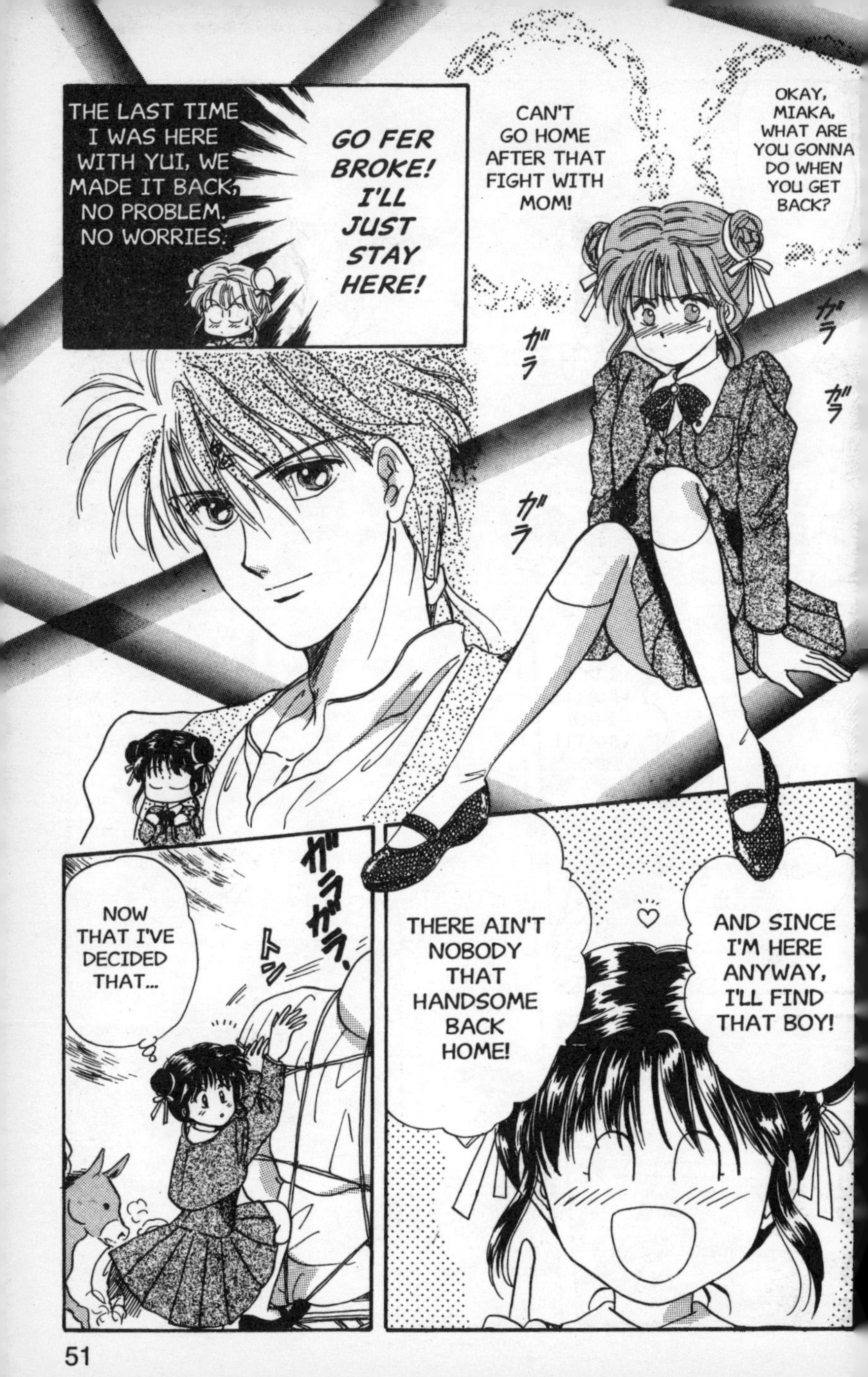

OKAY, MIAKA, WHAT ARE YOU GONNA DO WHEN YOU GET BACK?
CAN'T GO HOME AFTER THAT FIGHT WITH MOM!
THE LAST TIME I WAS HERE WITH YUI, WE MADE IT BACK, NO PROBLEM. NO WORRIES.
GO FER BROKE! I'LL JUST STAY HERE!
ガラ
ガラ
ガラ
ガラ
AND SINCE I'M HERE ANYWAY, I'LL FIND THAT BOY!
THERE AIN'T NOBODY THAT HANDSOME BACK HOME!
ガラガラ、
トッ
NOW THAT I'VE DECIDED THAT...

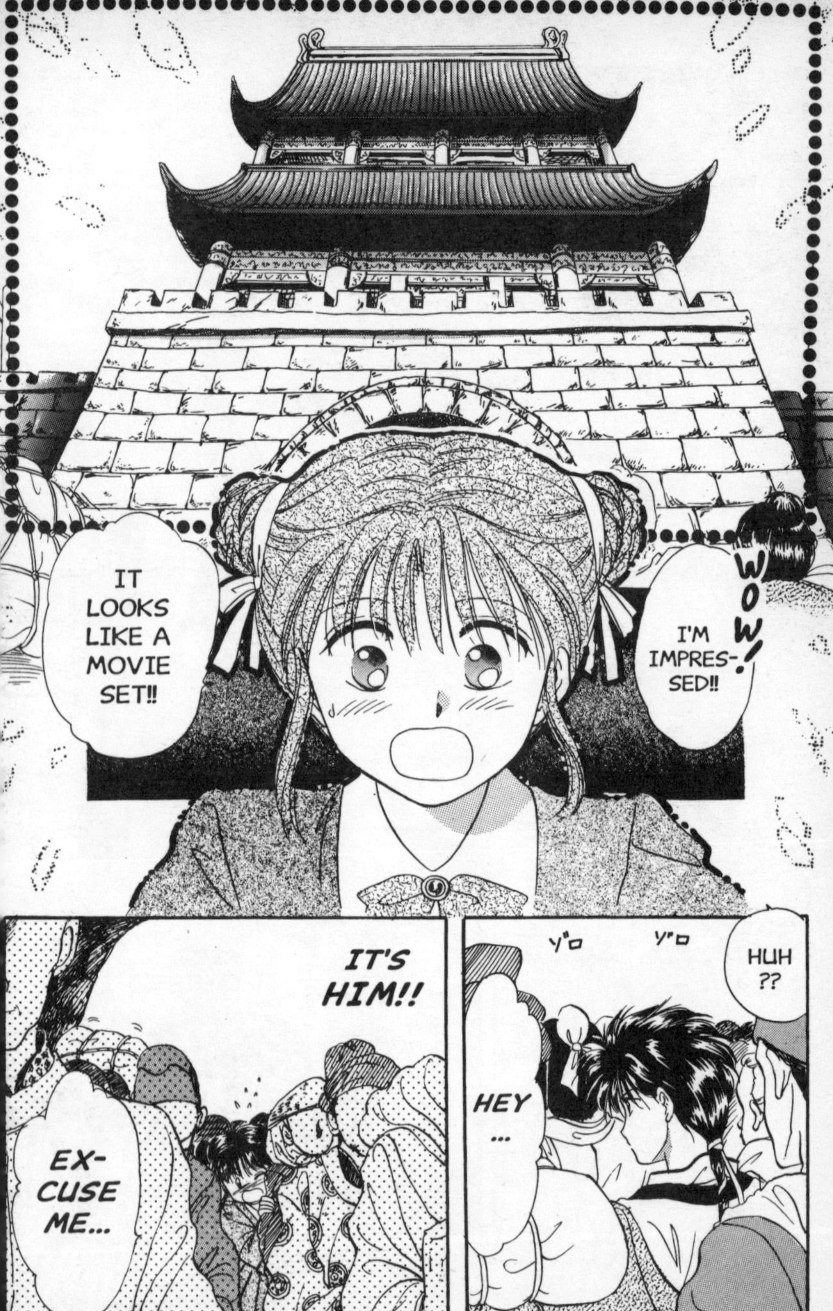
WOW!
I'M IMPRES-SED!!
IT LOOKS LIKE A MOVIE SET!!
HUH ??
ゾロ ゾロ
HEY ...
IT'S HIM!!
EX-CUSE ME...

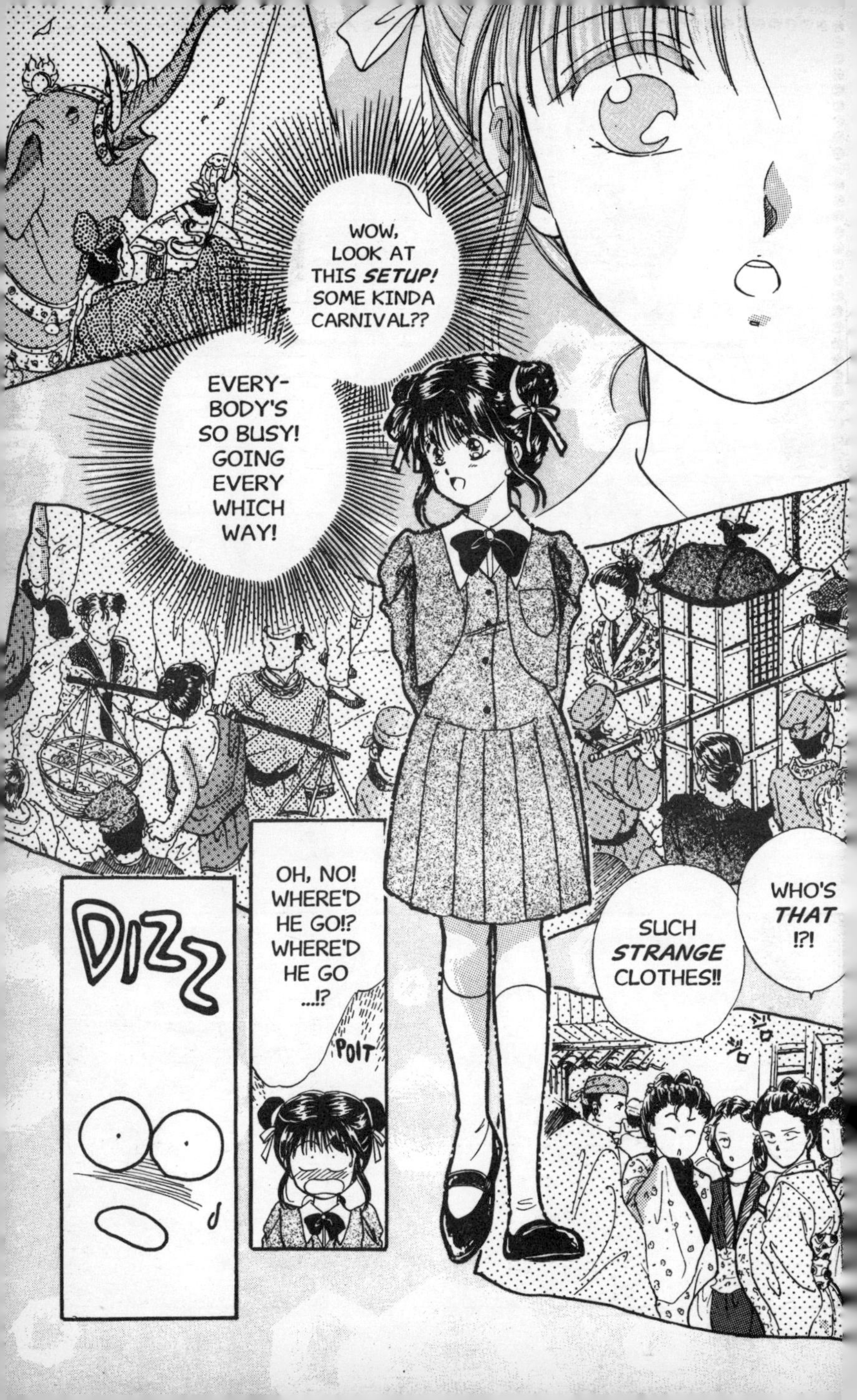
WOW, LOOK AT THIS *SETUP!* SOME KINDA CARNIVAL??
EVERY-BODY'S SO BUSY! GOING EVERY WHICH WAY!
WHO'S *THAT* !?!
SUCH *STRANGE* CLOTHES!!
OH, NO! WHERE'D HE GO!? WHERE'D HE GO ...!?
POIT
DIZZ

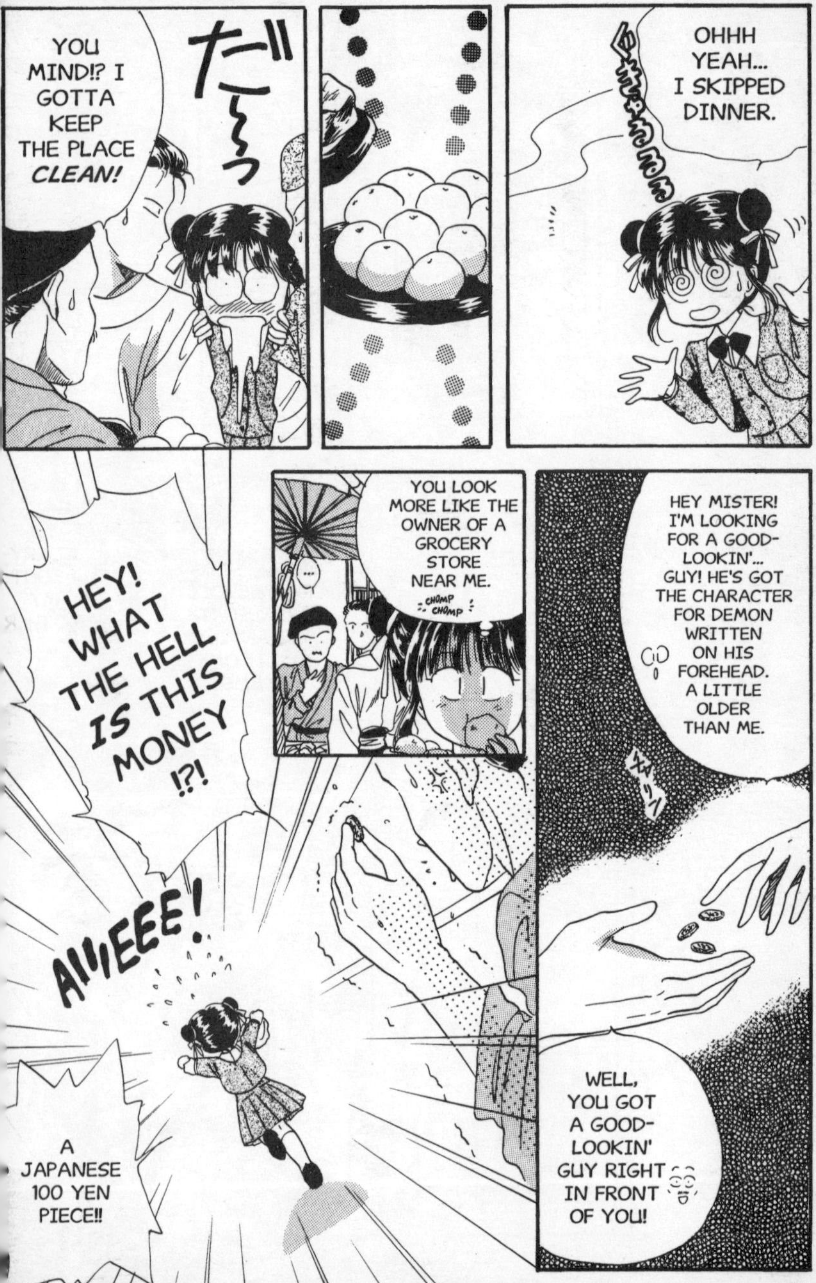
OHHH YEAH... I SKIPPED DINNER.
YOU MIND!? I GOTTA KEEP THE PLACE *CLEAN!*
HEY MISTER! I'M LOOKING FOR A GOOD-LOOKIN'... GUY! HE'S GOT THE CHARACTER FOR DEMON WRITTEN ON HIS FOREHEAD. A LITTLE OLDER THAN ME.
WELL, YOU GOT A GOOD-LOOKIN' GUY RIGHT IN FRONT OF YOU!
YOU LOOK MORE LIKE THE OWNER OF A GROCERY STORE NEAR ME.
CHOMP CHOMP
HEY! WHAT THE HELL *IS* THIS MONEY !?!
AIIIEEE!
A JAPANESE 100 YEN PIECE!!

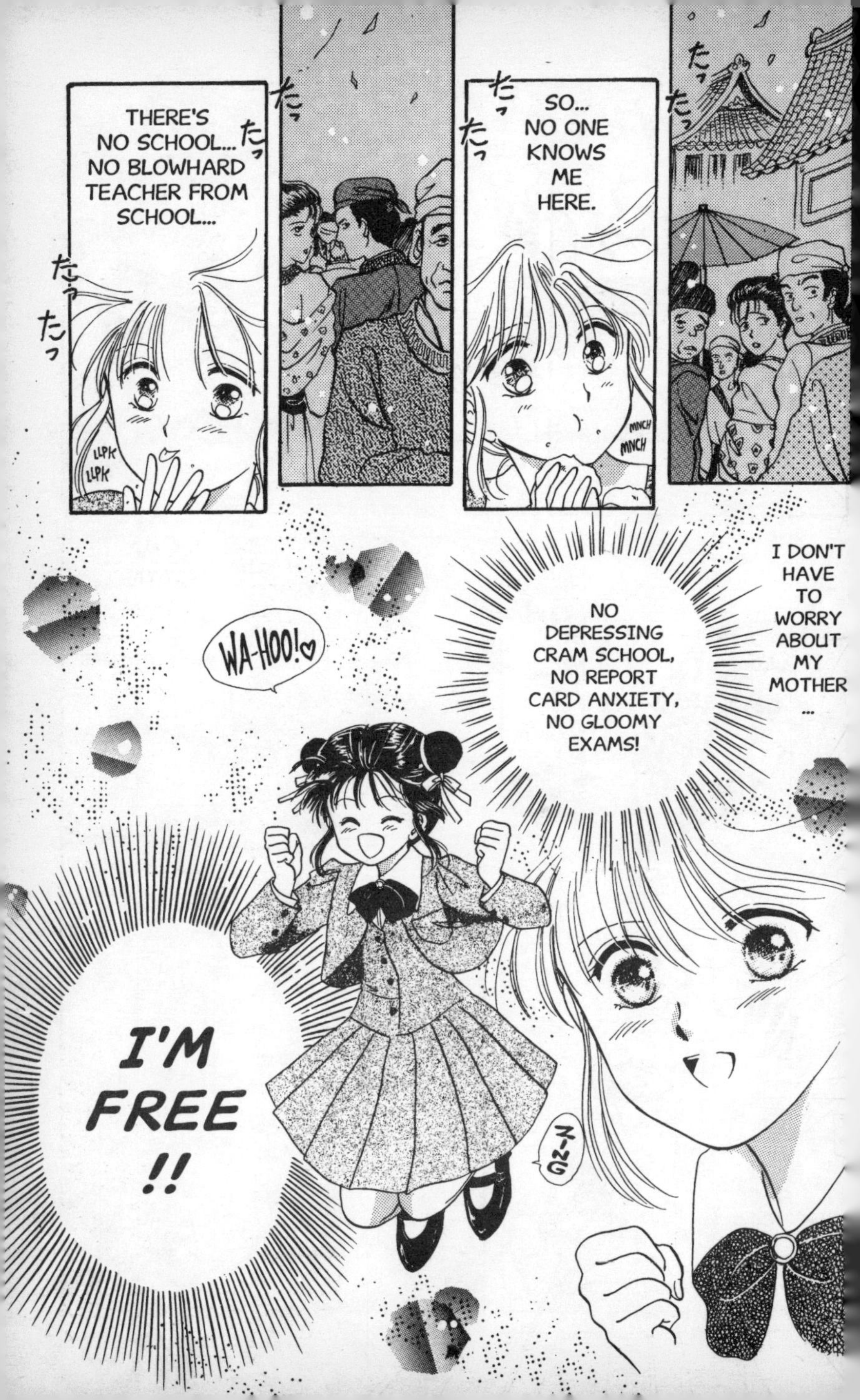

たっ
たっ
たっ
たっ
SO... NO ONE KNOWS ME HERE.
MNCH
MNCH
たっ
たっ
THERE'S NO SCHOOL... NO BLOWHARD TEACHER FROM SCHOOL...
たっ
たっ
LLPK
LLPK
I DON'T HAVE TO WORRY ABOUT MY MOTHER ...
NO DEPRESSING CRAM SCHOOL, NO REPORT CARD ANXIETY, NO GLOOMY EXAMS!
WA-HOO!♡
ZING
I'M FREE !!

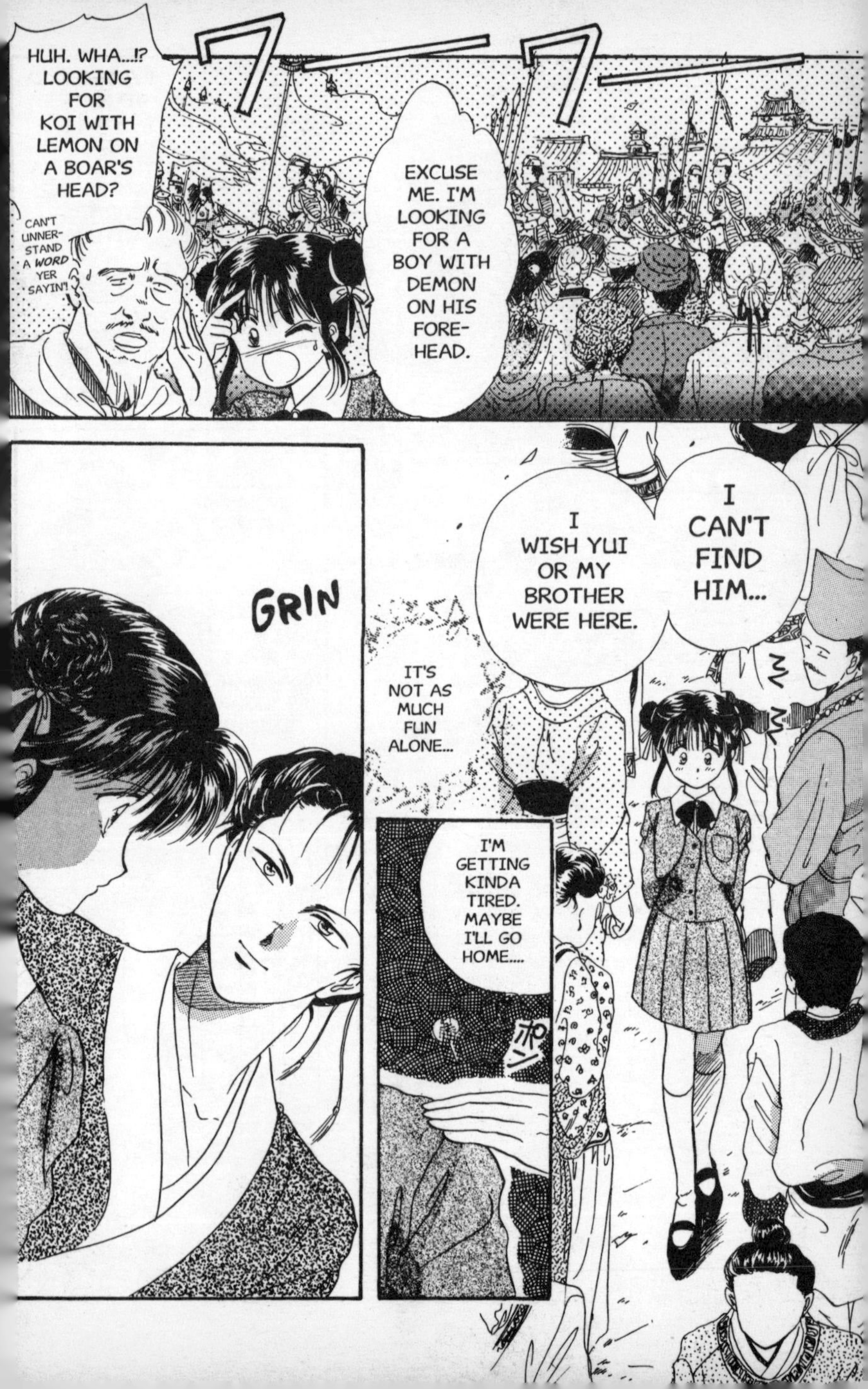
EXCUSE ME. I'M LOOKING FOR A BOY WITH DEMON ON HIS FORE-HEAD.
HUH. WHA...!? LOOKING FOR KOI WITH LEMON ON A BOAR'S HEAD?
CAN'T UNNER-STAND A WORD YER SAYIN'!
I CAN'T FIND HIM...
I WISH YUI OR MY BROTHER WERE HERE.
IT'S NOT AS MUCH FUN ALONE...
I'M GETTING KINDA TIRED. MAYBE I'LL GO HOME....
GRIN

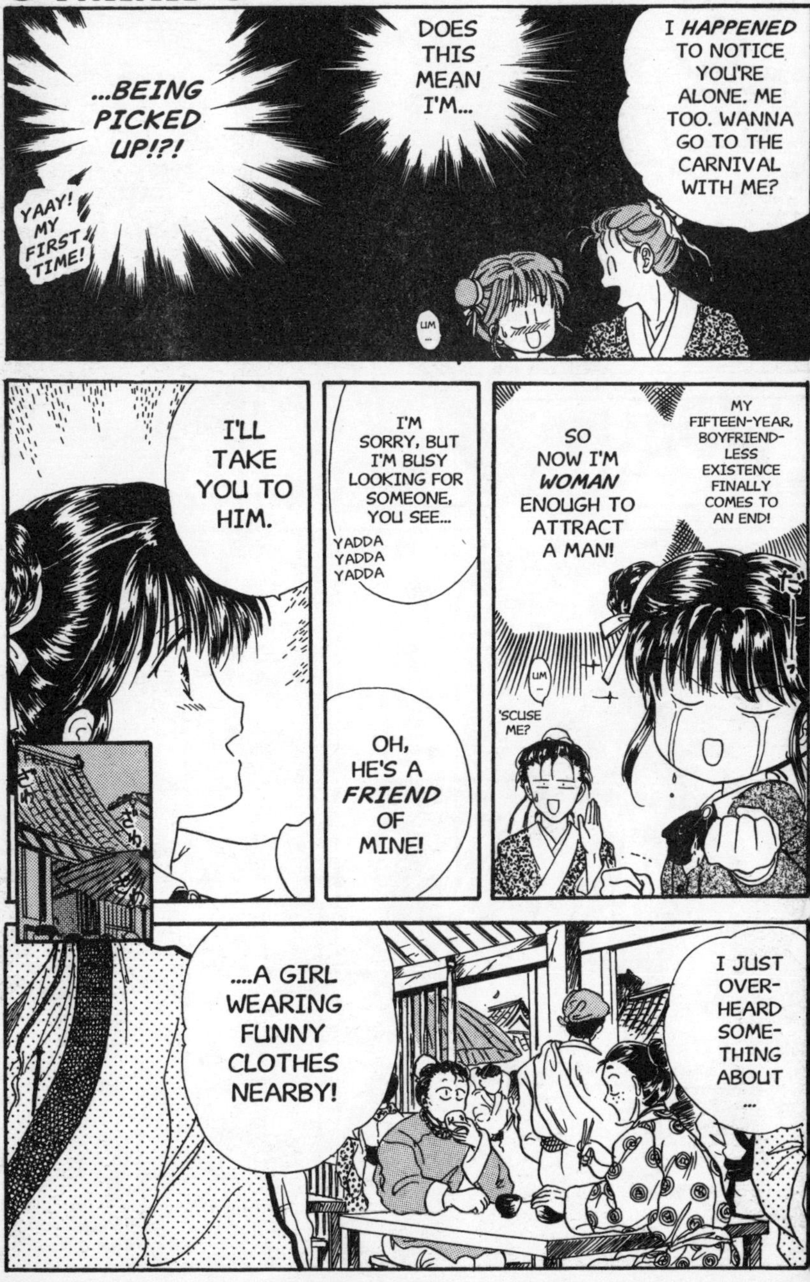
I HAPPENED TO NOTICE YOU'RE ALONE. ME TOO. WANNA GO TO THE CARNIVAL WITH ME?
UM...
DOES THIS MEAN I'M...
...BEING PICKED UP!?!
YAAY! MY FIRST TIME!
MY FIFTEEN-YEAR, BOYFRIEND-LESS EXISTENCE FINALLY COMES TO AN END!
SO NOW I'M WOMAN ENOUGH TO ATTRACT A MAN!
UM...
'SCUSE ME?
I'M SORRY, BUT I'M BUSY LOOKING FOR SOMEONE, YOU SEE...
YADDA YADDA YADDA
OH, HE'S A FRIEND OF MINE!
I'LL TAKE YOU TO HIM.
I JUST OVERHEARD SOMETHING ABOUT...
....A GIRL WEARING FUNNY CLOTHES NEARBY!

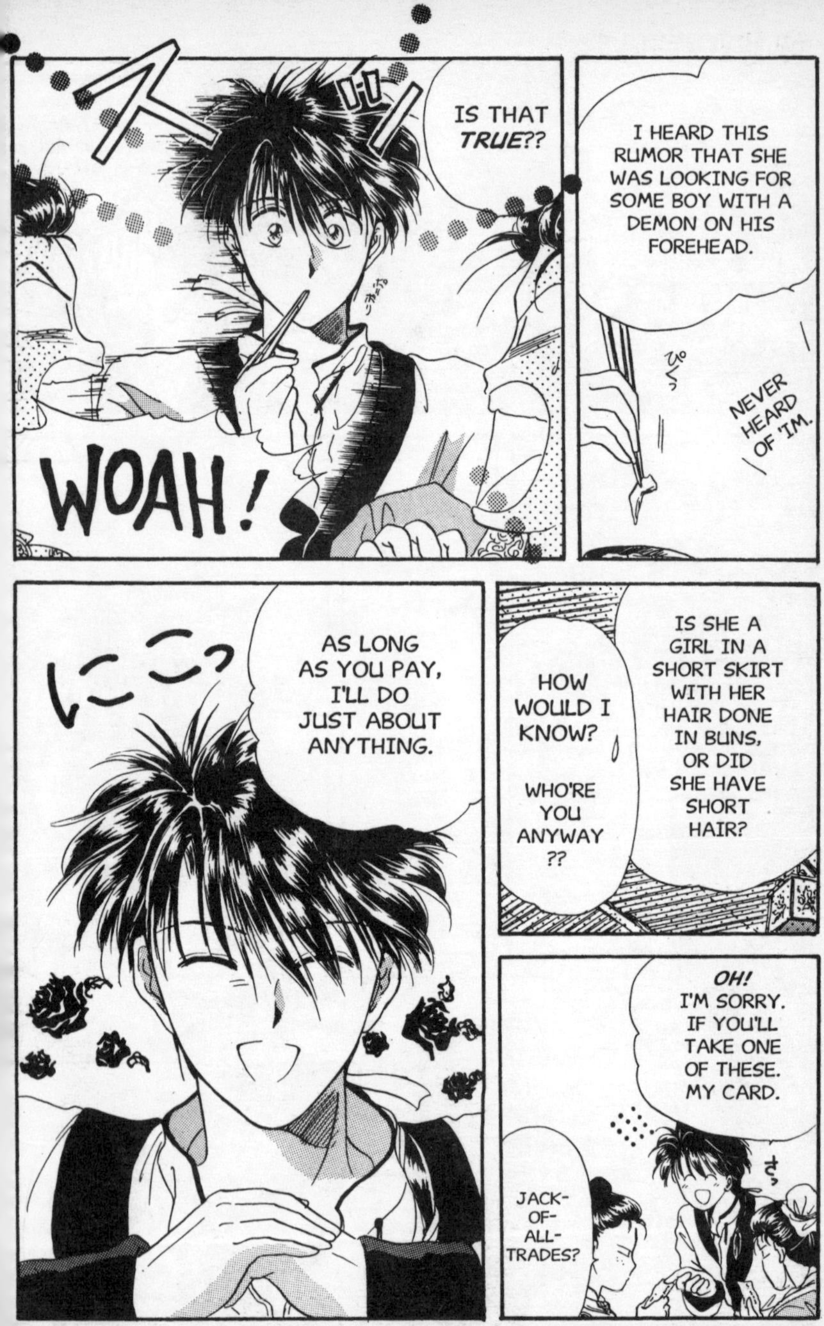
WOAH!
IS THAT *TRUE*??
I HEARD THIS RUMOR THAT SHE WAS LOOKING FOR SOME BOY WITH A DEMON ON HIS FOREHEAD.
NEVER HEARD OF 'IM.
AS LONG AS YOU PAY, I'LL DO JUST ABOUT ANYTHING.
IS SHE A GIRL IN A SHORT SKIRT WITH HER HAIR DONE IN BUNS, OR DID SHE HAVE SHORT HAIR?
HOW WOULD I KNOW?
WHO'RE YOU ANYWAY??
OH! I'M SORRY. IF YOU'LL TAKE ONE OF THESE. MY CARD.
JACK-OF-ALL-TRADES?

So I just want to clarify some things about my background. It seems I have to inform every reader that I'm a woman. ☺ As for how old I am...because I'm pretty young I'm not embarrassed about my age. Suffice to say I first got published at 18 and then "Prepubescence" came out when I was 20. You do the math.

I've had fans who tell me, "I want to be a manga artist just like you." Don't be just like me! "Lately I've been copying your drawings so much they look like yours." Well I suppose that's all right as long as you eventually acquire your own style. Every artist is always influenced by somebody else in the beginning. But I don't think it's such a good idea to continue copying other artists after you get published. Although they may seem the same, there's a big difference between being a big fan of an artist and unconsciously resembling that style, or parody, or reference, and PLAGIARISM. Lifting one or two ideas or scenes I can handle, but if you make a comic exactly like mine, I'll get mad at you!

I dunno, uh...

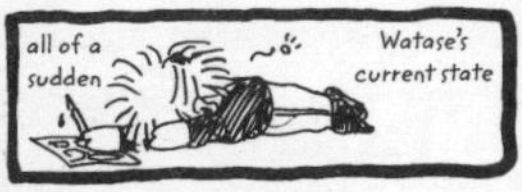
all of a sudden
Watase's current state

Now THAT'S something that can get me mad! (I'm still new to this.) I know that there are tons of ideas that resemble each other, but to steal an episode verbatim... and when I get upset it means I'm 10 times angrier than the average person. (Usually I'm laid back no matter what people say to me. Friends will say, "Why don't you get mad once in awhile," and get mad at me!) Guess I haven't grown up. For the past two years, I haven't read any of my favorite manga artists who have influenced me! (Actually I haven't been reading much manga in general.) I want to shed my influences. I just want to draw manga my own way. But my drawings aren't getting better! And I'm working on it so hard!

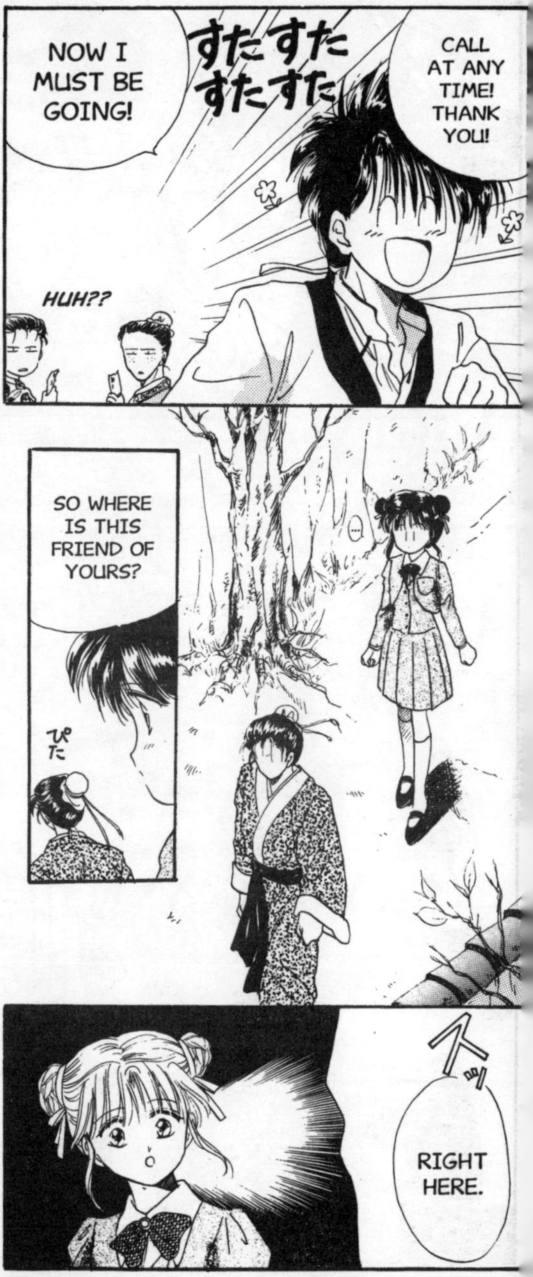
CALL AT ANY TIME! THANK YOU!
すたすたすたすた
NOW I MUST BE GOING!
HUH??
SO WHERE IS THIS FRIEND OF YOURS?
ぴた
RIGHT HERE.

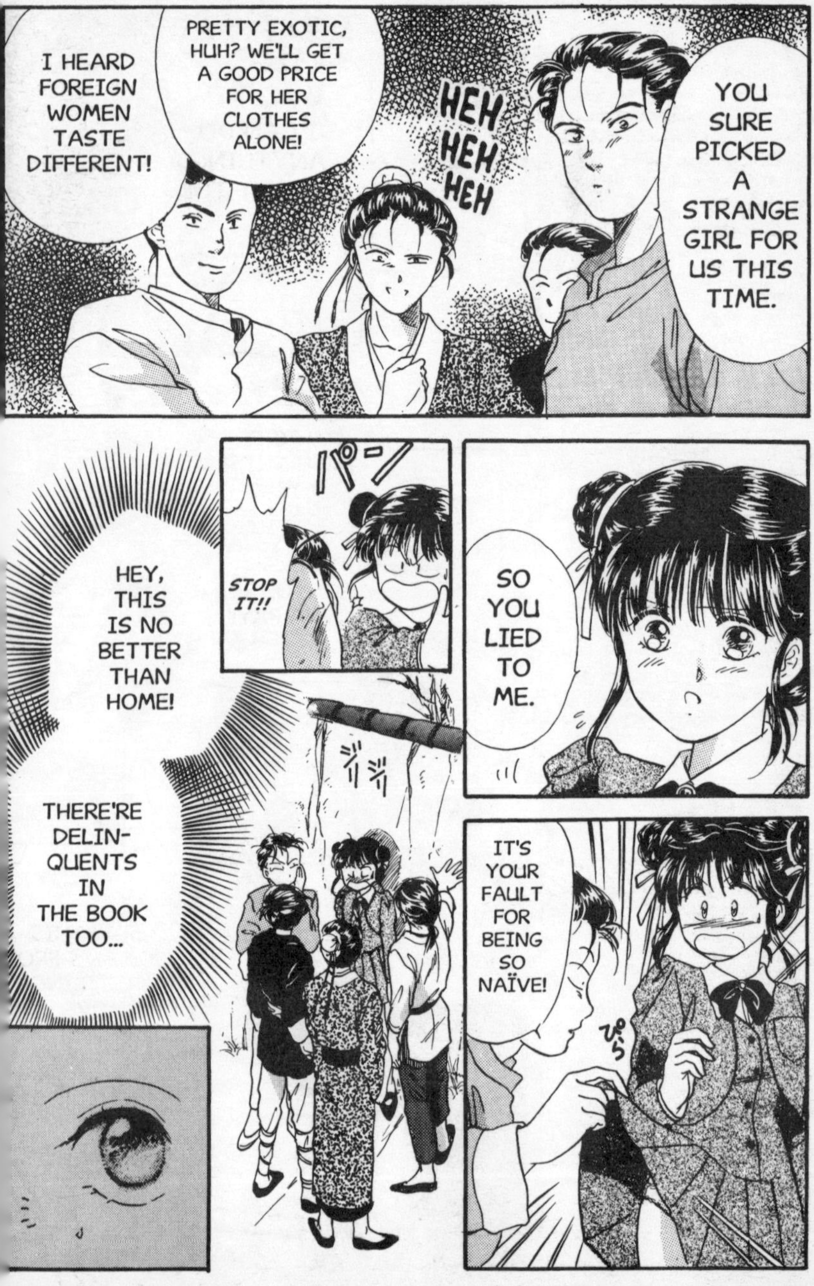
YOU SURE PICKED A STRANGE GIRL FOR US THIS TIME.
HEH HEH HEH
PRETTY EXOTIC, HUH? WE'LL GET A GOOD PRICE FOR HER CLOTHES ALONE!
I HEARD FOREIGN WOMEN TASTE DIFFERENT!
SO YOU LIED TO ME.
STOP IT!!
IT'S YOUR FAULT FOR BEING SO NAÏVE!
HEY, THIS IS NO BETTER THAN HOME!
THERE'RE DELIN-QUENTS IN THE BOOK TOO...

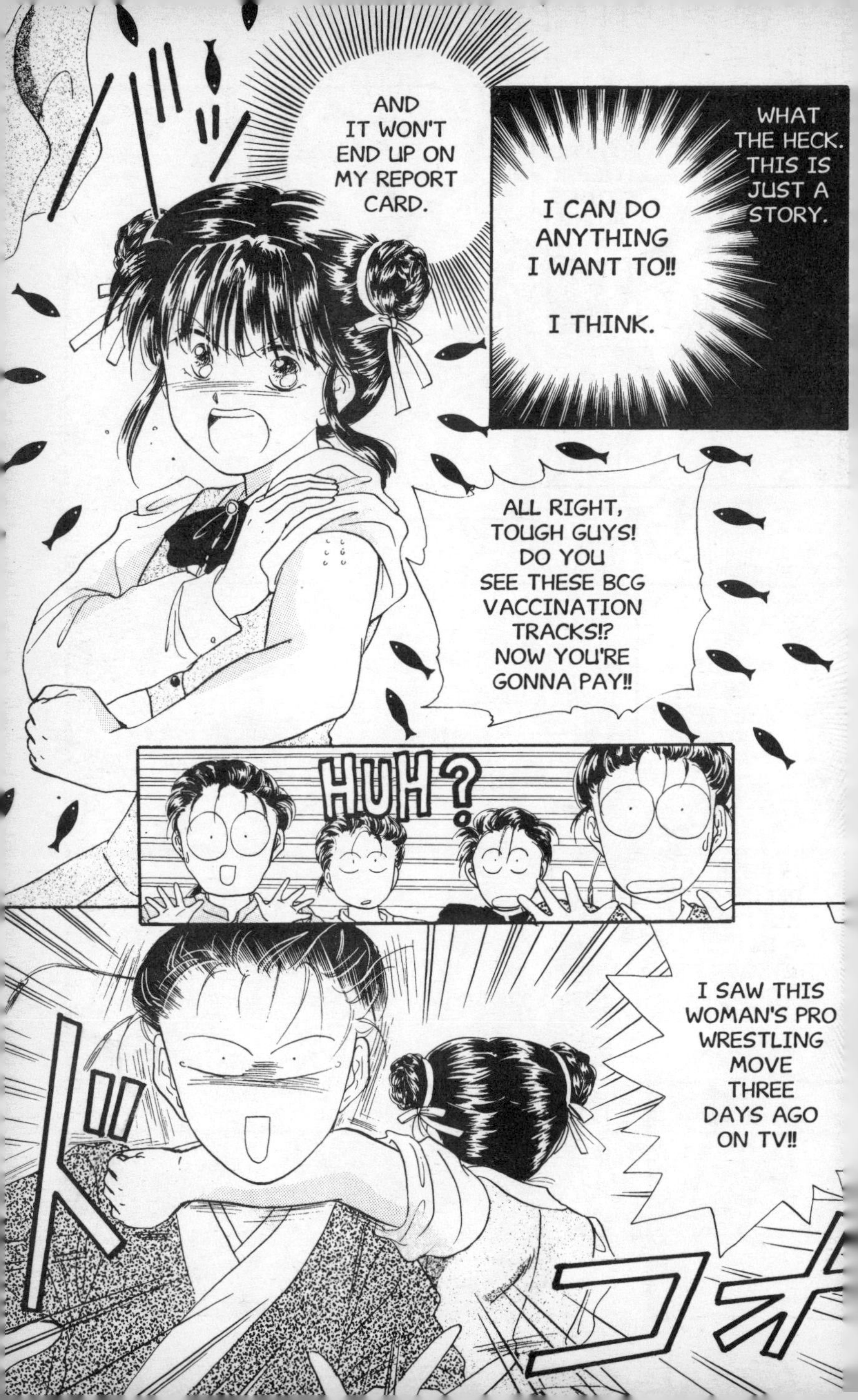
WHAT THE HECK. THIS IS JUST A STORY.
I CAN DO ANYTHING I WANT TO!!
I THINK.
AND IT WON'T END UP ON MY REPORT CARD.
ALL RIGHT, TOUGH GUYS! DO YOU SEE THESE BCG VACCINATION TRACKS!? NOW YOU'RE GONNA PAY!!
HUH?
I SAW THIS WOMAN'S PRO WRESTLING MOVE THREE DAYS AGO ON TV!!

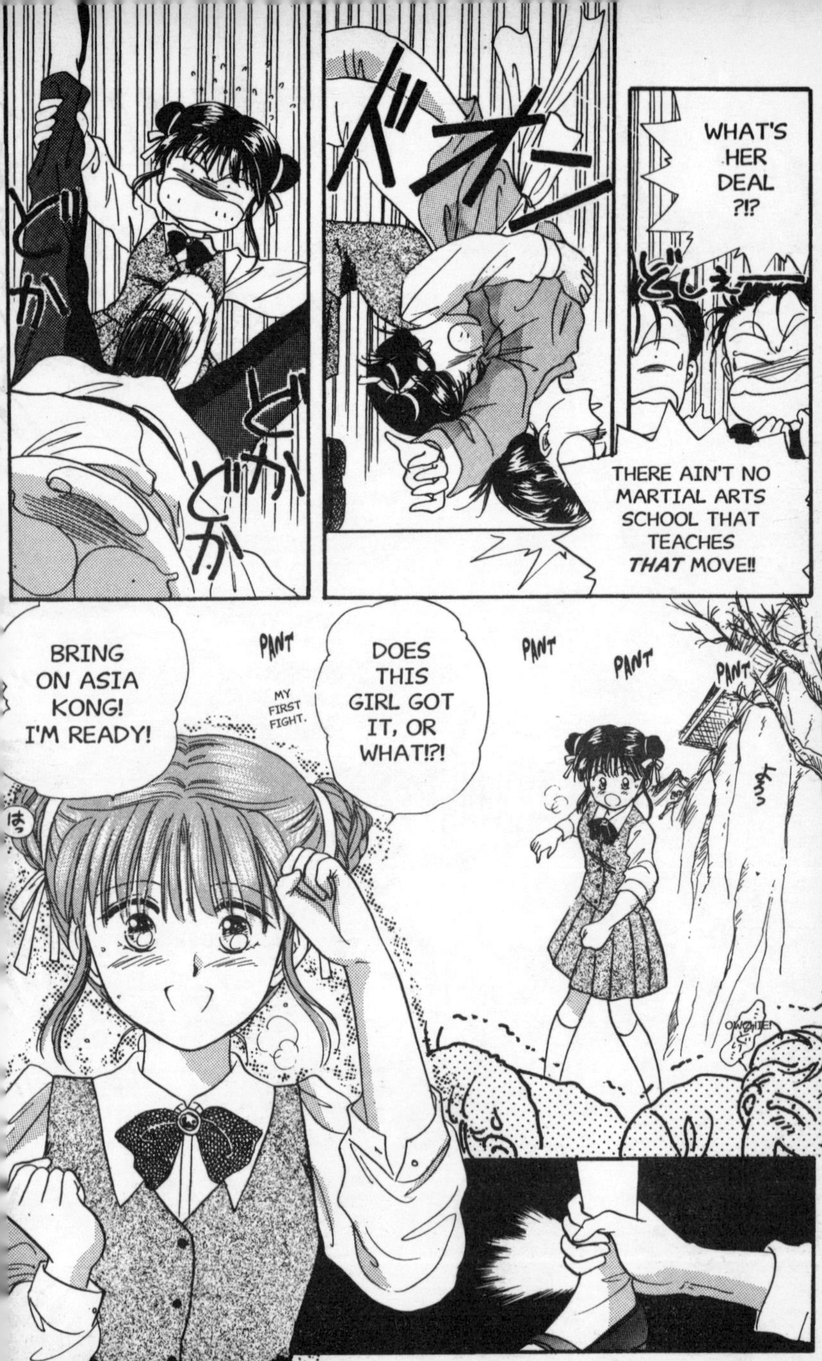
WHAT'S HER DEAL ?!?
THERE AIN'T NO MARTIAL ARTS SCHOOL THAT TEACHES *THAT* MOVE!!
PANT
PANT
PANT
PANT
DOES THIS GIRL GOT IT, OR WHAT!?!
MY FIRST FIGHT.
BRING ON ASIA KONG! I'M READY!

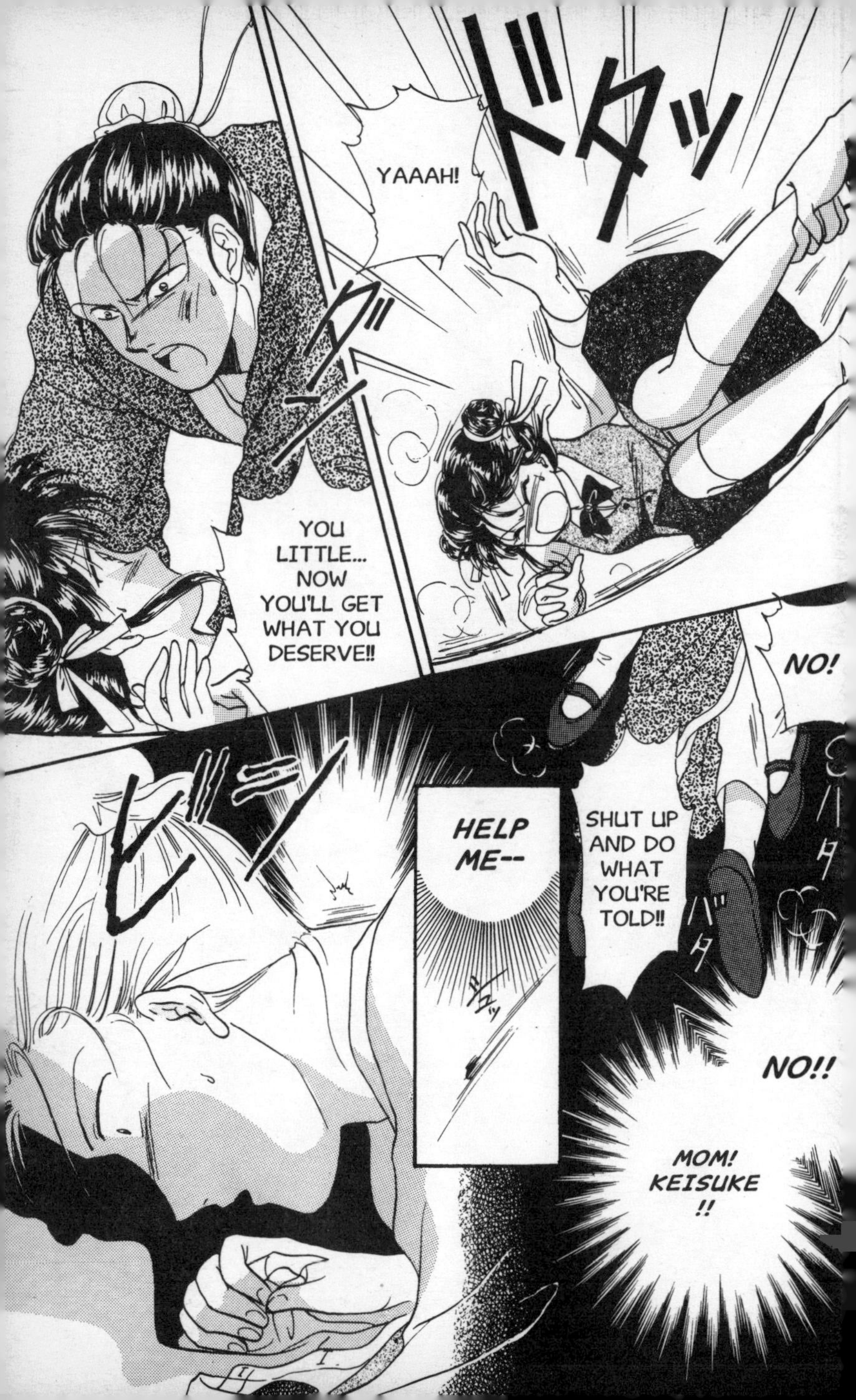
ドタッ
YAAAH!
YOU LITTLE... NOW YOU'LL GET WHAT YOU DESERVE!!
NO!
SHUT UP AND DO WHAT YOU'RE TOLD!!
NO!!
MOM! KEISUKE !!
HELP ME--

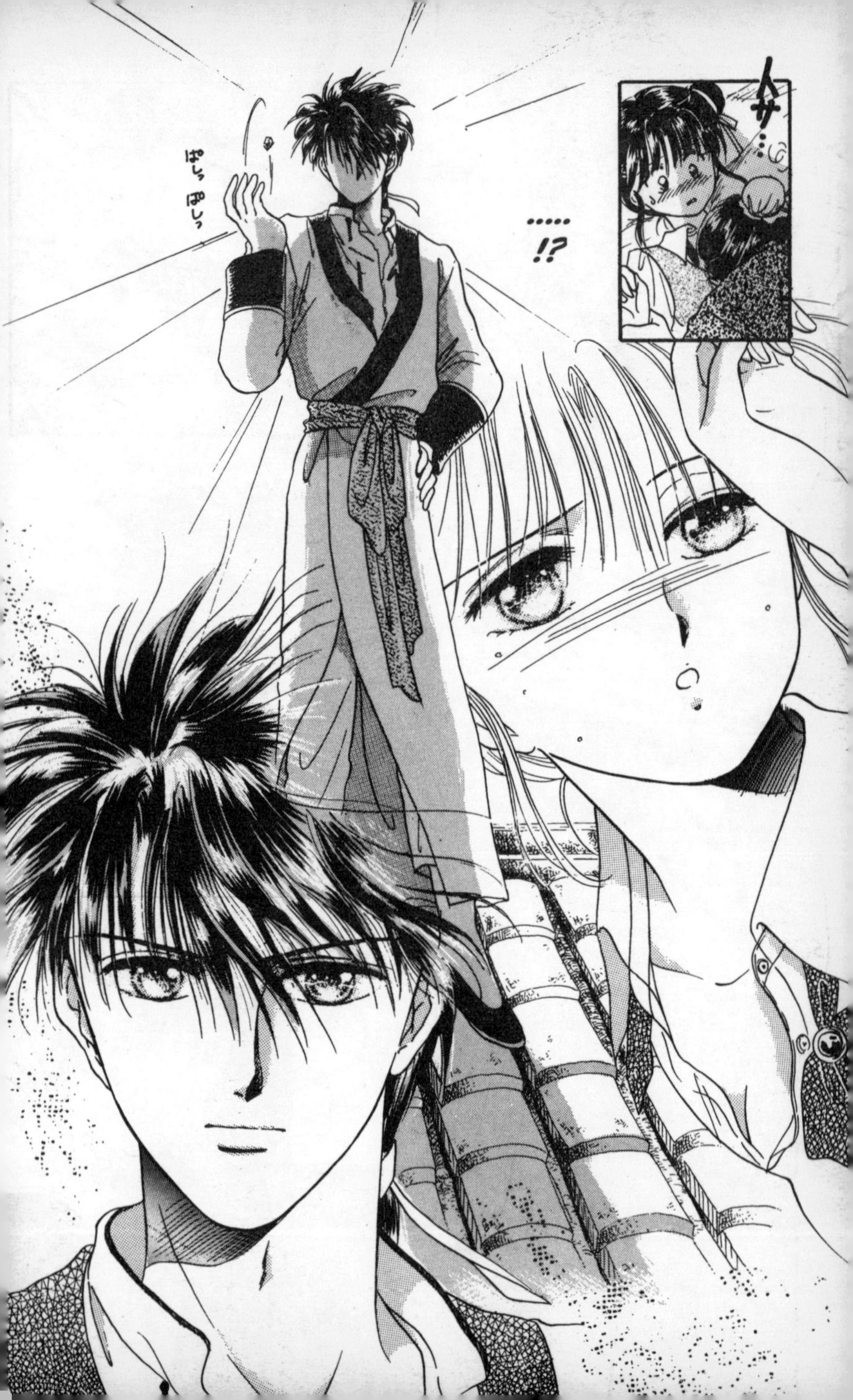
ムサ…
……!?
ぱしっ ぱしっ

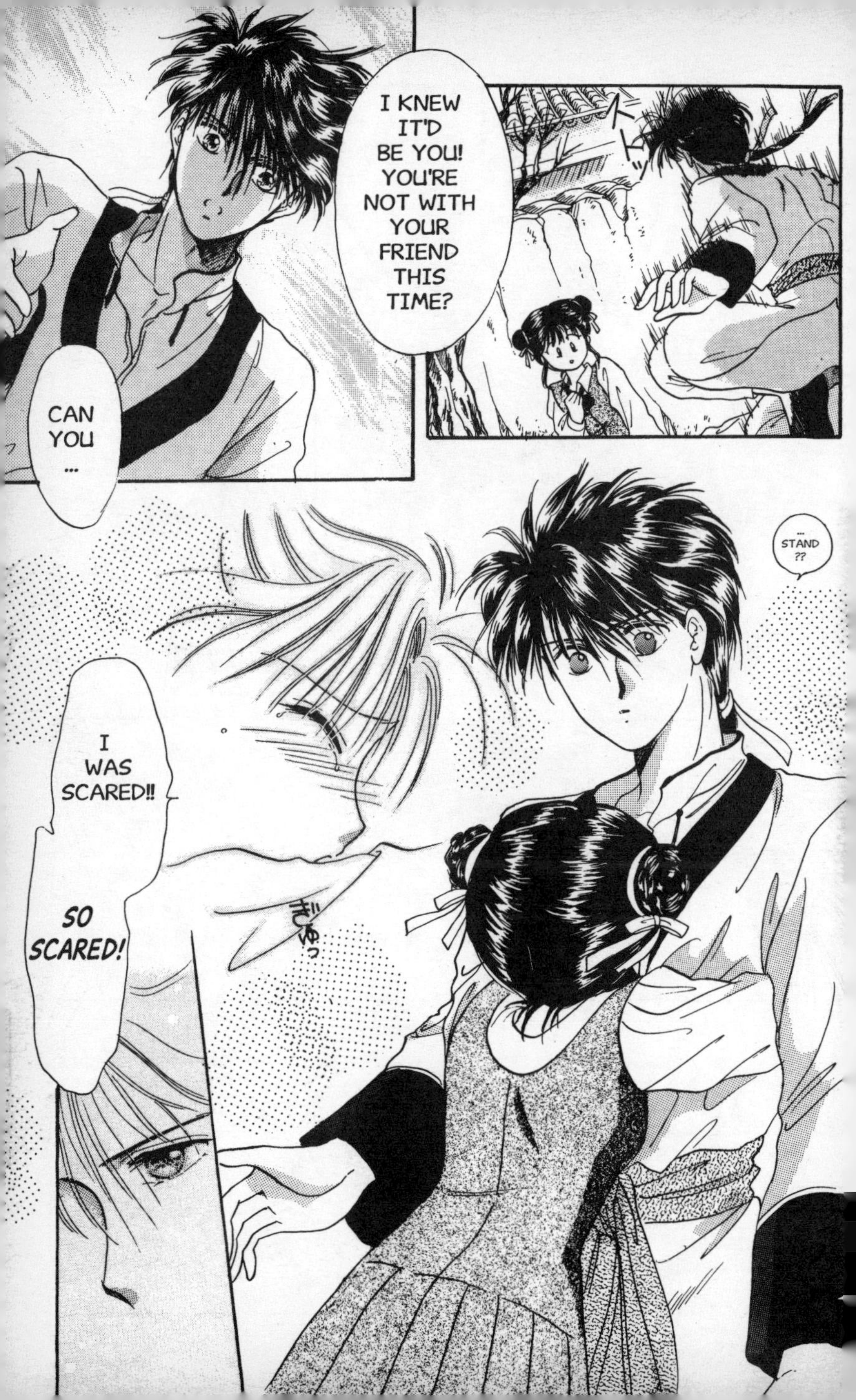
I KNEW IT'D BE YOU! YOU'RE NOT WITH YOUR FRIEND THIS TIME?
CAN YOU ...
... STAND ??
I WAS SCARED!!
SO SCARED!
ぎゅっ

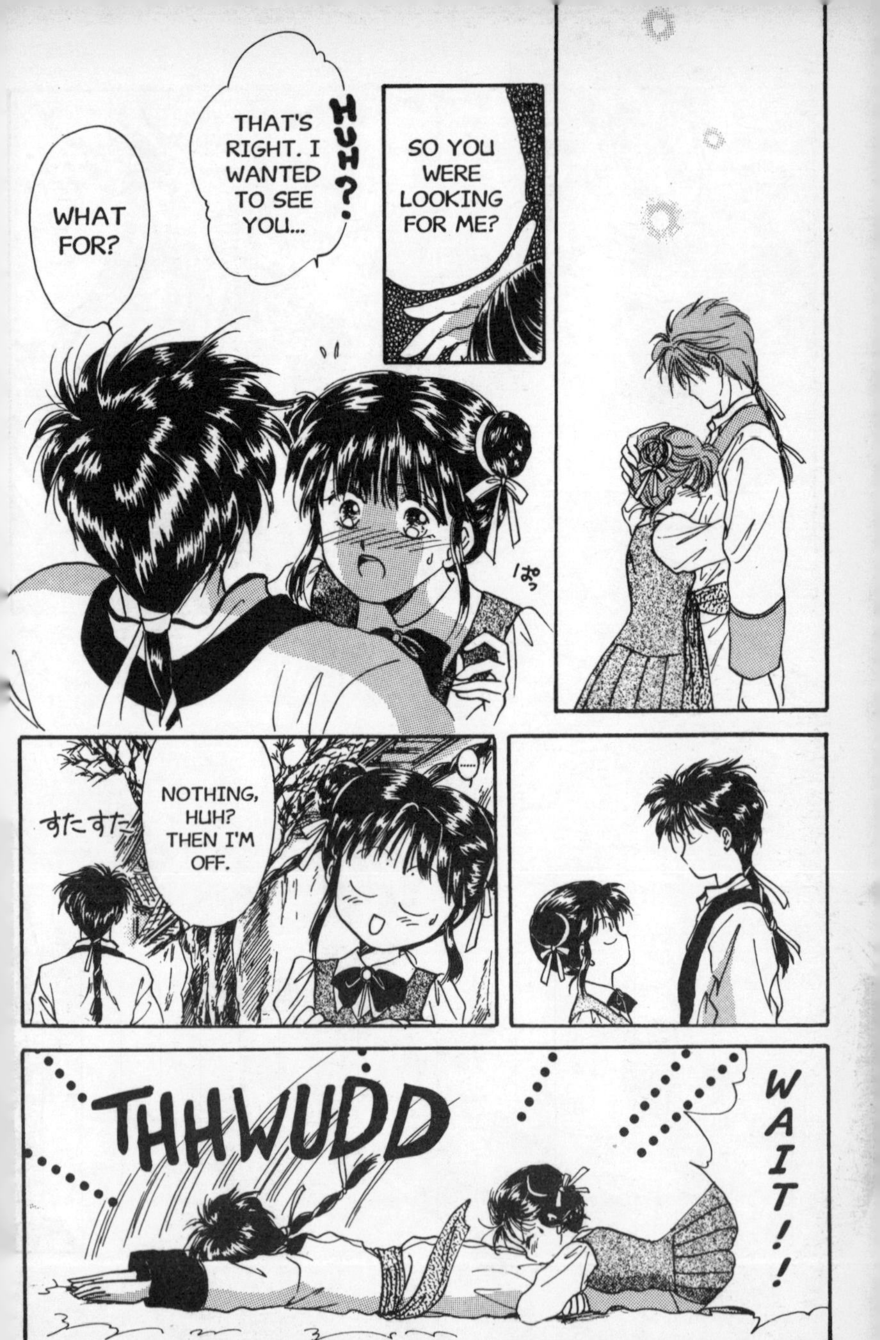
SO YOU WERE LOOKING FOR ME?
HUH?
THAT'S RIGHT. I WANTED TO SEE YOU...
WHAT FOR?
ぱっ
NOTHING, HUH? THEN I'M OFF.
すたすた
WAIT!!
THHWUDD

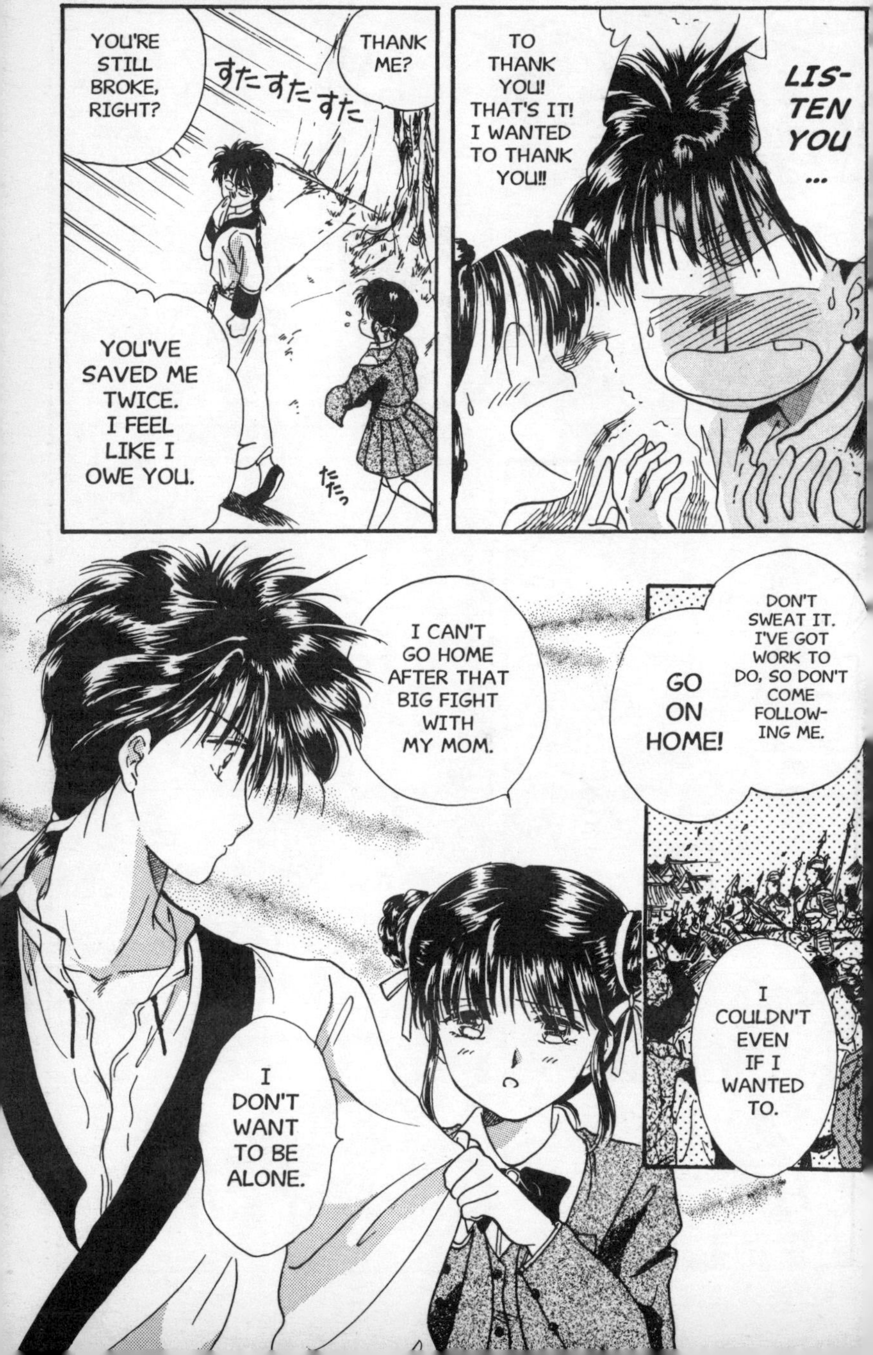
YOU'RE STILL BROKE, RIGHT?
すたすたすた
YOU'VE SAVED ME TWICE. I FEEL LIKE I OWE YOU.
たたっ
THANK ME?
TO THANK YOU! THAT'S IT! I WANTED TO THANK YOU!!
LIS-TEN YOU ...
DON'T SWEAT IT. I'VE GOT WORK TO DO, SO DON'T COME FOLLOW-ING ME.
GO ON HOME!
I CAN'T GO HOME AFTER THAT BIG FIGHT WITH MY MOM.
I COULDN'T EVEN IF I WANTED TO.
I DON'T WANT TO BE ALONE.

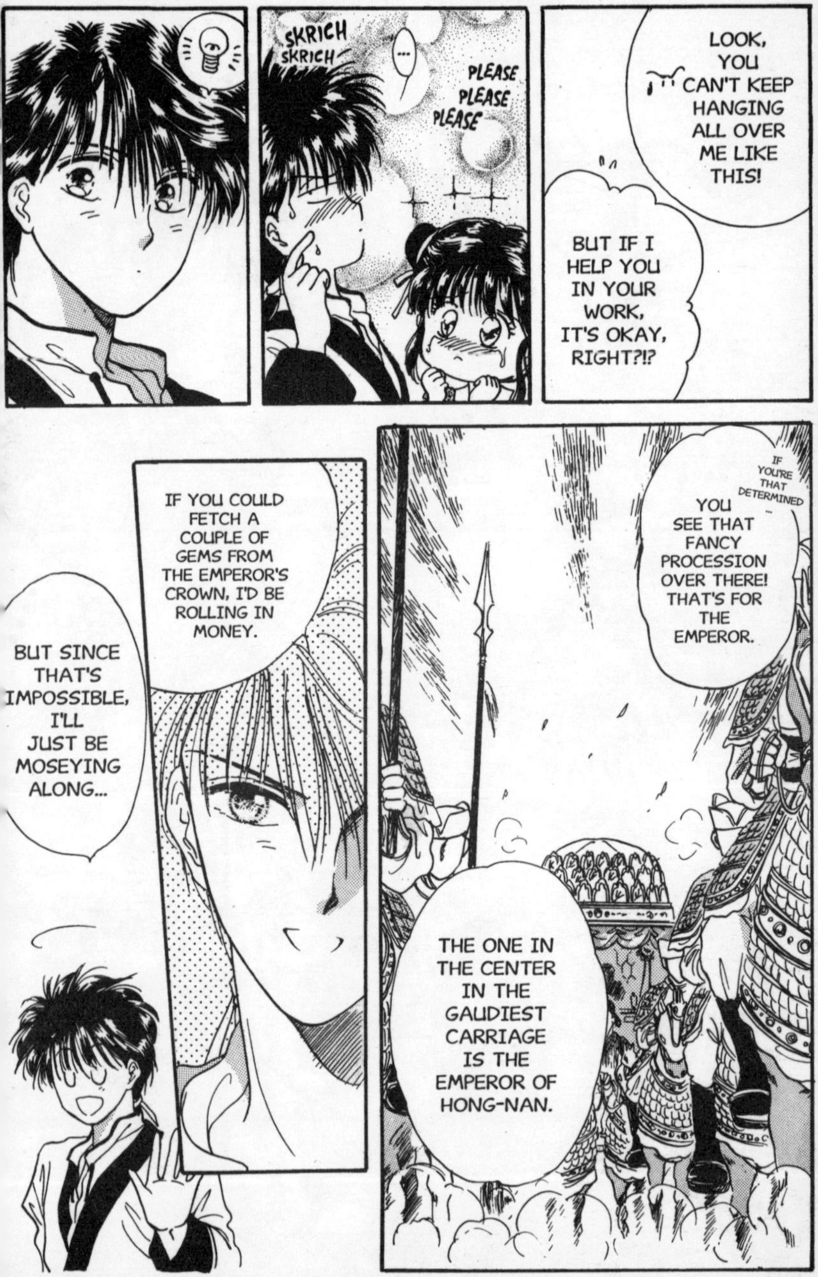
SKRICH
SKRICH
...
PLEASE
PLEASE
PLEASE
LOOK, YOU CAN'T KEEP HANGING ALL OVER ME LIKE THIS!
BUT IF I HELP YOU IN YOUR WORK, IT'S OKAY, RIGHT?!?
IF YOU'RE THAT DETERMINED...
YOU SEE THAT FANCY PROCESSION OVER THERE! THAT'S FOR THE EMPEROR.
THE ONE IN THE CENTER IN THE GAUDIEST CARRIAGE IS THE EMPEROR OF HONG-NAN.
IF YOU COULD FETCH A COUPLE OF GEMS FROM THE EMPEROR'S CROWN, I'D BE ROLLING IN MONEY.
BUT SINCE THAT'S IMPOSSIBLE, I'LL JUST BE MOSEYING ALONG...

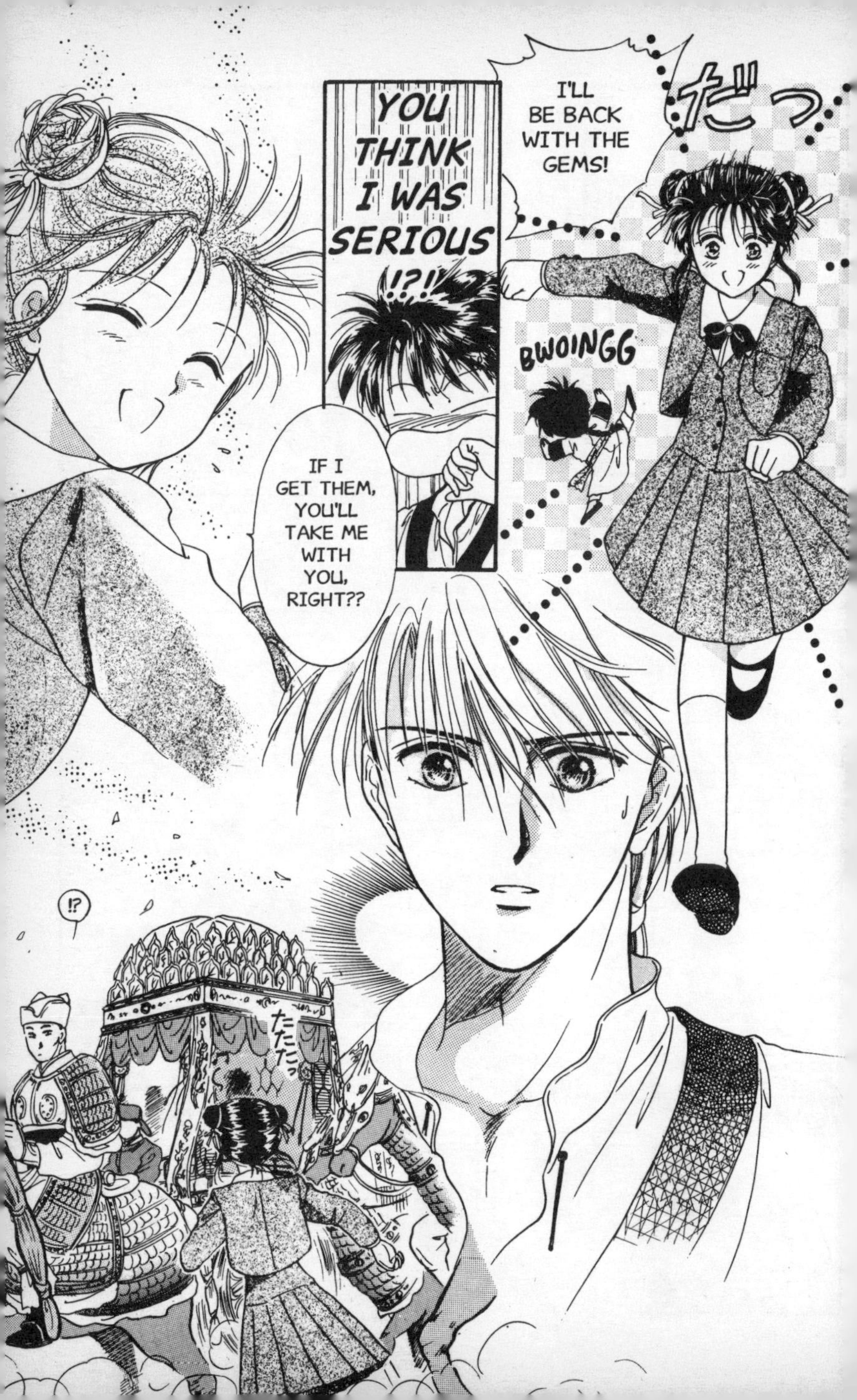
だっ
I'LL BE BACK WITH THE GEMS!
YOU THINK I WAS SERIOUS !?!
BWOINGG
IF I GET THEM, YOU'LL TAKE ME WITH YOU, RIGHT??
!?
たたたっ

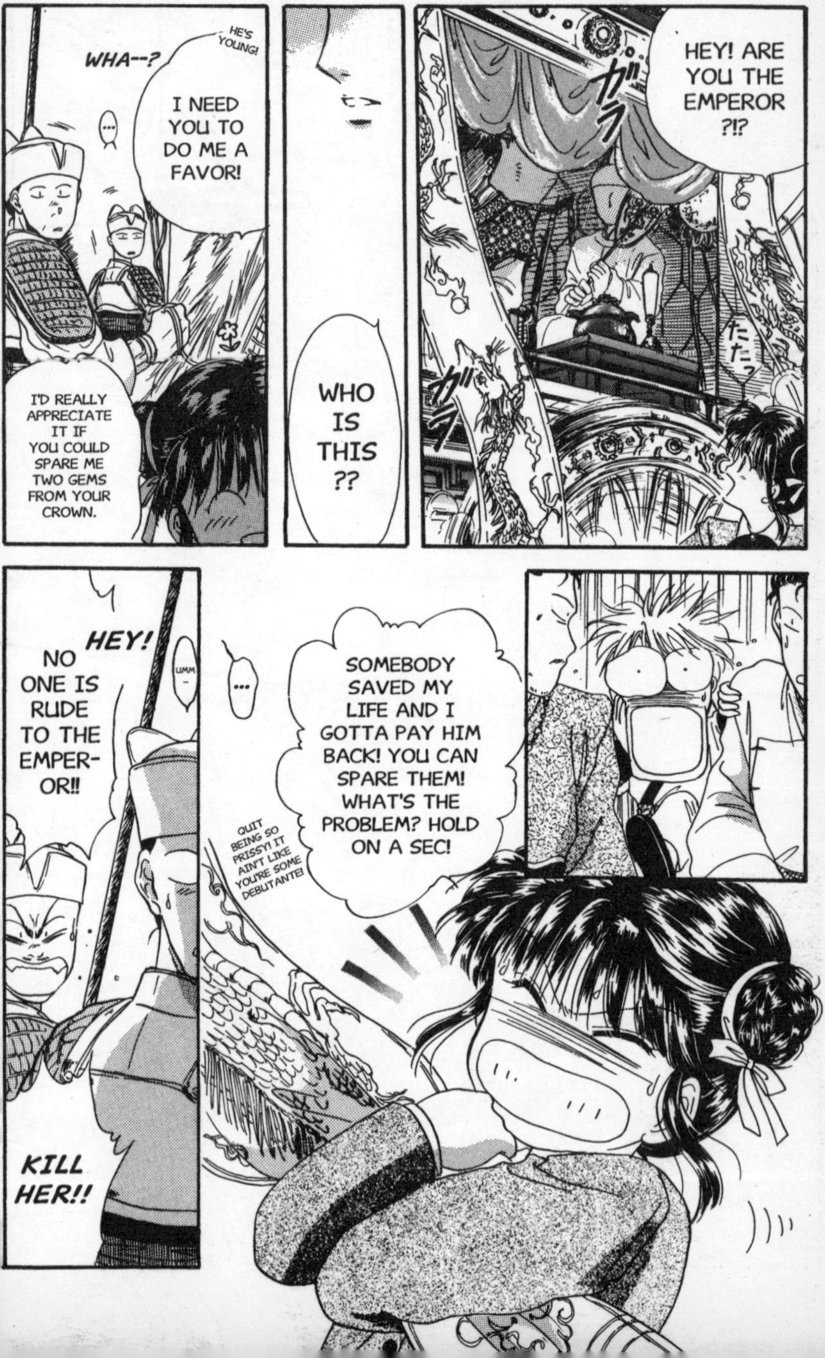

HEY! ARE YOU THE EMPEROR ?!?
ガラ
たたっ
WHO IS THIS ??
HE'S YOUNG!
WHA--?
I NEED YOU TO DO ME A FAVOR!
...
I'D REALLY APPRECIATE IT IF YOU COULD SPARE ME TWO GEMS FROM YOUR CROWN.
SOMEBODY SAVED MY LIFE AND I GOTTA PAY HIM BACK! YOU CAN SPARE THEM! WHAT'S THE PROBLEM? HOLD ON A SEC!
QUIT BEING SO PRISSY! IT AIN'T LIKE YOU'RE SOME DEBUTANTE!
...
UMM...
HEY! NO ONE IS RUDE TO THE EMPEROR!!
KILL HER!!

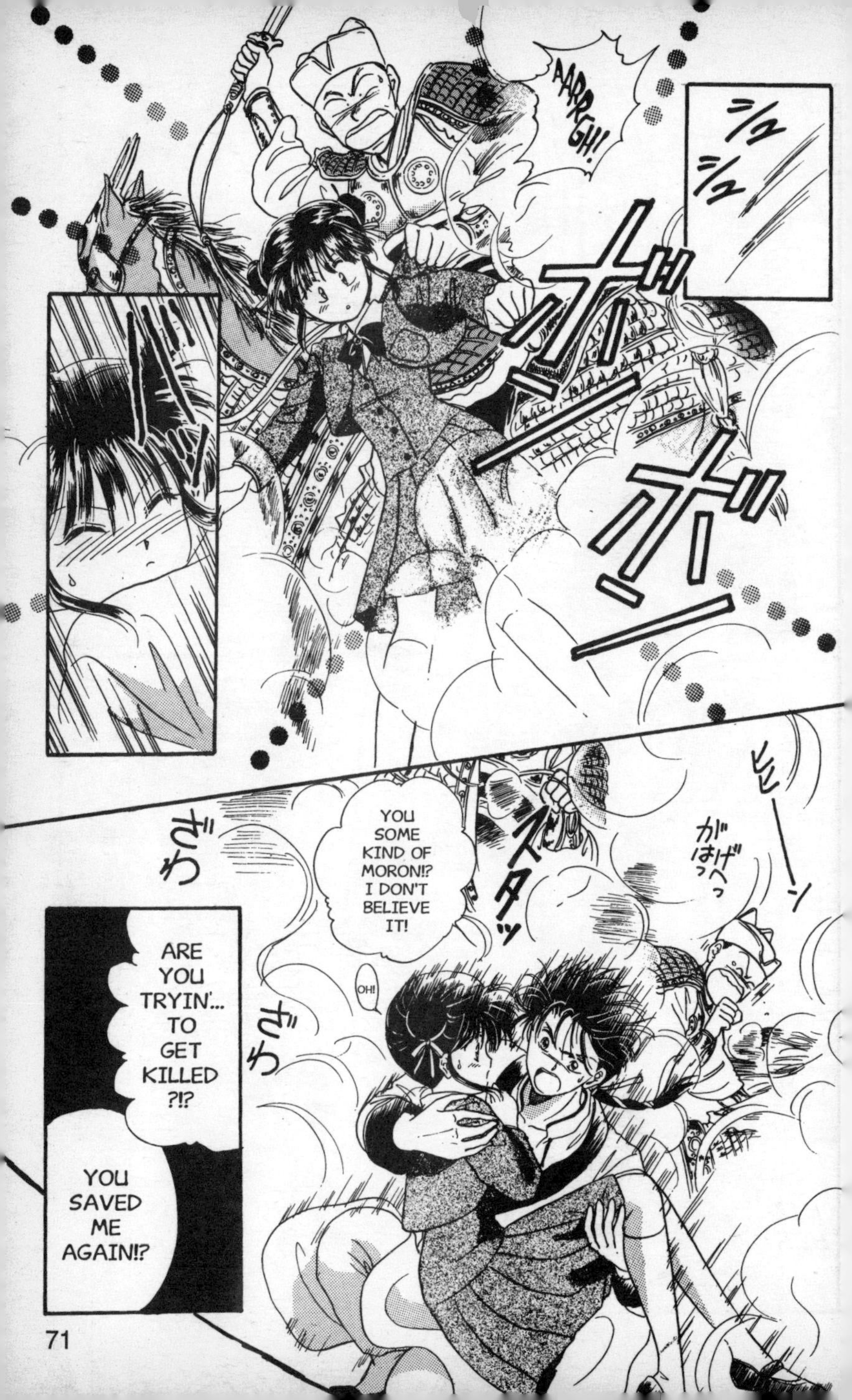

シュ
シュ
AARRGH!
ヒヒーン
げへっ
がばっ
スタッ
YOU SOME KIND OF MORON!? I DON'T BELIEVE IT!
ざわ
ざわ
OH!
ARE YOU TRYIN'... TO GET KILLED ?!?
YOU SAVED ME AGAIN!?

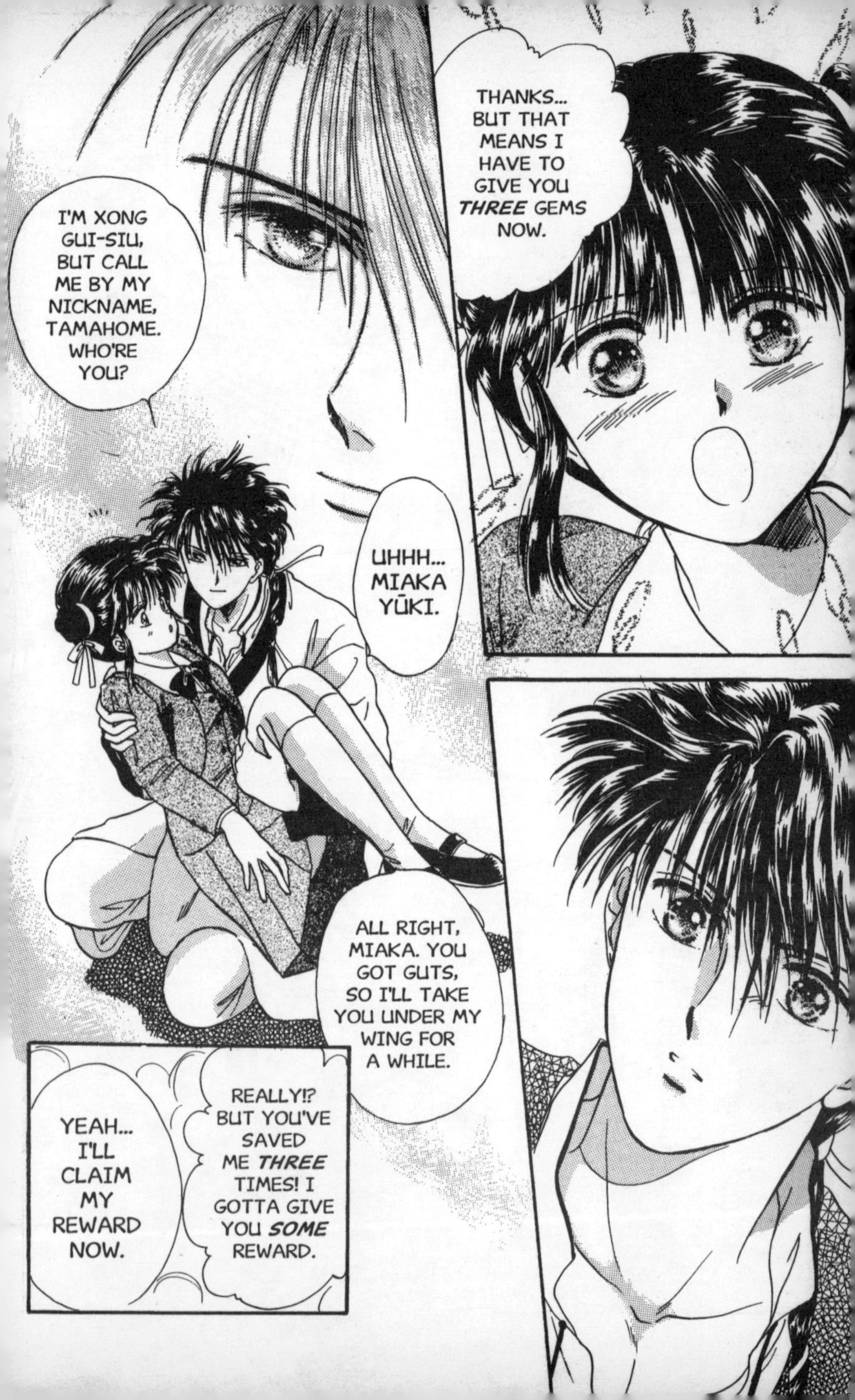
I'M XONG GUI-SIU, BUT CALL ME BY MY NICKNAME, TAMAHOME. WHO'RE YOU?
UHHH... MIAKA YŪKI.
ALL RIGHT, MIAKA. YOU GOT GUTS, SO I'LL TAKE YOU UNDER MY WING FOR A WHILE.
THANKS... BUT THAT MEANS I HAVE TO GIVE YOU *THREE* GEMS NOW.
REALLY!? BUT YOU'VE SAVED ME *THREE* TIMES! I GOTTA GIVE YOU *SOME* REWARD.
YEAH... I'LL CLAIM MY REWARD NOW.

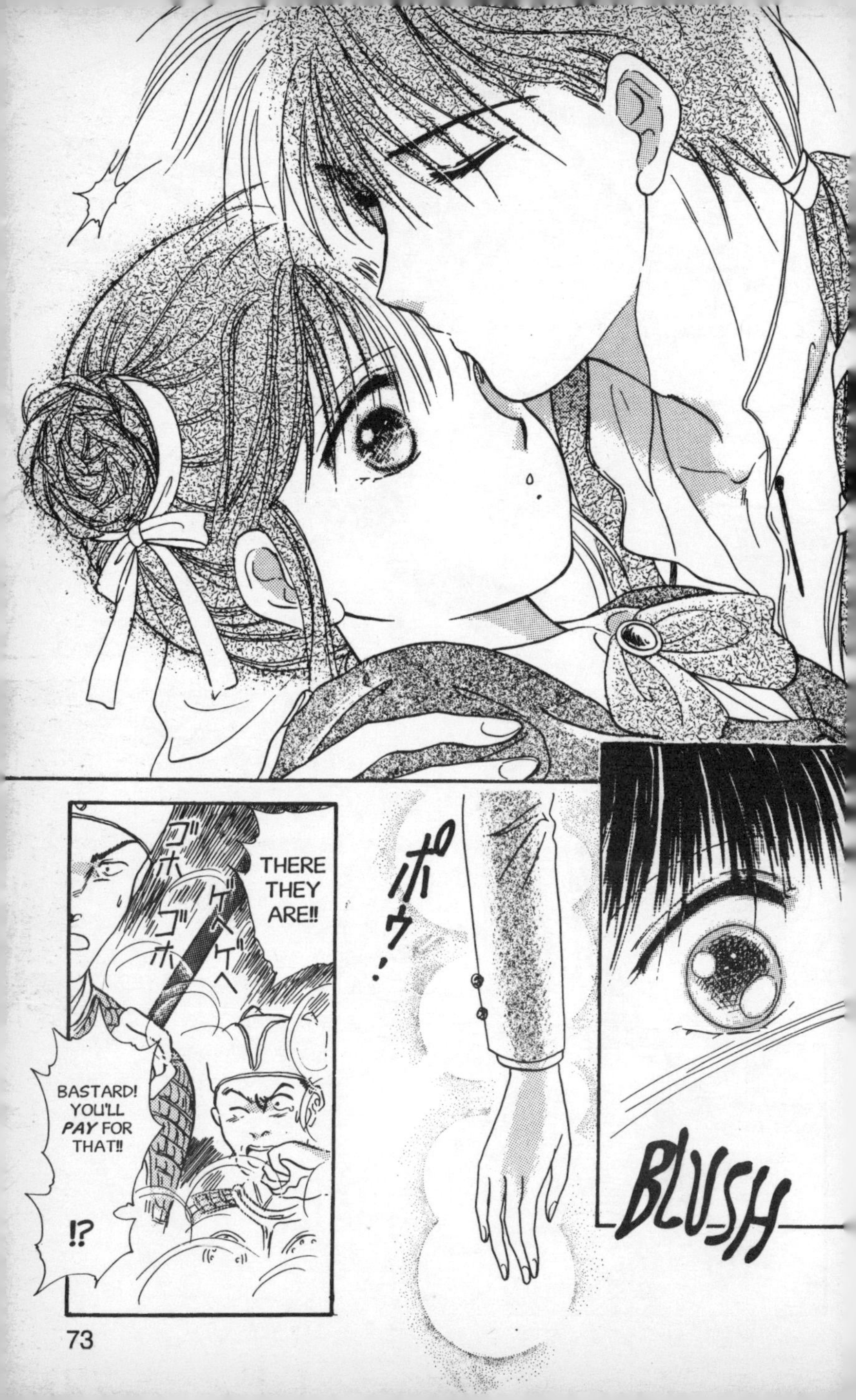
BLUSH
ポウ！
THERE THEY ARE!!
ゴホゴホ
ゲヘゲヘ
BASTARD! YOU'LL *PAY* FOR THAT!!
!?

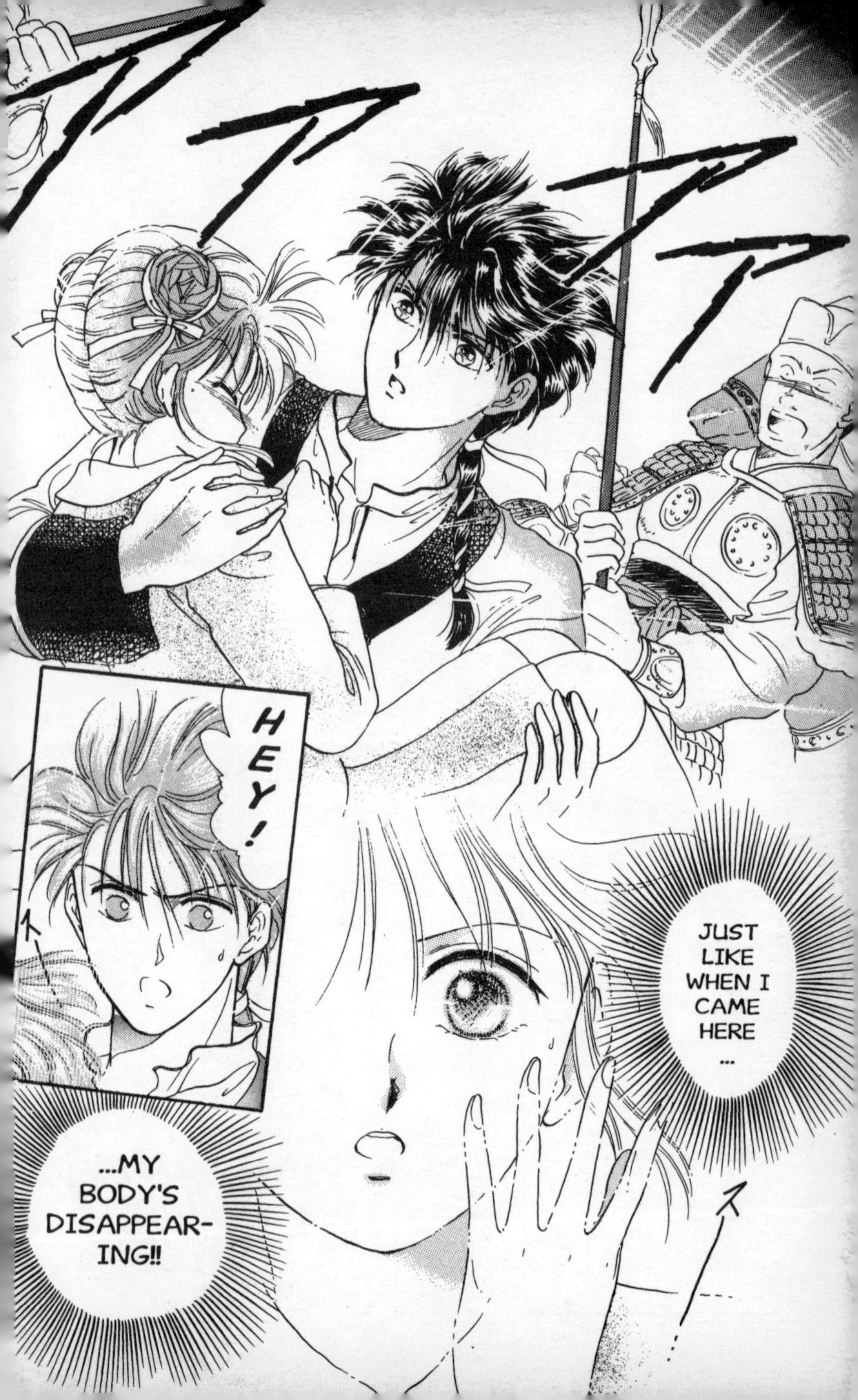

HEY!
JUST LIKE WHEN I CAME HERE ...
...MY BODY'S DISAPPEAR-ING!!

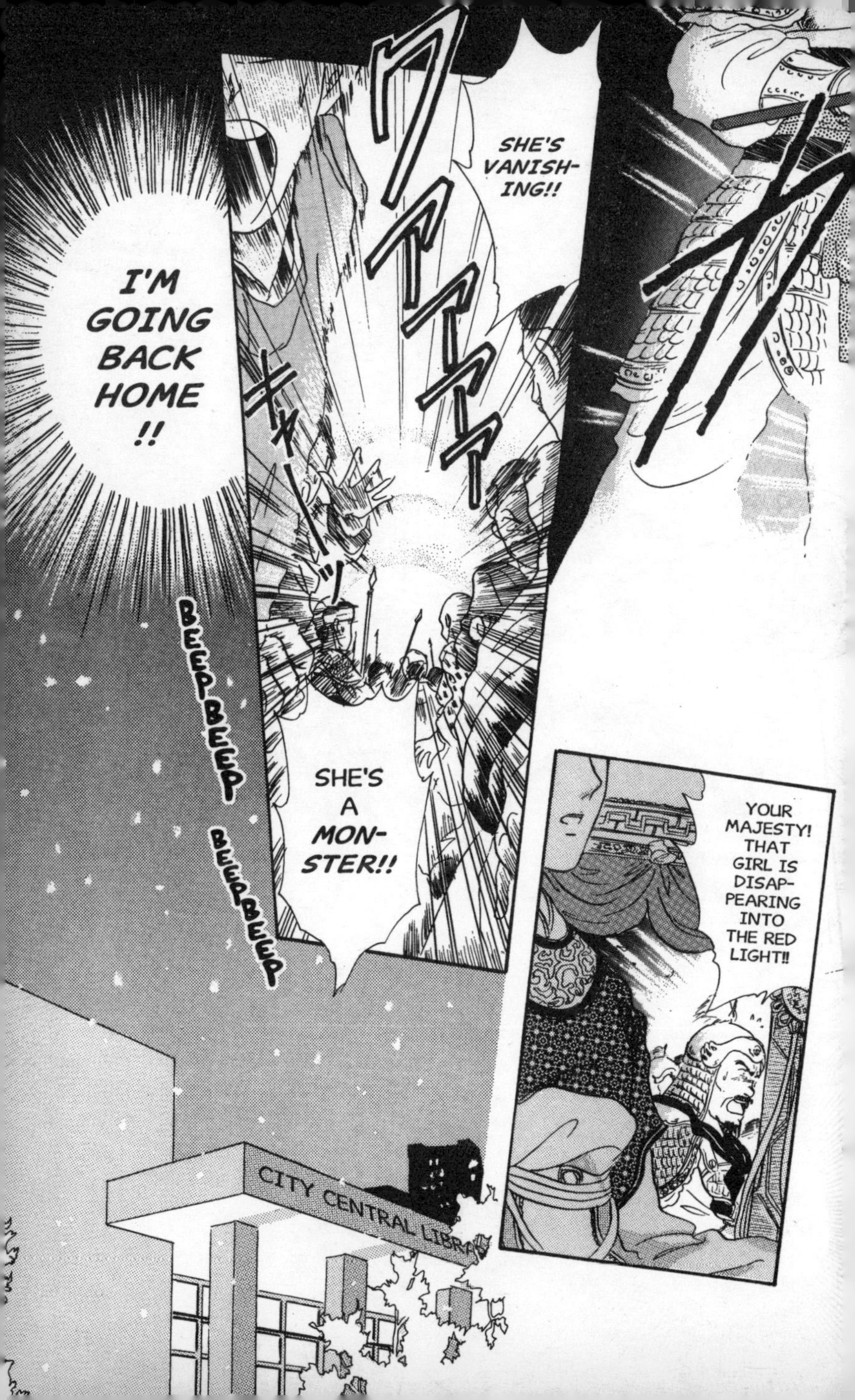
SHE'S VANISHING!!
SHE'S A MONSTER!!
YOUR MAJESTY! THAT GIRL IS DISAPPEARING INTO THE RED LIGHT!!
I'M GOING BACK HOME!!
BEEPBEEP BEEPBEEP
CITY CENTRAL LIBRA

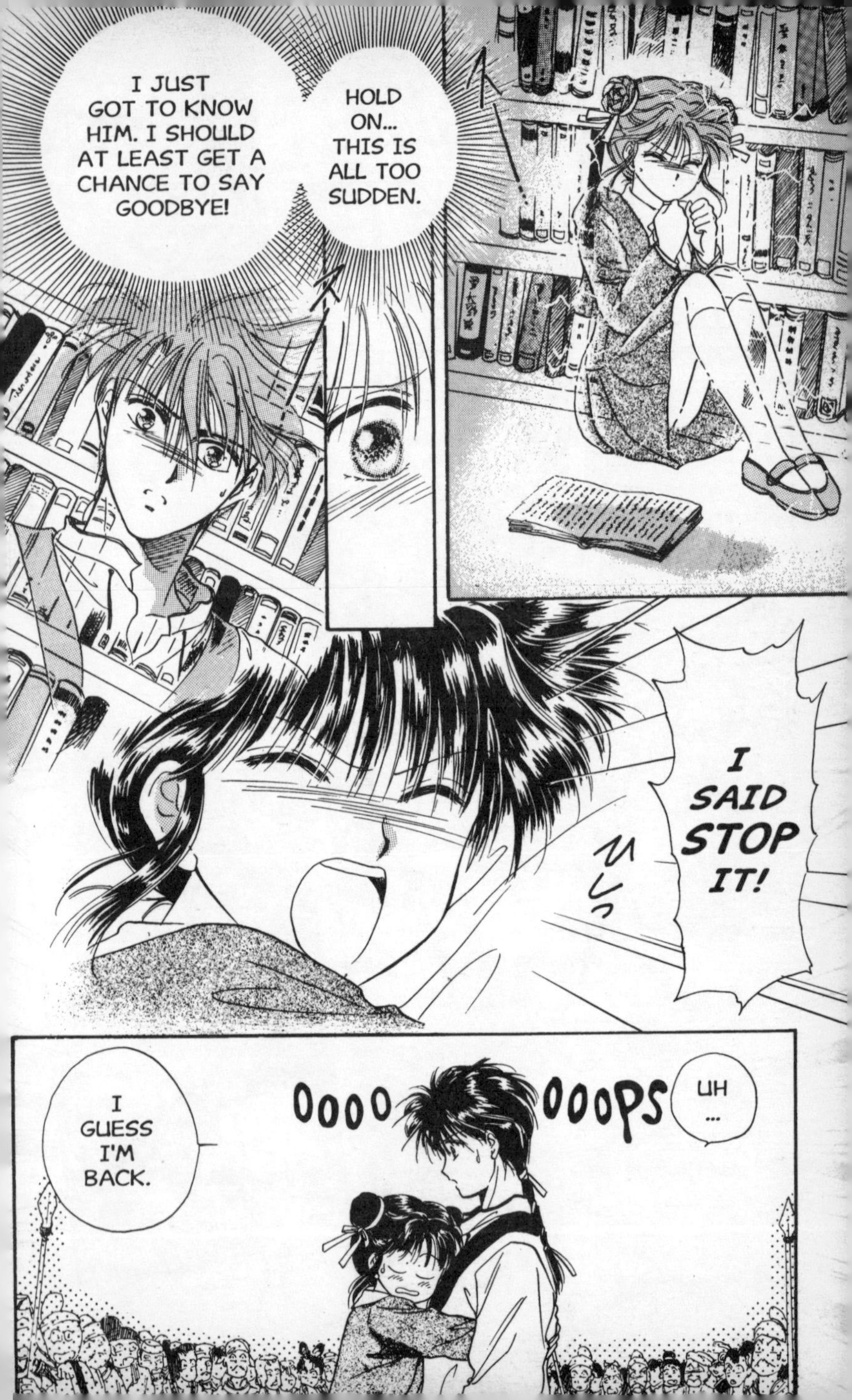
HOLD ON... THIS IS ALL TOO SUDDEN.
I JUST GOT TO KNOW HIM. I SHOULD AT LEAST GET A CHANCE TO SAY GOODBYE!
I SAID STOP IT!
UH ...
OOOOOOOPS
I GUESS I'M BACK.

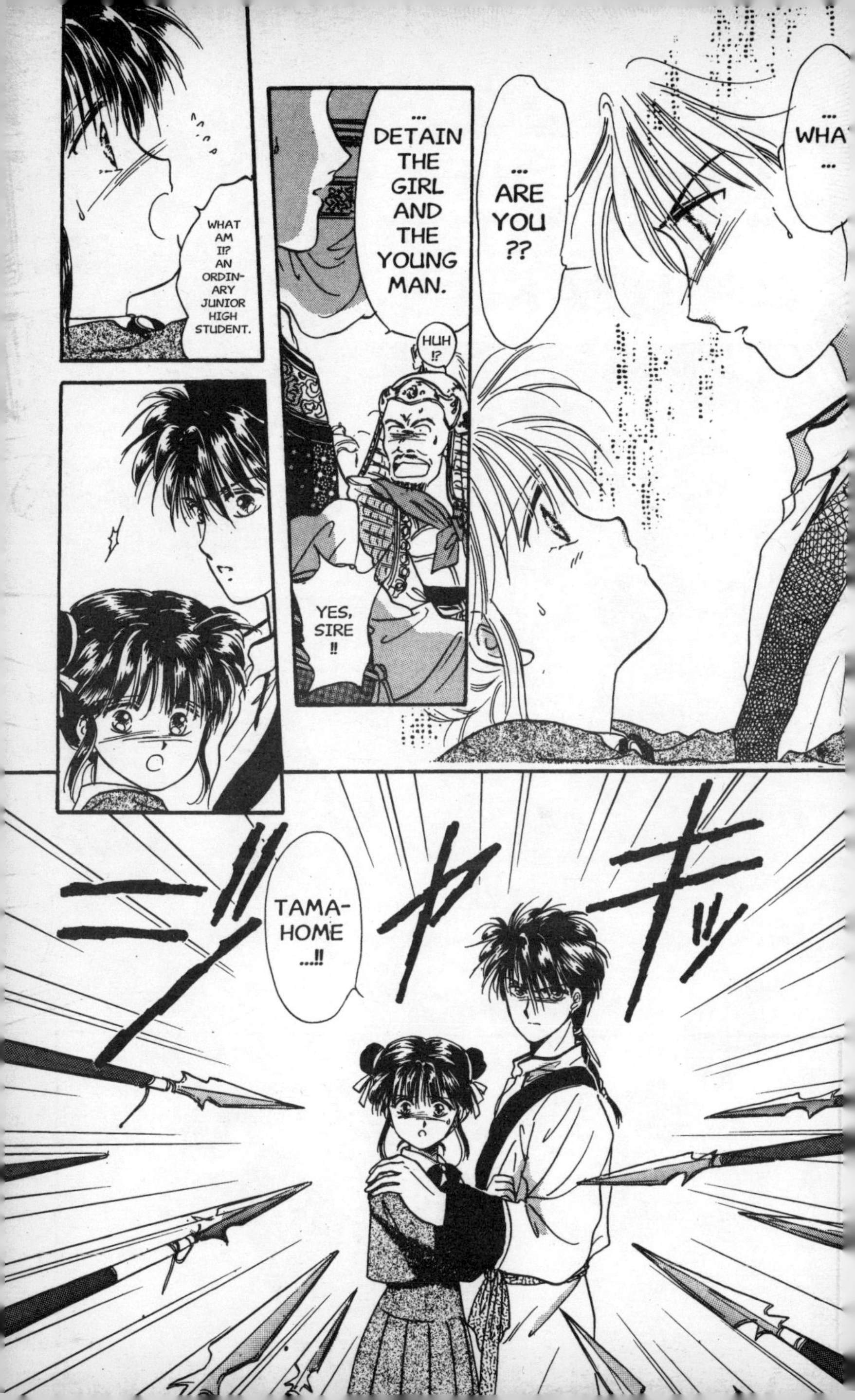

... WHAT ...
... ARE YOU ??
... DETAIN THE GIRL AND THE YOUNG MAN.
HUH !?
YES, SIRE !!
WHAT AM I!? AN ORDINARY JUNIOR HIGH STUDENT.
TAMA-HOME ...!!

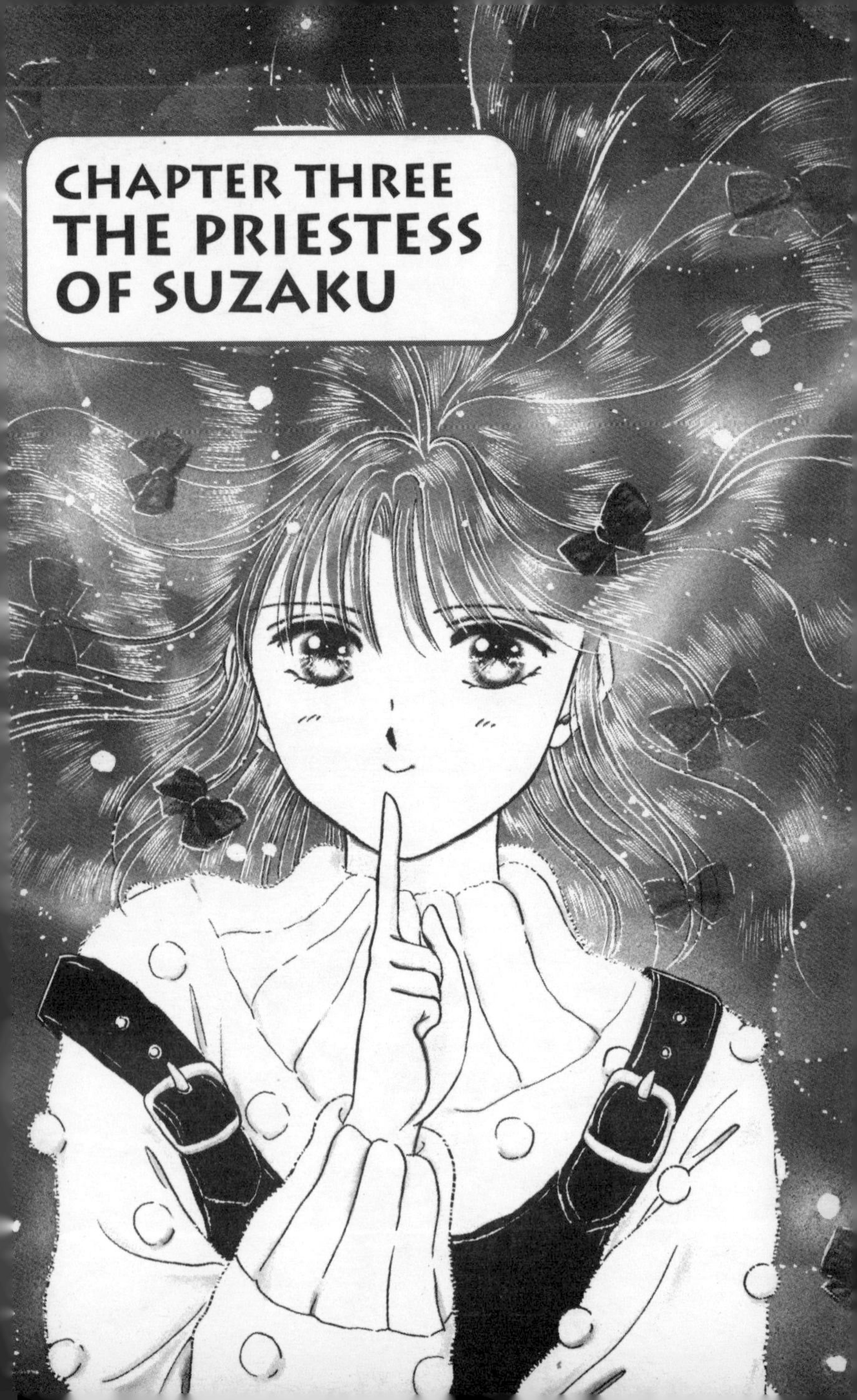
CHAPTER THREE
THE PRIESTESS
OF SUZAKU

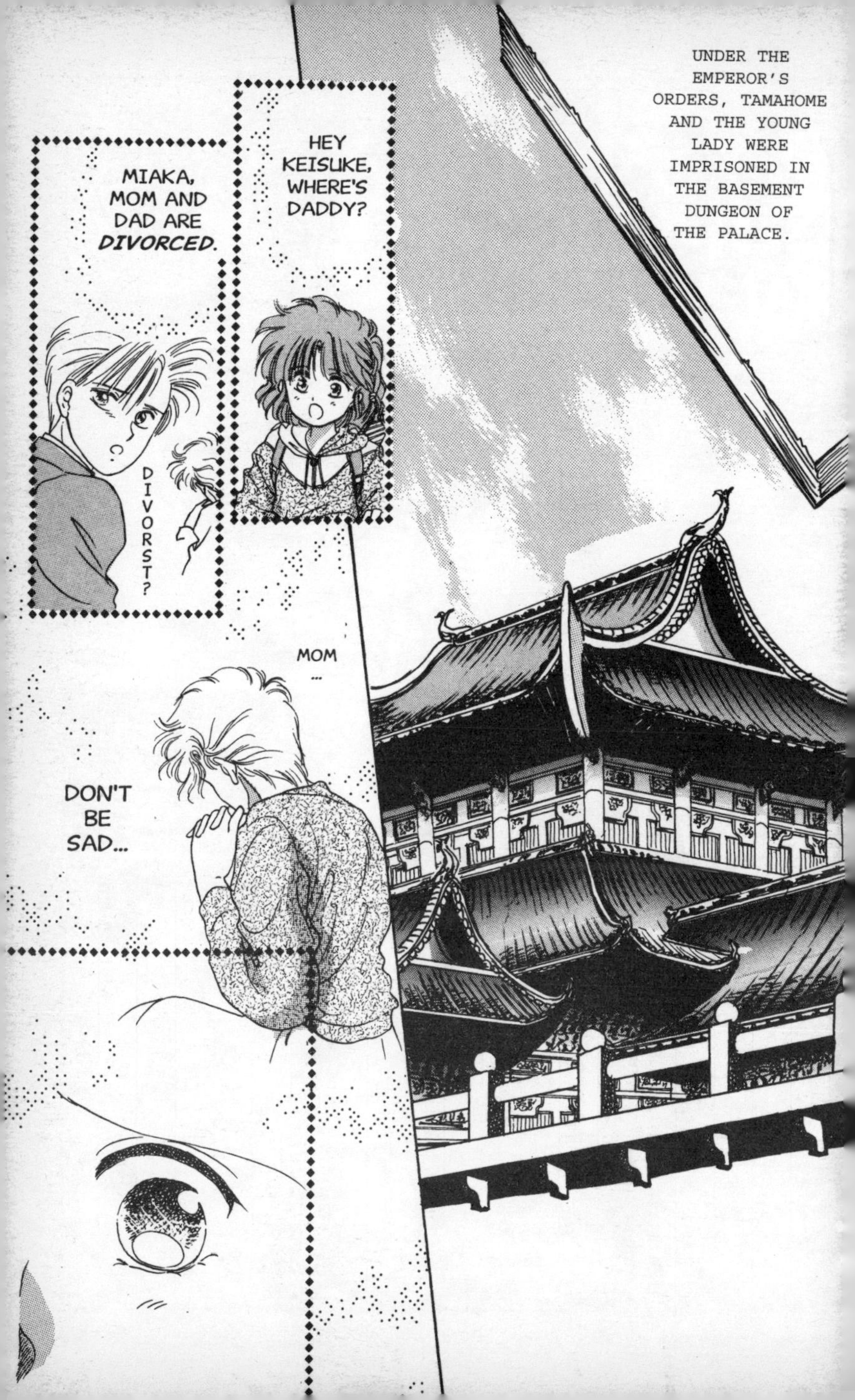
UNDER THE EMPEROR'S ORDERS, TAMAHOME AND THE YOUNG LADY WERE IMPRISONED IN THE BASEMENT DUNGEON OF THE PALACE.
HEY KEISUKE, WHERE'S DADDY?
MIAKA, MOM AND DAD ARE DIVORCED.
DIVORST?
MOM ...
DON'T BE SAD...

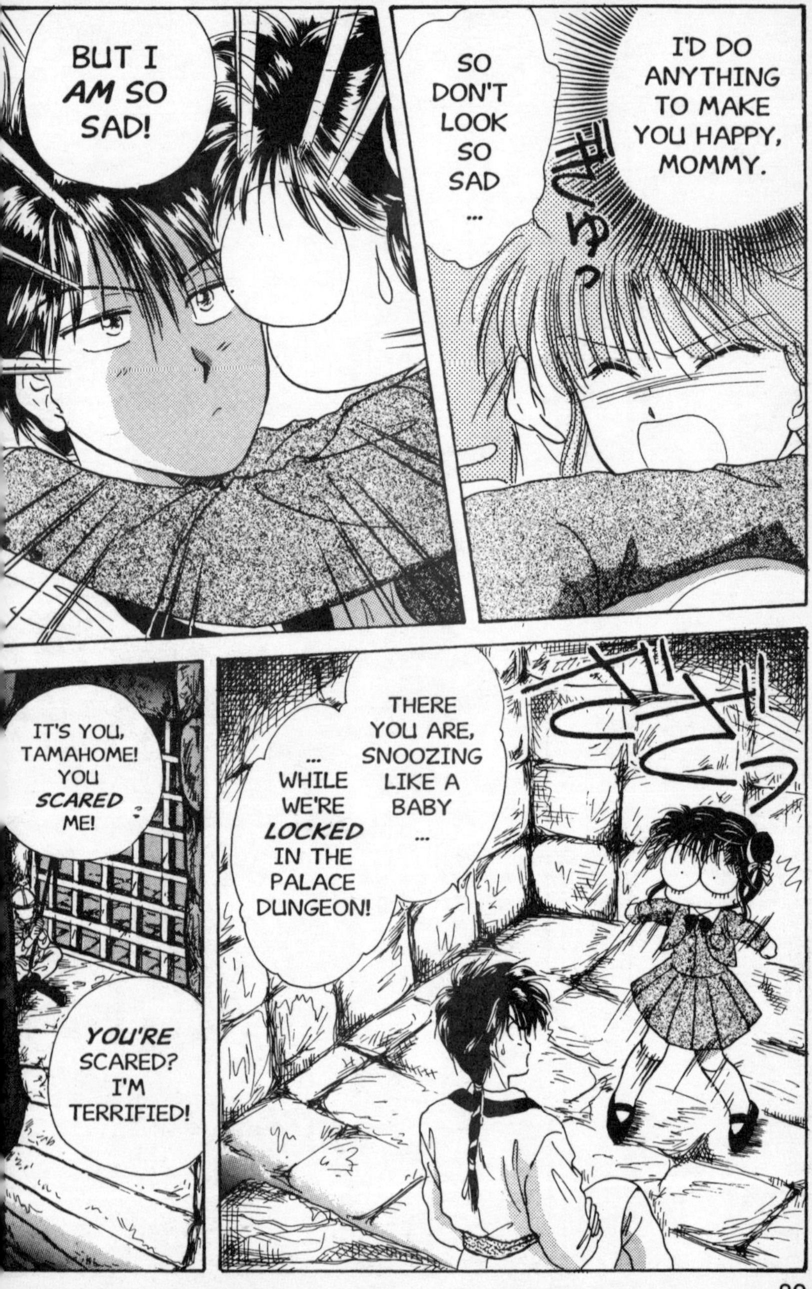
I'D DO ANYTHING TO MAKE YOU HAPPY, MOMMY.
ぎゅっ
SO DON'T LOOK SO SAD ...
BUT I AM SO SAD!
がさっ
THERE YOU ARE, SNOOZING LIKE A BABY ...
... WHILE WE'RE LOCKED IN THE PALACE DUNGEON!
IT'S YOU, TAMAHOME! YOU SCARED ME!
YOU'RE SCARED? I'M TERRIFIED!

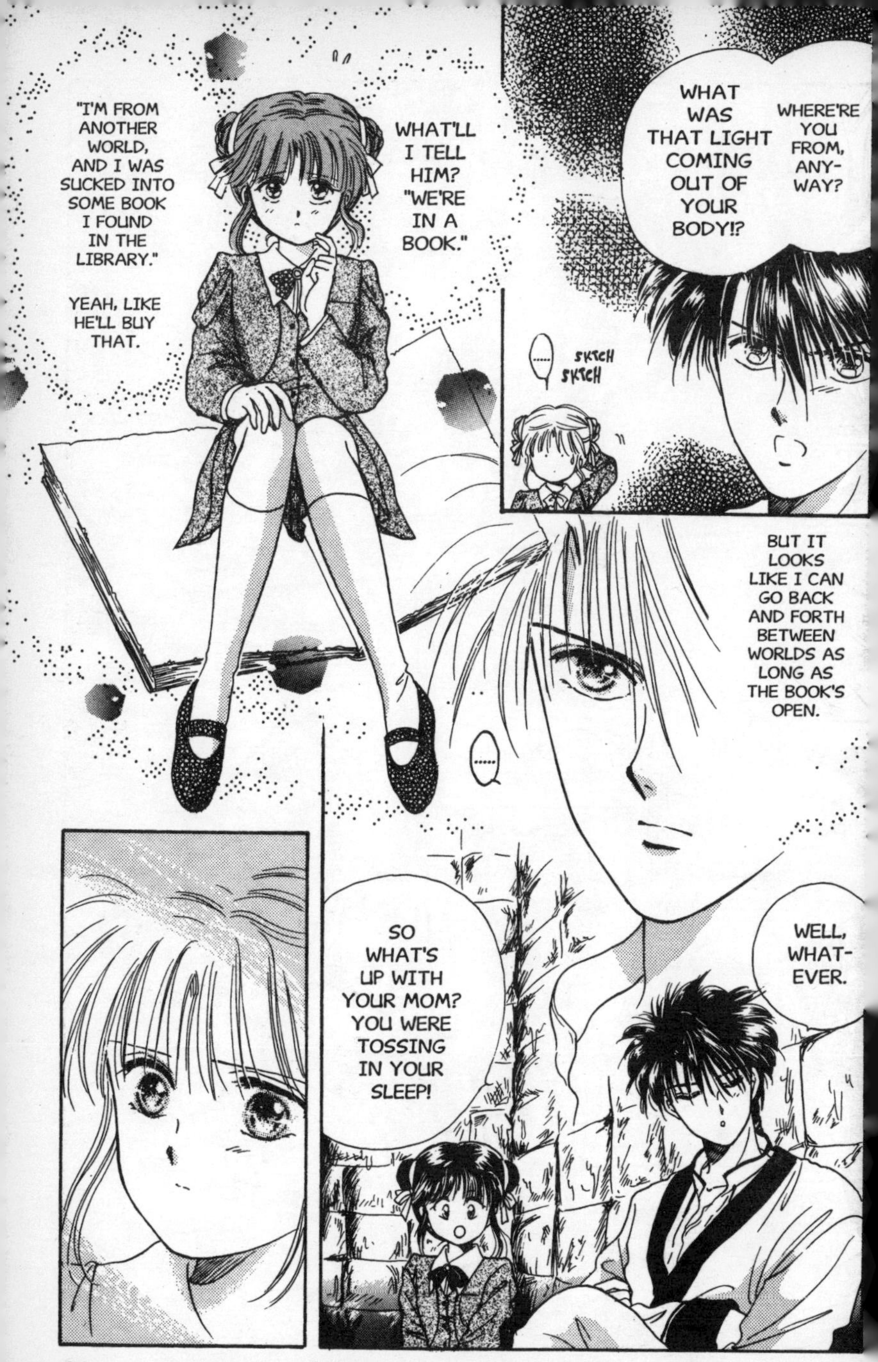
WHERE'RE YOU FROM, ANY-WAY?
WHAT WAS THAT LIGHT COMING OUT OF YOUR BODY!?
.....
SKTCH SKTCH
WHAT'LL I TELL HIM? "WE'RE IN A BOOK."
"I'M FROM ANOTHER WORLD, AND I WAS SUCKED INTO SOME BOOK I FOUND IN THE LIBRARY."
YEAH, LIKE HE'LL BUY THAT.
BUT IT LOOKS LIKE I CAN GO BACK AND FORTH BETWEEN WORLDS AS LONG AS THE BOOK'S OPEN.
.....
WELL, WHAT-EVER.
SO WHAT'S UP WITH YOUR MOM? YOU WERE TOSSING IN YOUR SLEEP!

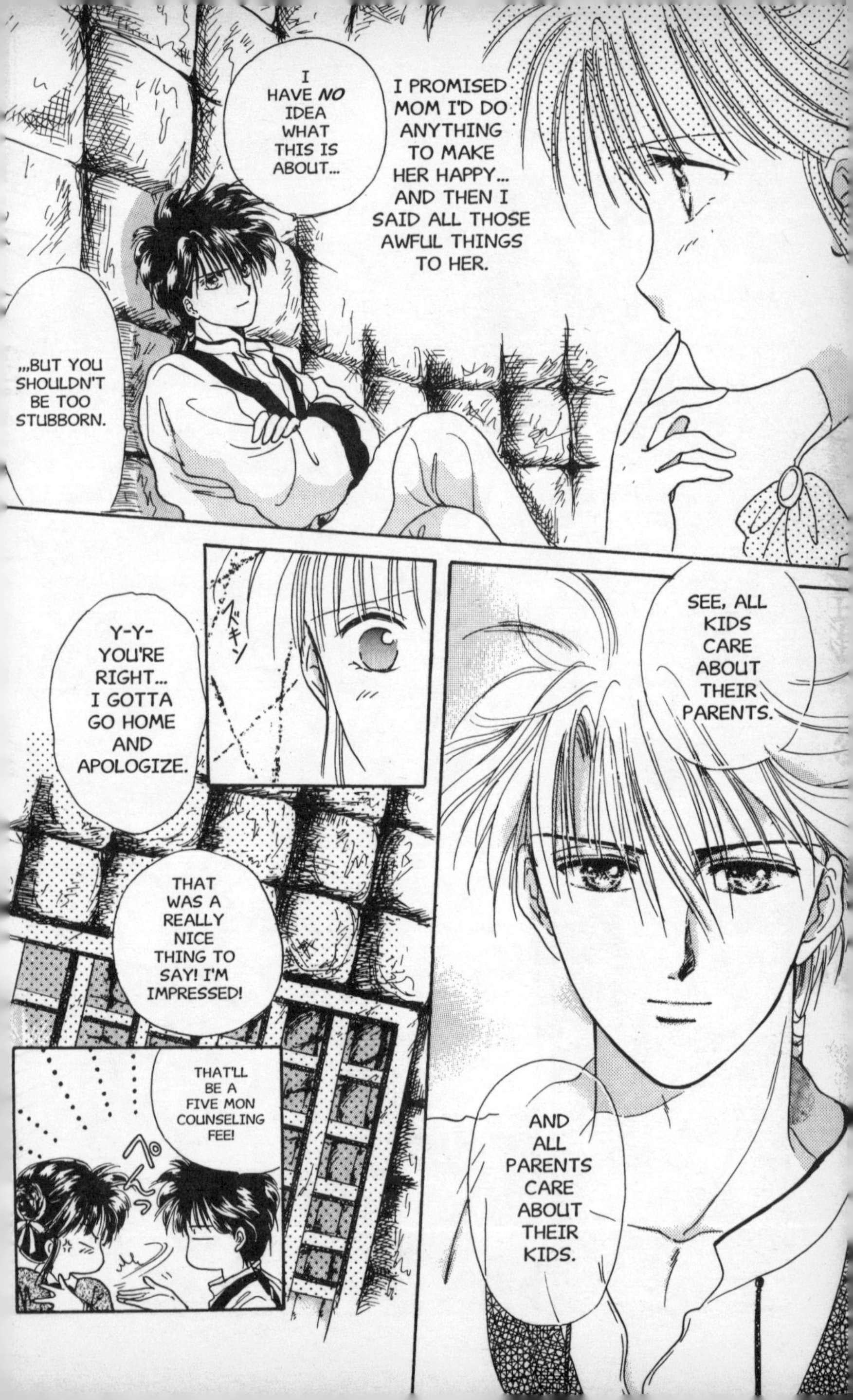
I PROMISED MOM I'D DO ANYTHING TO MAKE HER HAPPY... AND THEN I SAID ALL THOSE AWFUL THINGS TO HER.
I HAVE *NO* IDEA WHAT THIS IS ABOUT...
...BUT YOU SHOULDN'T BE TOO STUBBORN.
SEE, ALL KIDS CARE ABOUT THEIR PARENTS.
AND ALL PARENTS CARE ABOUT THEIR KIDS.
ズキン
Y-Y-YOU'RE RIGHT... I GOTTA GO HOME AND APOLOGIZE.
THAT WAS A REALLY NICE THING TO SAY! I'M IMPRESSED!
THAT'LL BE A FIVE MON COUNSELING FEE!

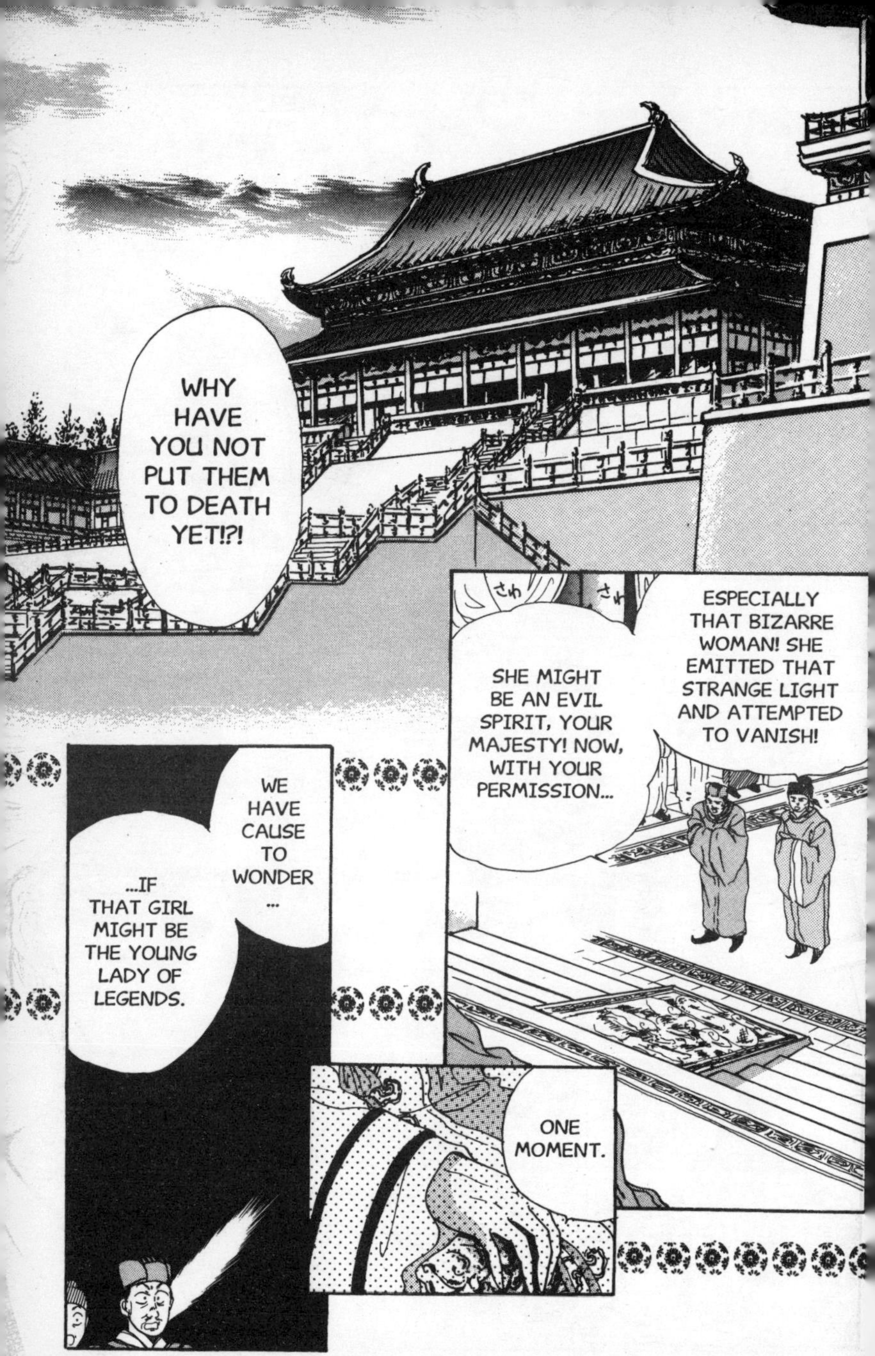

WHY HAVE YOU NOT PUT THEM TO DEATH YET!?!
さわ
さわ
ESPECIALLY THAT BIZARRE WOMAN! SHE EMITTED THAT STRANGE LIGHT AND ATTEMPTED TO VANISH!
SHE MIGHT BE AN EVIL SPIRIT, YOUR MAJESTY! NOW, WITH YOUR PERMISSION...
ONE MOMENT.
WE HAVE CAUSE TO WONDER...
...IF THAT GIRL MIGHT BE THE YOUNG LADY OF LEGENDS.

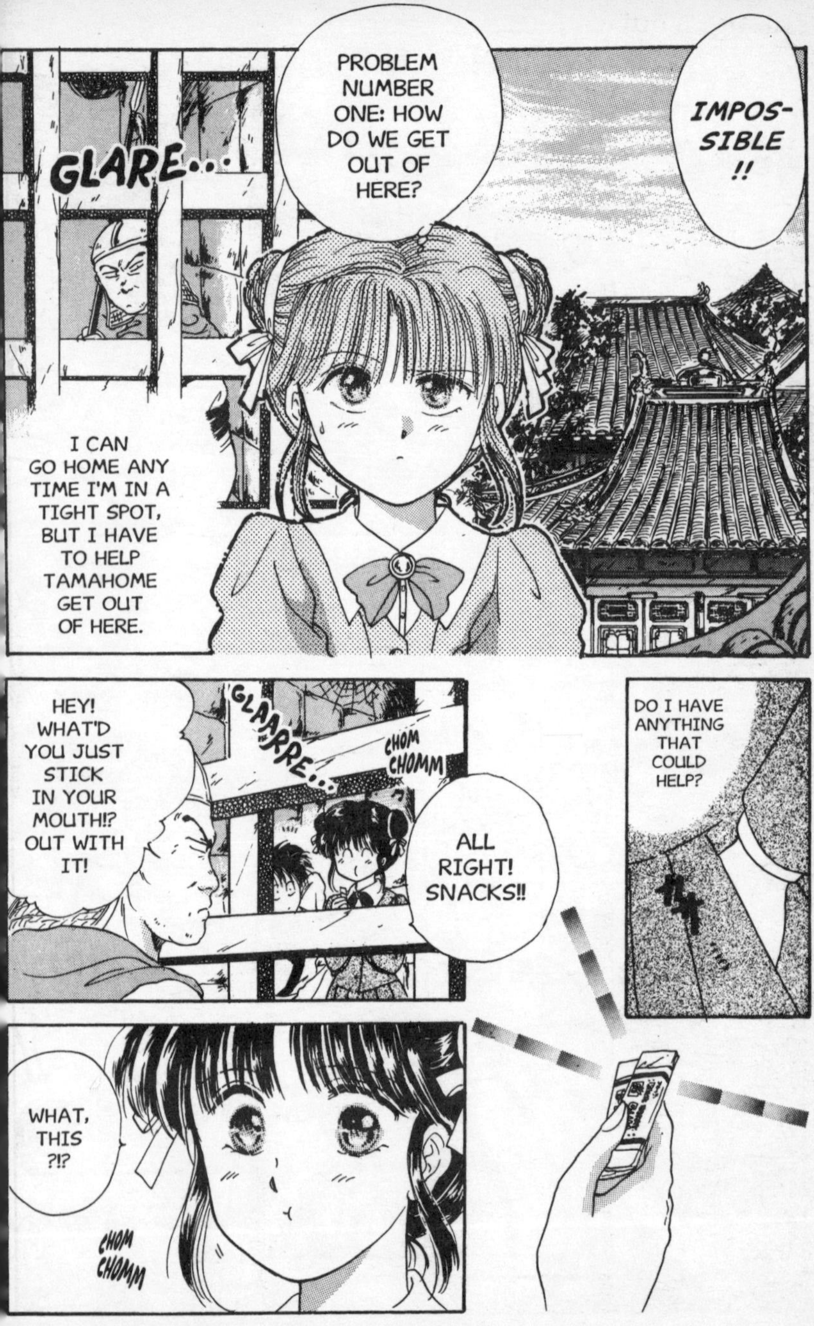
IMPOSSIBLE!!
PROBLEM NUMBER ONE: HOW DO WE GET OUT OF HERE?
GLARE...
I CAN GO HOME ANY TIME I'M IN A TIGHT SPOT, BUT I HAVE TO HELP TAMAHOME GET OUT OF HERE.
DO I HAVE ANYTHING THAT COULD HELP?
ALL RIGHT! SNACKS!!
CHOM CHOMM
GLAAARRE...
HEY! WHAT'D YOU JUST STICK IN YOUR MOUTH!? OUT WITH IT!
WHAT, THIS?!?
CHOM CHOMM

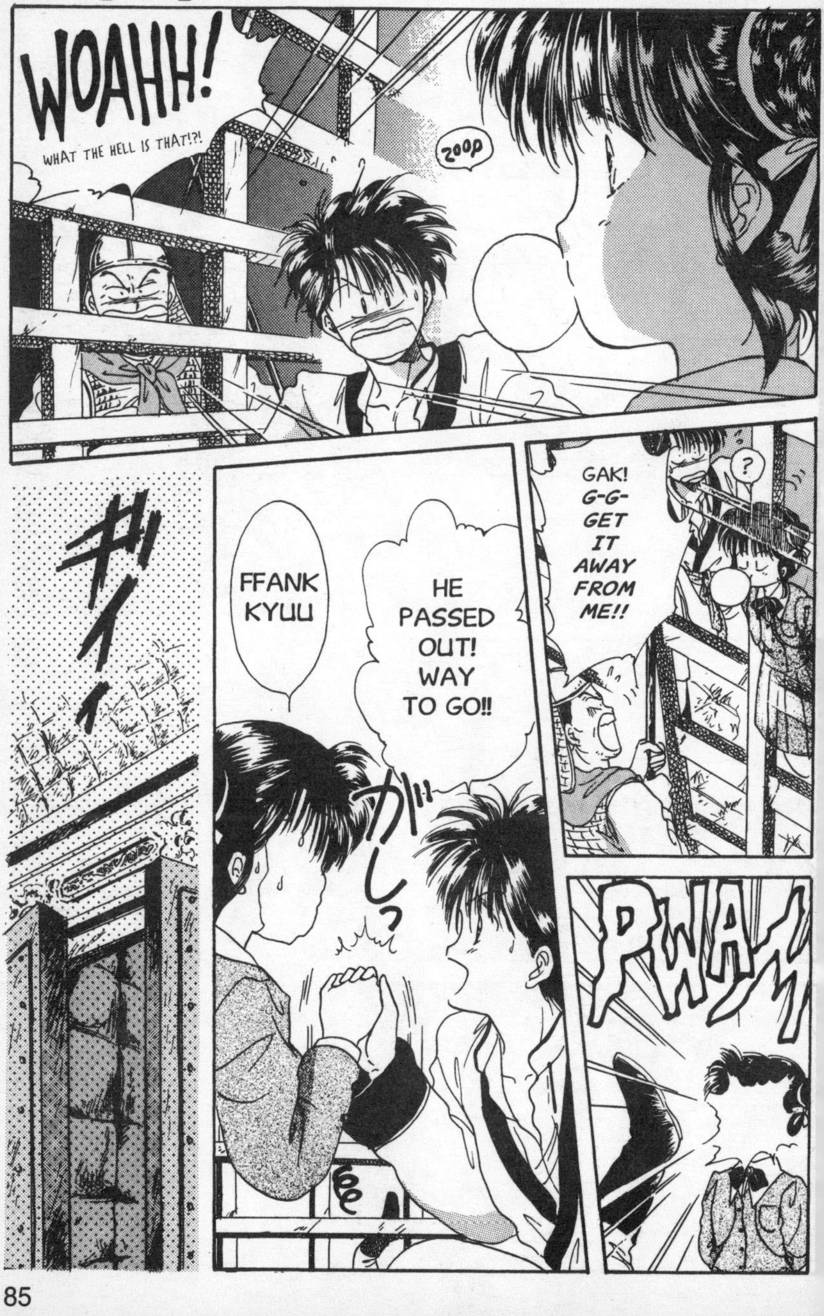
WOAHH!
WHAT THE HELL IS THAT!?!
zoop
FFANK KYUU
HE PASSED OUT! WAY TO GO!!
かしっ
GAK! G-G-GET IT AWAY FROM ME!!
?
PWAH

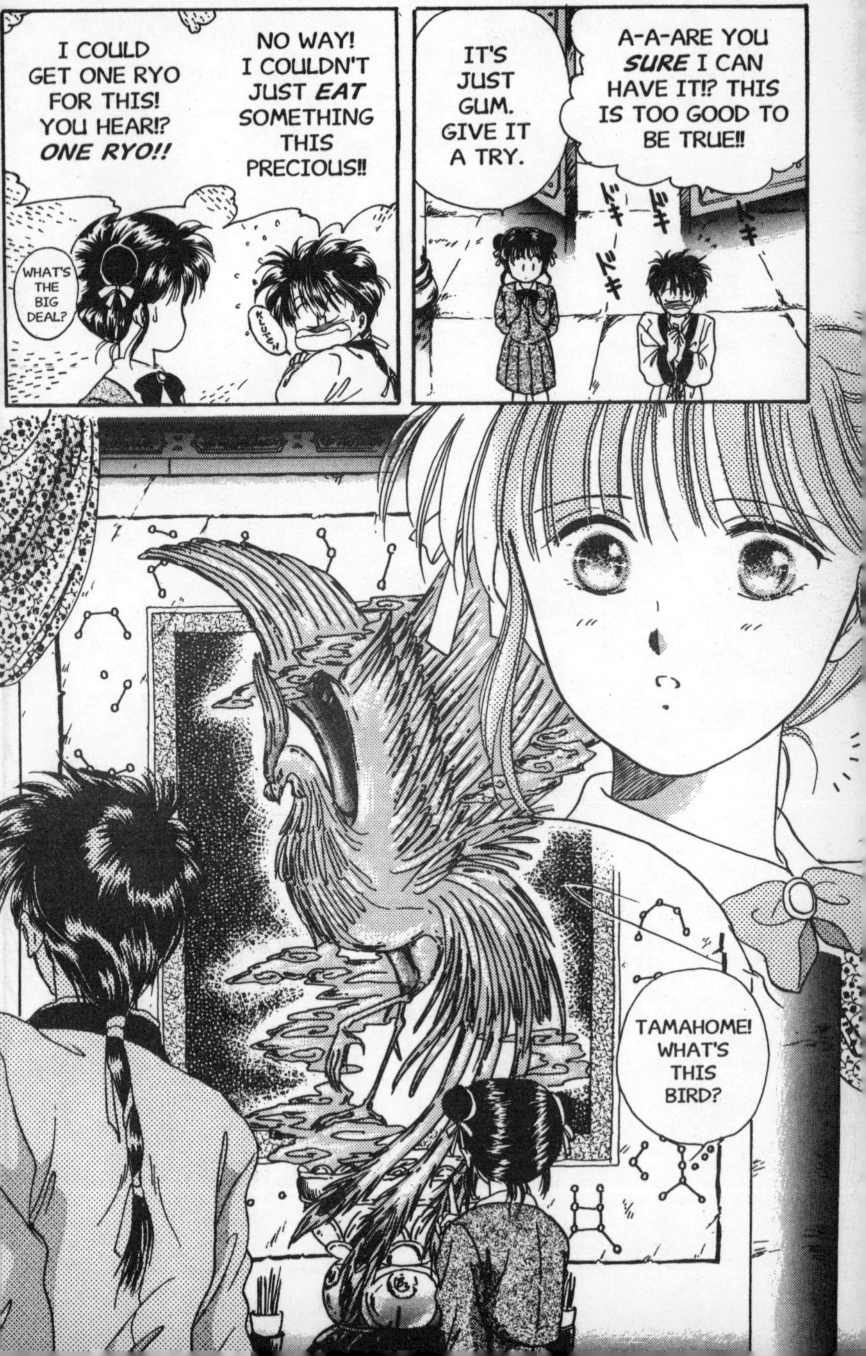
A-A-ARE YOU SURE I CAN HAVE IT!? THIS IS TOO GOOD TO BE TRUE!!
IT'S JUST GUM. GIVE IT A TRY.
ドキ ドキ ドキ ドキ
NO WAY! I COULDN'T JUST EAT SOMETHING THIS PRECIOUS!!
I COULD GET ONE RYO FOR THIS! YOU HEAR!? ONE RYO!!
KLUTCH
WHAT'S THE BIG DEAL?
TAMAHOME! WHAT'S THIS BIRD?

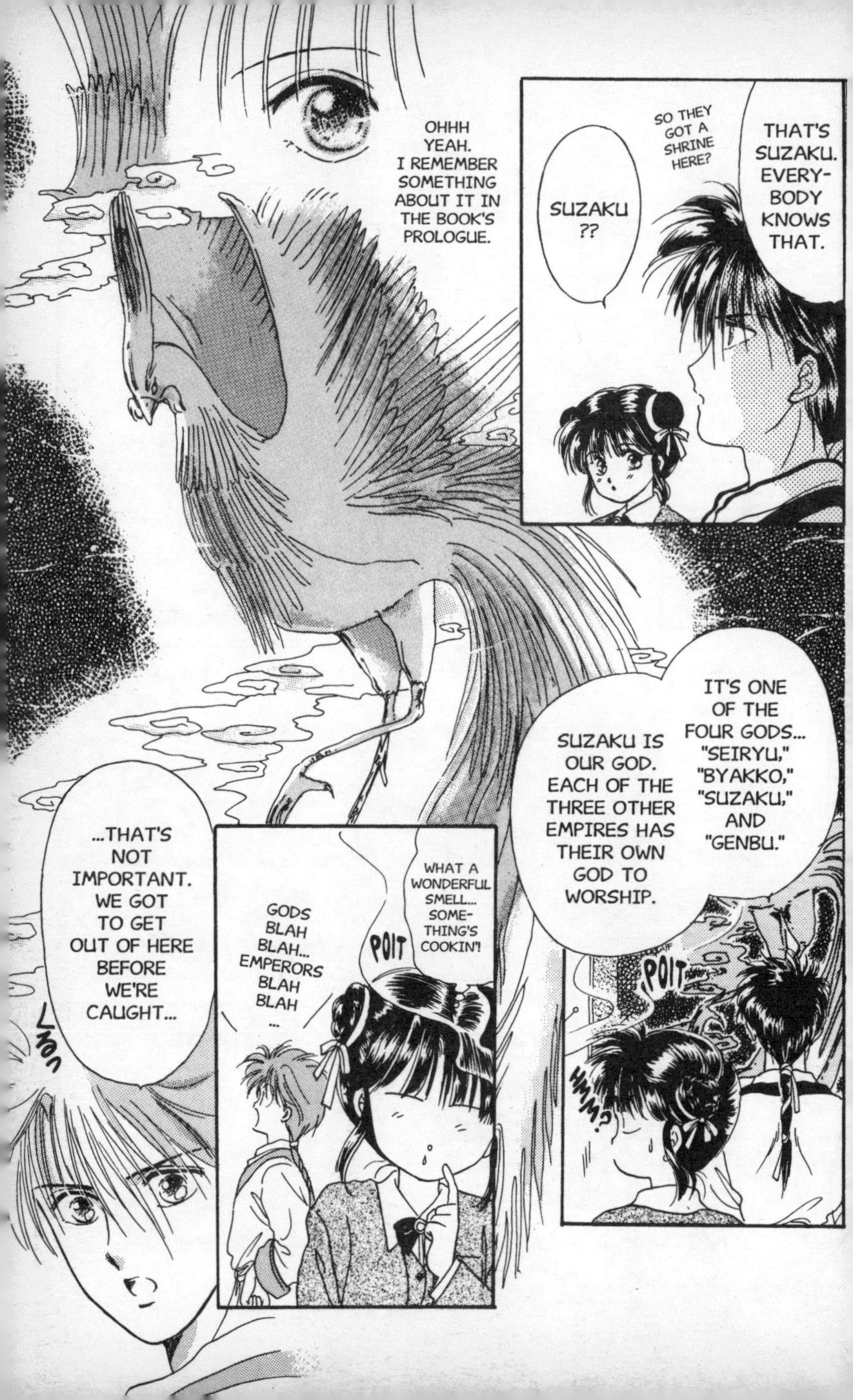
THAT'S SUZAKU. EVERY-BODY KNOWS THAT.
SO THEY GOT A SHRINE HERE?
SUZAKU ??
OHHH YEAH. I REMEMBER SOMETHING ABOUT IT IN THE BOOK'S PROLOGUE.
IT'S ONE OF THE FOUR GODS... "SEIRYU," "BYAKKO," "SUZAKU," AND "GENBU."
SUZAKU IS OUR GOD. EACH OF THE THREE OTHER EMPIRES HAS THEIR OWN GOD TO WORSHIP.
POIT
HMM?
WHAT A WONDERFUL SMELL... SOME-THING'S COOKIN'!
POIT
GODS BLAH BLAH... EMPERORS BLAH BLAH ...
...THAT'S NOT IMPORTANT. WE GOT TO GET OUT OF HERE BEFORE WE'RE CAUGHT...

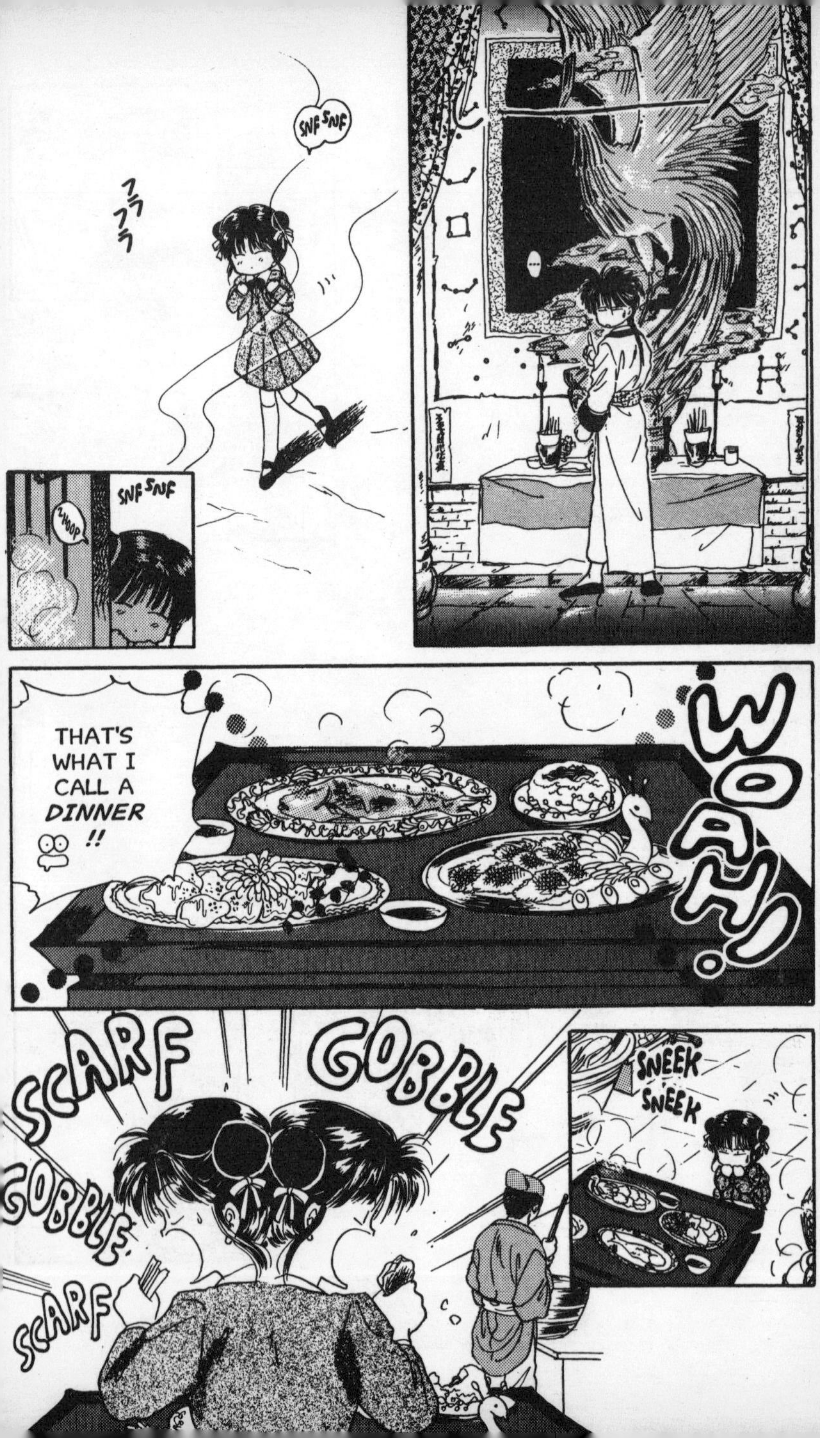
SNF SNF
フラフラ
SNF SNF
ZHOOP
WOAH!
THAT'S WHAT I CALL A *DINNER* !!
SNEEK SNEEK
GOBBLE
SCARF
GOBBLE
SCARF

Priestess

Getting back to where we left off, I'm sure some of my work reminds the readers of other comics. Of course I never do it consciously! (Even I have some pride). Someone ends up pointing it out, and then I'm like "oh my god!" wait. "Magical Nan" ♪ was different. That came from a book my editor gave me. Although I tried to make my version totally different, due to limitations on the number of pages, I was told to imitate the book. I really do try not to copy scenes. During junior high and high school I was influenced mostly by people like Toyoo Ashida (director, animation director: Yamato, Minky Momo and Vampire Hunter D) and Akemi Takada (character designer: Creamy Mami, Urusei Yatsura, Kimagure Orange Road) (My older drawings from "Prepubescence Vol. 3", I was really into Takada at the time) and Mutsumi Inomata (character designer: Windaria, Leda, Brain-Powerd), anime artists rather than comic artists. Now I hardly get a chance to watch animation at all, so I don't know what's going on these days. I really loved animation. Seems so long ago. I tried to cram these animation influences into a shôjo manga drawing style that never really existed before. (I've asked many people, and there's nobody else who draws like I do).

It's really hard to find a balance. I have many fellow artists who can give me advice, but I just can't change at this point.

I think that my own pictures are too complicated! I was really into boys' comics so everyone thought I'd be writing for shonen manga magazines such as Shonen Sunday. But can you believe that maybe after three years of hard work, I finally managed to draw shôjo manga effectively? ♥ I still have a long way to go. Okay, okay, I'm getting a little long-winded here but most of my fan letters come from people who want to become comic artists, so you guys can use this as a reference (maybe). To sum up, I recommend you study and incorporate all the elements of artists you admire in your unique way into your own drawings (without ripping them off). I tend to discard those elements that don't fit with my style. You should also read as many novels, see as many films and dramas as possible. Remember the great Osamu Tezuka once said, "If you want to write a new manga then don't bother reading another manga!" Of course, this is coming from someone who bought his "How To Draw Manga" AFTER getting published! Sorry!

My friends razzed me about it. But I don't know how to do effects work. So sue me!! ♪

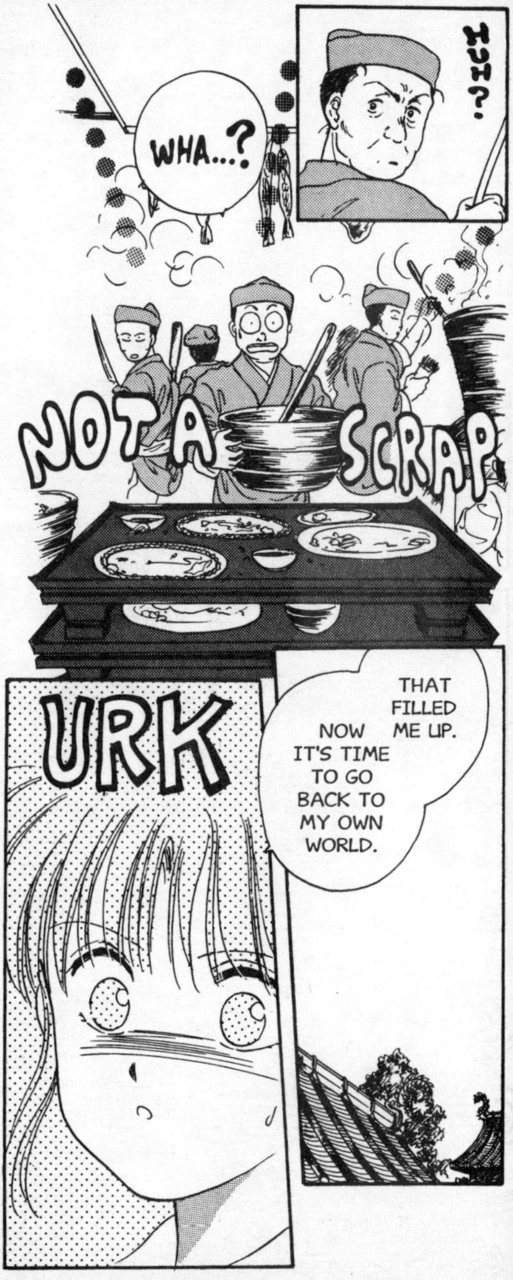
HUH?
WHA...?
NOT A SCRAP
THAT FILLED ME UP.
NOW IT'S TIME TO GO BACK TO MY OWN WORLD.
URK

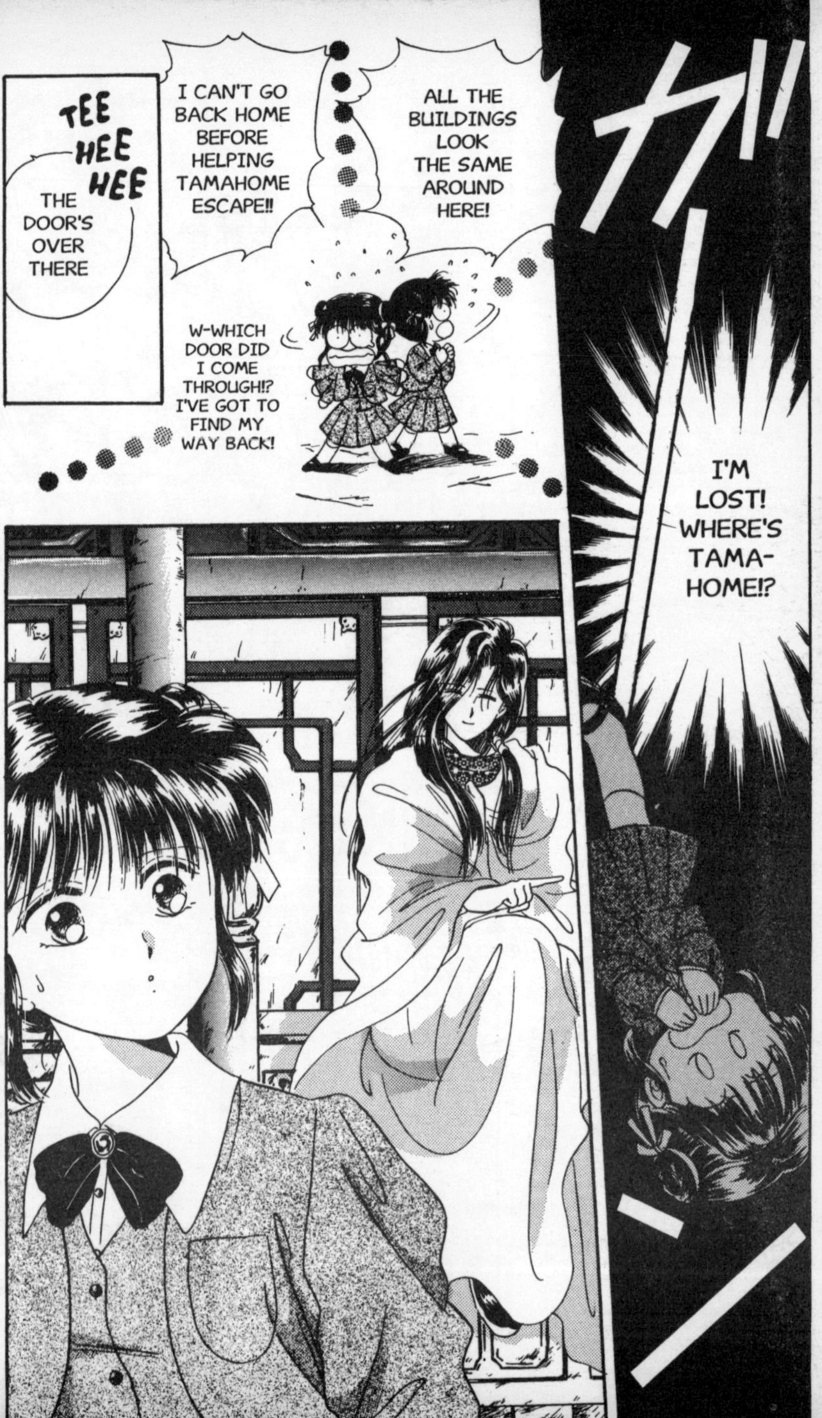

ガーン
I'M LOST! WHERE'S TAMA-HOME!?
ALL THE BUILDINGS LOOK THE SAME AROUND HERE!
I CAN'T GO BACK HOME BEFORE HELPING TAMAHOME ESCAPE!!
W-WHICH DOOR DID I COME THROUGH!? I'VE GOT TO FIND MY WAY BACK!
TEE HEE HEE
THE DOOR'S OVER THERE

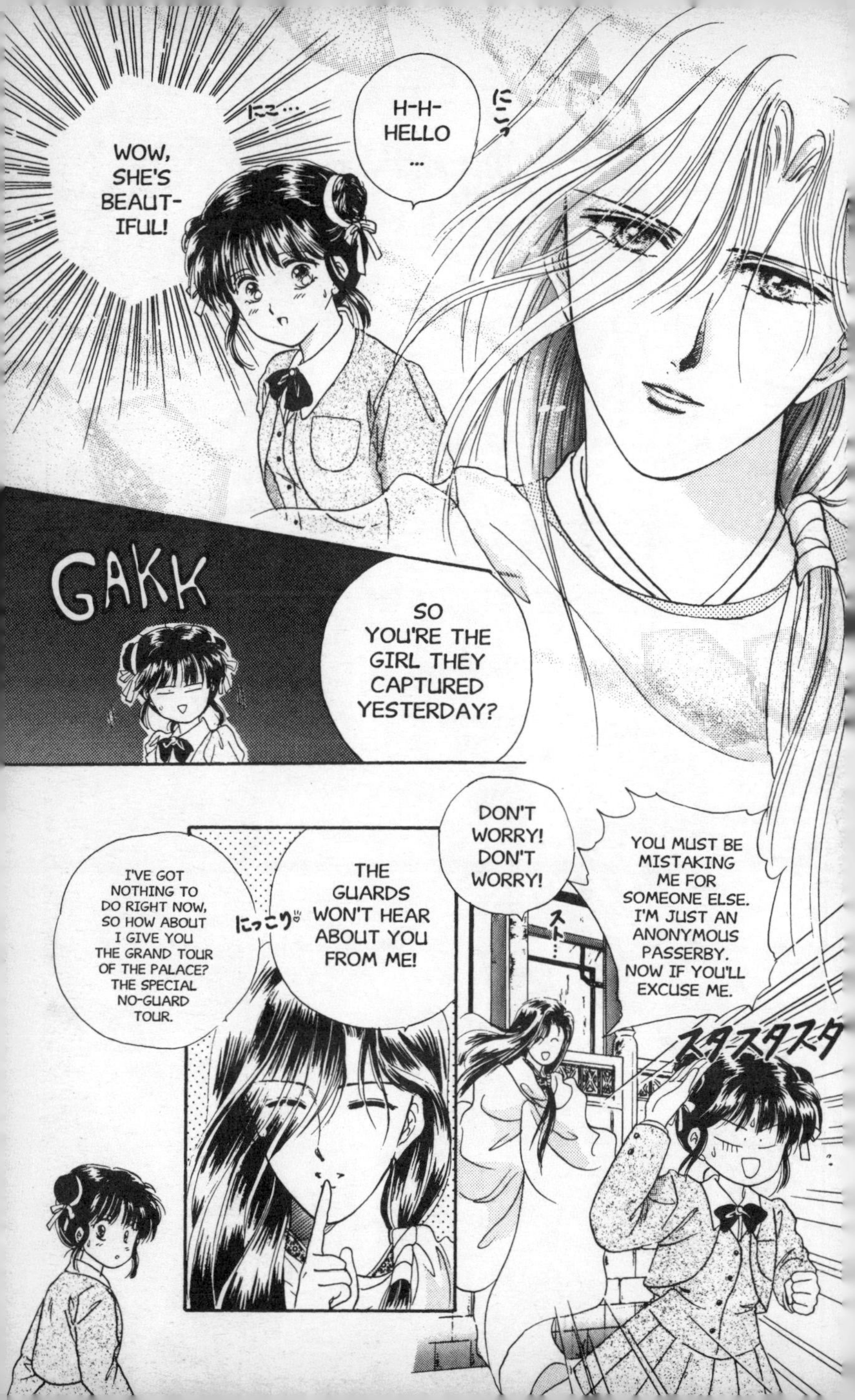
にこっ
H-H-HELLO ...
にこ…
WOW, SHE'S BEAUTIFUL!
SO YOU'RE THE GIRL THEY CAPTURED YESTERDAY?
GAKK
YOU MUST BE MISTAKING ME FOR SOMEONE ELSE. I'M JUST AN ANONYMOUS PASSERBY. NOW IF YOU'LL EXCUSE ME.
スタスタスタ
スト…
DON'T WORRY! DON'T WORRY!
THE GUARDS WON'T HEAR ABOUT YOU FROM ME!
にっこり
I'VE GOT NOTHING TO DO RIGHT NOW, SO HOW ABOUT I GIVE YOU THE GRAND TOUR OF THE PALACE? THE SPECIAL NO-GUARD TOUR.

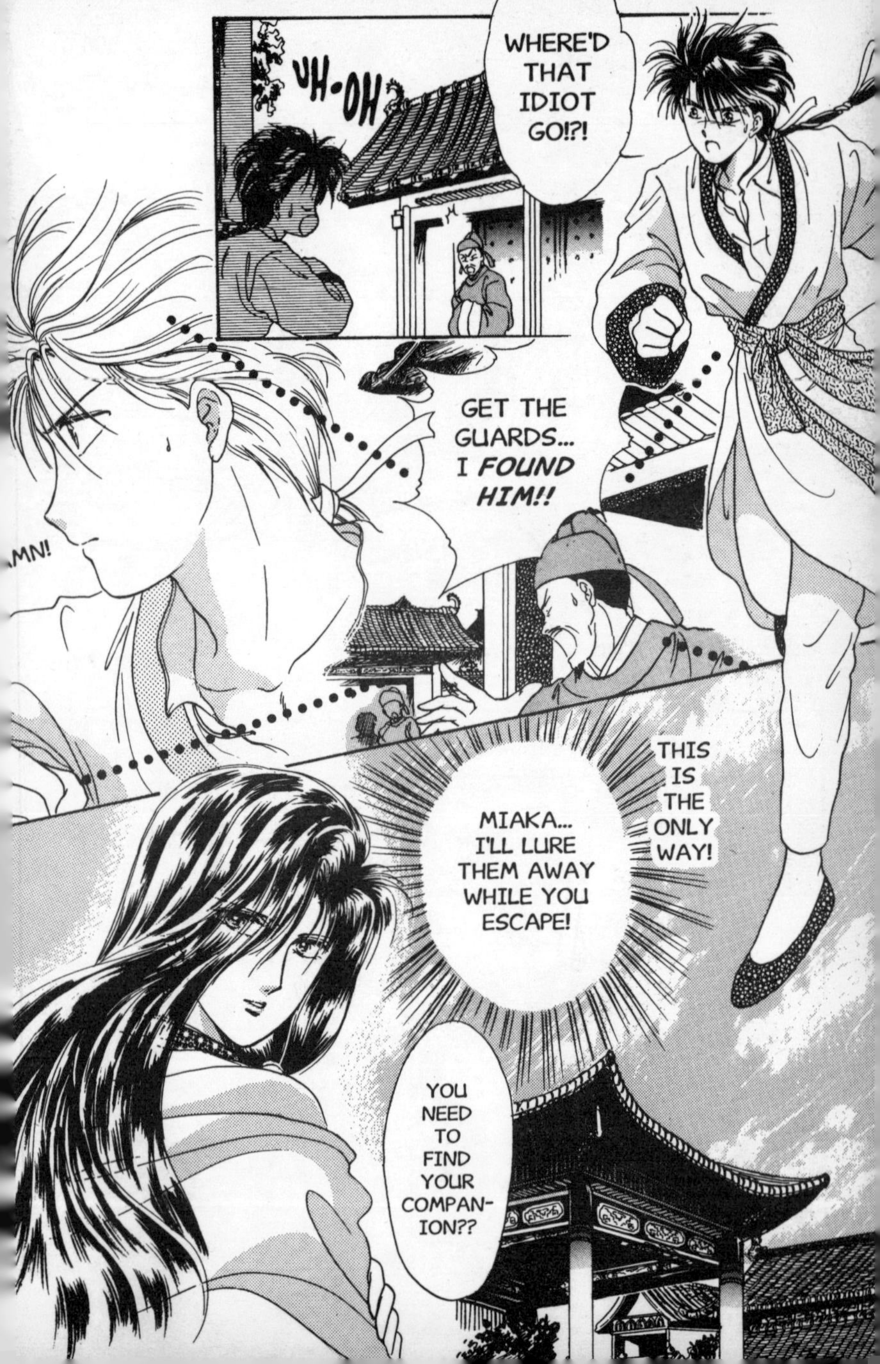
WHERE'D THAT IDIOT GO!?!
UH-OH
GET THE GUARDS... I FOUND HIM!!
THIS IS THE ONLY WAY!
MIAKA... I'LL LURE THEM AWAY WHILE YOU ESCAPE!
YOU NEED TO FIND YOUR COMPANION??

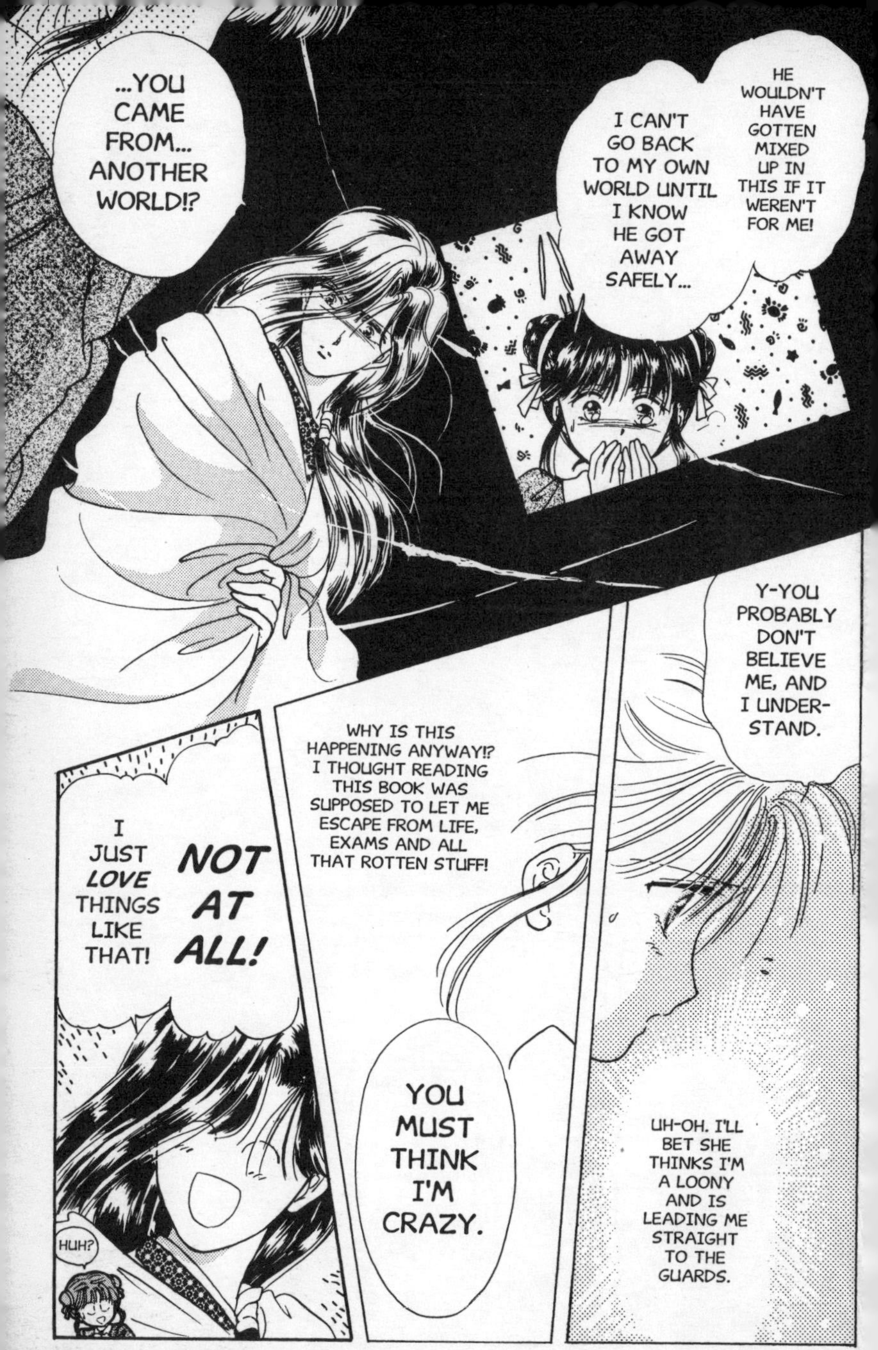
...YOU CAME FROM... ANOTHER WORLD!?
I CAN'T GO BACK TO MY OWN WORLD UNTIL I KNOW HE GOT AWAY SAFELY...
HE WOULDN'T HAVE GOTTEN MIXED UP IN THIS IF IT WEREN'T FOR ME!
Y-YOU PROBABLY DON'T BELIEVE ME, AND I UNDER-STAND.
UH-OH. I'LL BET SHE THINKS I'M A LOONY AND IS LEADING ME STRAIGHT TO THE GUARDS.
WHY IS THIS HAPPENING ANYWAY!? I THOUGHT READING THIS BOOK WAS SUPPOSED TO LET ME ESCAPE FROM LIFE, EXAMS AND ALL THAT ROTTEN STUFF!
YOU MUST THINK I'M CRAZY.
NOT AT ALL!
I JUST *LOVE* THINGS LIKE THAT!
HUH?

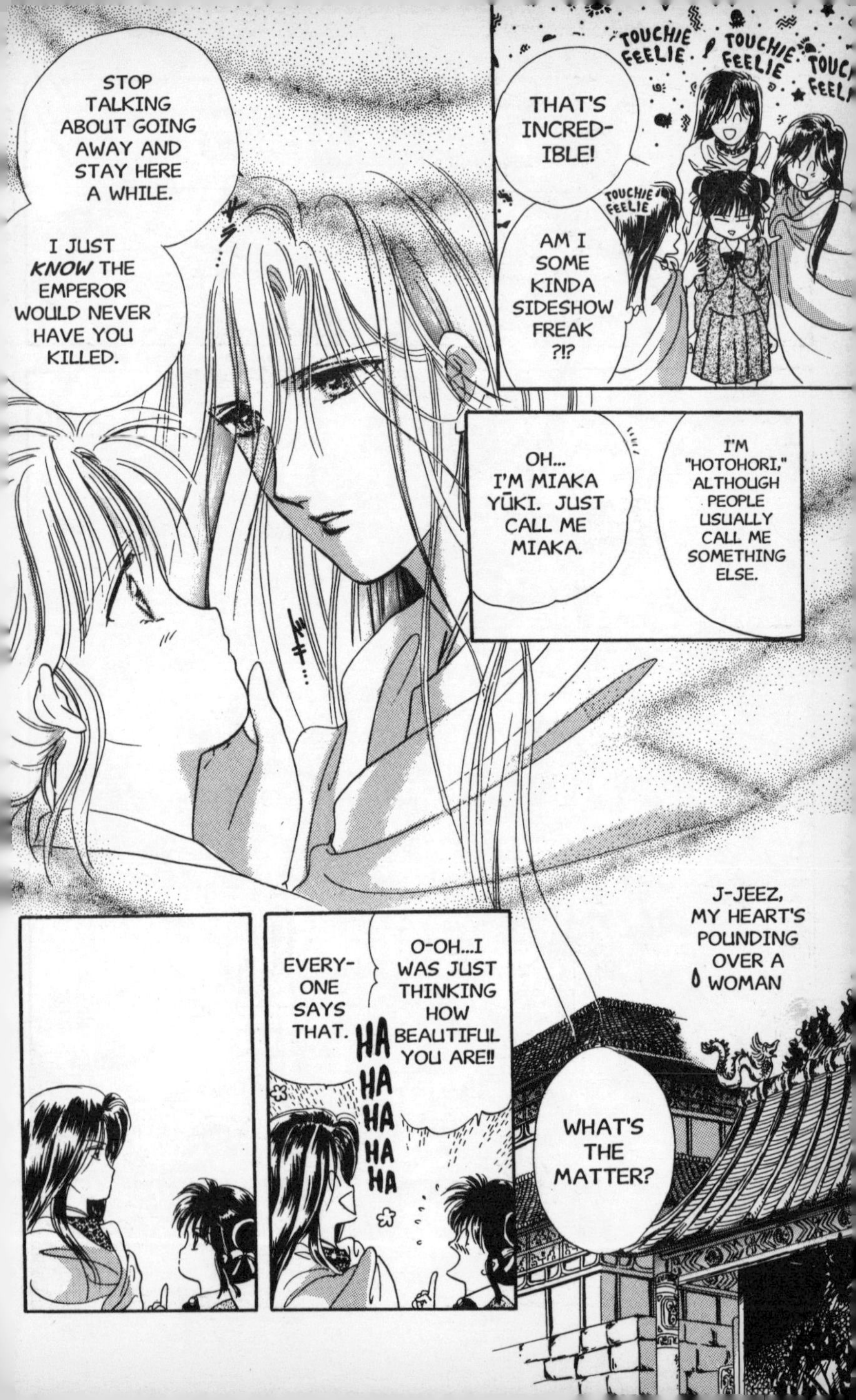
STOP TALKING ABOUT GOING AWAY AND STAY HERE A WHILE.
I JUST *KNOW* THE EMPEROR WOULD NEVER HAVE YOU KILLED.
TOUCHIE FEELIE
TOUCHIE FEELIE
TOUCHIE FEELIE
THAT'S INCRED-IBLE!
TOUCHIE FEELIE
AM I SOME KINDA SIDESHOW FREAK ?!?
I'M "HOTOHORI," ALTHOUGH PEOPLE USUALLY CALL ME SOMETHING ELSE.
OH... I'M MIAKA YŪKI. JUST CALL ME MIAKA.
J-JEEZ, MY HEART'S POUNDING OVER A WOMAN
WHAT'S THE MATTER?
O-OH...I WAS JUST THINKING HOW BEAUTIFUL YOU ARE!!
HA HA HA HA HA HA
EVERY-ONE SAYS THAT.

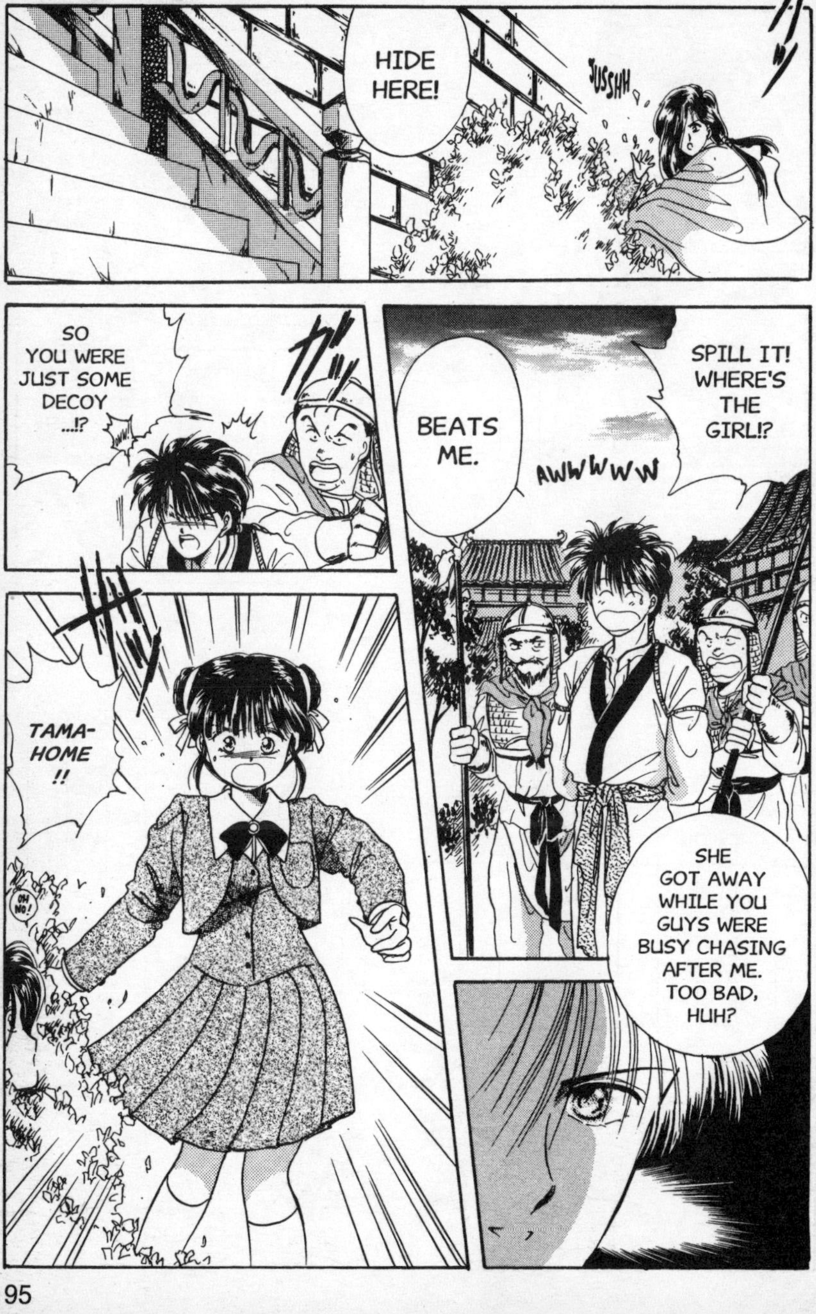
HIDE HERE!
JUSSHH
SPILL IT! WHERE'S THE GIRL!?
AWWWWWW
BEATS ME.
SHE GOT AWAY WHILE YOU GUYS WERE BUSY CHASING AFTER ME. TOO BAD, HUH?
SO YOU WERE JUST SOME DECOY ...!?
TAMA-HOME !!
OH NO!

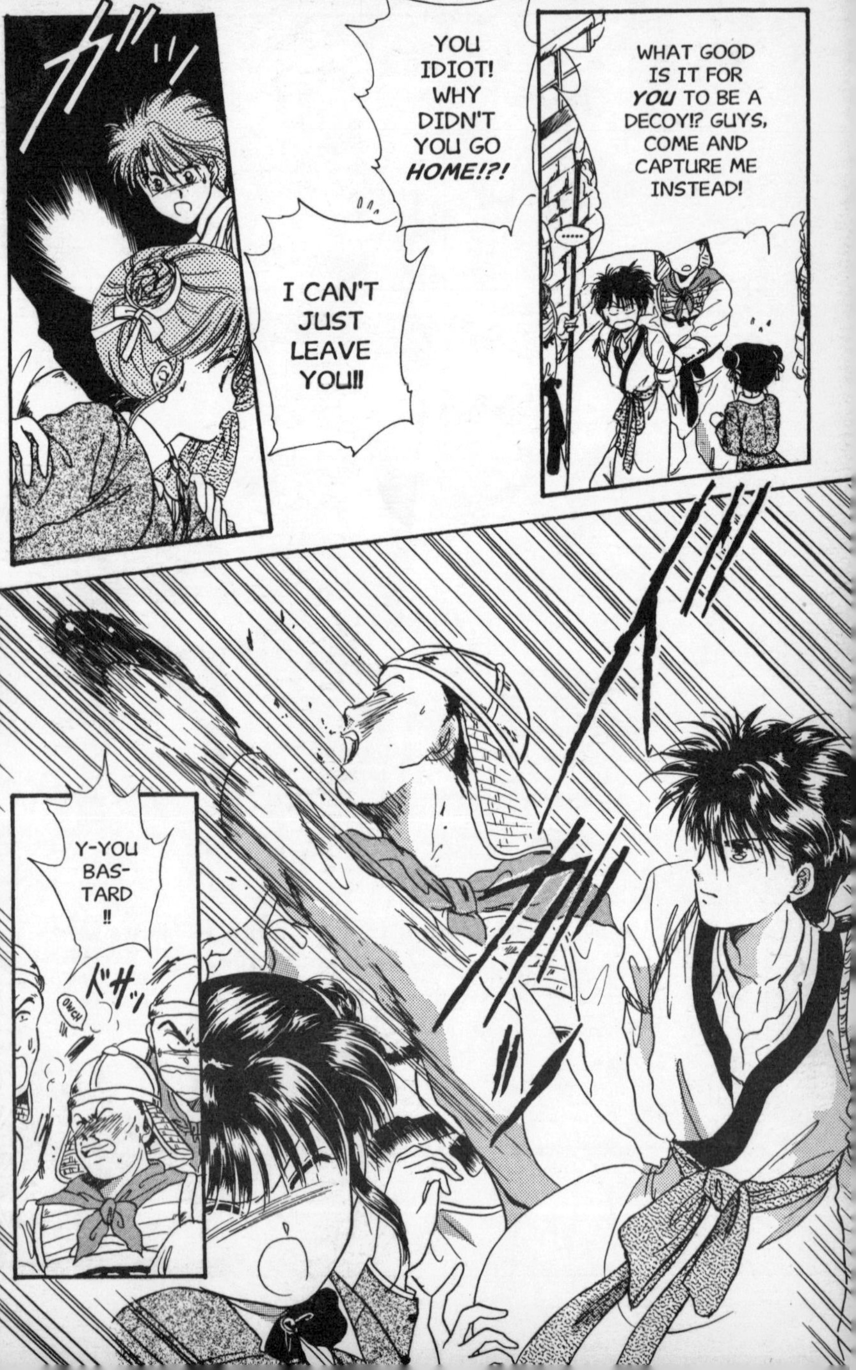
WHAT GOOD IS IT FOR *YOU* TO BE A DECOY!? GUYS, COME AND CAPTURE ME INSTEAD!
......
YOU IDIOT! WHY DIDN'T YOU GO *HOME!?!*
I CAN'T JUST LEAVE YOU!!
ガッ
Y-YOU BAS-TARD !!
ドサッ

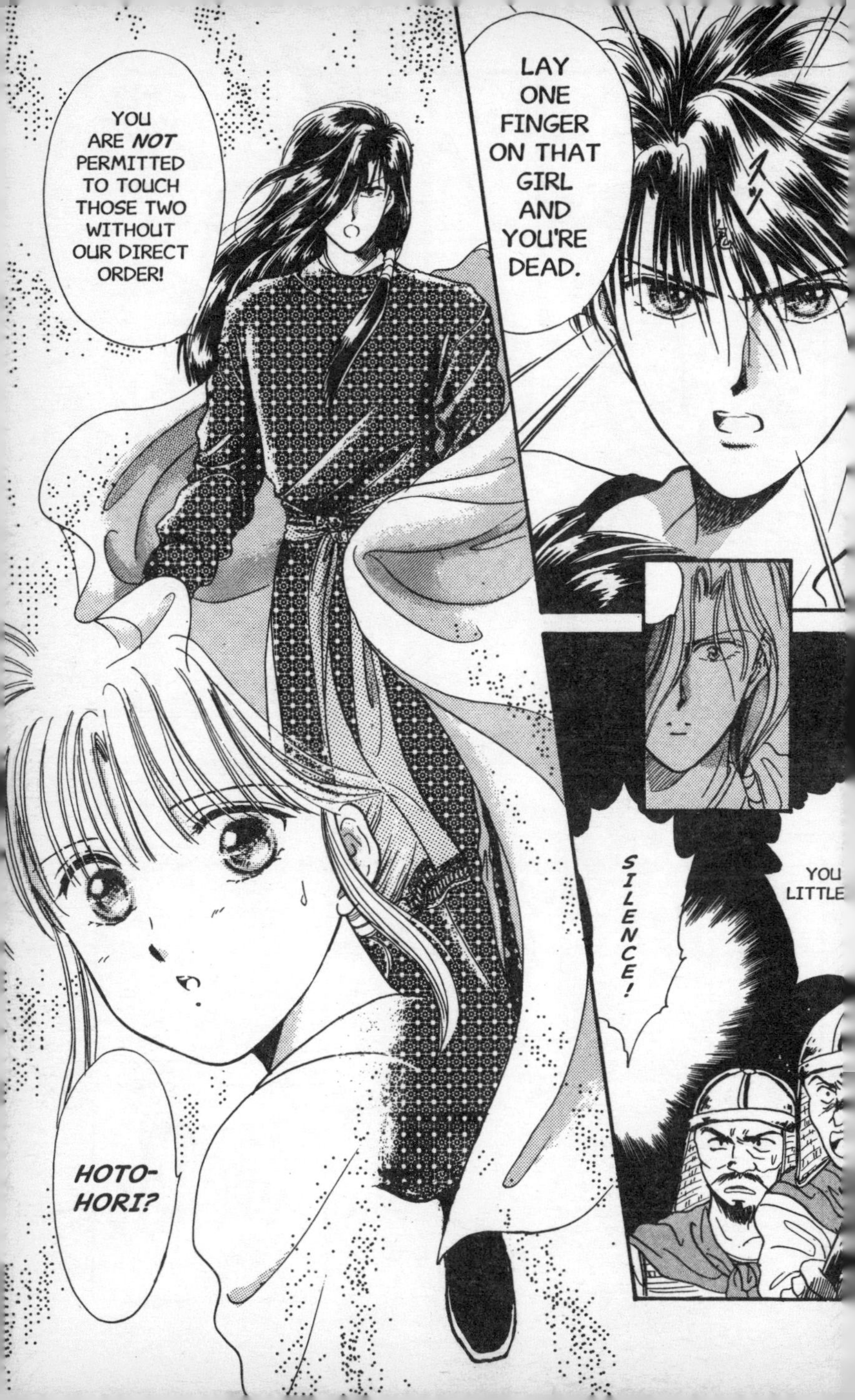
LAY ONE FINGER ON THAT GIRL AND YOU'RE DEAD.
YOU ARE NOT PERMITTED TO TOUCH THOSE TWO WITHOUT OUR DIRECT ORDER!
YOU LITTLE
SILENCE!
HOTO-HORI?

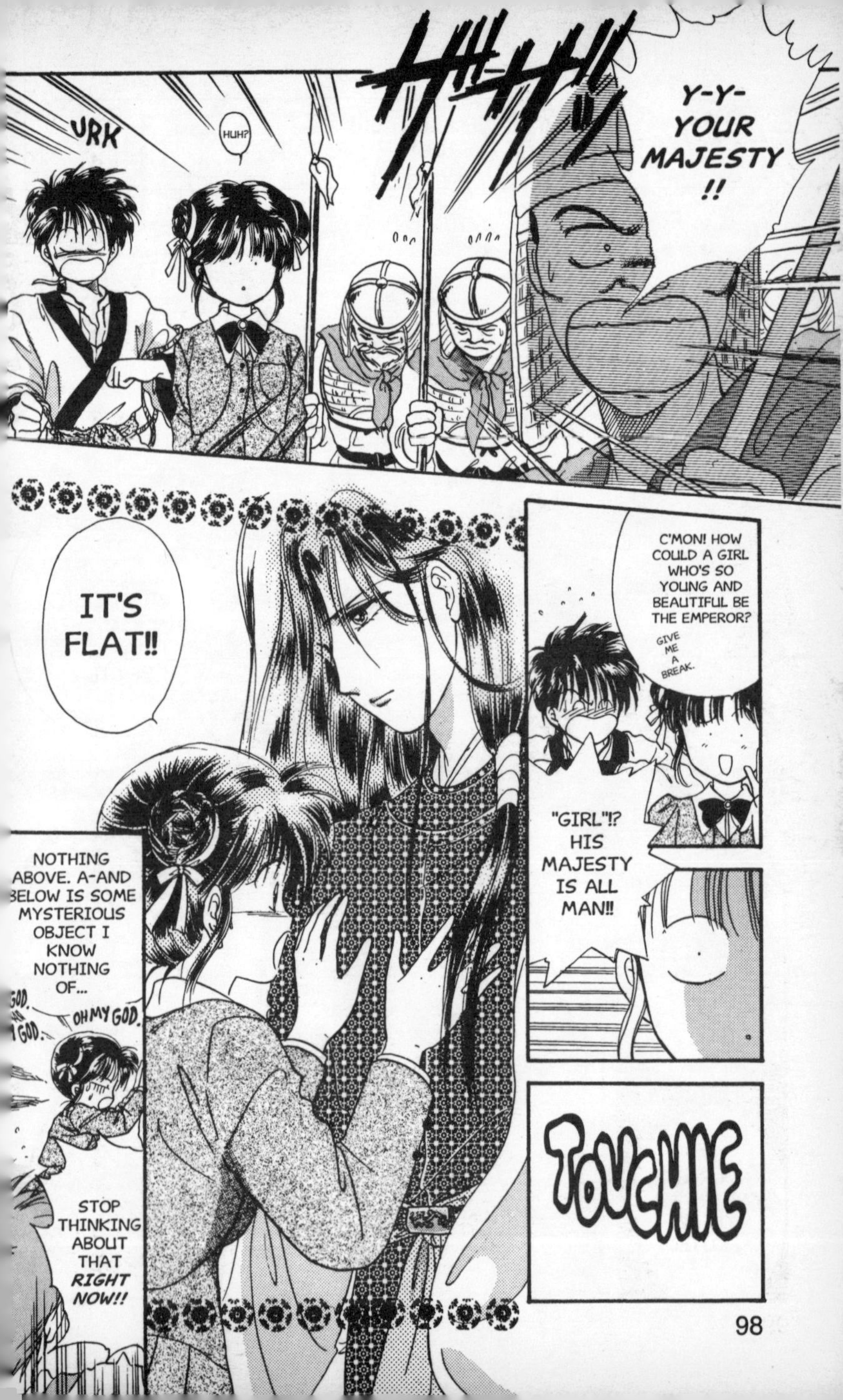
Y-Y-YOUR MAJESTY!!
HUH?
URK
C'MON! HOW COULD A GIRL WHO'S SO YOUNG AND BEAUTIFUL BE THE EMPEROR?
GIVE ME A BREAK.
"GIRL"!? HIS MAJESTY IS ALL MAN!!
TOUCHIE
IT'S FLAT!!
NOTHING ABOVE. A-AND BELOW IS SOME MYSTERIOUS OBJECT I KNOW NOTHING OF...
OH MY GOD.
STOP THINKING ABOUT THAT RIGHT NOW!!

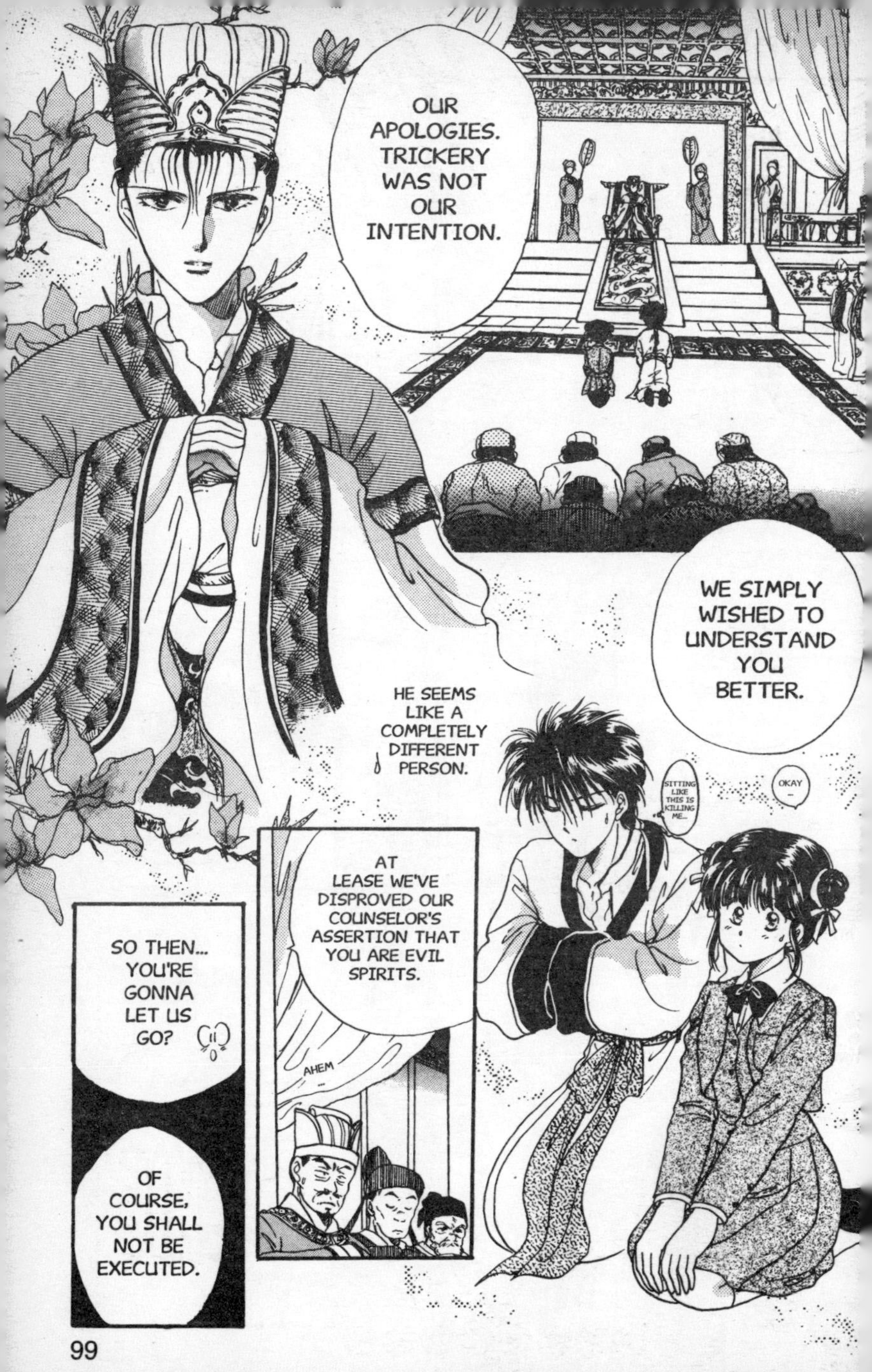
OUR APOLOGIES. TRICKERY WAS NOT OUR INTENTION.
WE SIMPLY WISHED TO UNDERSTAND YOU BETTER.
HE SEEMS LIKE A COMPLETELY DIFFERENT PERSON.
SITTING LIKE THIS IS KILLING ME...
OKAY –
AT LEASE WE'VE DISPROVED OUR COUNSELOR'S ASSERTION THAT YOU ARE EVIL SPIRITS.
AHEM ...
SO THEN... YOU'RE GONNA LET US GO?
OF COURSE, YOU SHALL NOT BE EXECUTED.

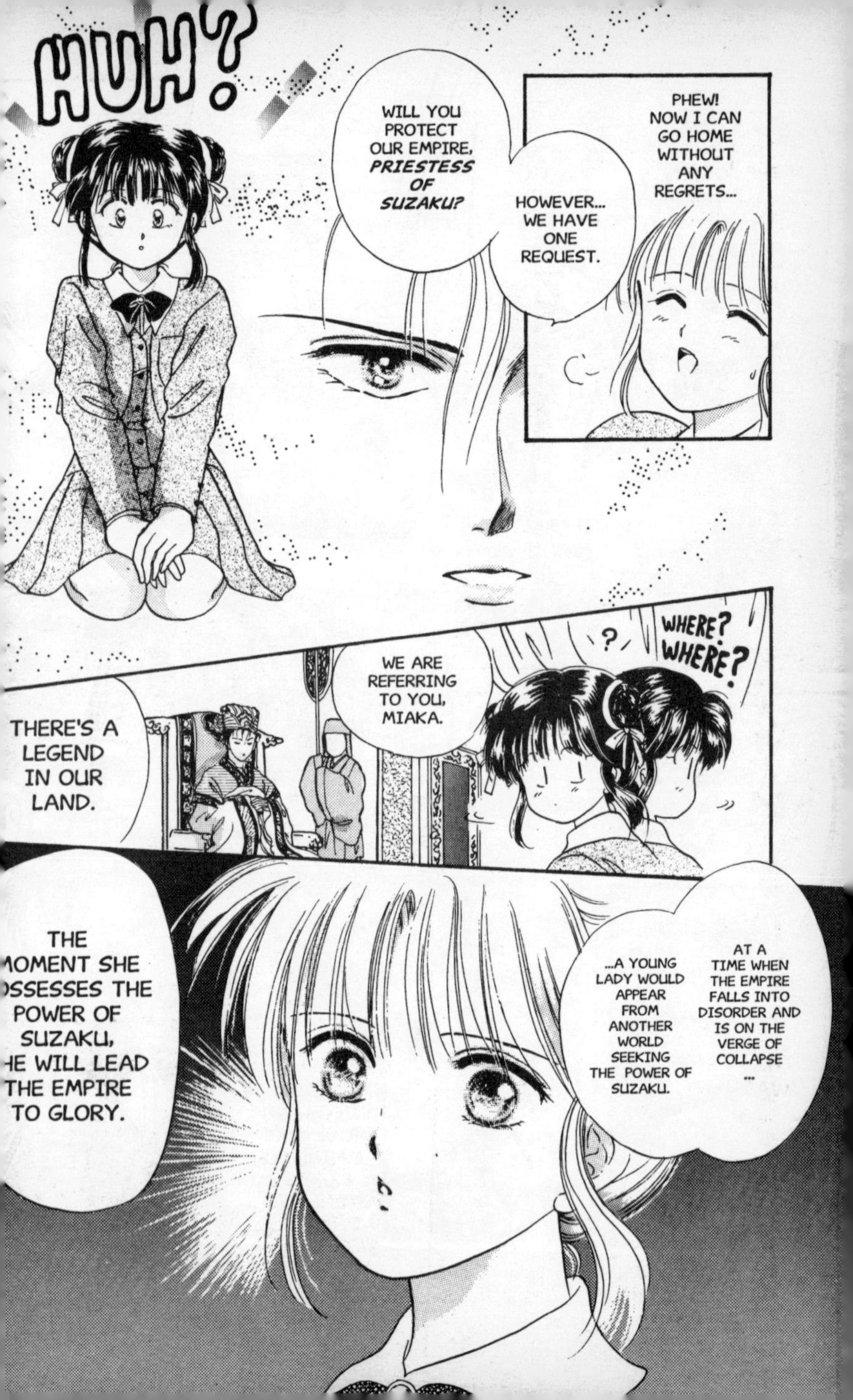
PHEW! NOW I CAN GO HOME WITHOUT ANY REGRETS...
HOWEVER... WE HAVE ONE REQUEST.
WILL YOU PROTECT OUR EMPIRE, PRIESTESS OF SUZAKU?
HUH?
WHERE? WHERE?
?
WE ARE REFERRING TO YOU, MIAKA.
THERE'S A LEGEND IN OUR LAND.
AT A TIME WHEN THE EMPIRE FALLS INTO DISORDER AND IS ON THE VERGE OF COLLAPSE ...
...A YOUNG LADY WOULD APPEAR FROM ANOTHER WORLD SEEKING THE POWER OF SUZAKU.
THE OMENT SHE OSSESSES THE POWER OF SUZAKU, HE WILL LEAD THE EMPIRE TO GLORY.

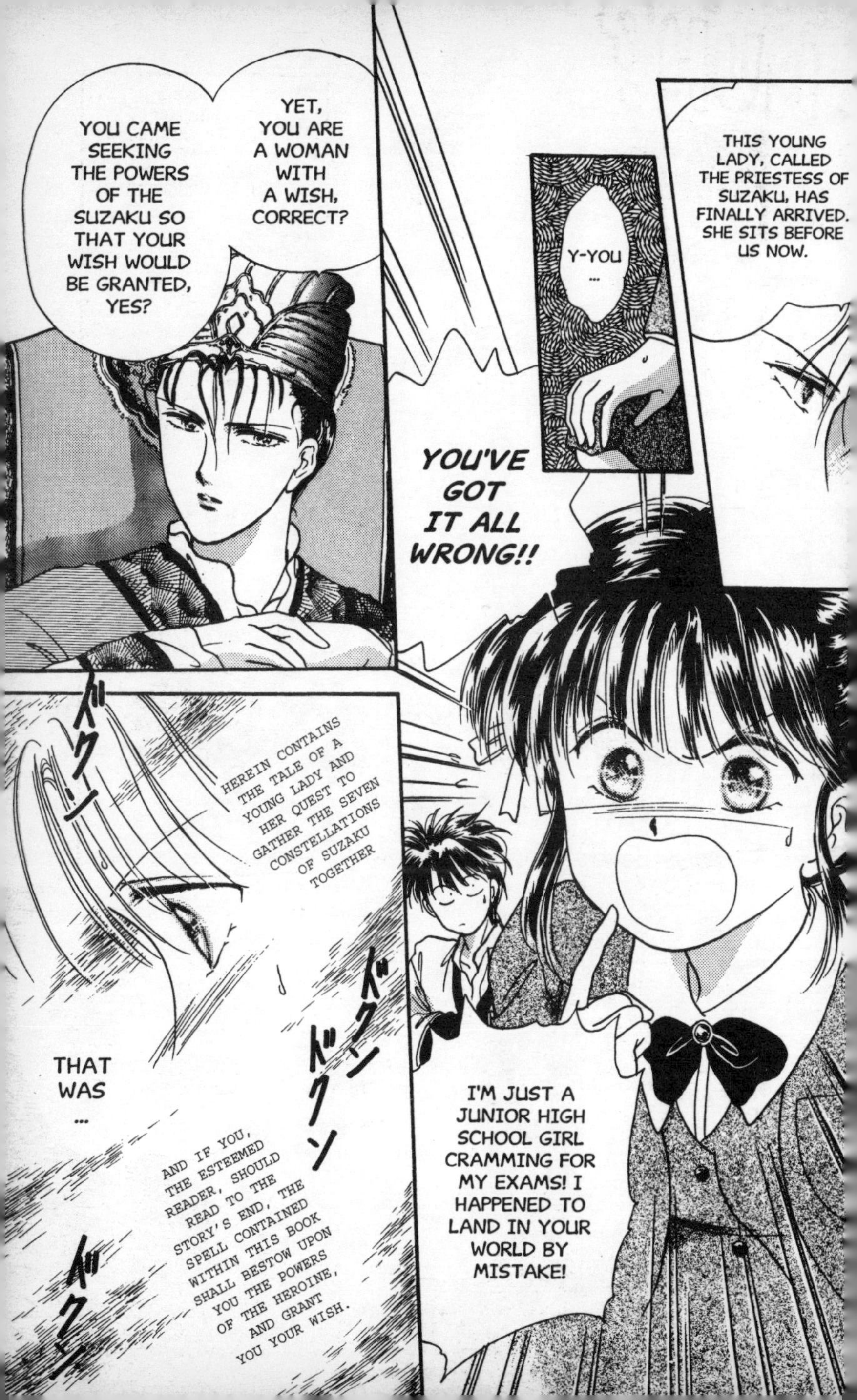
YOU CAME SEEKING THE POWERS OF THE SUZAKU SO THAT YOUR WISH WOULD BE GRANTED, YES?
YET, YOU ARE A WOMAN WITH A WISH, CORRECT?
THIS YOUNG LADY, CALLED THE PRIESTESS OF SUZAKU, HAS FINALLY ARRIVED. SHE SITS BEFORE US NOW.
Y-YOU ...
YOU'VE GOT IT ALL WRONG!!
I'M JUST A JUNIOR HIGH SCHOOL GIRL CRAMMING FOR MY EXAMS! I HAPPENED TO LAND IN YOUR WORLD BY MISTAKE!
ドクン
HEREIN CONTAINS THE TALE OF A YOUNG LADY AND HER QUEST TO GATHER THE SEVEN CONSTELLATIONS OF SUZAKU TOGETHER
ドクン ドクン
THAT WAS ...
AND IF YOU, THE ESTEEMED READER, SHOULD READ TO THE STORY'S END, THE SPELL CONTAINED WITHIN THIS BOOK SHALL BESTOW UPON YOU THE POWERS OF THE HEROINE, AND GRANT YOU YOUR WISH.
ドクン

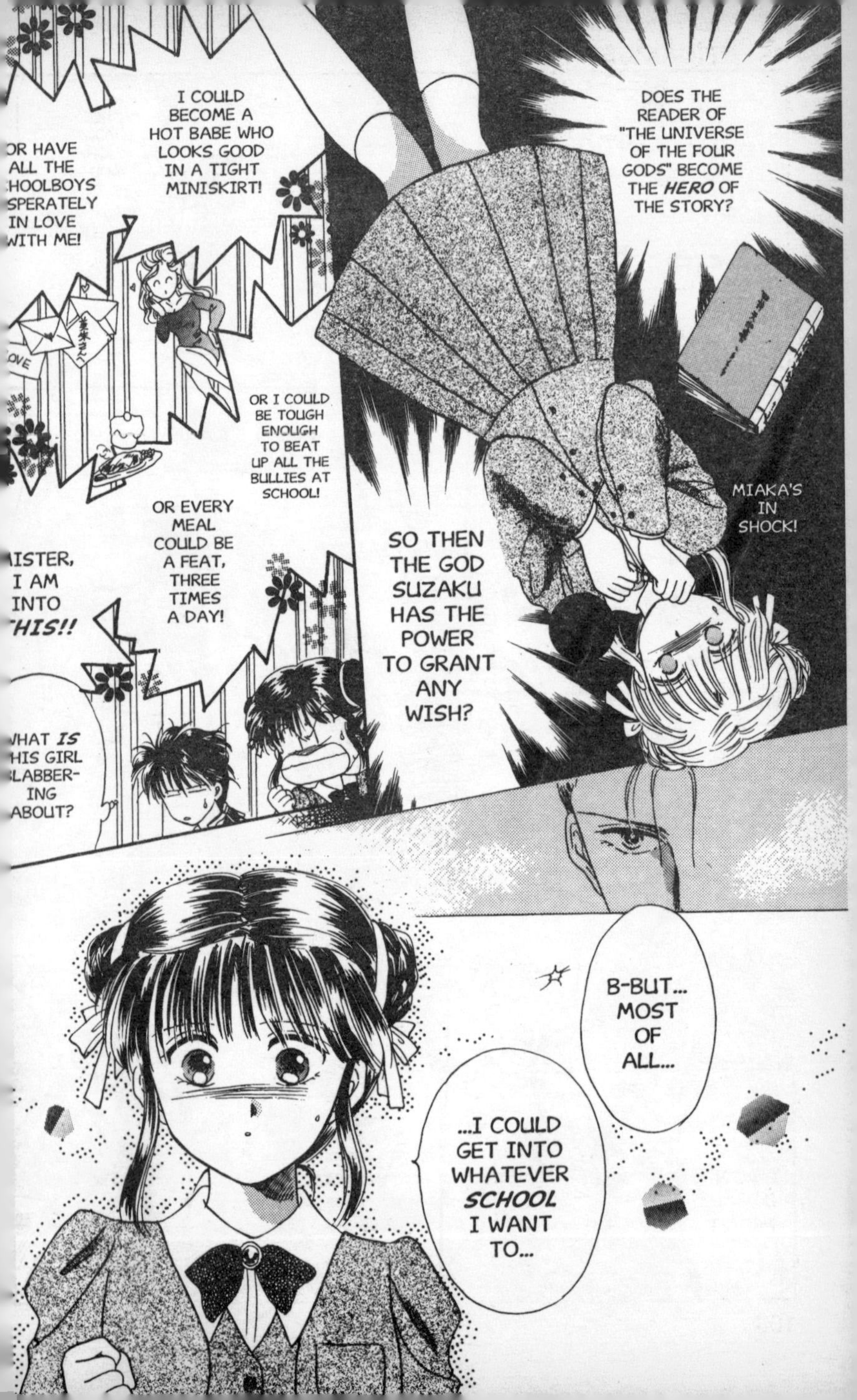

DOES THE READER OF "THE UNIVERSE OF THE FOUR GODS" BECOME THE *HERO* OF THE STORY?
SO THEN THE GOD SUZAKU HAS THE POWER TO GRANT ANY WISH?
MIAKA'S IN SHOCK!
I COULD BECOME A HOT BABE WHO LOOKS GOOD IN A TIGHT MINISKIRT!
OR HAVE ALL THE HOOLBOYS SPERATELY IN LOVE WITH ME!
OR I COULD BE TOUGH ENOUGH TO BEAT UP ALL THE BULLIES AT SCHOOL!
OR EVERY MEAL COULD BE A FEAT, THREE TIMES A DAY!
ISTER, I AM INTO HIS!!
HAT *IS* HIS GIRL LABBER-ING ABOUT?
LOVE
B-BUT... MOST OF ALL...
...I COULD GET INTO WHATEVER *SCHOOL* I WANT TO...

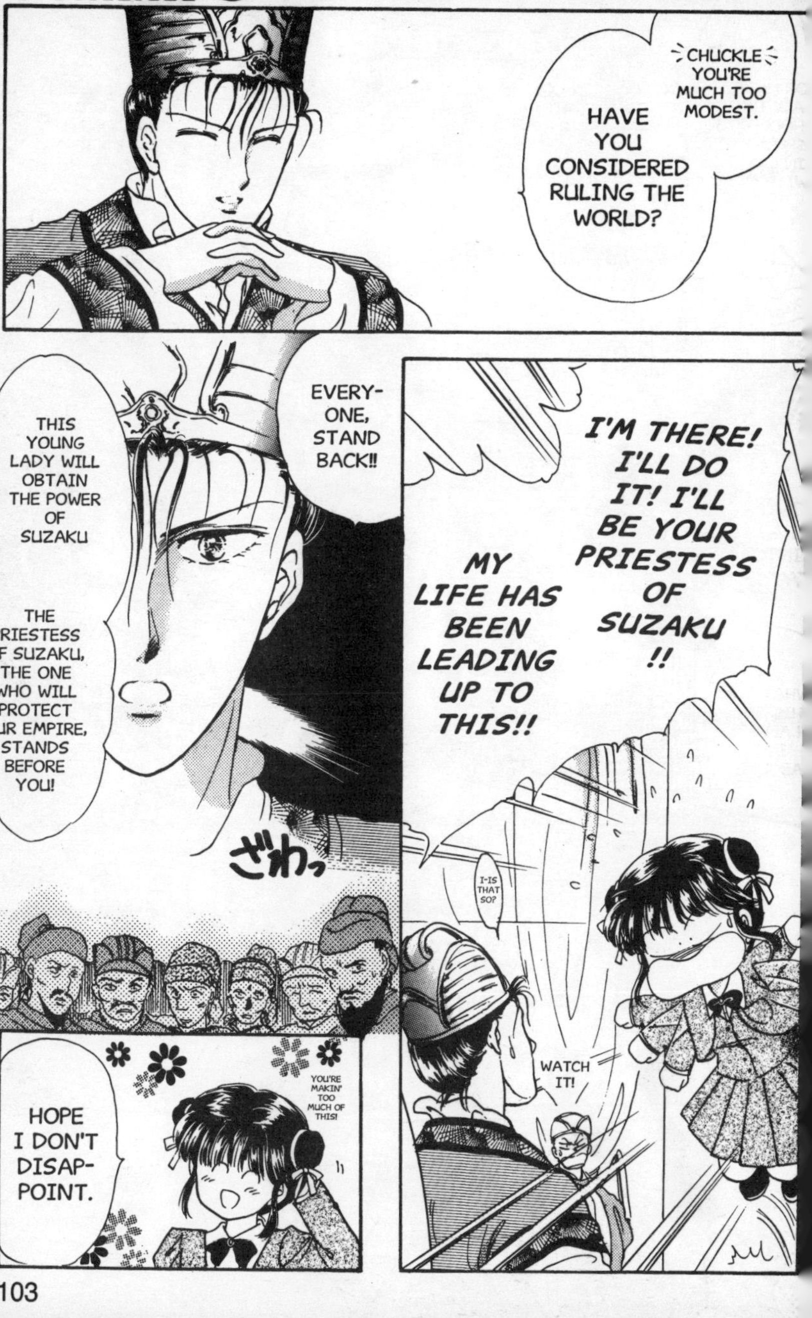
CHUCKLE YOU'RE MUCH TOO MODEST.
HAVE YOU CONSIDERED RULING THE WORLD?
EVERY-ONE, STAND BACK!!
THIS YOUNG LADY WILL OBTAIN THE POWER OF SUZAKU
THE PRIESTESS OF SUZAKU, THE ONE WHO WILL PROTECT OUR EMPIRE, STANDS BEFORE YOU!
ざわっ
HOPE I DON'T DISAP-POINT.
YOU'RE MAKIN' TOO MUCH OF THIS!
I-IS THAT SO?
MY LIFE HAS BEEN LEADING UP TO THIS!!
I'M THERE! I'LL DO IT! I'LL BE YOUR PRIESTESS OF SUZAKU !!
WATCH IT!

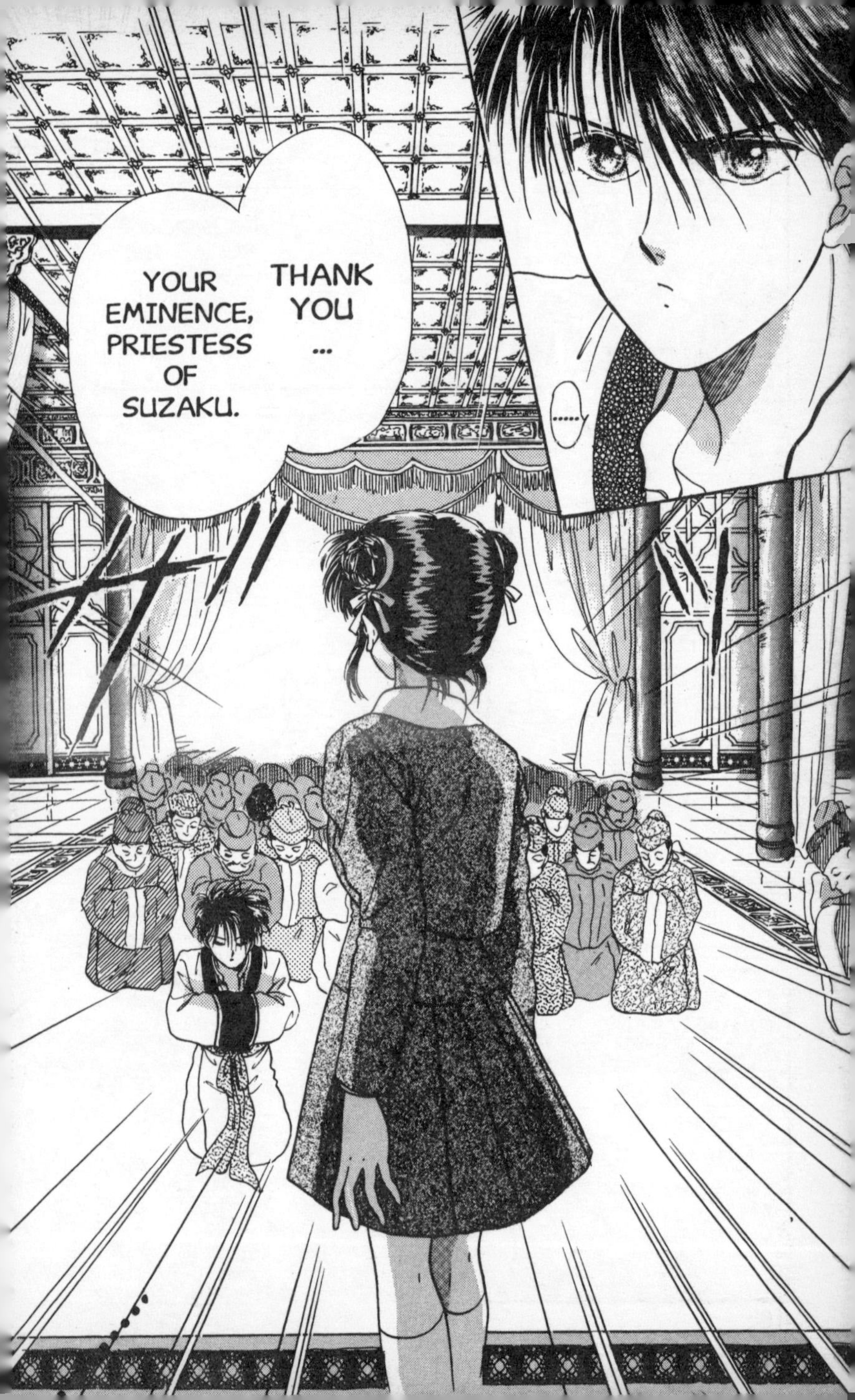
......
THANK YOU ... YOUR EMINENCE, PRIESTESS OF SUZAKU.

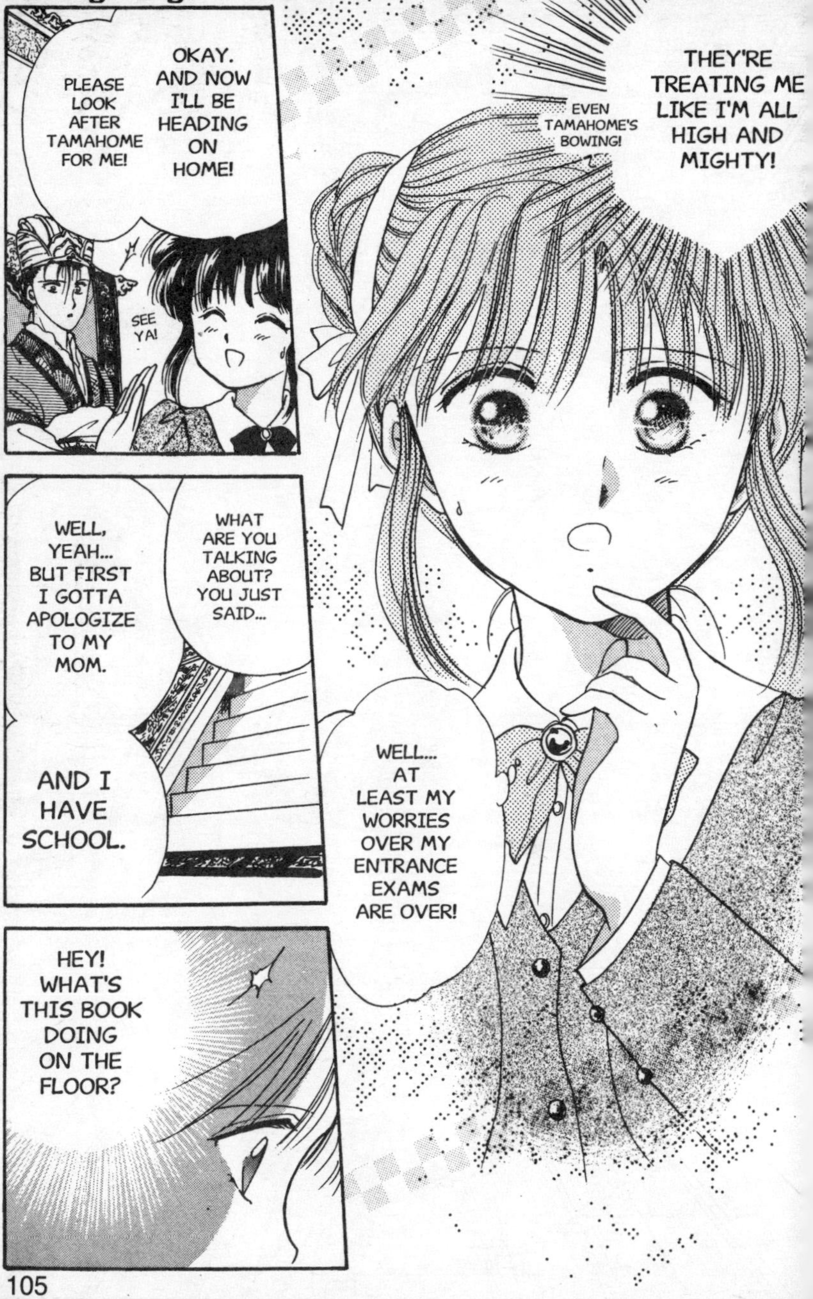
OKAY. AND NOW I'LL BE HEADING ON HOME!
PLEASE LOOK AFTER TAMAHOME FOR ME!
SEE YA!
THEY'RE TREATING ME LIKE I'M ALL HIGH AND MIGHTY!
EVEN TAMAHOME'S BOWING!
WHAT ARE YOU TALKING ABOUT? YOU JUST SAID...
WELL, YEAH... BUT FIRST I GOTTA APOLOGIZE TO MY MOM.
AND I HAVE SCHOOL.
WELL... AT LEAST MY WORRIES OVER MY ENTRANCE EXAMS ARE OVER!
HEY! WHAT'S THIS BOOK DOING ON THE FLOOR?

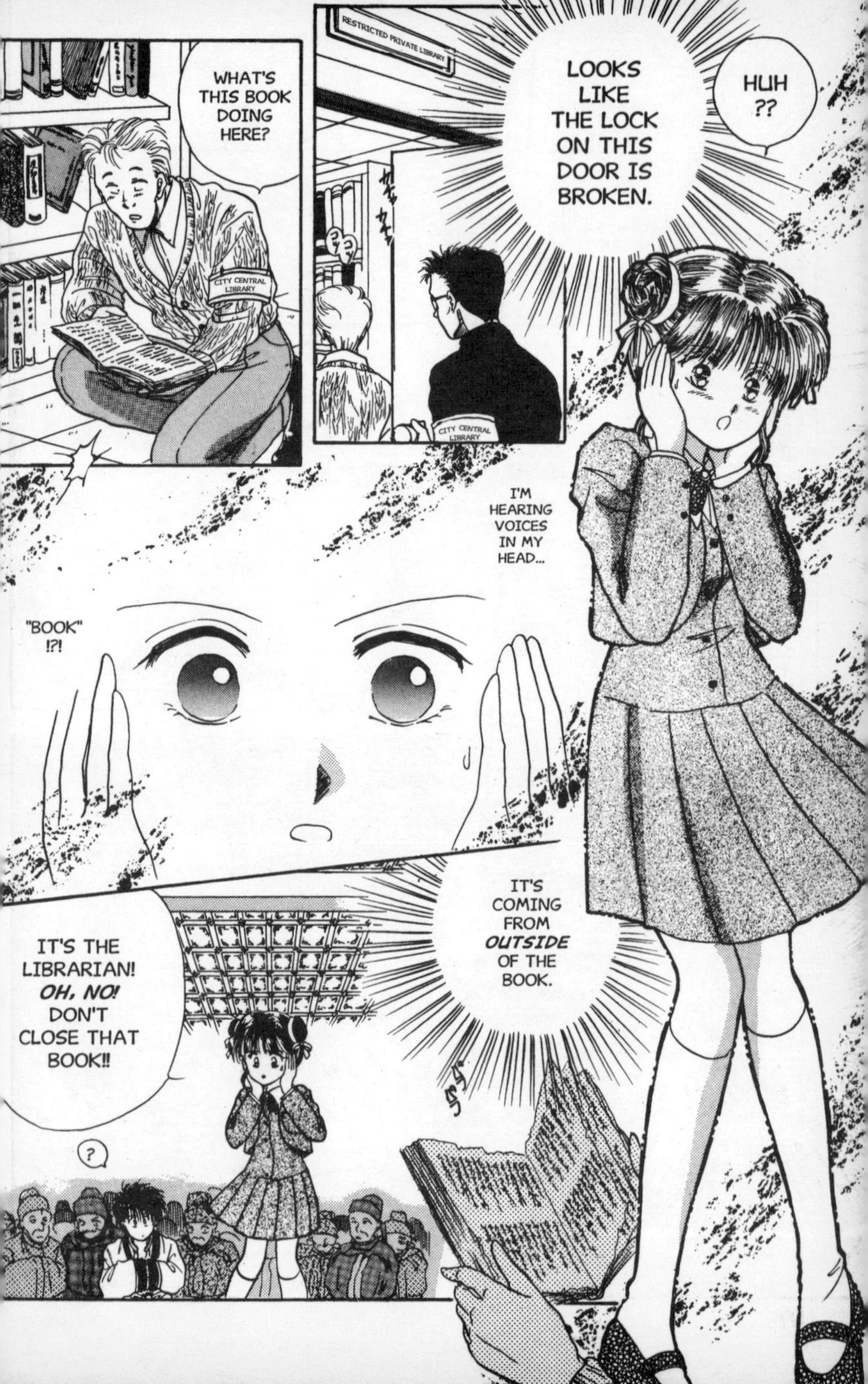
CITY CENTRAL LIBRARY
WHAT'S THIS BOOK DOING HERE?
RESTRICTED PRIVATE LIBRARY
CITY CENTRAL LIBRARY
LOOKS LIKE THE LOCK ON THIS DOOR IS BROKEN.
HUH ??
I'M HEARING VOICES IN MY HEAD...
"BOOK" !?!
IT'S COMING FROM *OUTSIDE* OF THE BOOK.
IT'S THE LIBRARIAN! *OH, NO!* DON'T CLOSE THAT BOOK!!
?

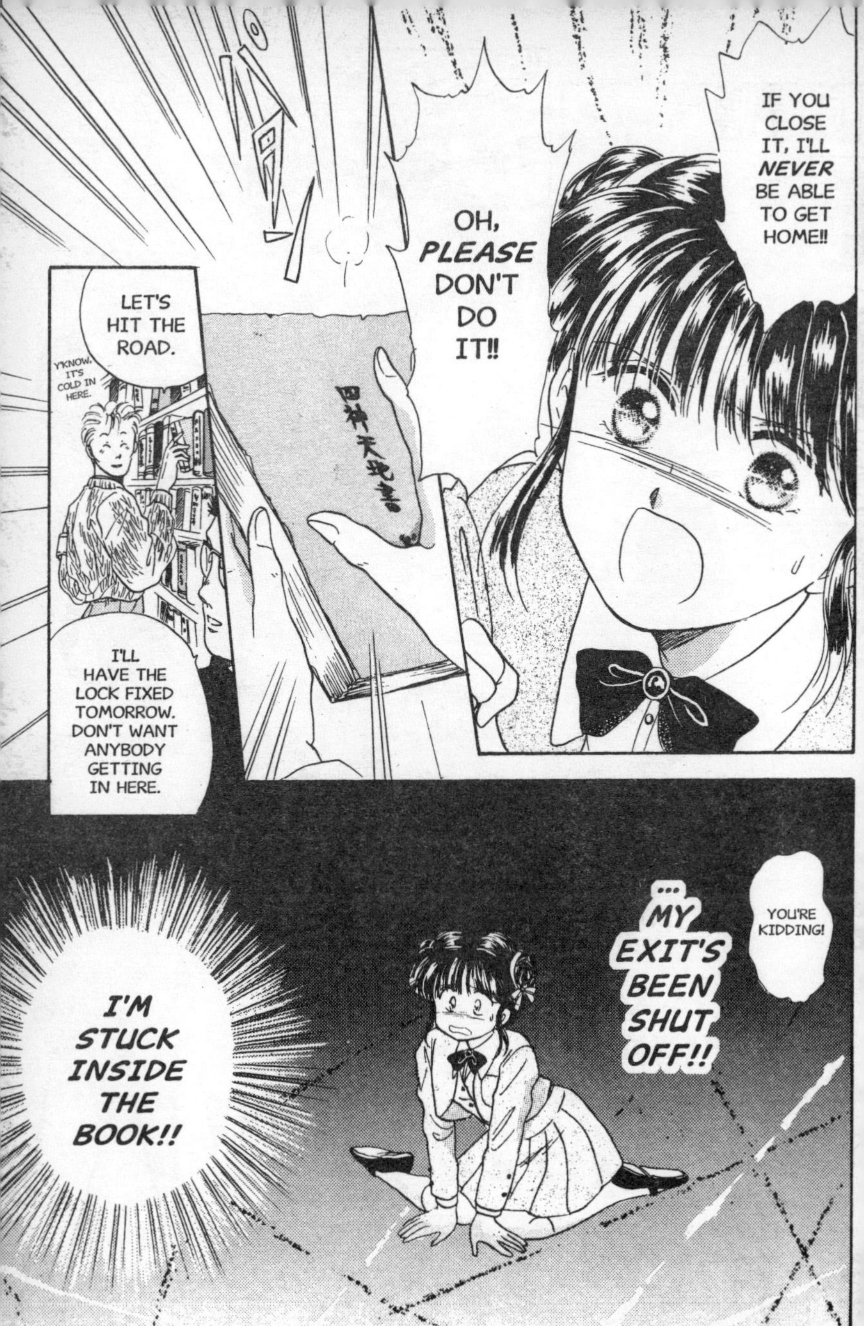
IF YOU CLOSE IT, I'LL *NEVER* BE ABLE TO GET HOME!!
OH, *PLEASE* DON'T DO IT!!
四神天地書
LET'S HIT THE ROAD.
Y'KNOW, IT'S COLD IN HERE.
I'LL HAVE THE LOCK FIXED TOMORROW. DON'T WANT ANYBODY GETTING IN HERE.
YOU'RE KIDDING!
...MY EXIT'S BEEN SHUT OFF!!
I'M STUCK INSIDE THE BOOK!!

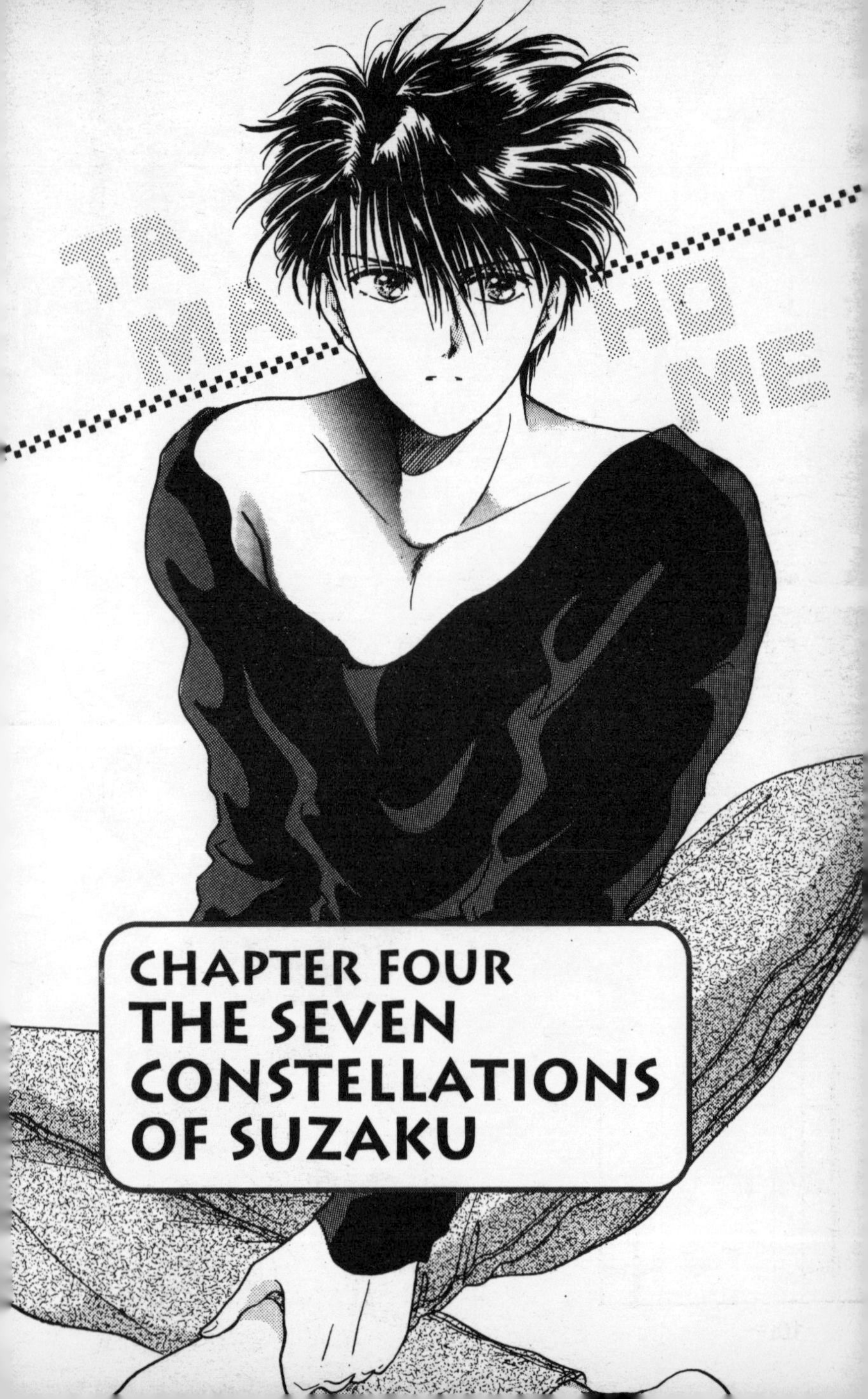
CHAPTER FOUR
THE SEVEN CONSTELLATIONS OF SUZAKU

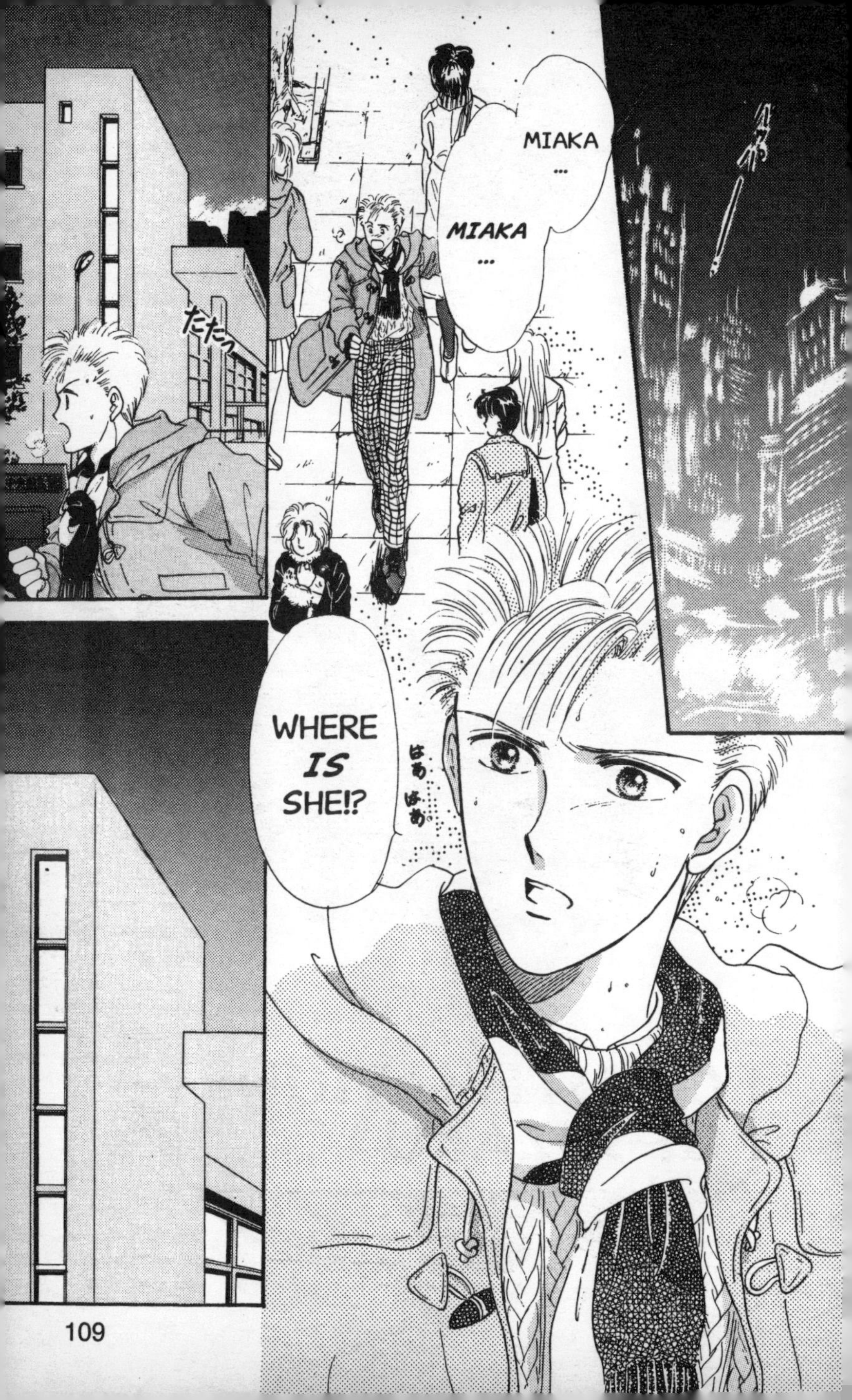
MIAKA ...
MIAKA ...
たたっ
WHERE *IS* SHE!?
はあ はあ

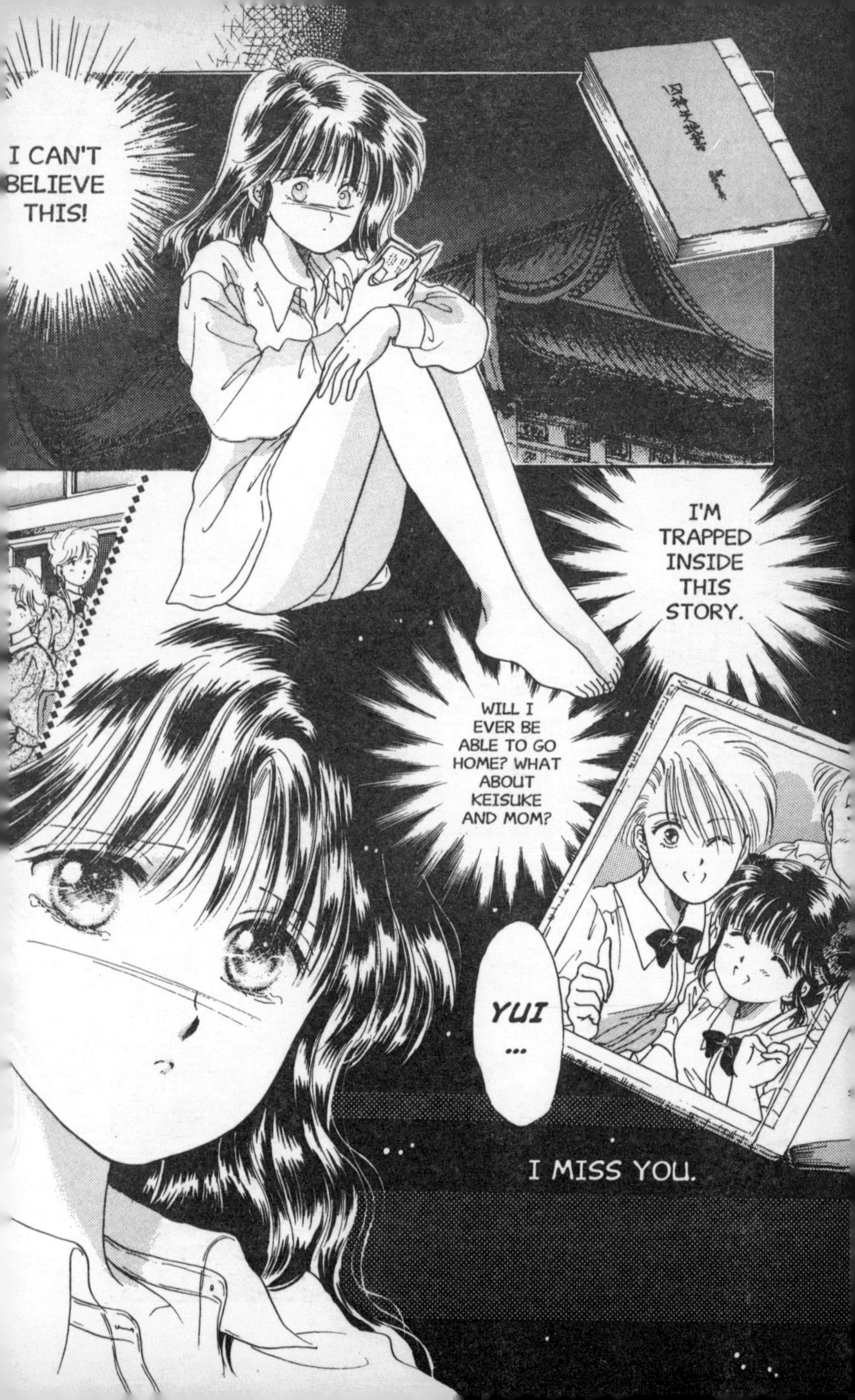
I CAN'T BELIEVE THIS!
I'M TRAPPED INSIDE THIS STORY.
WILL I EVER BE ABLE TO GO HOME? WHAT ABOUT KEISUKE AND MOM?
YUI ...
I MISS YOU.

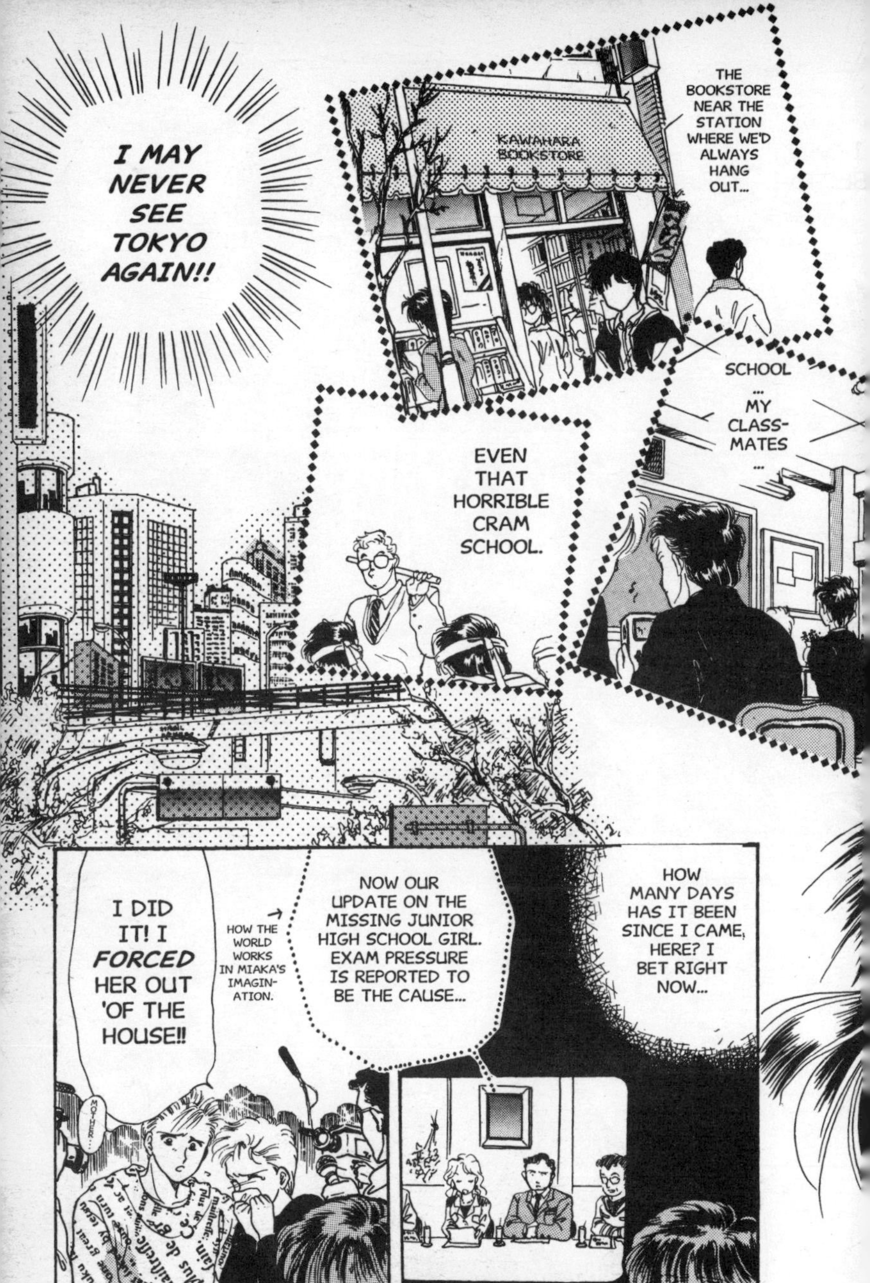
I MAY NEVER SEE TOKYO AGAIN!!
THE BOOKSTORE NEAR THE STATION WHERE WE'D ALWAYS HANG OUT...
KAWAHARA BOOKSTORE
SCHOOL ... MY CLASSMATES ...
EVEN THAT HORRIBLE CRAM SCHOOL.
HOW MANY DAYS HAS IT BEEN SINCE I CAME HERE? I BET RIGHT NOW...
NOW OUR UPDATE ON THE MISSING JUNIOR HIGH SCHOOL GIRL. EXAM PRESSURE IS REPORTED TO BE THE CAUSE...
HOW THE WORLD WORKS IN MIAKA'S IMAGINATION.
I DID IT! I FORCED HER OUT 'OF THE HOUSE!!
MOTHER...

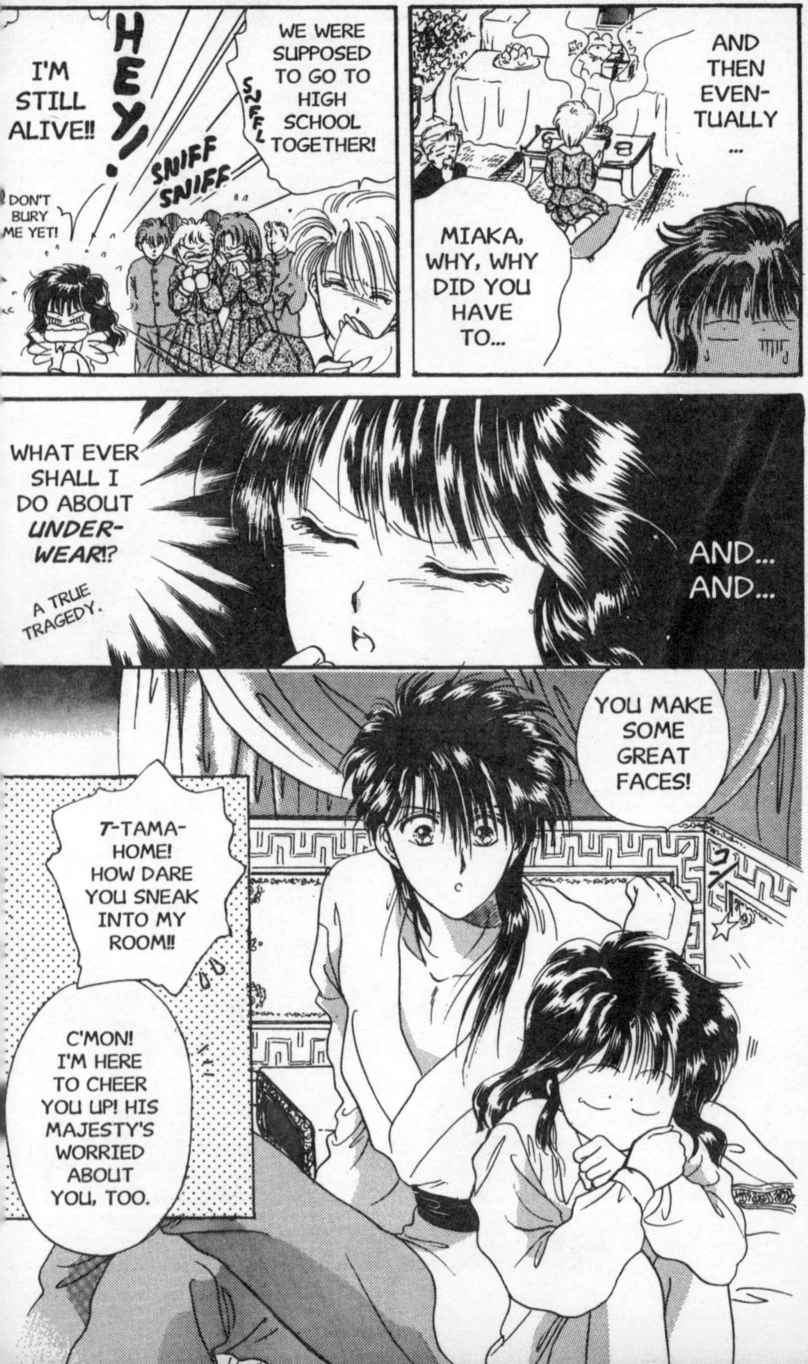
AND THEN EVENTUALLY...
MIAKA, WHY, WHY DID YOU HAVE TO...
WE WERE SUPPOSED TO GO TO HIGH SCHOOL TOGETHER!
SNIFFL
SNIFF SNIFF
HEY!
I'M STILL ALIVE!!
DON'T BURY ME YET!
AND... AND...
WHAT EVER SHALL I DO ABOUT UNDERWEAR!?
A TRUE TRAGEDY.
YOU MAKE SOME GREAT FACES!
T-TAMAHOME! HOW DARE YOU SNEAK INTO MY ROOM!!
C'MON! I'M HERE TO CHEER YOU UP! HIS MAJESTY'S WORRIED ABOUT YOU, TOO.

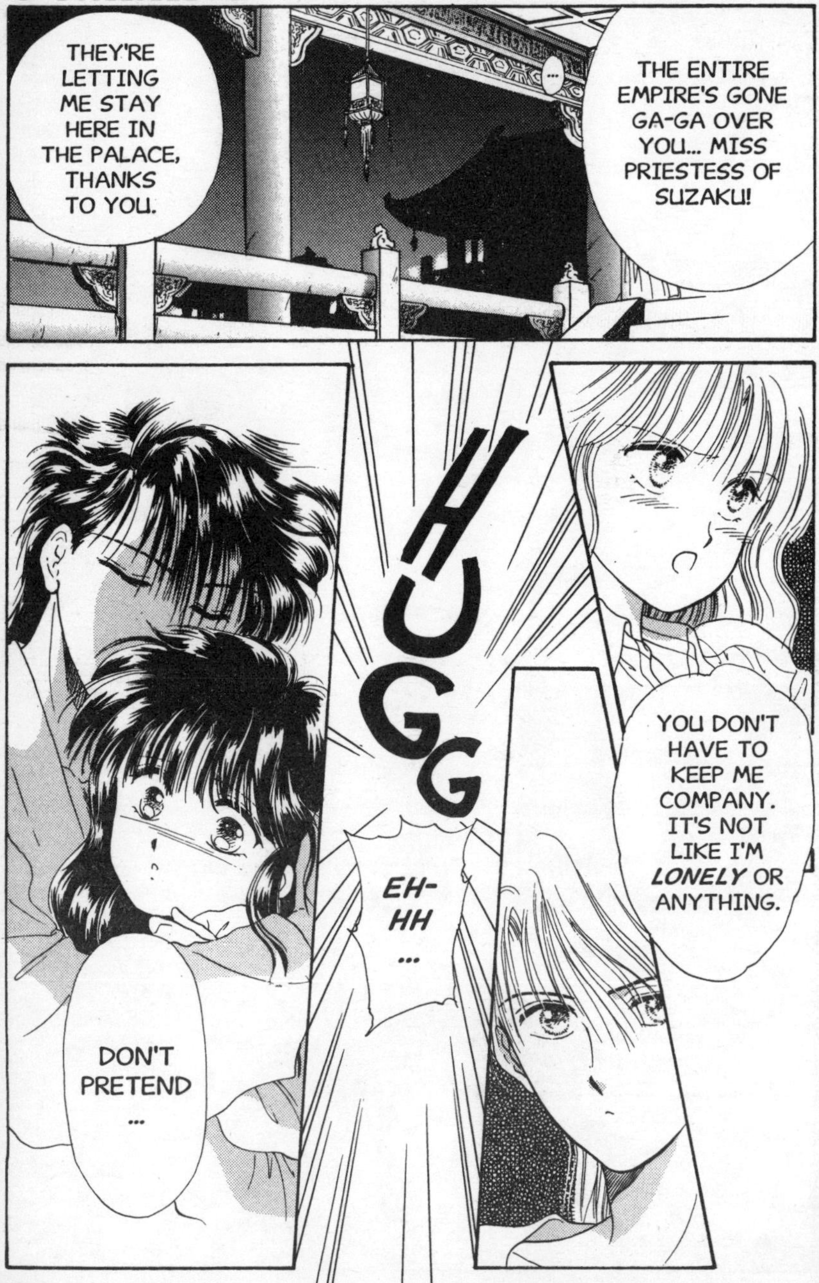
THE ENTIRE EMPIRE'S GONE GA-GA OVER YOU... MISS PRIESTESS OF SUZAKU!
...
THEY'RE LETTING ME STAY HERE IN THE PALACE, THANKS TO YOU.
YOU DON'T HAVE TO KEEP ME COMPANY. IT'S NOT LIKE I'M *LONELY* OR ANYTHING.
HUGG
EH-HH ...
DON'T PRETEND ...

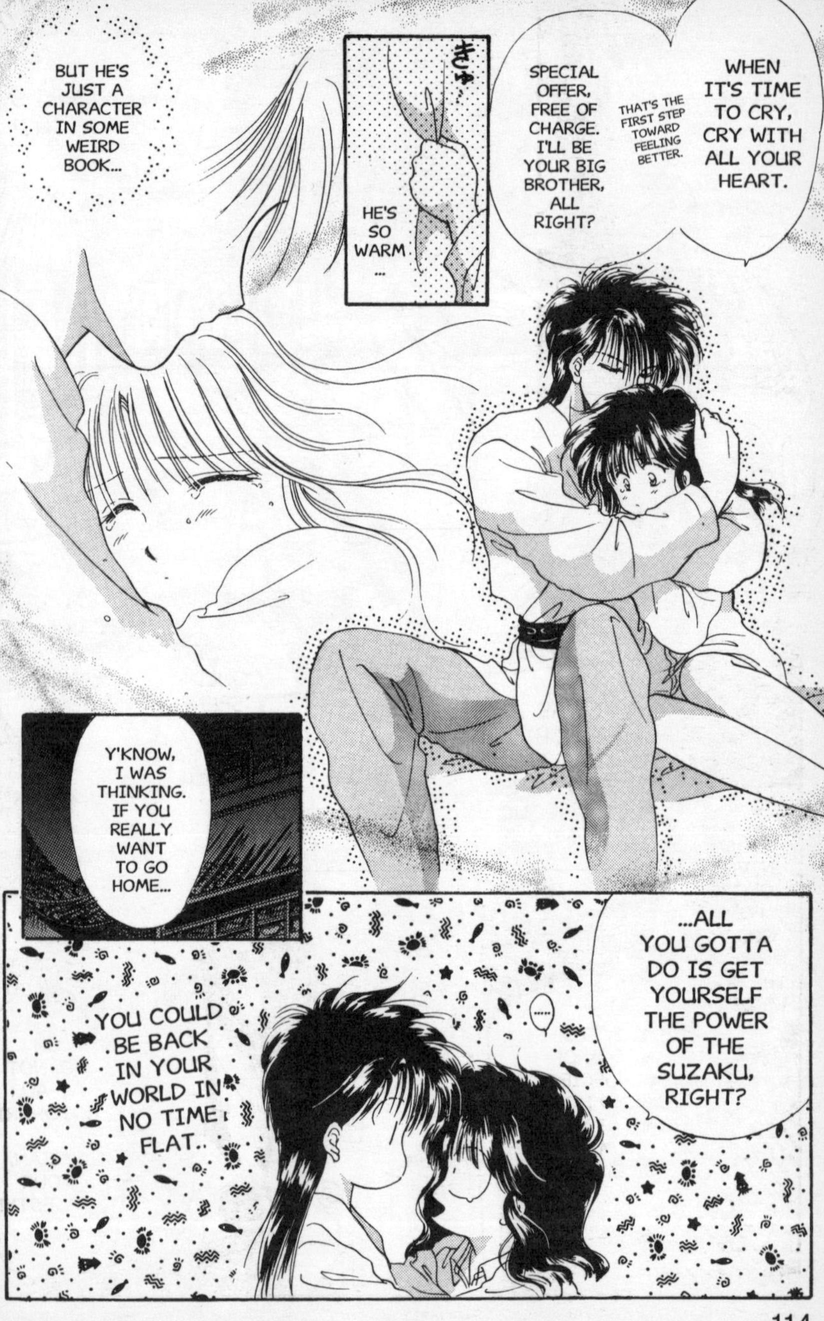
WHEN IT'S TIME TO CRY, CRY WITH ALL YOUR HEART.
THAT'S THE FIRST STEP TOWARD FEELING BETTER.
SPECIAL OFFER, FREE OF CHARGE. I'LL BE YOUR BIG BROTHER, ALL RIGHT?
きゅ
HE'S SO WARM ...
BUT HE'S JUST A CHARACTER IN SOME WEIRD BOOK...
Y'KNOW, I WAS THINKING. IF YOU REALLY WANT TO GO HOME...
...ALL YOU GOTTA DO IS GET YOURSELF THE POWER OF THE SUZAKU, RIGHT?
......
YOU COULD BE BACK IN YOUR WORLD IN NO TIME FLAT.

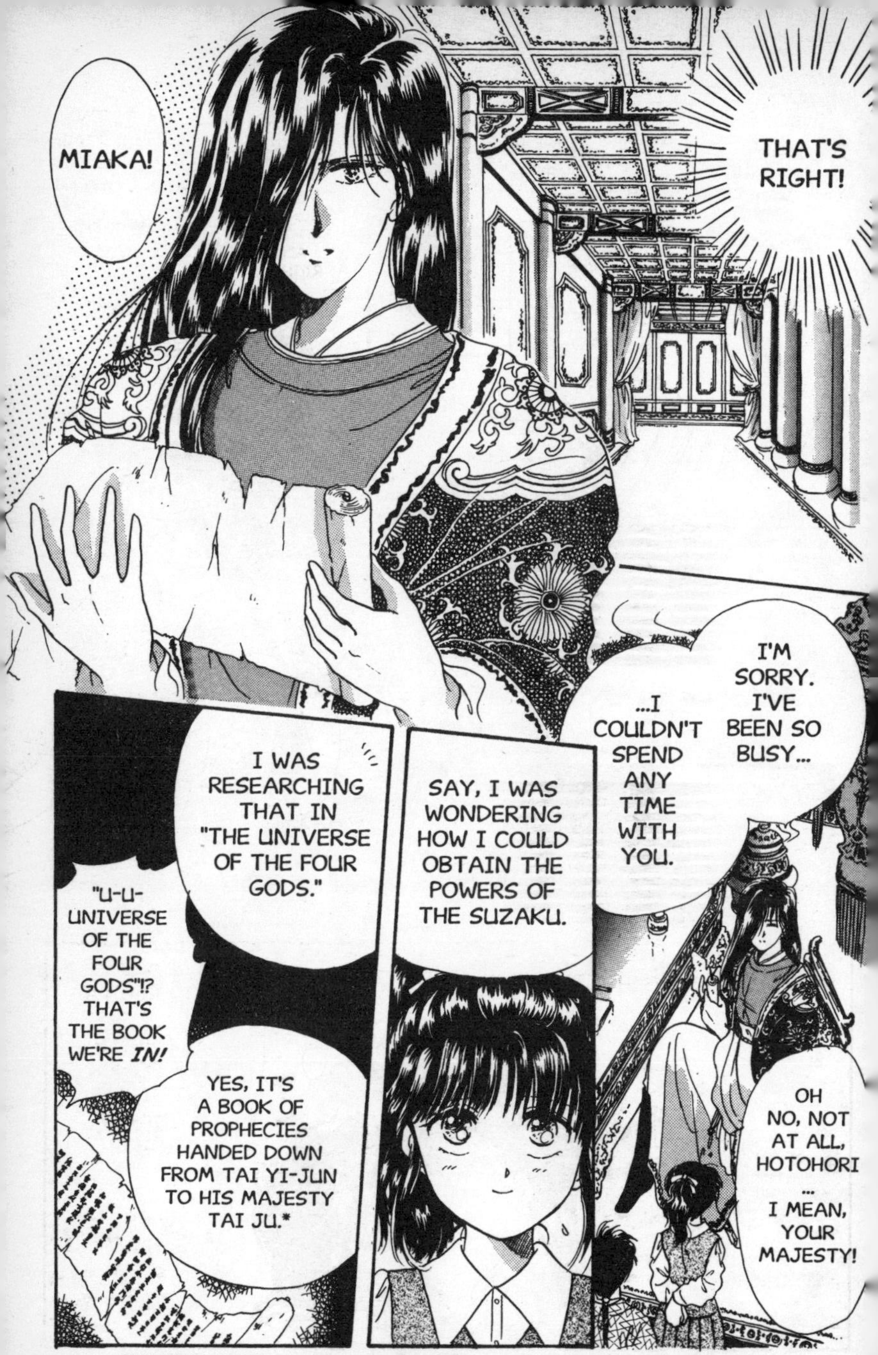
MIAKA!
THAT'S RIGHT!
I'M SORRY. I'VE BEEN SO BUSY...
...I COULDN'T SPEND ANY TIME WITH YOU.
OH NO, NOT AT ALL, HOTOHORI ... I MEAN, YOUR MAJESTY!
SAY, I WAS WONDERING HOW I COULD OBTAIN THE POWERS OF THE SUZAKU.
I WAS RESEARCHING THAT IN "THE UNIVERSE OF THE FOUR GODS."
"U-U-UNIVERSE OF THE FOUR GODS"!? THAT'S THE BOOK WE'RE *IN!*
YES, IT'S A BOOK OF PROPHECIES HANDED DOWN FROM TAI YI-JUN TO HIS MAJESTY TAI JU.*

*THE FIRST EMPEROR OF HOTOHORI'S DYNASTY.

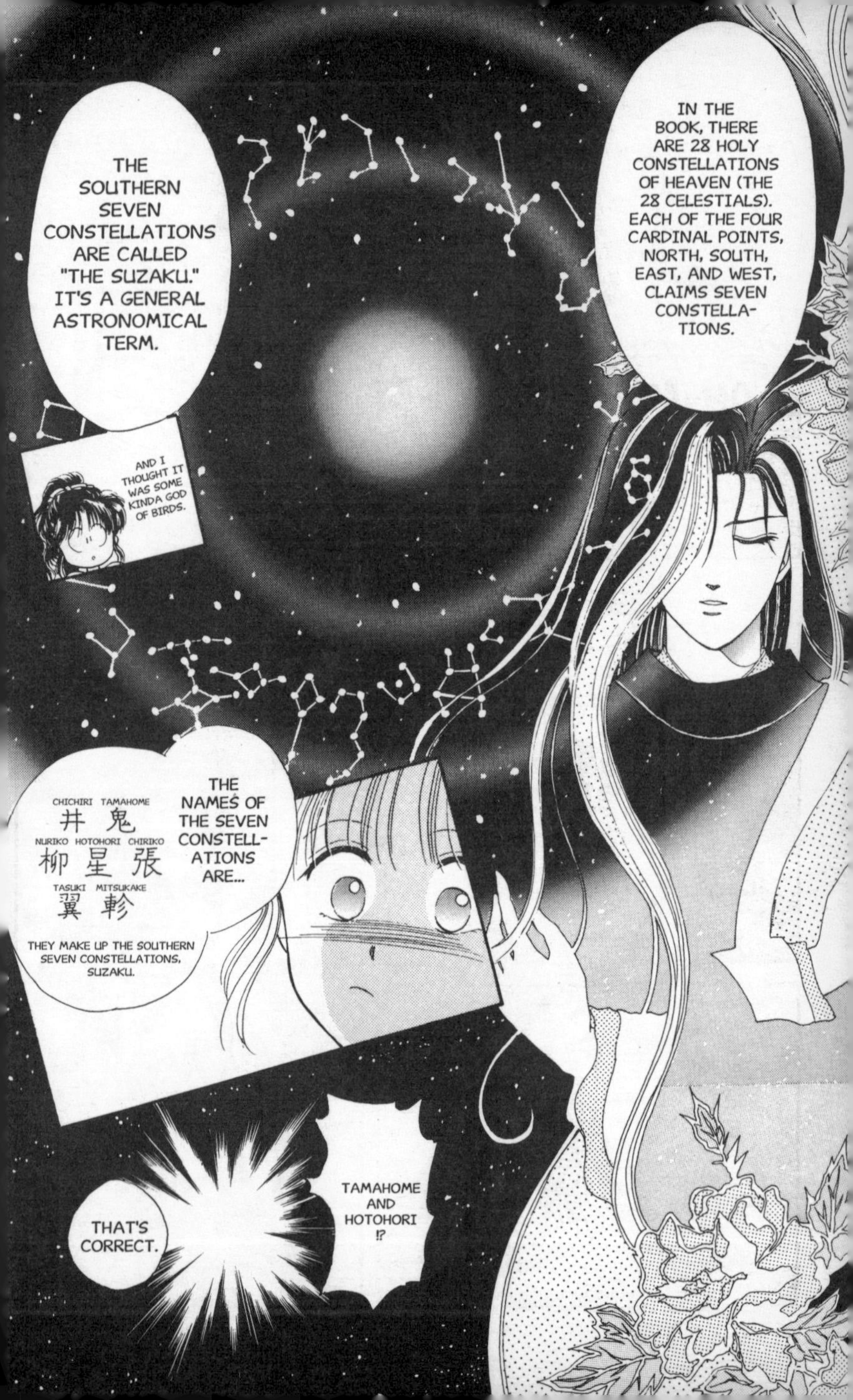
IN THE BOOK, THERE ARE 28 HOLY CONSTELLATIONS OF HEAVEN (THE 28 CELESTIALS). EACH OF THE FOUR CARDINAL POINTS, NORTH, SOUTH, EAST, AND WEST, CLAIMS SEVEN CONSTELLA-TIONS.
THE SOUTHERN SEVEN CONSTELLATIONS ARE CALLED "THE SUZAKU." IT'S A GENERAL ASTRONOMICAL TERM.
AND I THOUGHT IT WAS SOME KINDA GOD OF BIRDS.
THE NAMES OF THE SEVEN CONSTELL-ATIONS ARE...
CHICHIRI 井 TAMAHOME 鬼
NURIKO 柳 HOTOHORI 星 CHIRIKO 張
TASUKI 翼 MITSUKAKE 軫
THEY MAKE UP THE SOUTHERN SEVEN CONSTELLATIONS, SUZAKU.
TAMAHOME AND HOTOHORI !?
THAT'S CORRECT.

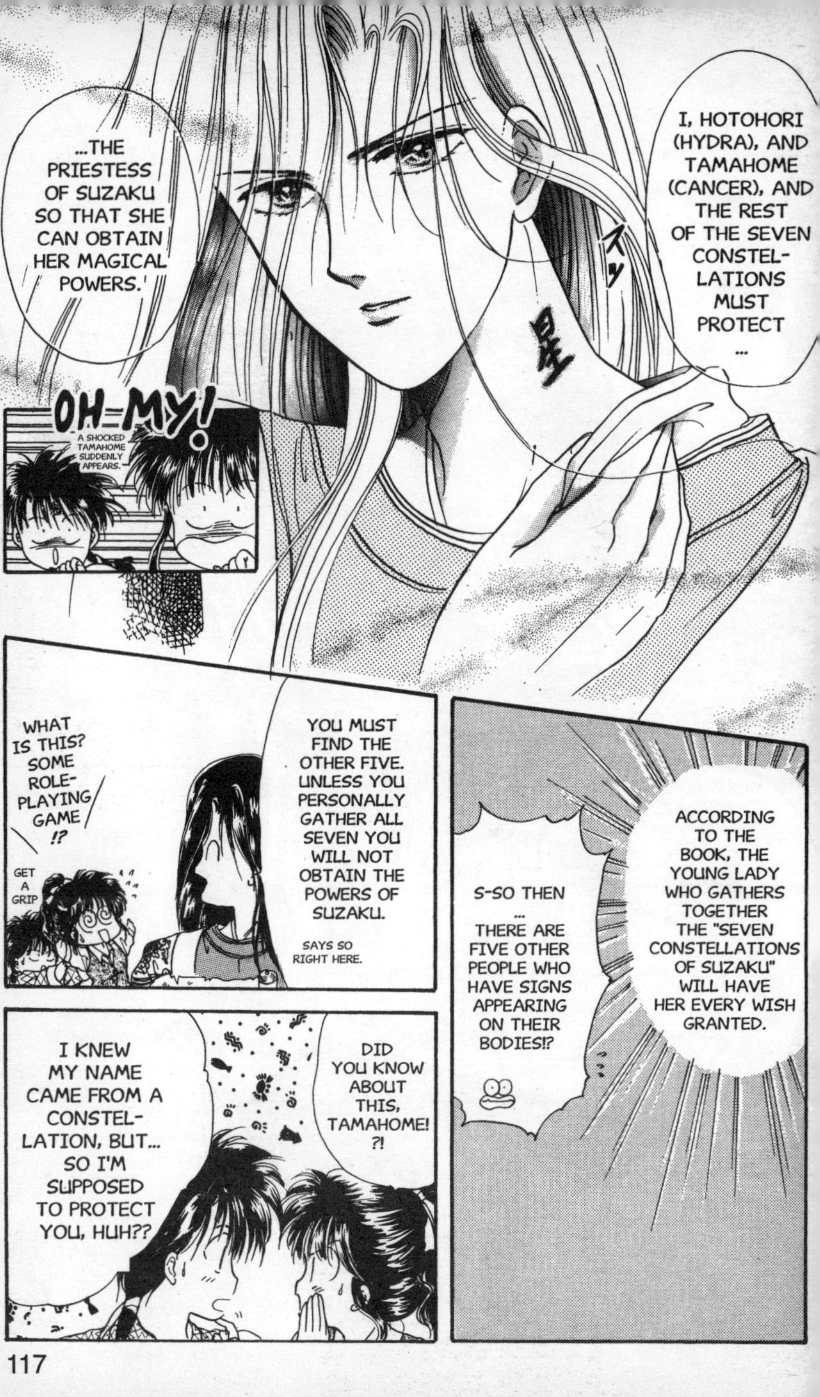

I, HOTOHORI (HYDRA), AND TAMAHOME (CANCER), AND THE REST OF THE SEVEN CONSTELLATIONS MUST PROTECT ...
...THE PRIESTESS OF SUZAKU SO THAT SHE CAN OBTAIN HER MAGICAL POWERS.'
スッ
星
OH-MY!
A SHOCKED TAMAHOME SUDDENLY APPEARS.
ACCORDING TO THE BOOK, THE YOUNG LADY WHO GATHERS TOGETHER THE "SEVEN CONSTELLATIONS OF SUZAKU" WILL HAVE HER EVERY WISH GRANTED.
S-SO THEN ... THERE ARE FIVE OTHER PEOPLE WHO HAVE SIGNS APPEARING ON THEIR BODIES!?
YOU MUST FIND THE OTHER FIVE. UNLESS YOU PERSONALLY GATHER ALL SEVEN YOU WILL NOT OBTAIN THE POWERS OF SUZAKU.
SAYS SO RIGHT HERE.
WHAT IS THIS? SOME ROLE-PLAYING GAME !?
GET A GRIP
DID YOU KNOW ABOUT THIS, TAMAHOME! ?!
I KNEW MY NAME CAME FROM A CONSTELLATION, BUT... SO I'M SUPPOSED TO PROTECT YOU, HUH??

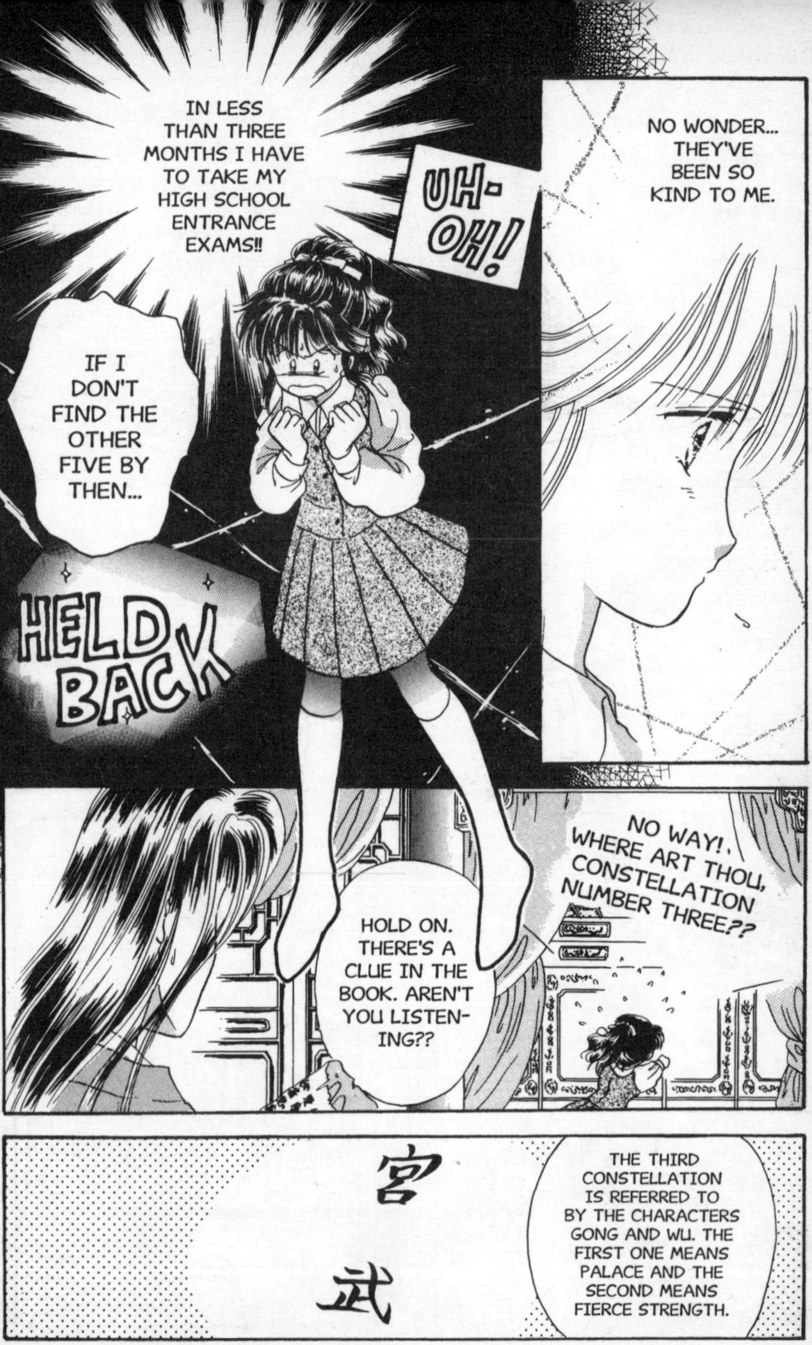
NO WONDER... THEY'VE BEEN SO KIND TO ME.
UH-OH!
IN LESS THAN THREE MONTHS I HAVE TO TAKE MY HIGH SCHOOL ENTRANCE EXAMS!!
IF I DON'T FIND THE OTHER FIVE BY THEN...
HELD BACK
NO WAY!. WHERE ART THOU, CONSTELLATION NUMBER THREE??
HOLD ON. THERE'S A CLUE IN THE BOOK. AREN'T YOU LISTEN-ING??
THE THIRD CONSTELLATION IS REFERRED TO BY THE CHARACTERS GONG AND WU. THE FIRST ONE MEANS PALACE AND THE SECOND MEANS FIERCE STRENGTH.
宮
武

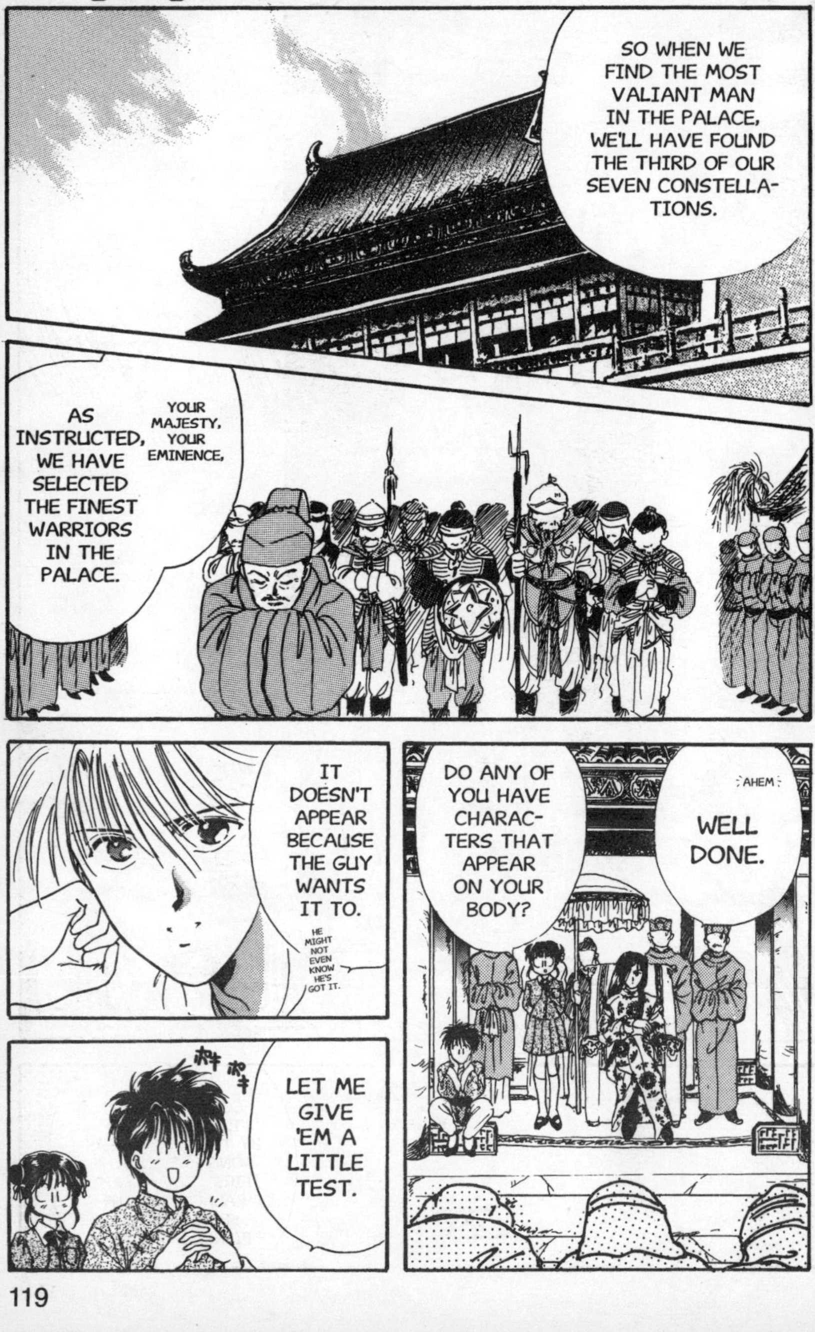
SO WHEN WE FIND THE MOST VALIANT MAN IN THE PALACE, WE'LL HAVE FOUND THE THIRD OF OUR SEVEN CONSTELLATIONS.
YOUR MAJESTY, YOUR EMINENCE,
AS INSTRUCTED, WE HAVE SELECTED THE FINEST WARRIORS IN THE PALACE.
WELL DONE.
AHEM
DO ANY OF YOU HAVE CHARACTERS THAT APPEAR ON YOUR BODY?
IT DOESN'T APPEAR BECAUSE THE GUY WANTS IT TO.
HE MIGHT NOT EVEN KNOW HE'S GOT IT.
LET ME GIVE 'EM A LITTLE TEST.

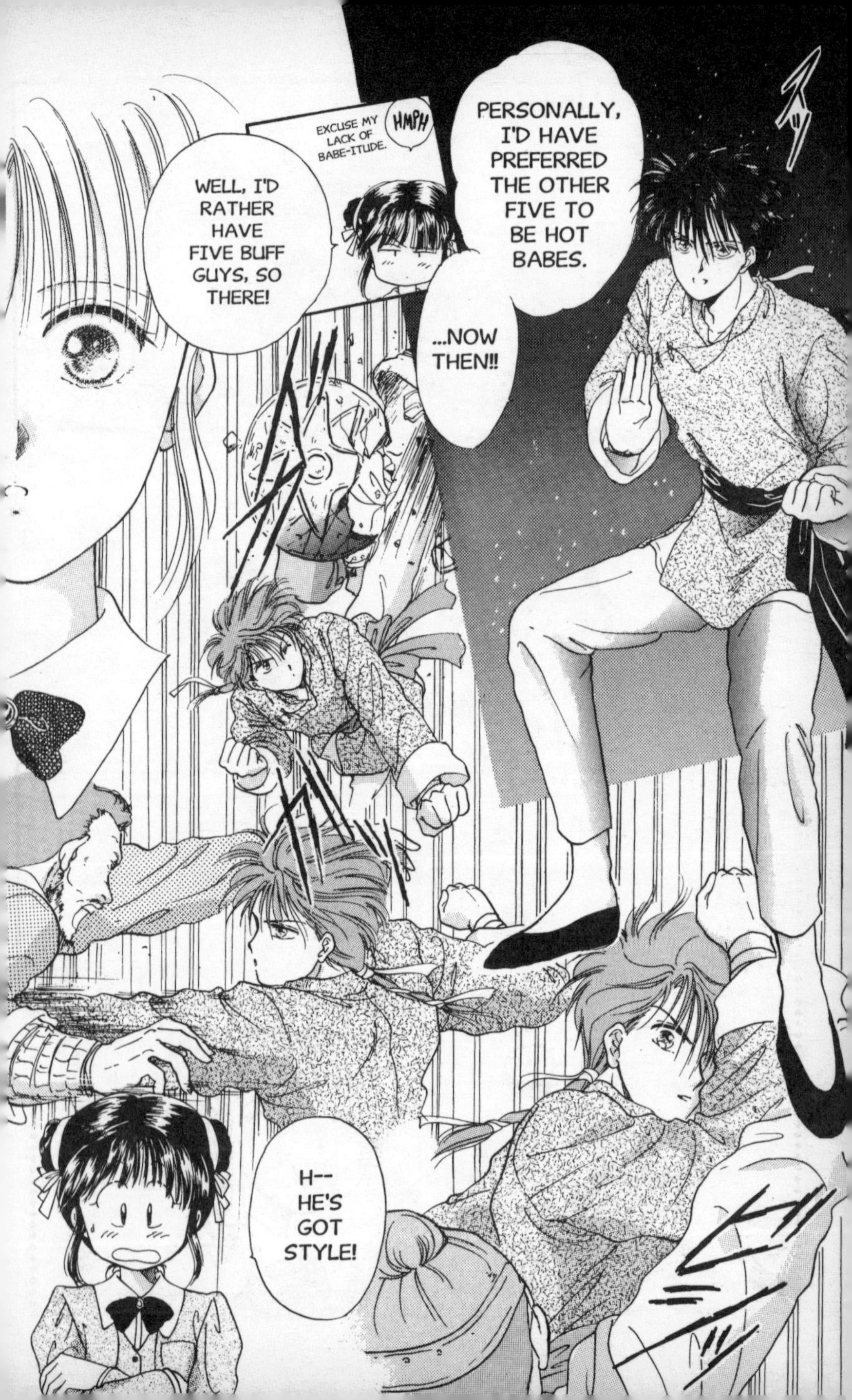

PERSONALLY, I'D HAVE PREFERRED THE OTHER FIVE TO BE HOT BABES.
WELL, I'D RATHER HAVE FIVE BUFF GUYS, SO THERE!
HMPH
EXCUSE MY LACK OF BABE-ITUDE.
...NOW THEN!!
H-- HE'S GOT STYLE!

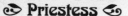

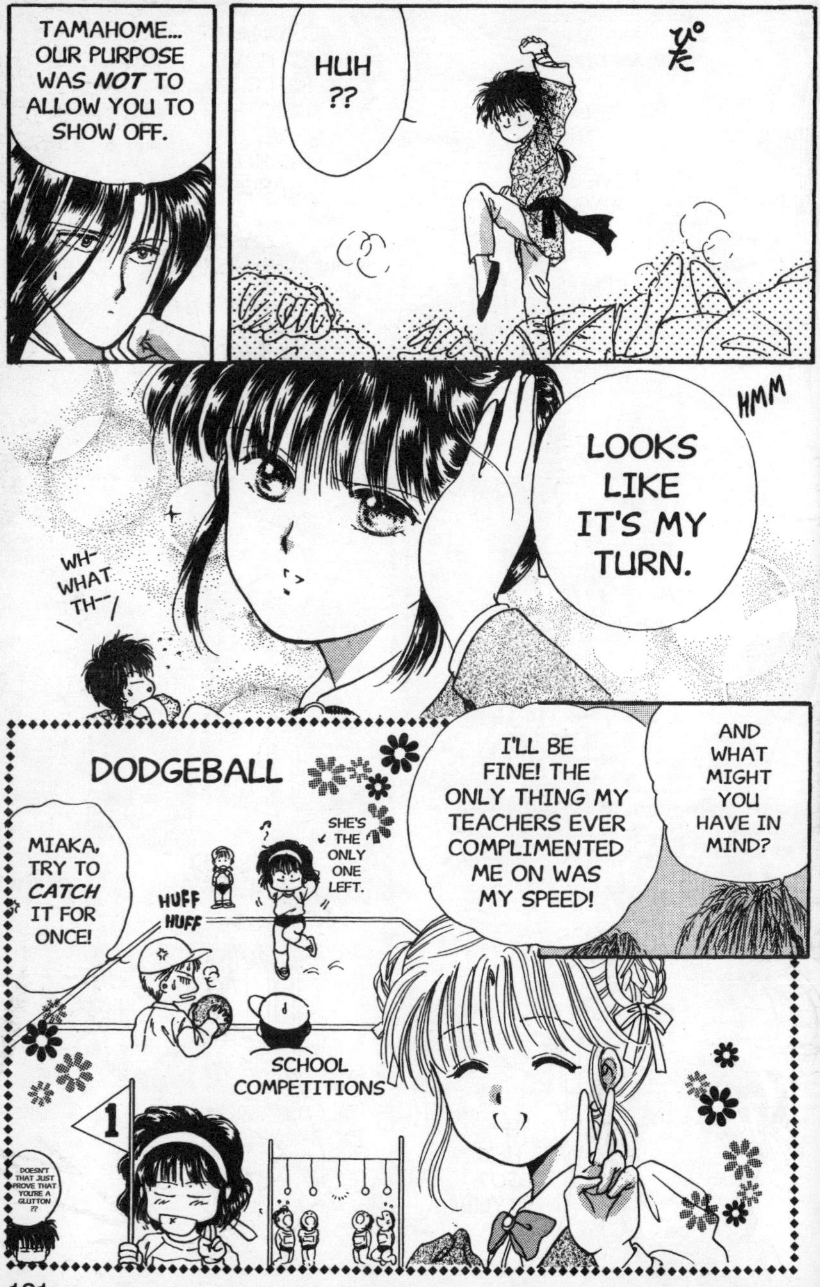
TAMAHOME... OUR PURPOSE WAS *NOT* TO ALLOW YOU TO SHOW OFF.
HUH ??
ぴた
HMM
LOOKS LIKE IT'S MY TURN.
WH- WHAT TH--!
AND WHAT MIGHT YOU HAVE IN MIND?
I'LL BE FINE! THE ONLY THING MY TEACHERS EVER COMPLIMENTED ME ON WAS MY SPEED!
DODGEBALL
MIAKA, TRY TO *CATCH* IT FOR ONCE!
HUFF HUFF
SHE'S THE ONLY ONE LEFT.
SCHOOL COMPETITIONS
1
DOESN'T THAT JUST PROVE THAT YOU'RE A GLUTTON ??

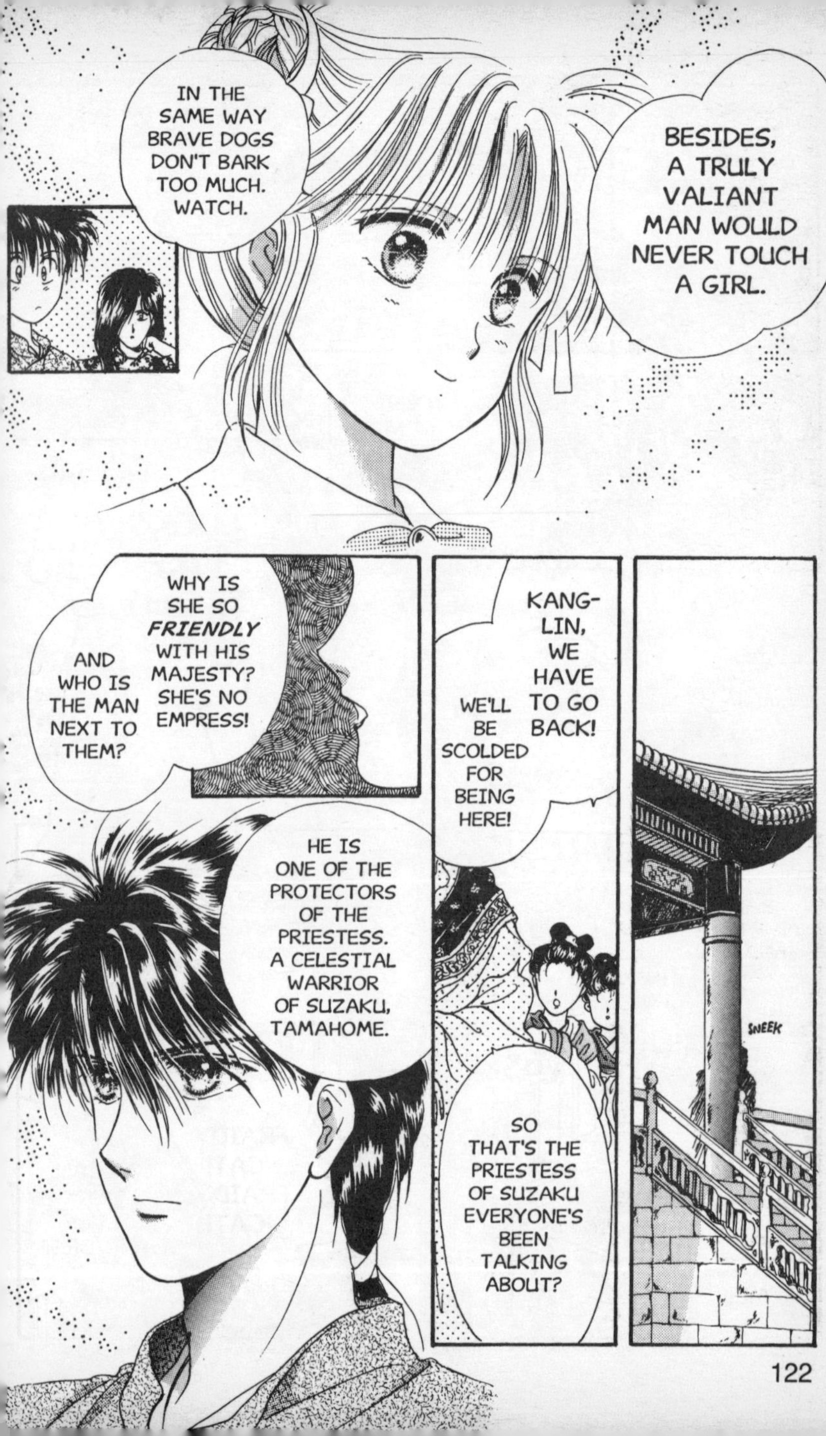
BESIDES, A TRULY VALIANT MAN WOULD NEVER TOUCH A GIRL.
IN THE SAME WAY BRAVE DOGS DON'T BARK TOO MUCH. WATCH.
SNEEK
KANG-LIN, WE HAVE TO GO BACK!
WE'LL BE SCOLDED FOR BEING HERE!
SO THAT'S THE PRIESTESS OF SUZAKU EVERYONE'S BEEN TALKING ABOUT?
WHY IS SHE SO ***FRIENDLY*** WITH HIS MAJESTY? SHE'S NO EMPRESS!
AND WHO IS THE MAN NEXT TO THEM?
HE IS ONE OF THE PROTECTORS OF THE PRIESTESS. A CELESTIAL WARRIOR OF SUZAKU, TAMAHOME.

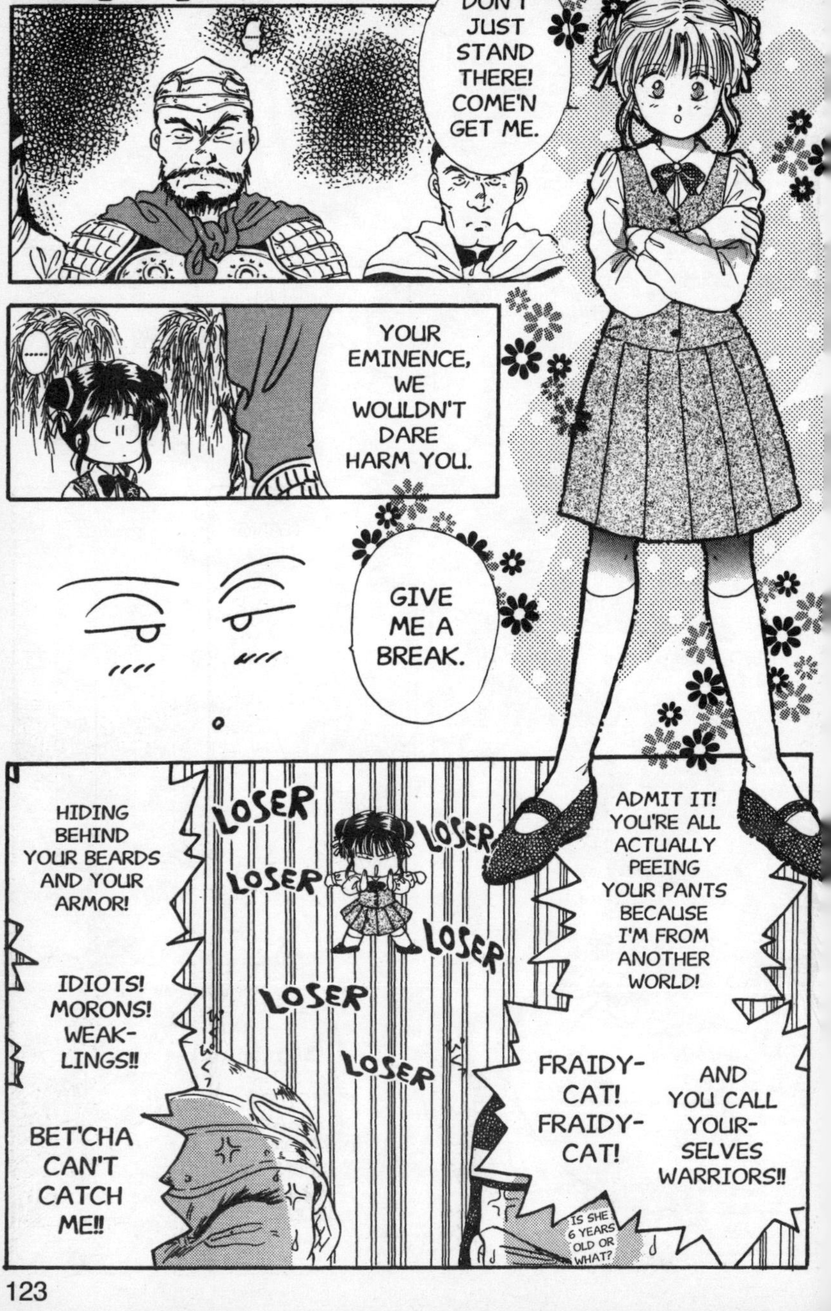
DON'T JUST STAND THERE! COME'N GET ME.
......
YOUR EMINENCE, WE WOULDN'T DARE HARM YOU.
GIVE ME A BREAK.
ADMIT IT! YOU'RE ALL ACTUALLY PEEING YOUR PANTS BECAUSE I'M FROM ANOTHER WORLD!
AND YOU CALL YOUR-SELVES WARRIORS!!
FRAIDY-CAT! FRAIDY-CAT!
IS SHE 6 YEARS OLD OR WHAT?
LOSER LOSER LOSER LOSER LOSER LOSER
HIDING BEHIND YOUR BEARDS AND YOUR ARMOR!
IDIOTS! MORONS! WEAK-LINGS!!
BET'CHA CAN'T CATCH ME!!

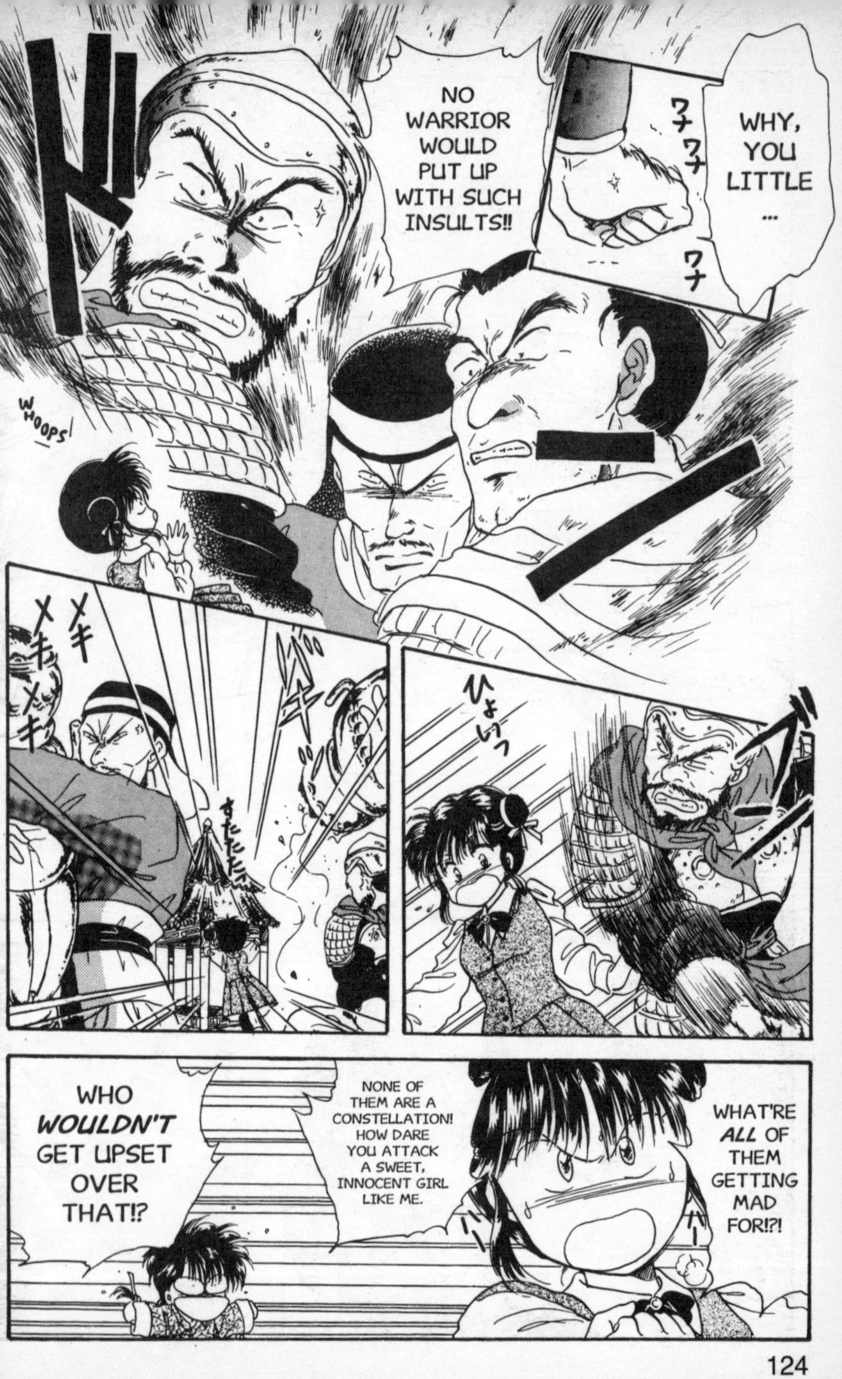
WHY, YOU LITTLE ...
ワナ ワナ
ワナ
NO WARRIOR WOULD PUT UP WITH SUCH INSULTS!!
WHOOPS!
ひょいっ
メキメキ
WHAT'RE *ALL* OF THEM GETTING MAD FOR!?!
NONE OF THEM ARE A CONSTELLATION! HOW DARE YOU ATTACK A SWEET, INNOCENT GIRL LIKE ME.
WHO *WOULDN'T* GET UPSET OVER THAT!?

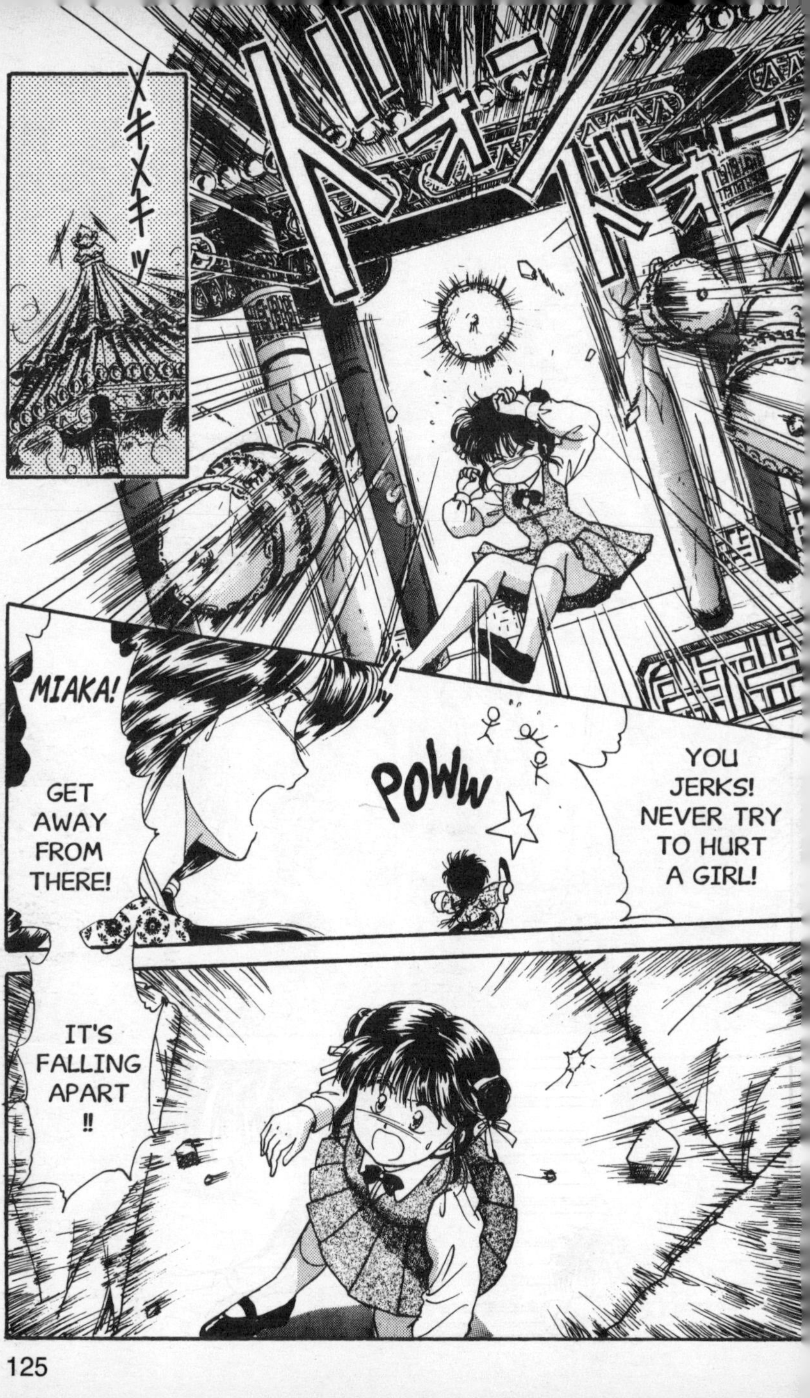

メキメキッ
YOU JERKS! NEVER TRY TO HURT A GIRL!
POWW
MIAKA!
GET AWAY FROM THERE!
IT'S FALLING APART !!

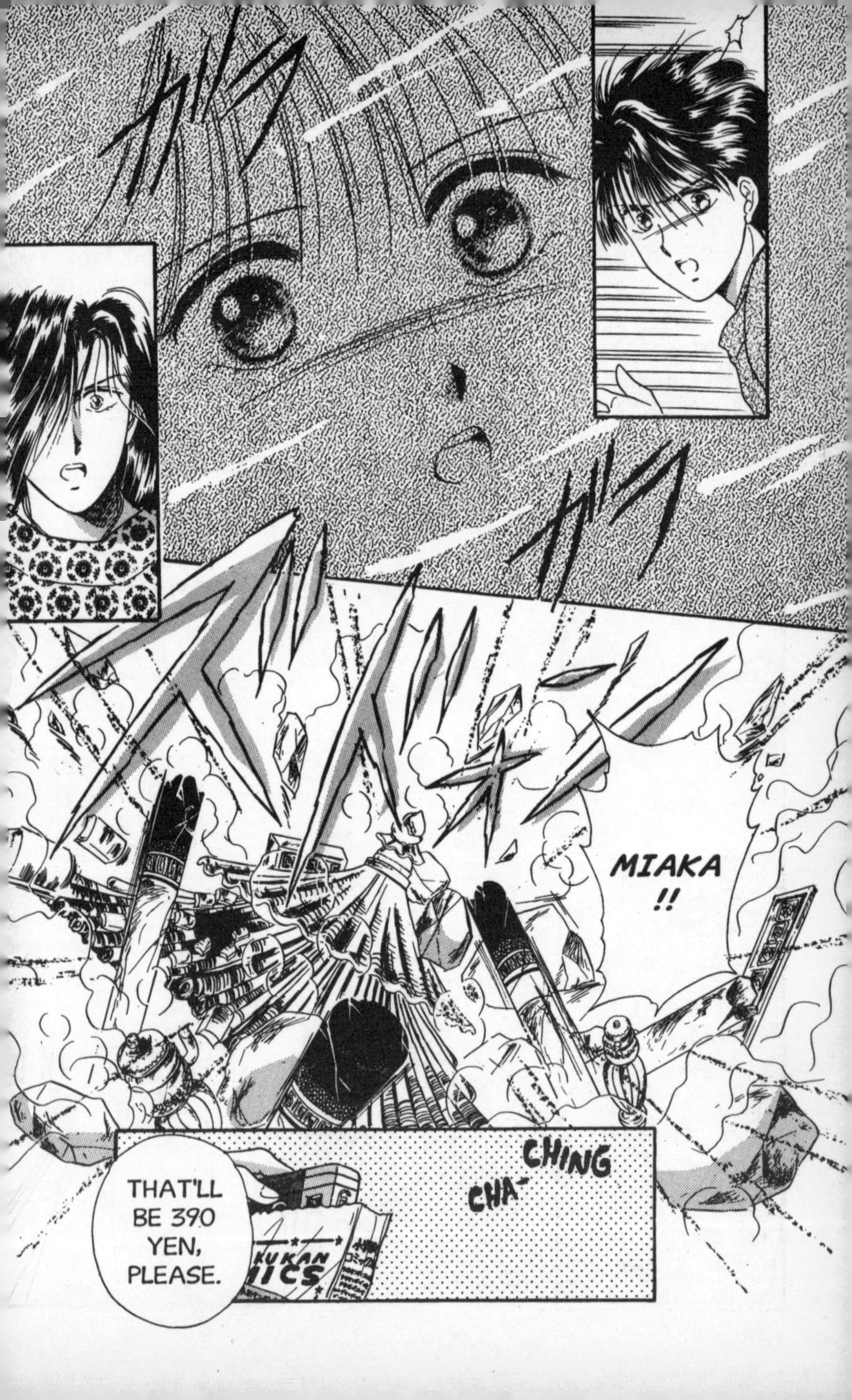
MIAKA !!
CHA-CHING
THAT'LL BE 390 YEN, PLEASE.

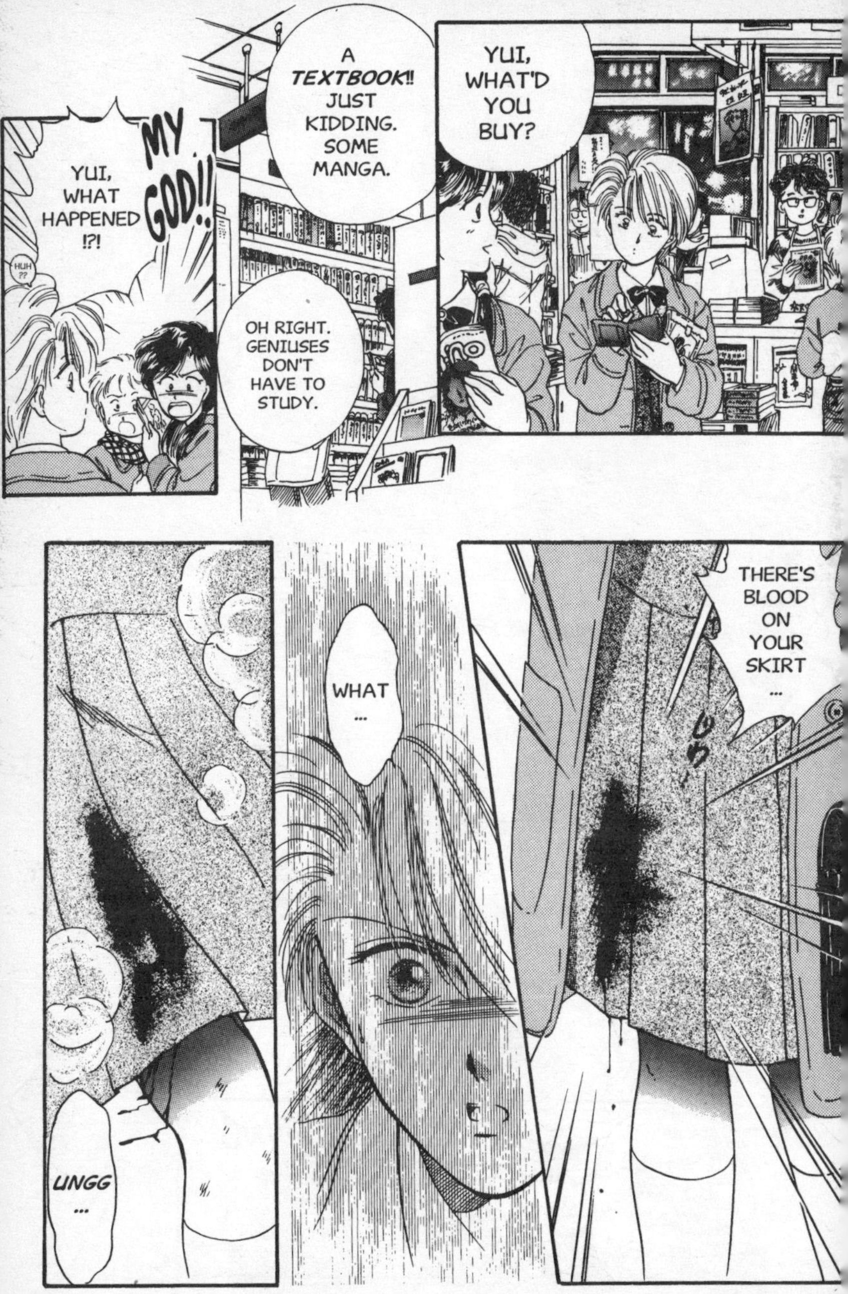

YUI, WHAT'D YOU BUY?
A TEXTBOOK!! JUST KIDDING. SOME MANGA.
OH RIGHT. GENIUSES DON'T HAVE TO STUDY.
MY GOD!!..
YUI, WHAT HAPPENED !?!
HUH ??
THERE'S BLOOD ON YOUR SKIRT ...
WHAT ...
UNGG ...

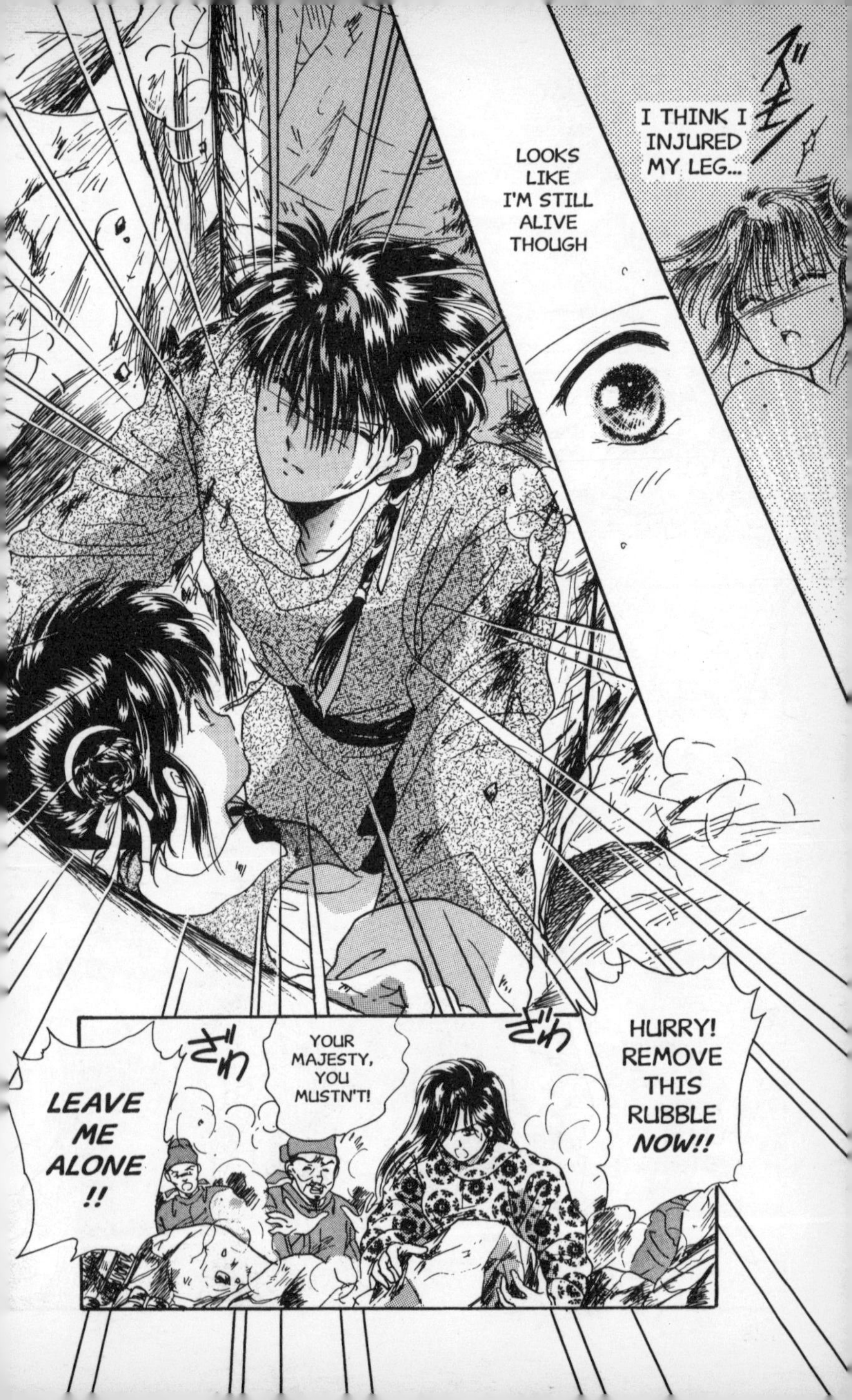

I THINK I INJURED MY LEG...
LOOKS LIKE I'M STILL ALIVE THOUGH
ざわ
HURRY! REMOVE THIS RUBBLE NOW!!
YOUR MAJESTY, YOU MUSTN'T!
ざわ
LEAVE ME ALONE !!

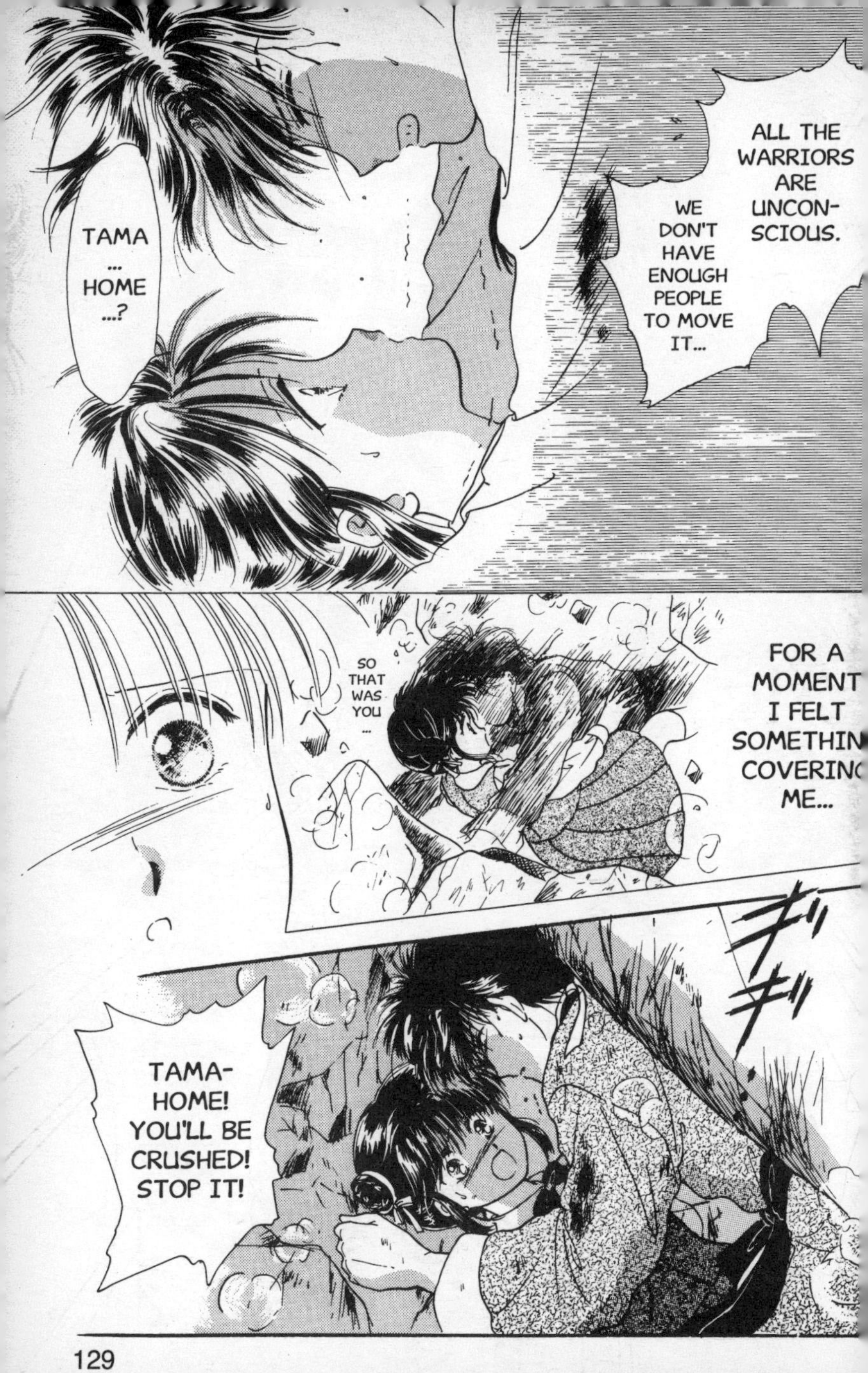
ALL THE WARRIORS ARE UNCON-SCIOUS.
WE DON'T HAVE ENOUGH PEOPLE TO MOVE IT...
TAMA ... HOME ...?
FOR A MOMENT I FELT SOMETHIN COVERIN ME...
SO THAT WAS YOU ...
ギギ
TAMA-HOME! YOU'LL BE CRUSHED! STOP IT!

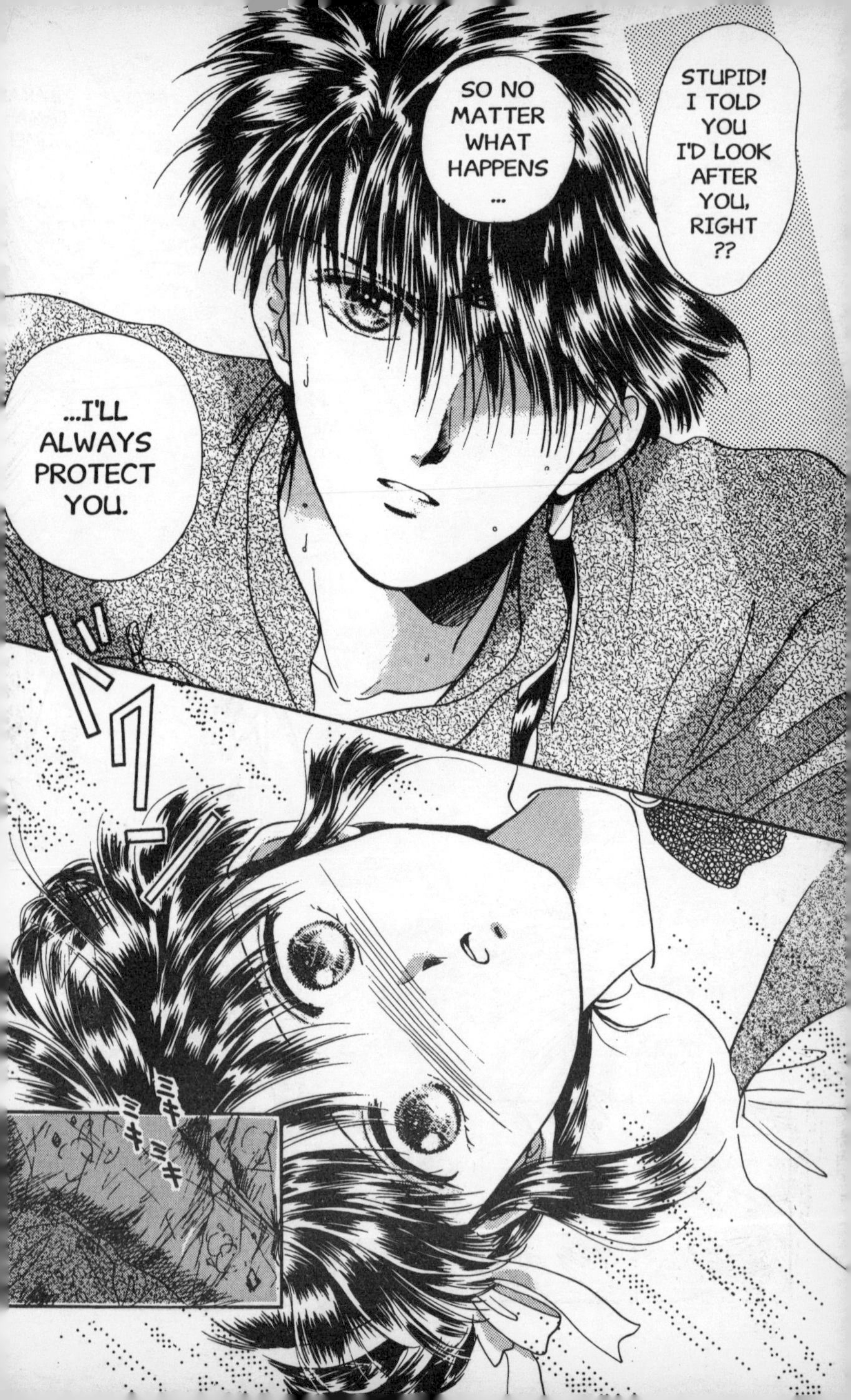
STUPID! I TOLD YOU I'D LOOK AFTER YOU, RIGHT ??
SO NO MATTER WHAT HAPPENS ...
...I'LL ALWAYS PROTECT YOU.
ドクーン
ミキ
ミキミキ

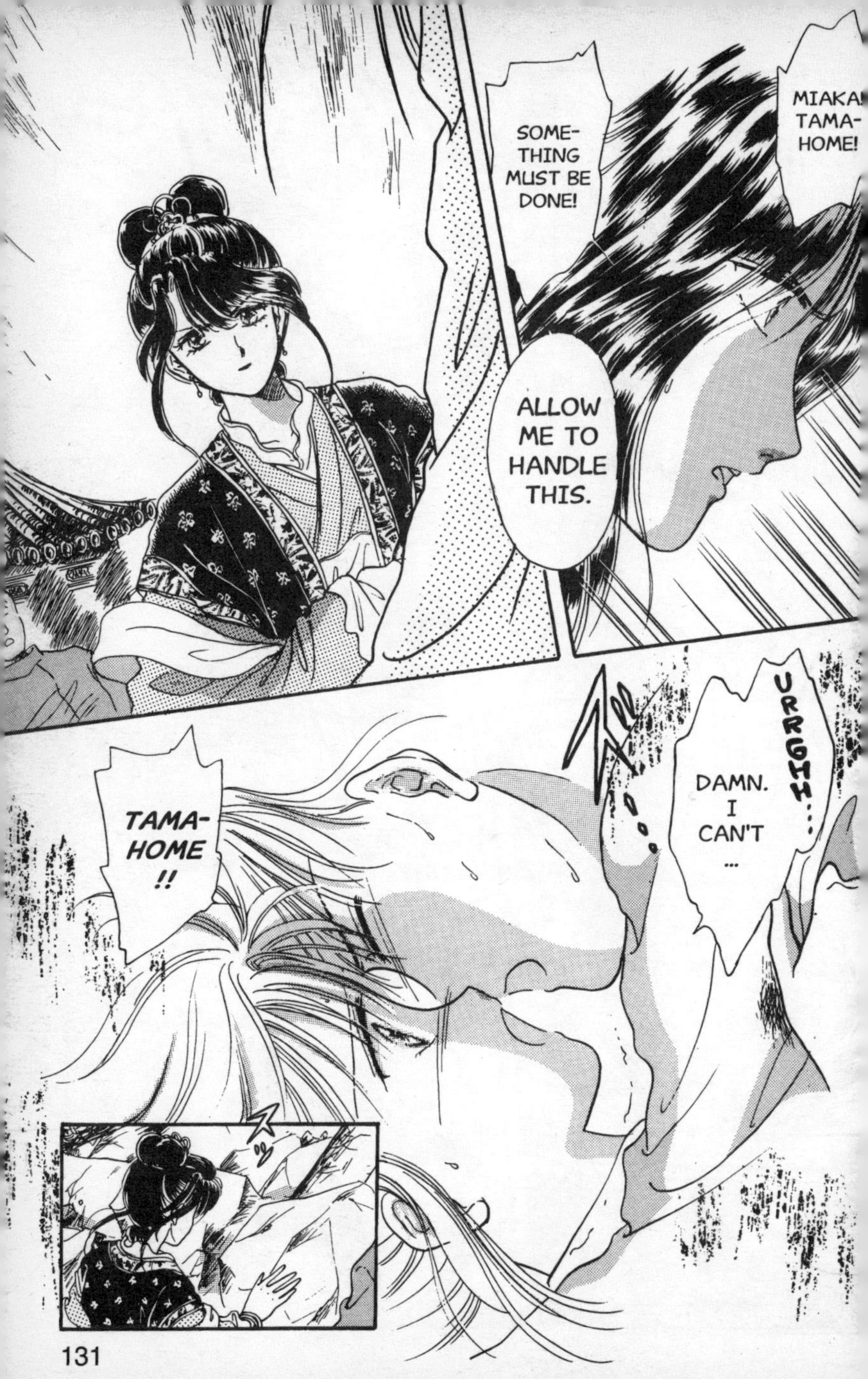
MIAKA! TAMA-HOME!
SOME-THING MUST BE DONE!
ALLOW ME TO HANDLE THIS.
URRGHH...
DAMN. I CAN'T ...
TAMA-HOME!!

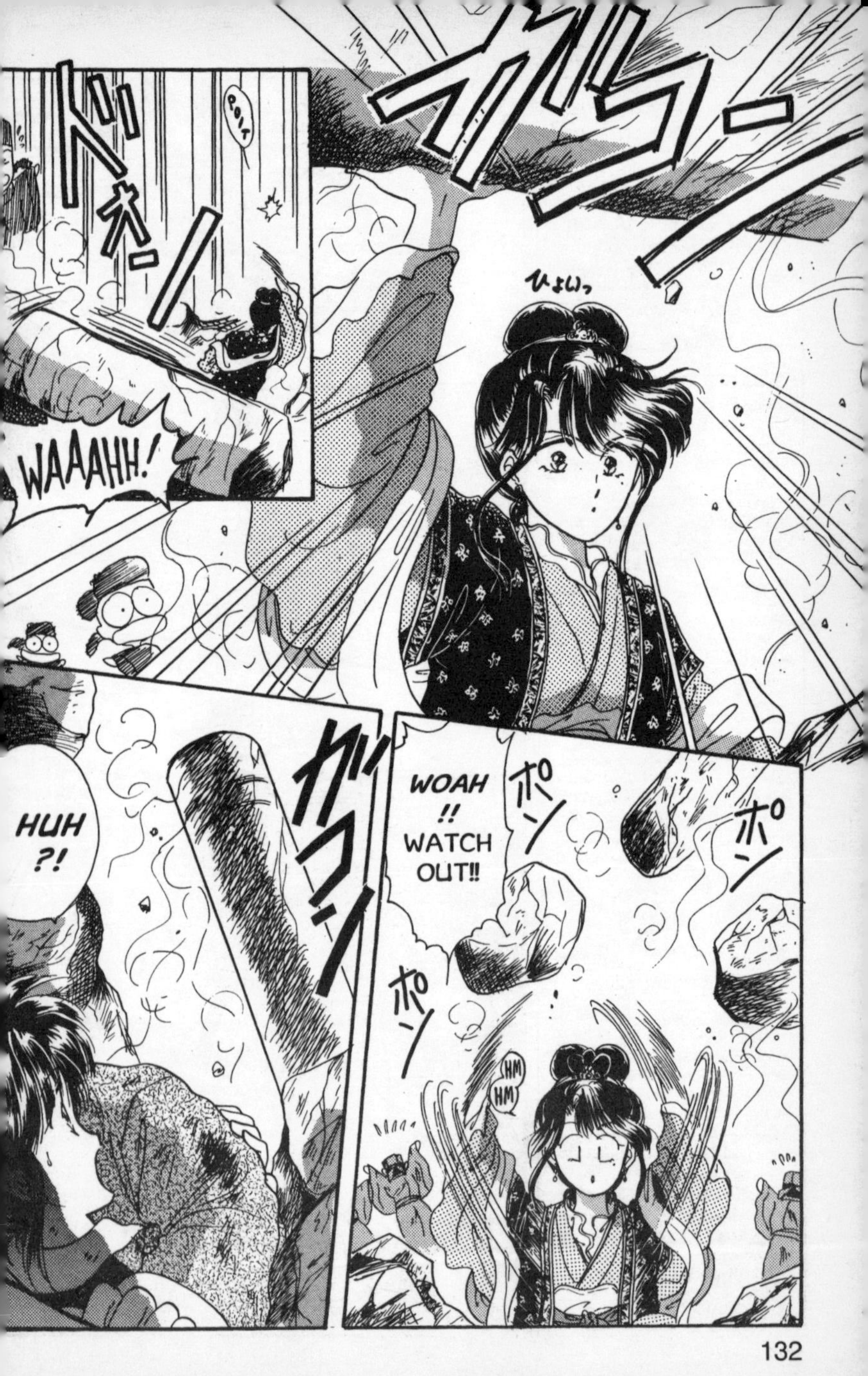
ズバーン
ドゥオーン
POIT
WAAAHH!
ひょいっ
ガコーン
HUH ?!
ポン
ポン
ポン
WOAH !! WATCH OUT!!
HM HM

Let me just say that drawing the buildings in this chapter was no easy task. I did all this research to draw them (although I didn't want it to look exactly the same as in my reference, so I'd alter some of the designs and layouts). It was a real pain for my assistants but also for me as well. (I do as much of the backgrounds as I possibly can.) Hey, Chinese architecture, why're you such a pain!? And these outfits are no easier. Not to mention the mob scenes. And I've had it up to here with the soldiers' armor! (I was gonna use "Romance of the Three Kingdoms" as reference material, but that story's set too far back in time. ♪ There's not a whole lot of changes over time in China but we're talking about a difference of a thousand years. ♪ At least I want the armor to be right. The armor is kind of a pastiche between different periods, mostly the period between the Sung and Ming dynasties but also a little bit of Tang all mixed up together. But this China is supposed to be a work of the imagination. Even my editor's been telling me not to be too particular.

When I was in elementary school, I loved the TV live drama show "Saiyuki." Then they started doing re-runs when I was eighteen. All of a sudden I realized how great the action, characters, and comedy were. So I'd look forward to 8 p.m. every Sunday. That's really the kind of project I'd like to work on.

By the way, I really wanted to have Tamahome wear an outfit with Chinese buttons, but the style only came into existence in modern China. I might eventually draw it in anyway. In the ↘ 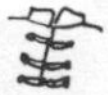 first graphic novel, maybe! The kimono style just isn't much fun. When were the "Mr. Vampire" and "Chinese Ghost Story" series set? I'd like Tamahome to wear the same clothes worn by the guy in "Mr. Vampire," but maybe that outfit would be too recent. I know, I know. I'm not supposed to be so particular, but I am. Oh, I also pay a lot of attention to hair. The bun style is just too boring.

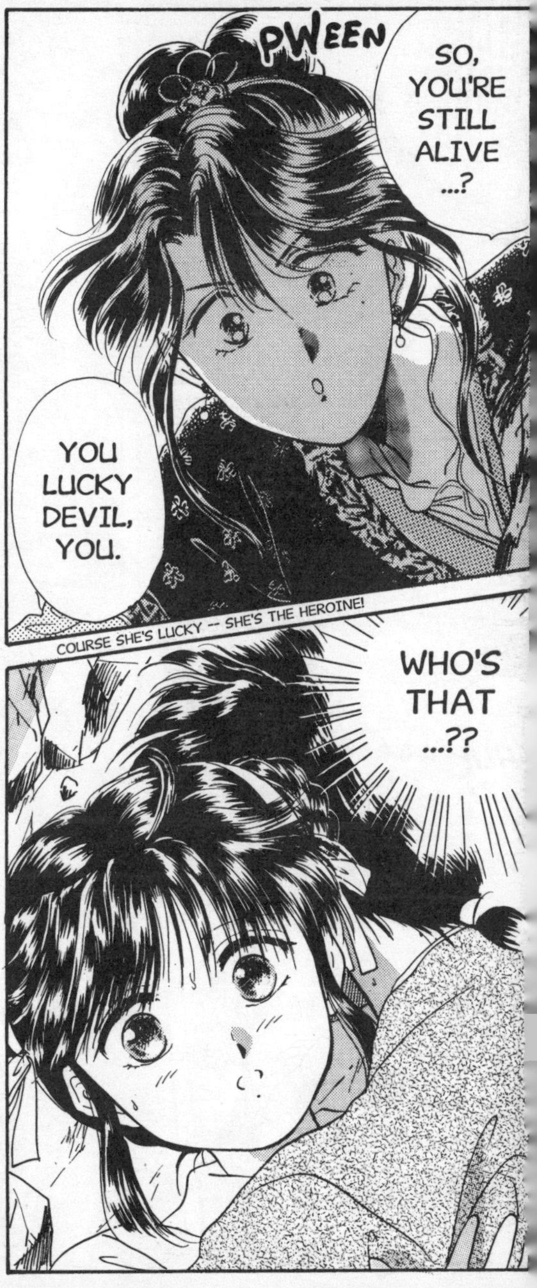
PWEEN
SO, YOU'RE STILL ALIVE ...?
YOU LUCKY DEVIL, YOU.
COURSE SHE'S LUCKY -- SHE'S THE HEROINE!
WHO'S THAT ...??

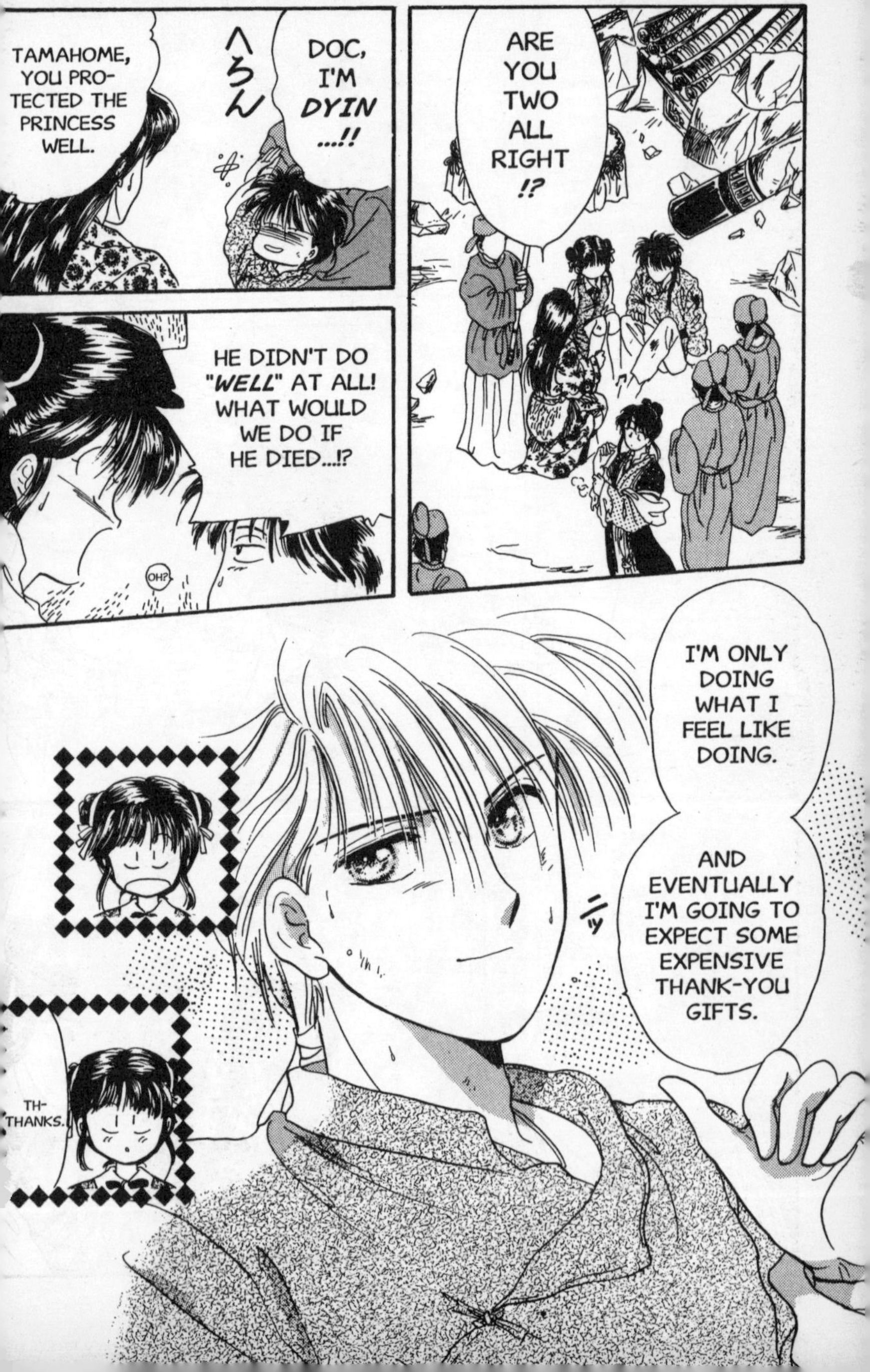
ARE YOU TWO ALL RIGHT !?
へろん
DOC, I'M DYIN ...!!
TAMAHOME, YOU PROTECTED THE PRINCESS WELL.
HE DIDN'T DO "WELL" AT ALL! WHAT WOULD WE DO IF HE DIED...!?
OH?
I'M ONLY DOING WHAT I FEEL LIKE DOING.
AND EVENTUALLY I'M GOING TO EXPECT SOME EXPENSIVE THANK-YOU GIFTS.
ニッ
TH-THANKS.

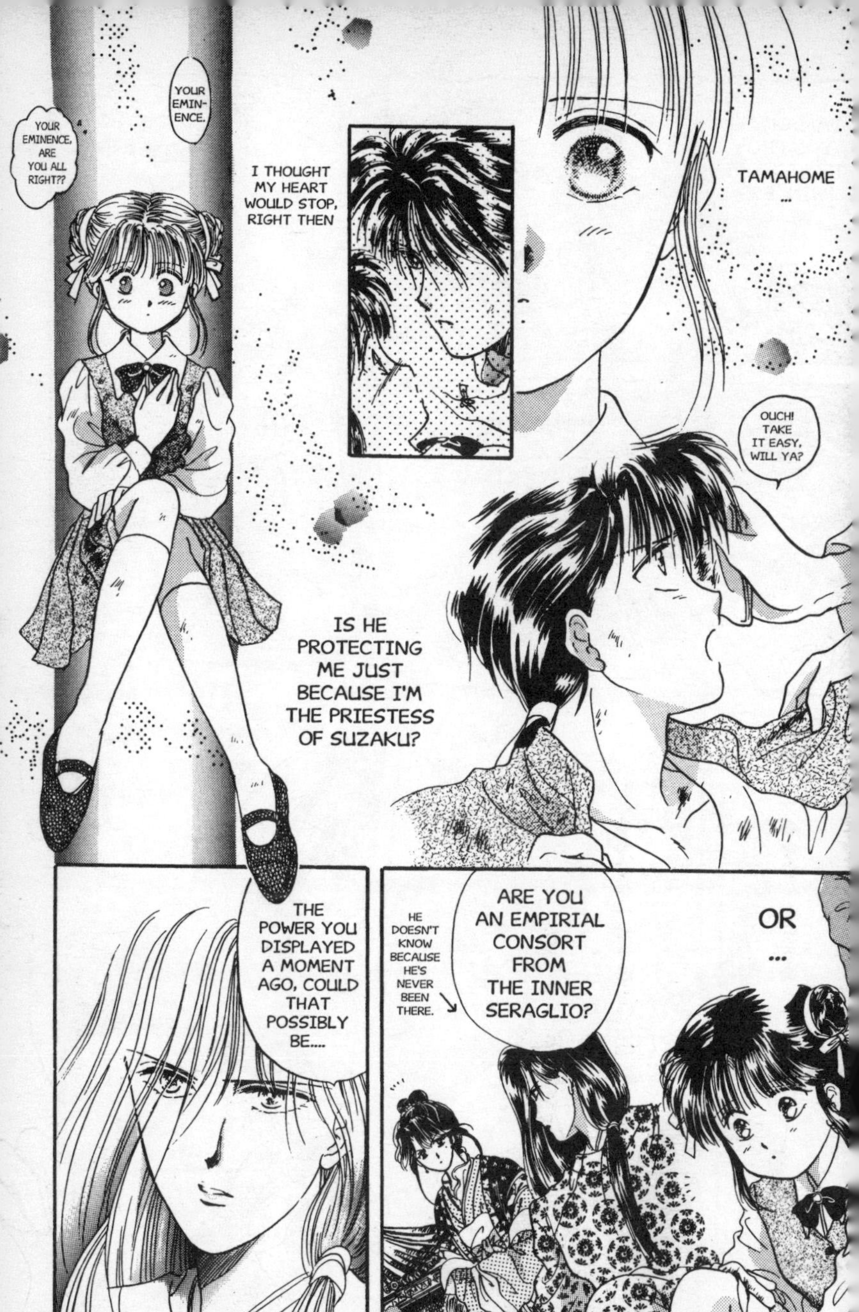
YOUR EMINENCE, ARE YOU ALL RIGHT??
YOUR EMIN-ENCE.
I THOUGHT MY HEART WOULD STOP, RIGHT THEN
TAMAHOME ...
OUCH! TAKE IT EASY, WILL YA?
IS HE PROTECTING ME JUST BECAUSE I'M THE PRIESTESS OF SUZAKU?
THE POWER YOU DISPLAYED A MOMENT AGO, COULD THAT POSSIBLY BE....
HE DOESN'T KNOW BECAUSE HE'S NEVER BEEN THERE.
ARE YOU AN EMPIRIAL CONSORT FROM THE INNER SERAGLIO?
OR ...

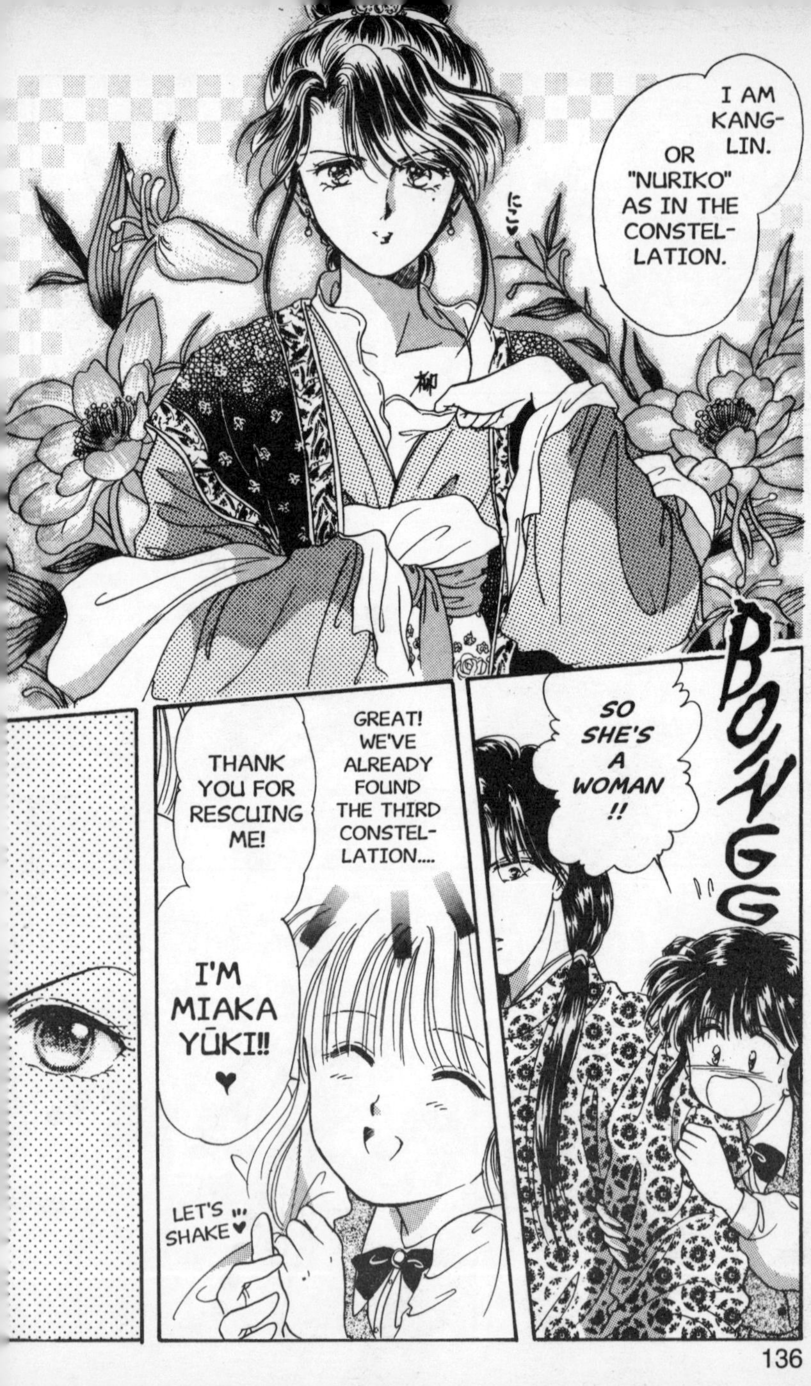
I AM KANG-LIN.
OR "NURIKO" AS IN THE CONSTEL-LATION.
にこ♥
BOINGG
SO SHE'S A WOMAN !!
GREAT! WE'VE ALREADY FOUND THE THIRD CONSTEL-LATION....
THANK YOU FOR RESCUING ME!
I'M MIAKA YŪKI!! ♥
LET'S SHAKE ♥

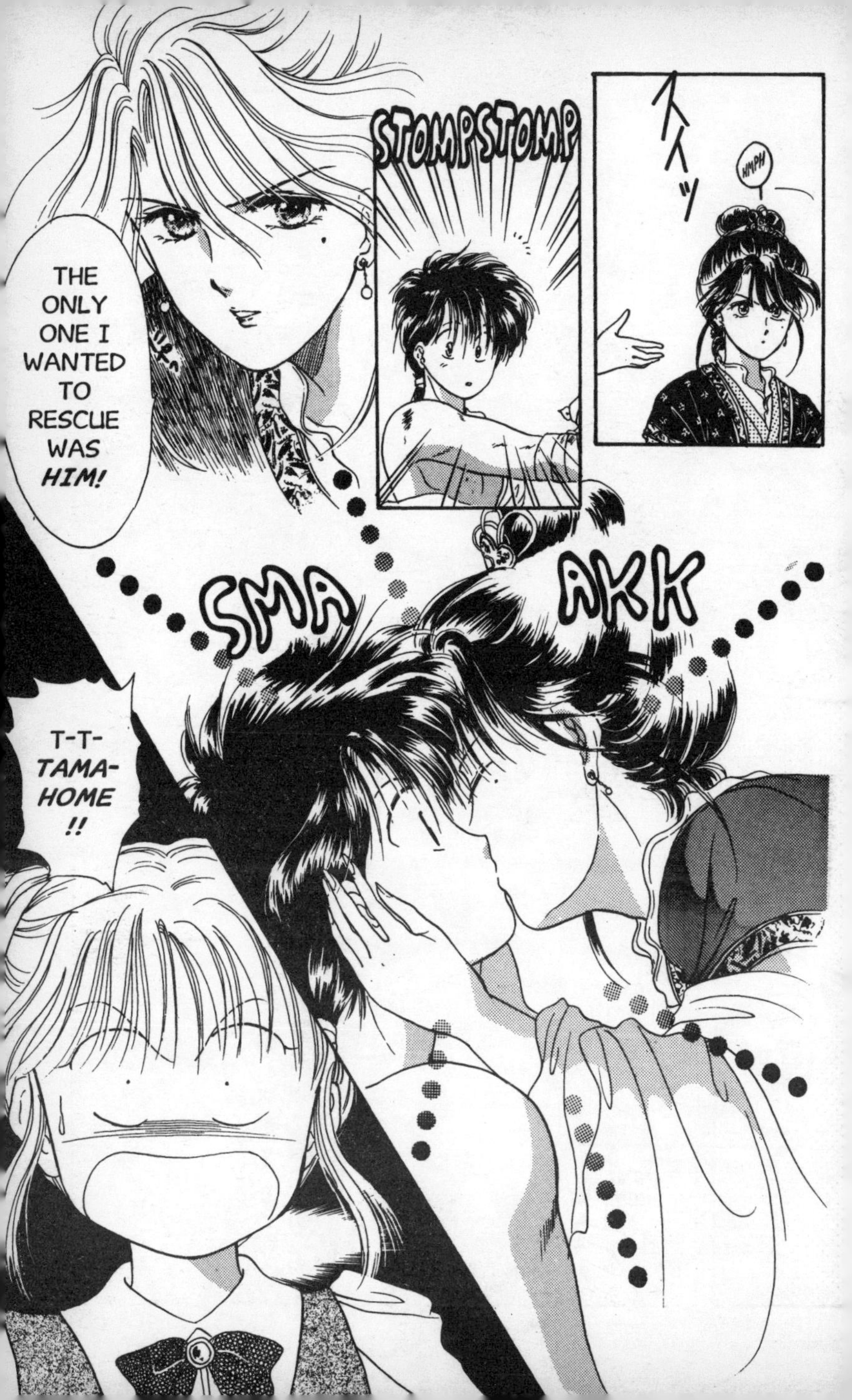
HMPH
STOMPSTOMP
THE ONLY ONE I WANTED TO RESCUE WAS *HIM!*
SMAAKK
T-T-TAMA-HOME!!

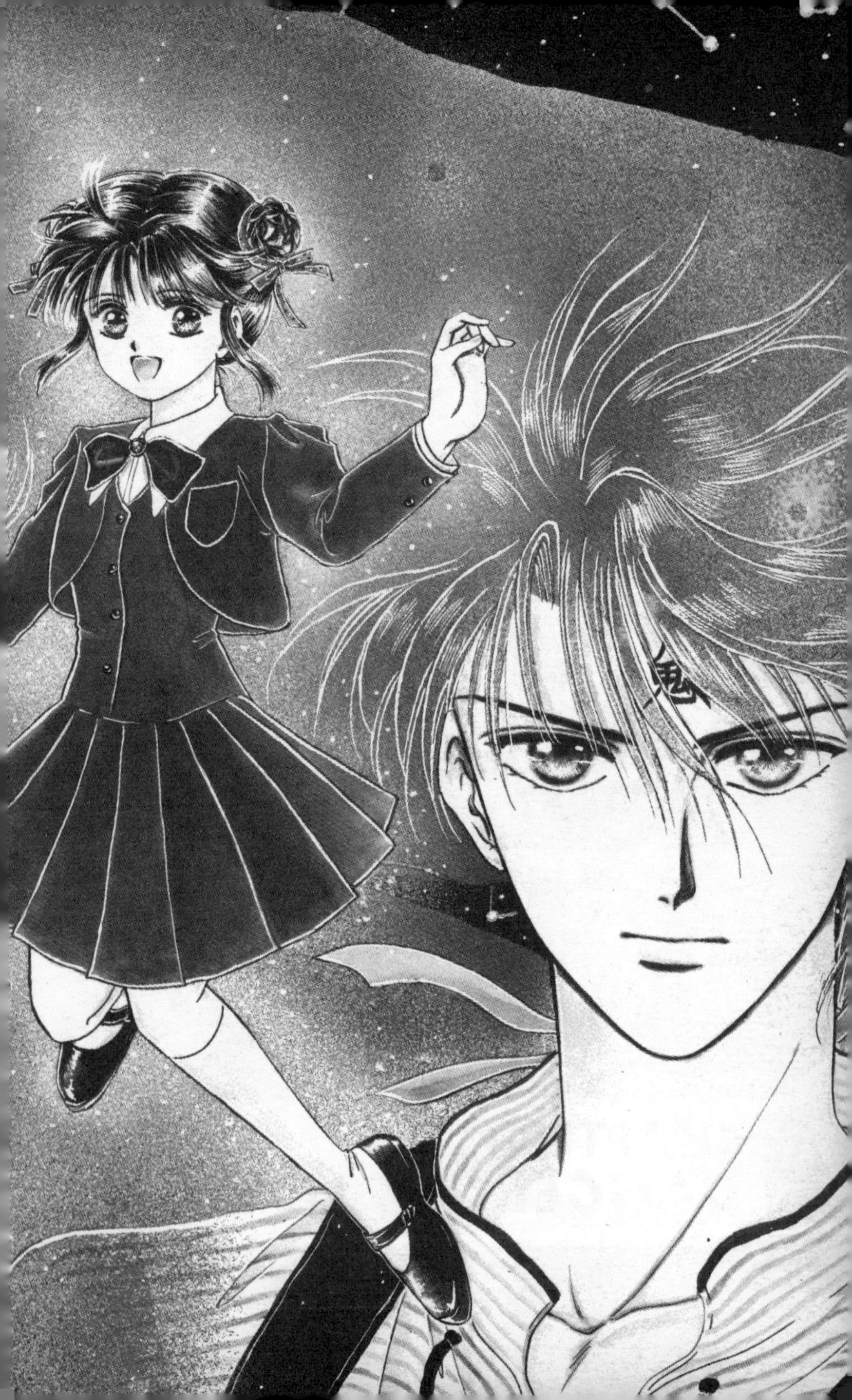

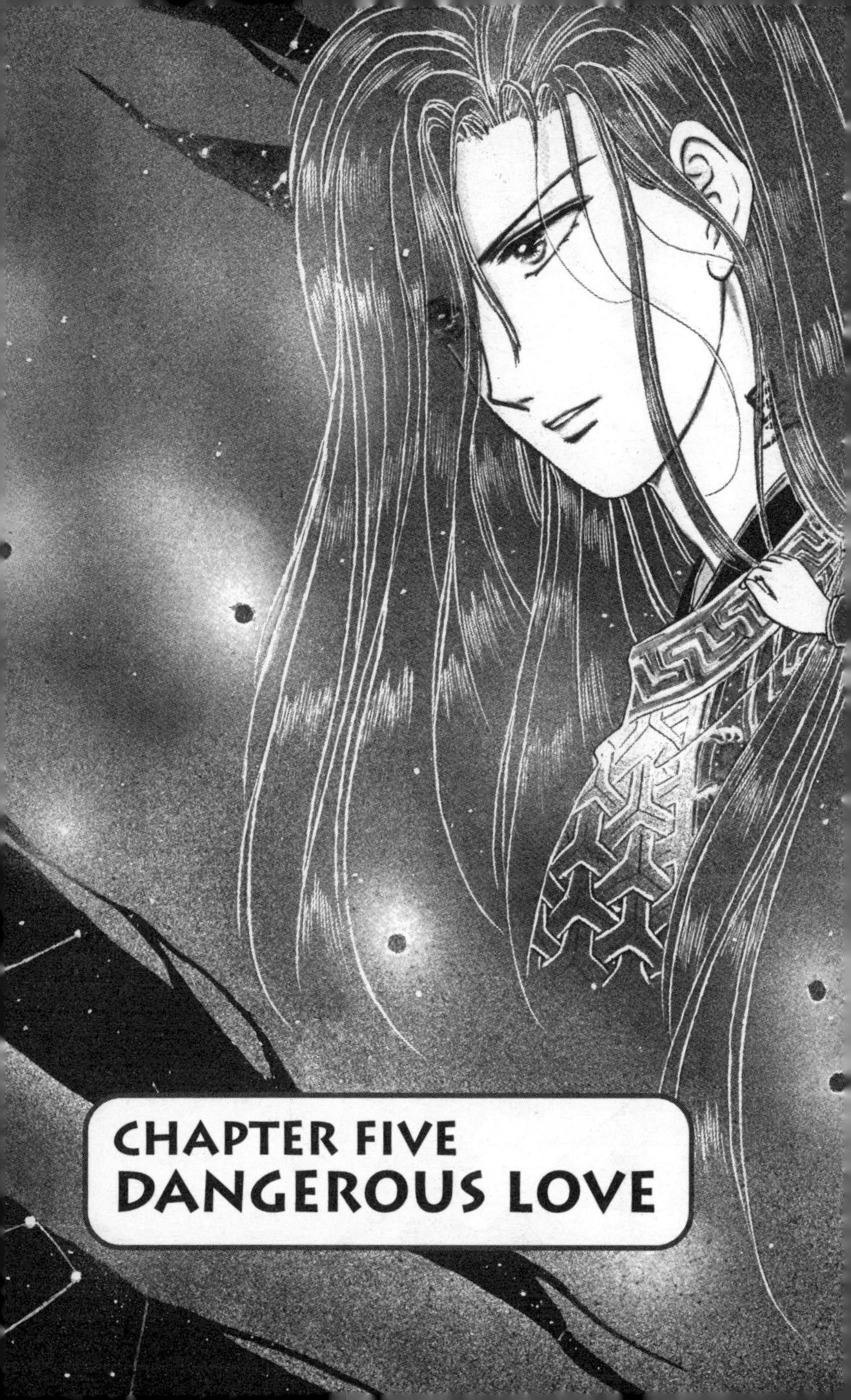
CHAPTER FIVE
DANGEROUS LOVE

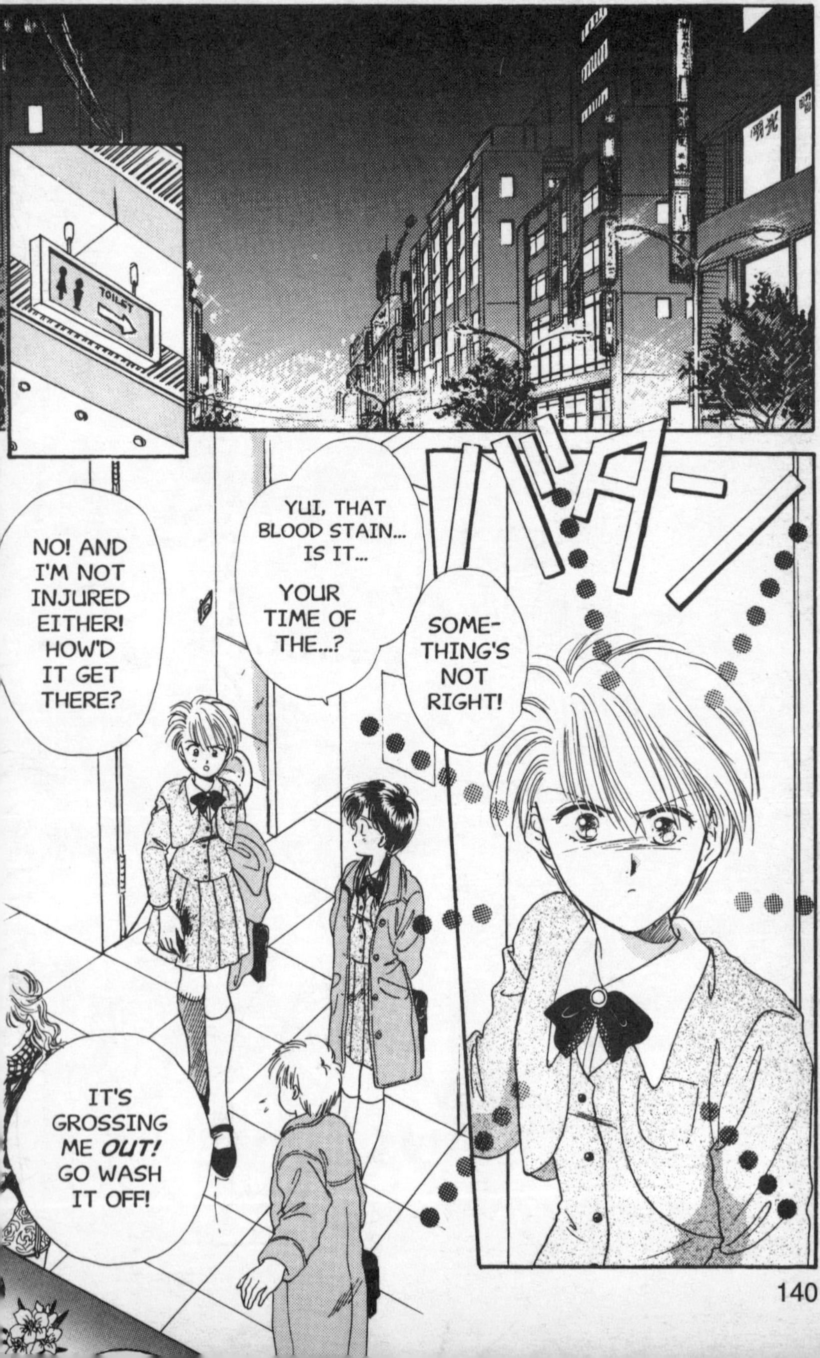
TOILET
YUI, THAT BLOOD STAIN... IS IT...
YOUR TIME OF THE...?
NO! AND I'M NOT INJURED EITHER! HOW'D IT GET THERE?
IT'S GROSSING ME *OUT!* GO WASH IT OFF!
バーン
SOME-THING'S NOT RIGHT!

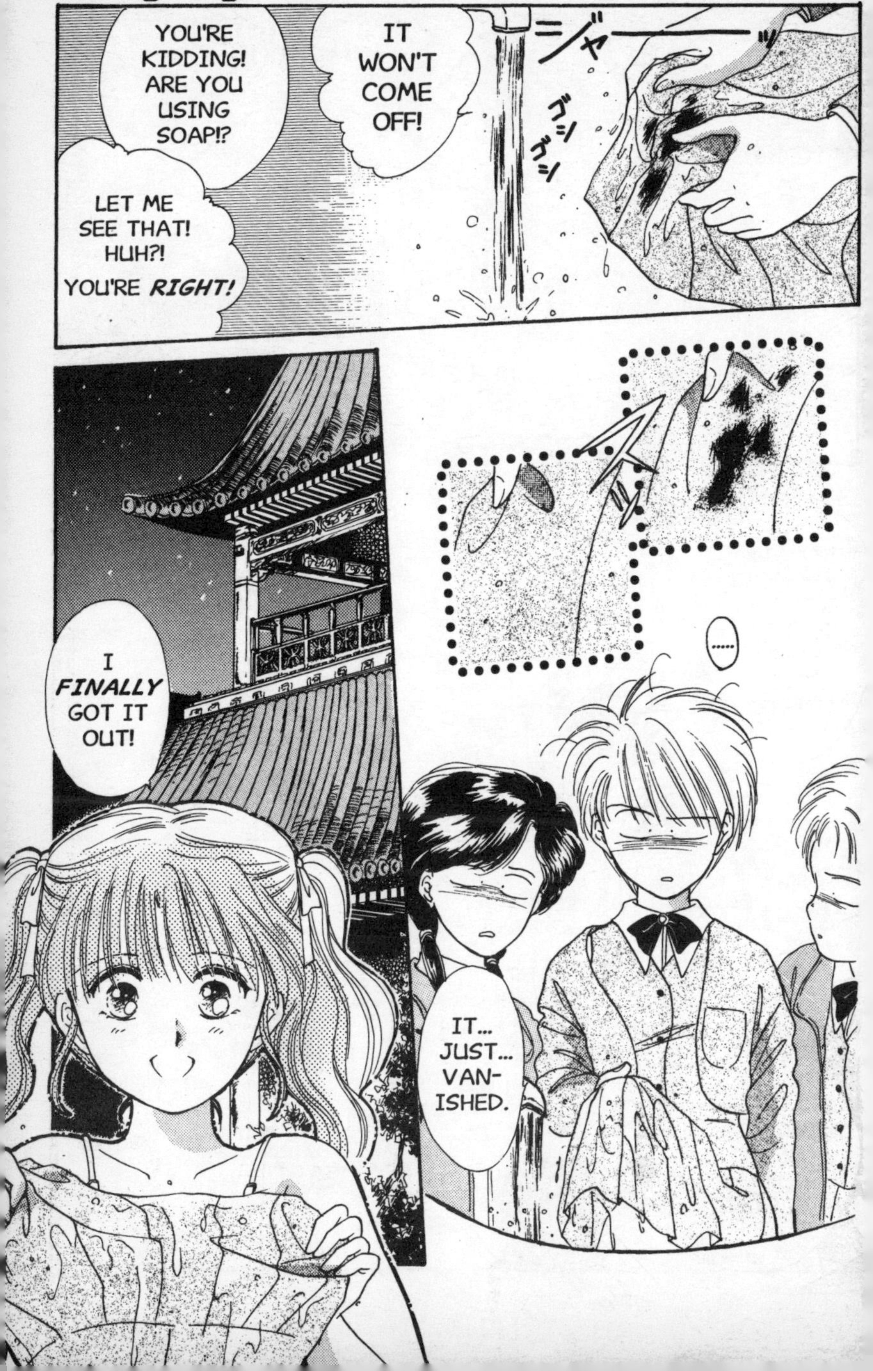
ジャーーーッ
ゴシゴシ
IT WON'T COME OFF!
YOU'RE KIDDING! ARE YOU USING SOAP!?
LET ME SEE THAT! HUH?! YOU'RE *RIGHT!*
......
IT... JUST... VAN-ISHED.
I *FINALLY* GOT IT OUT!

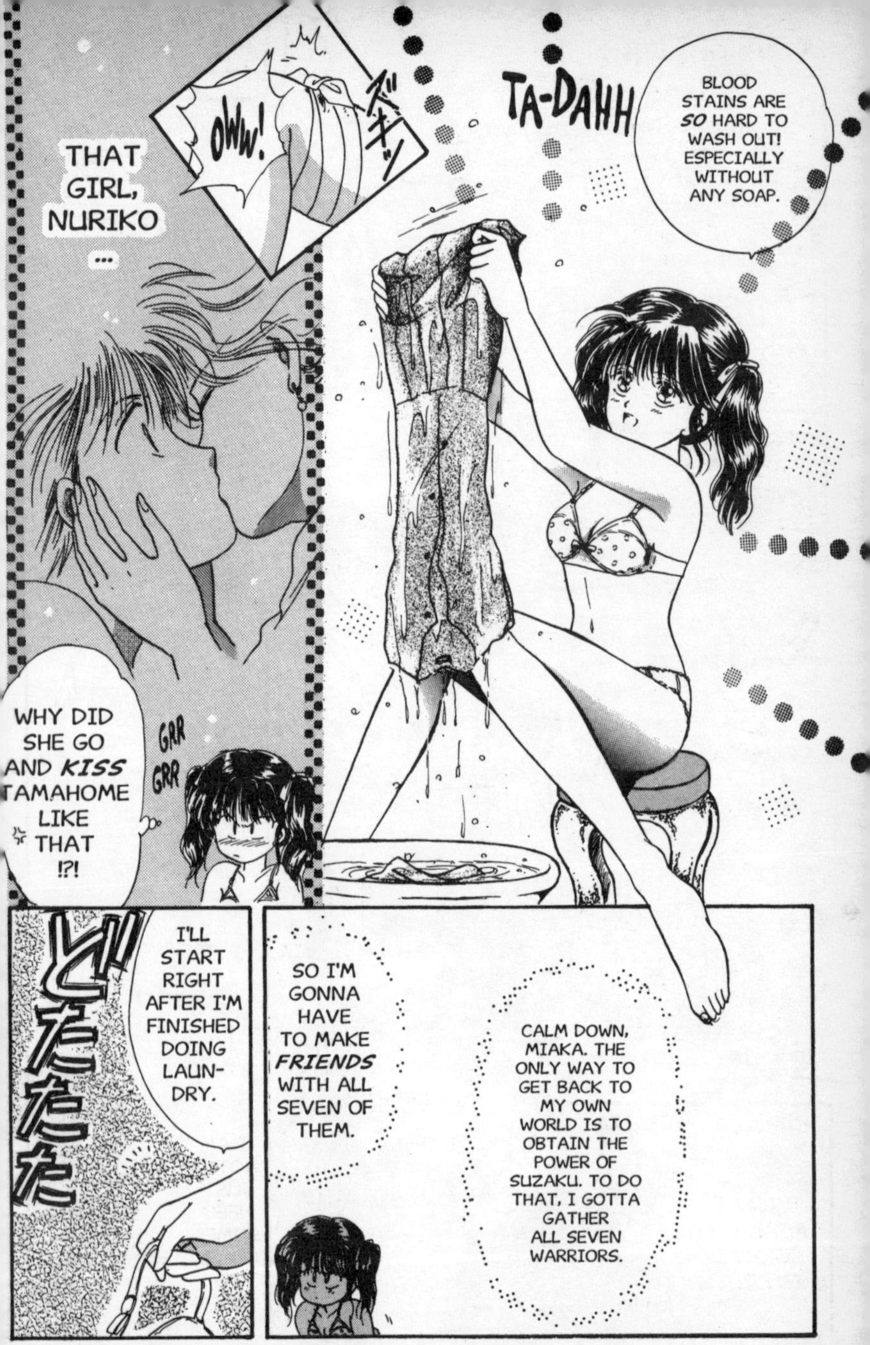
TA-DAHH
BLOOD STAINS ARE *SO* HARD TO WASH OUT! ESPECIALLY WITHOUT ANY SOAP.
ズキッ
OWW!
THAT GIRL, NURIKO ...
WHY DID SHE GO AND *KISS* TAMAHOME LIKE THAT !?!
GRR GRR
CALM DOWN, MIAKA. THE ONLY WAY TO GET BACK TO MY OWN WORLD IS TO OBTAIN THE POWER OF SUZAKU. TO DO THAT, I GOTTA GATHER ALL SEVEN WARRIORS.
SO I'M GONNA HAVE TO MAKE *FRIENDS* WITH ALL SEVEN OF THEM.
I'LL START RIGHT AFTER I'M FINISHED DOING LAUN-DRY.
どたたたた

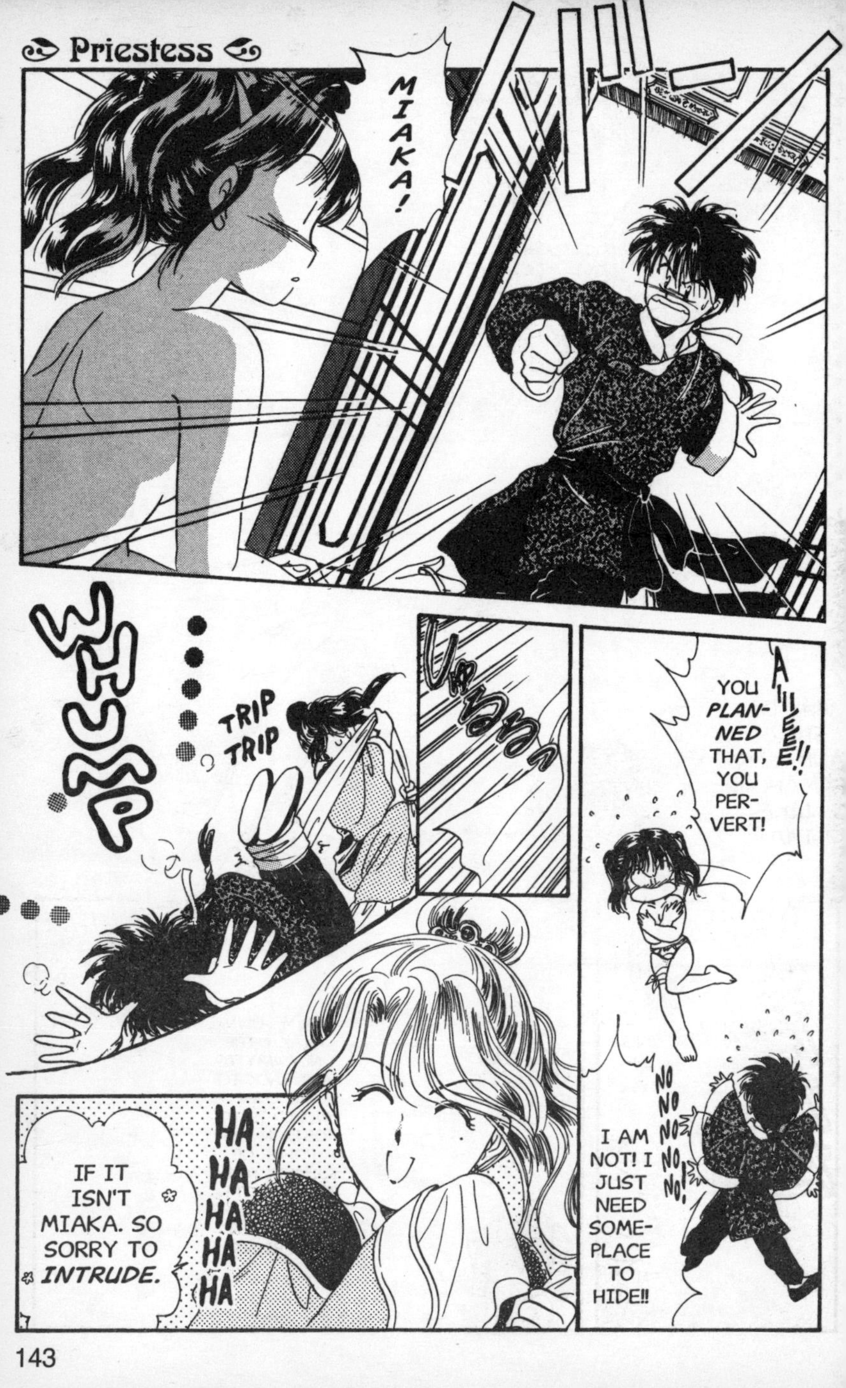
MIAKA!
WHUMP...
TRIP TRIP
AIIIEEE!!
YOU PLANNED THAT, YOU PERVERT!
NO NO NO NO NO NO!
I AM NOT! I JUST NEED SOMEPLACE TO HIDE!!
IF IT ISN'T MIAKA. SO SORRY TO INTRUDE.
HA HA HA HA HA HA

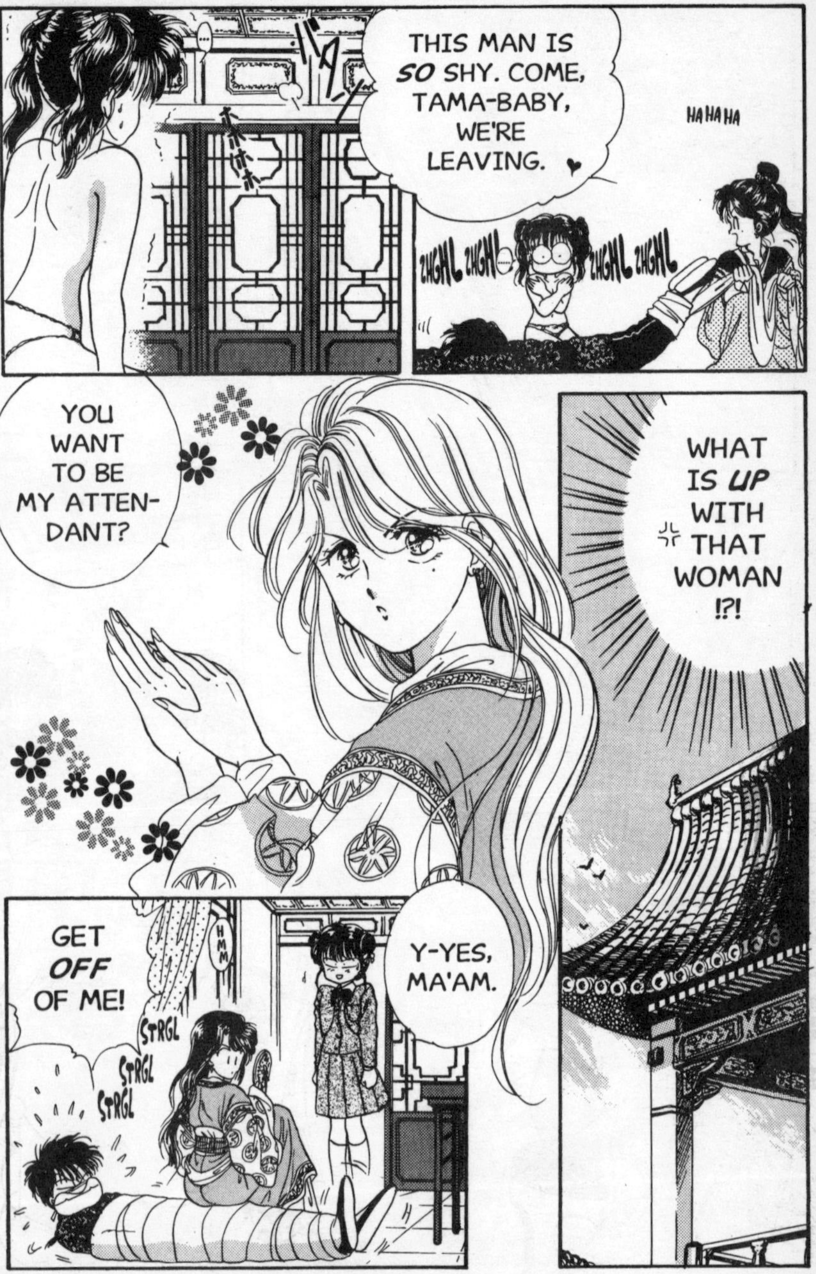
...
THIS MAN IS SO SHY. COME, TAMA-BABY, WE'RE LEAVING.
HA HA HA
ZHGHL ZHGHL
.....
ZHGHL ZHGHL
WHAT IS UP WITH THAT WOMAN !?!
YOU WANT TO BE MY ATTEN-DANT?
Y-YES, MA'AM.
GET OFF OF ME!
HMM
STRGL
STRGL
STRGL

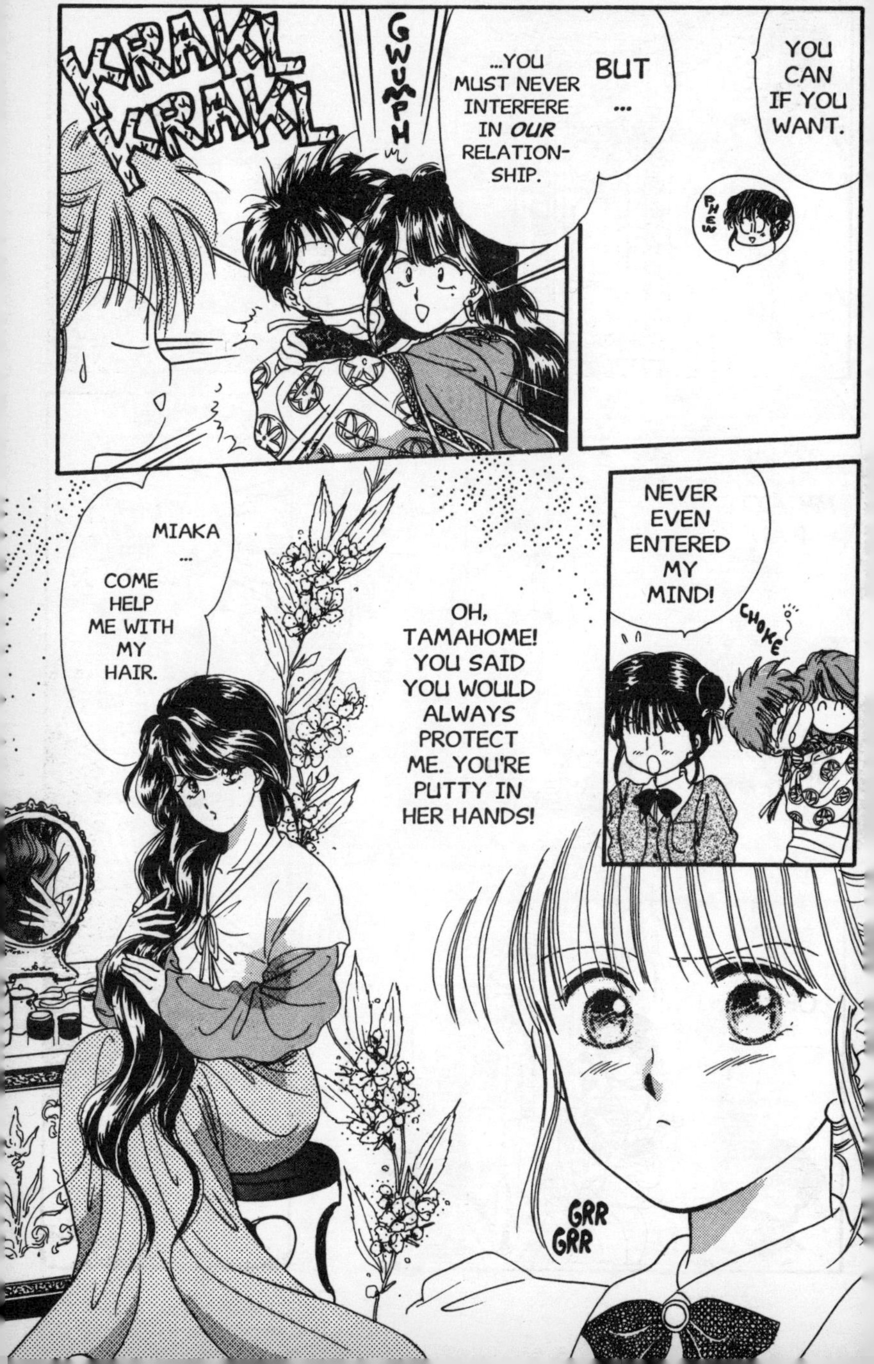
YOU CAN IF YOU WANT.
PHEW
BUT ...
...YOU MUST NEVER INTERFERE IN *OUR* RELATIONSHIP.
GWUMPH
KRAKL KRAKL
NEVER EVEN ENTERED MY MIND!
CHOKE
OH, TAMAHOME! YOU SAID YOU WOULD ALWAYS PROTECT ME. YOU'RE PUTTY IN HER HANDS!
MIAKA ... COME HELP ME WITH MY HAIR.
GRR GRR

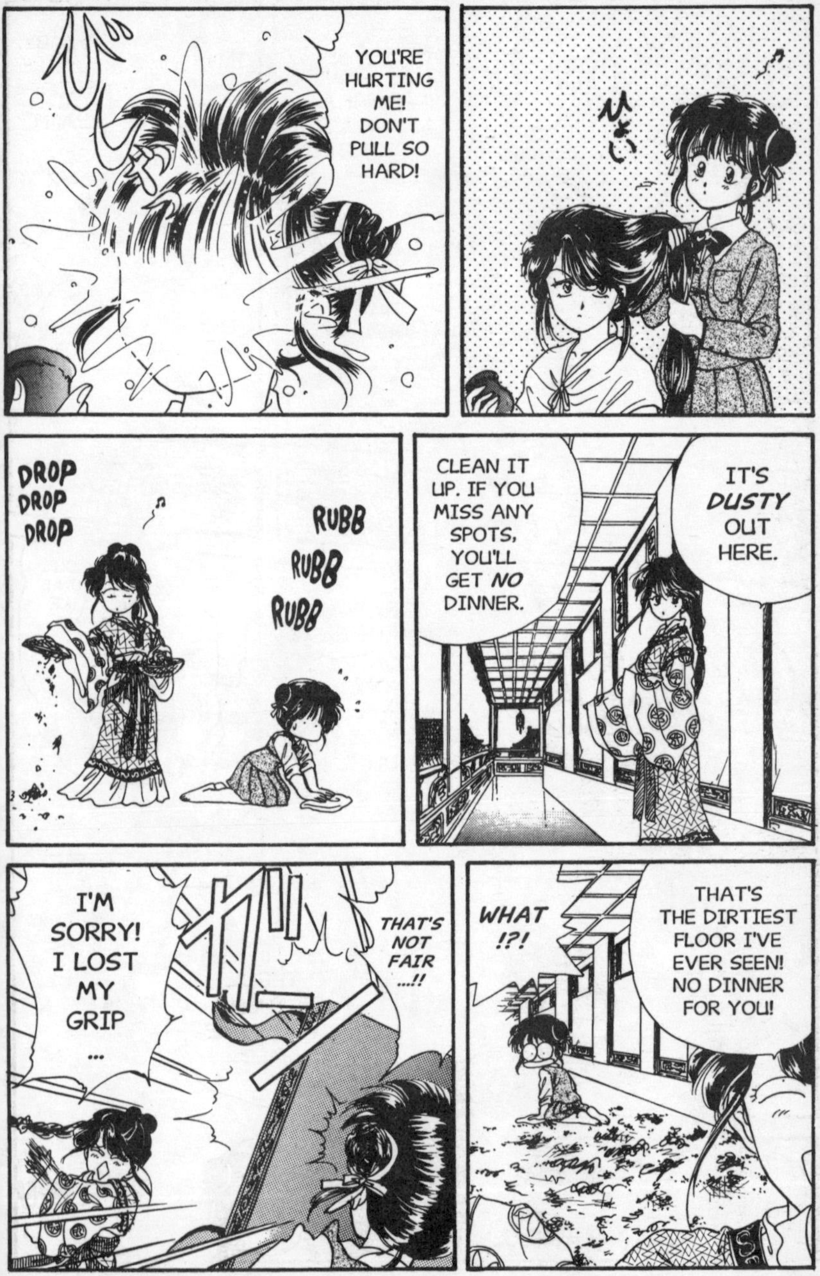

ひょい
YOU'RE HURTING ME! DON'T PULL SO HARD!
IT'S DUSTY OUT HERE.
CLEAN IT UP. IF YOU MISS ANY SPOTS, YOU'LL GET NO DINNER.
DROP DROP DROP
RUBB RUBB RUBB
THAT'S THE DIRTIEST FLOOR I'VE EVER SEEN! NO DINNER FOR YOU!
WHAT !?!
THAT'S NOT FAIR ...!!
I'M SORRY! I LOST MY GRIP ...

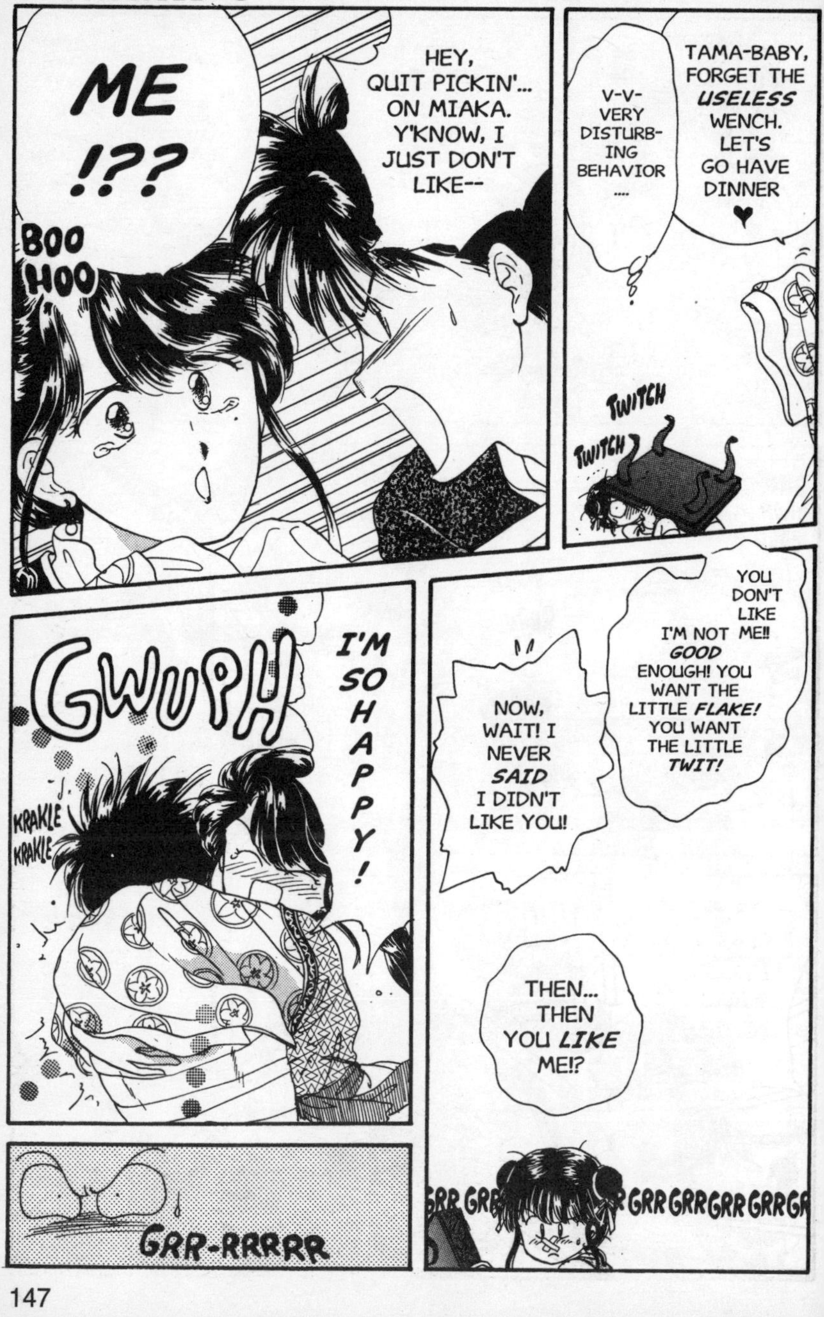
TAMA-BABY, FORGET THE *USELESS* WENCH. LET'S GO HAVE DINNER ♥
V-V-VERY DISTURBING BEHAVIOR ....
TWITCH
TWITCH
HEY, QUIT PICKIN'... ON MIAKA. Y'KNOW, I JUST DON'T LIKE--
ME !??
BOO HOO
YOU DON'T LIKE ME!! I'M NOT *GOOD* ENOUGH! YOU WANT THE LITTLE *FLAKE!* YOU WANT THE LITTLE *TWIT!*
NOW, WAIT! I NEVER *SAID* I DIDN'T LIKE YOU!
THEN... THEN YOU *LIKE* ME!?
GRR GRR GRR GRR GRR GRR GR
GWUPH
I'M SO HAPPY!
KRAKLE KRAKLE
GRR-RRRRR

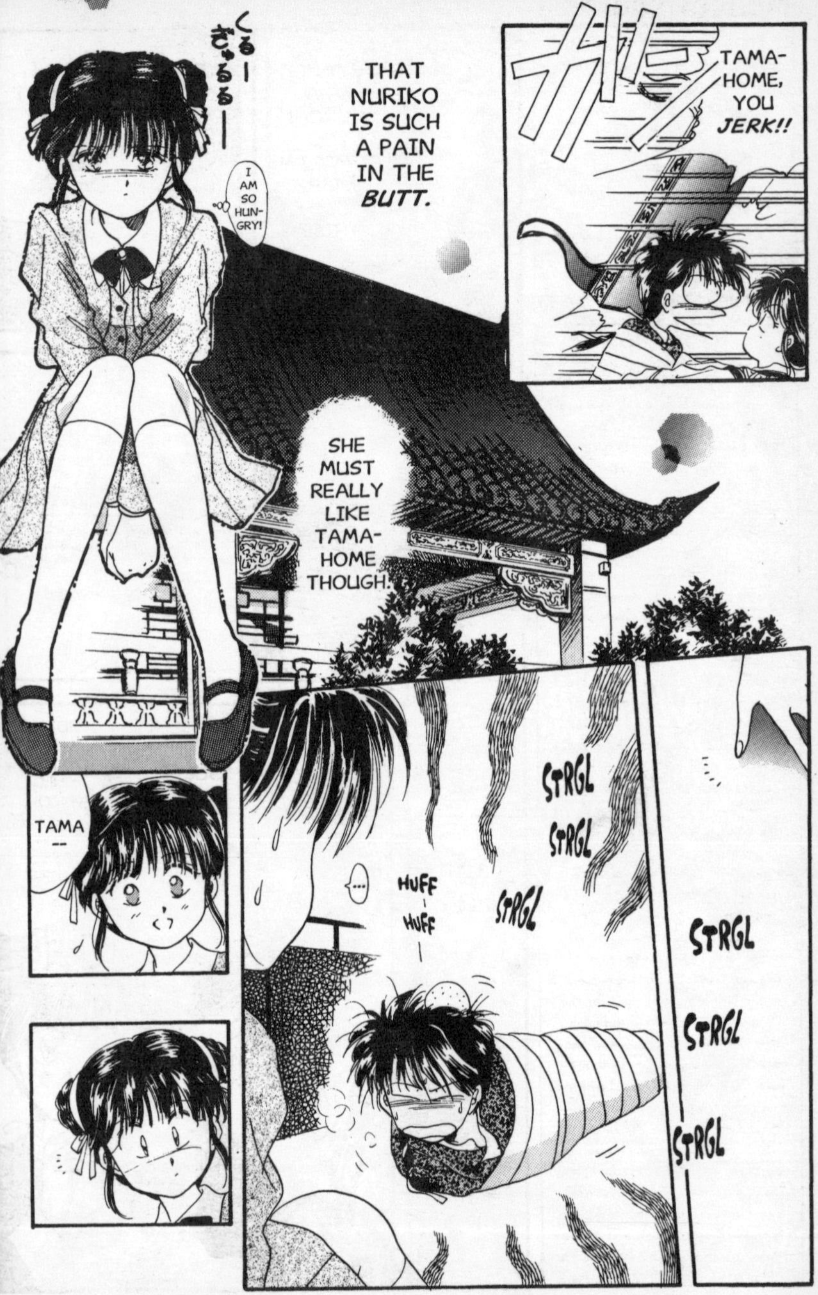
TAMA-HOME, YOU JERK!!
THAT NURIKO IS SUCH A PAIN IN THE BUTT.
くるーぎゅるる—
I AM SO HUNGRY!
SHE MUST REALLY LIKE TAMA-HOME THOUGH.
...
STRGL
STRGL
STRGL
STRGL
STRGL
STRGL
STRGL
HUFF HUFF
...
TAMA --

So I was reading some fan mail informing me that "Prepubescence" was voted second place in the top 20 manga poll of an anime magazine in Taiwan (I think). Can it really be true? A friend in the bookstore business told me that it was ranked in the top 10, 20, 30, or something. I dunno what it was, but I'm just happy to be ranked! Sniff! sniff! Thank you everyone, so much! I received some fan mail from Taiwan, from a 15-year-old named Li. So I have readers abroad! A girl who was half Chinese and half Japanese wrote me when I was working on "Treasure of the Heart," Yui Len (I could have the wrong spelling), and she's studying martial arts with a real master. That's awesome! Her name is so cute, I'll have to use it in a future manga. I once got a letter from someone who's half British/half Japanese... very international. I have to admit I'm a little nervous about having native Chinese reading "Fushigi Yûgi." Oh, and thanks so much for the tapes. I'm changing the subject. I listen to them all! There's B'z, TMN, Ranma soundtracks, recorded letters, Lodoss soundtracks, etc. Oh, when I mentioned COCO in "Prepubescence," I had lots of people writing back! They're really popular! A special thanks to the people who made compilation tapes of COCO songs dedicated to scenes in "Prepubescence." They were great! It's true that "Your Song, My Song" is really appropriate as Manato's song right around the "to live in the present" scene. "Melody" is perfect for the scene where Asuka is hiding in the rain, watching Manato. The best song though is "Circus Game"!! I was thinking how much I wanted it to be the theme song! But I found out that the "No Interest in Prepubescence" CD is coming out!! I'm on it too, so please listen to it. For those who are just now being introduced to my work, "No Interest in Prepubescence" is a three-volume comic. Check it out!! ♥

But why wasn't the COCO tune "Why?" On the tape. "Why?" Oh, I get it, just so I'd make a silly pun.

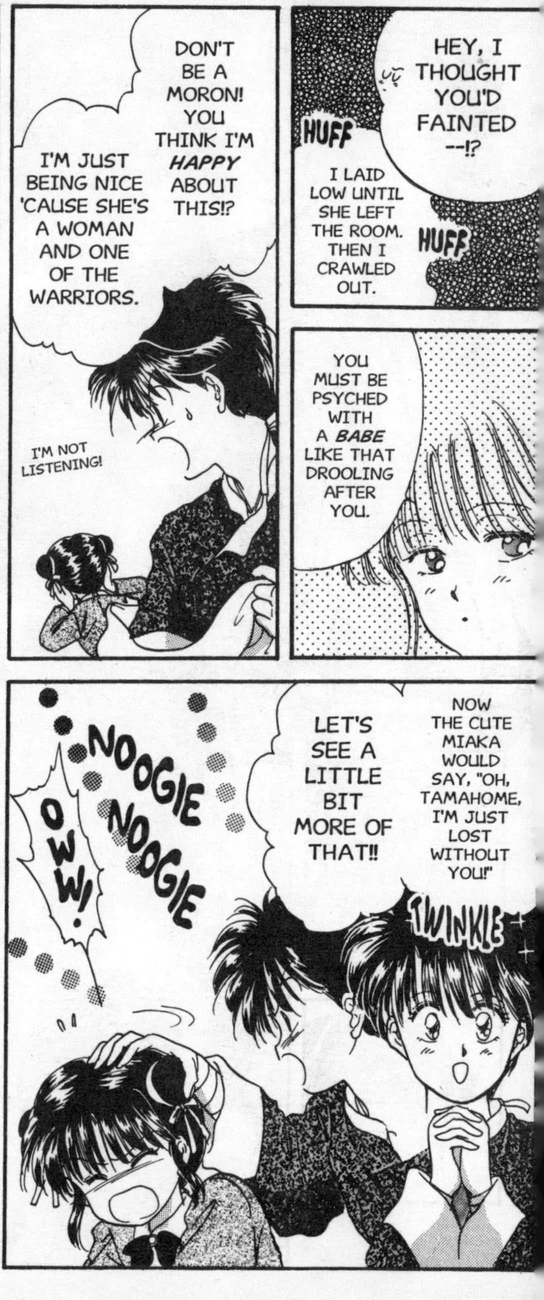
HEY, I THOUGHT YOU'D FAINTED--!?
HUFF
I LAID LOW UNTIL SHE LEFT THE ROOM. THEN I CRAWLED OUT.
HUFF
DON'T BE A MORON! YOU THINK I'M *HAPPY* ABOUT THIS!?
I'M JUST BEING NICE 'CAUSE SHE'S A WOMAN AND ONE OF THE WARRIORS.
I'M NOT LISTENING!
YOU MUST BE PSYCHED WITH A *BABE* LIKE THAT DROOLING AFTER YOU.
NOW THE CUTE MIAKA WOULD SAY, "OH, TAMAHOME, I'M JUST LOST WITHOUT YOU!"
LET'S SEE A LITTLE BIT MORE OF THAT!!
TWINKLE
NOOGIE NOOGIE
OWW!

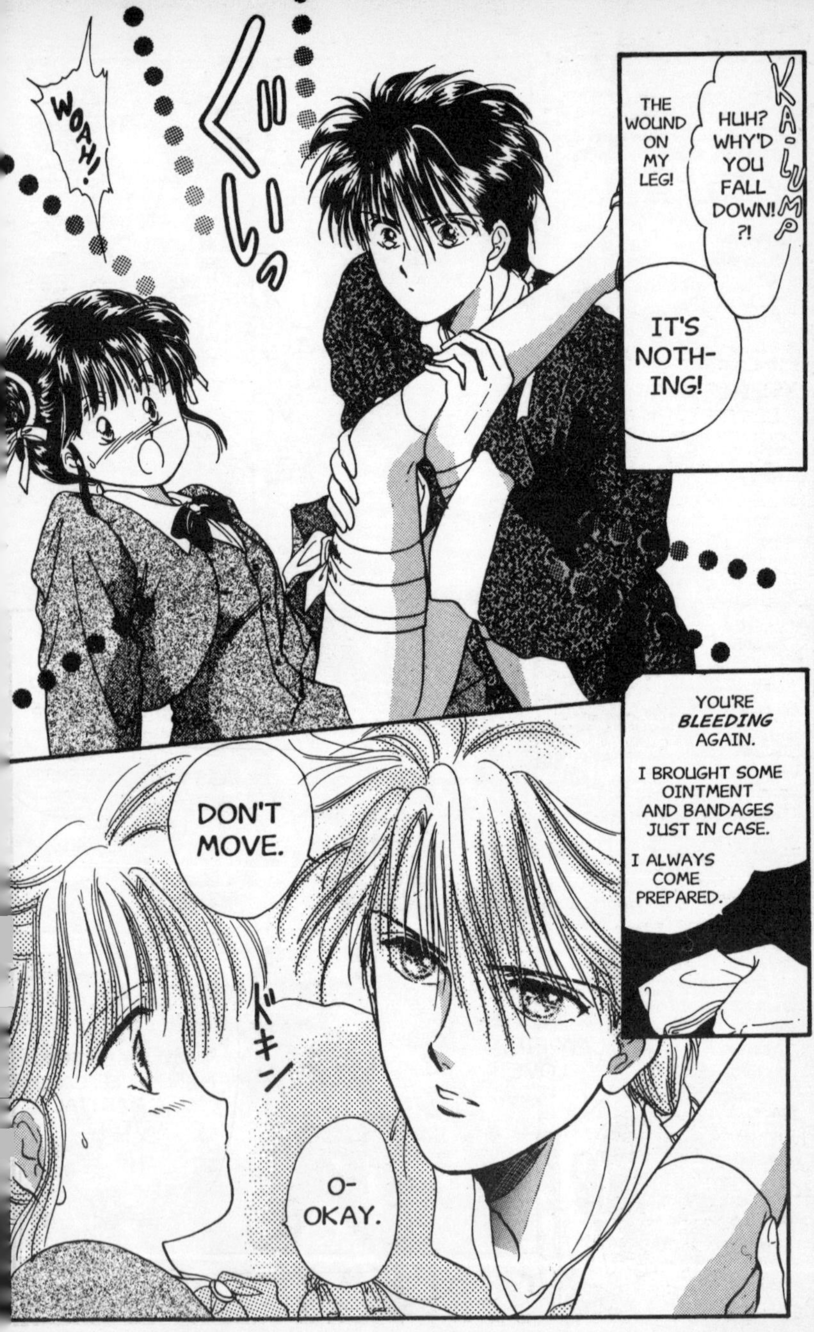

KALUMP
HUH? WHY'D YOU FALL DOWN!?!
THE WOUND ON MY LEG!
IT'S NOTHING!
WOAH!
YOU'RE *BLEEDING* AGAIN.
I BROUGHT SOME OINTMENT AND BANDAGES JUST IN CASE.
I ALWAYS COME PREPARED.
DON'T MOVE.
ドキン
O-OKAY.

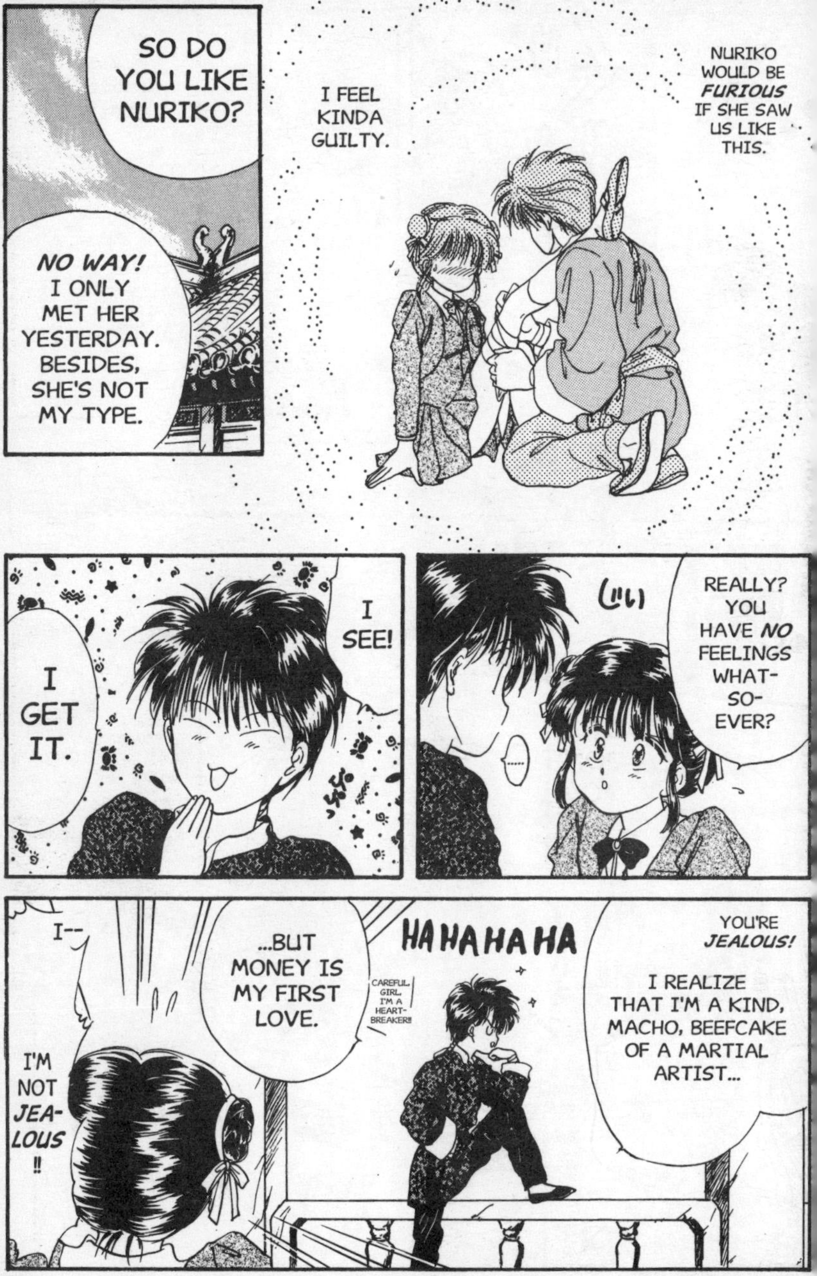
SO DO YOU LIKE NURIKO?
NO WAY! I ONLY MET HER YESTERDAY. BESIDES, SHE'S NOT MY TYPE.
I FEEL KINDA GUILTY.
NURIKO WOULD BE FURIOUS IF SHE SAW US LIKE THIS.
I GET IT.
I SEE!
REALLY? YOU HAVE NO FEELINGS WHAT-SO-EVER?
......
YOU'RE JEALOUS!
I REALIZE THAT I'M A KIND, MACHO, BEEFCAKE OF A MARTIAL ARTIST...
HAHAHAHA
CAREFUL, GIRL, I'M A HEART-BREAKER!!
...BUT MONEY IS MY FIRST LOVE.
I--
I'M NOT JEA-LOUS!!

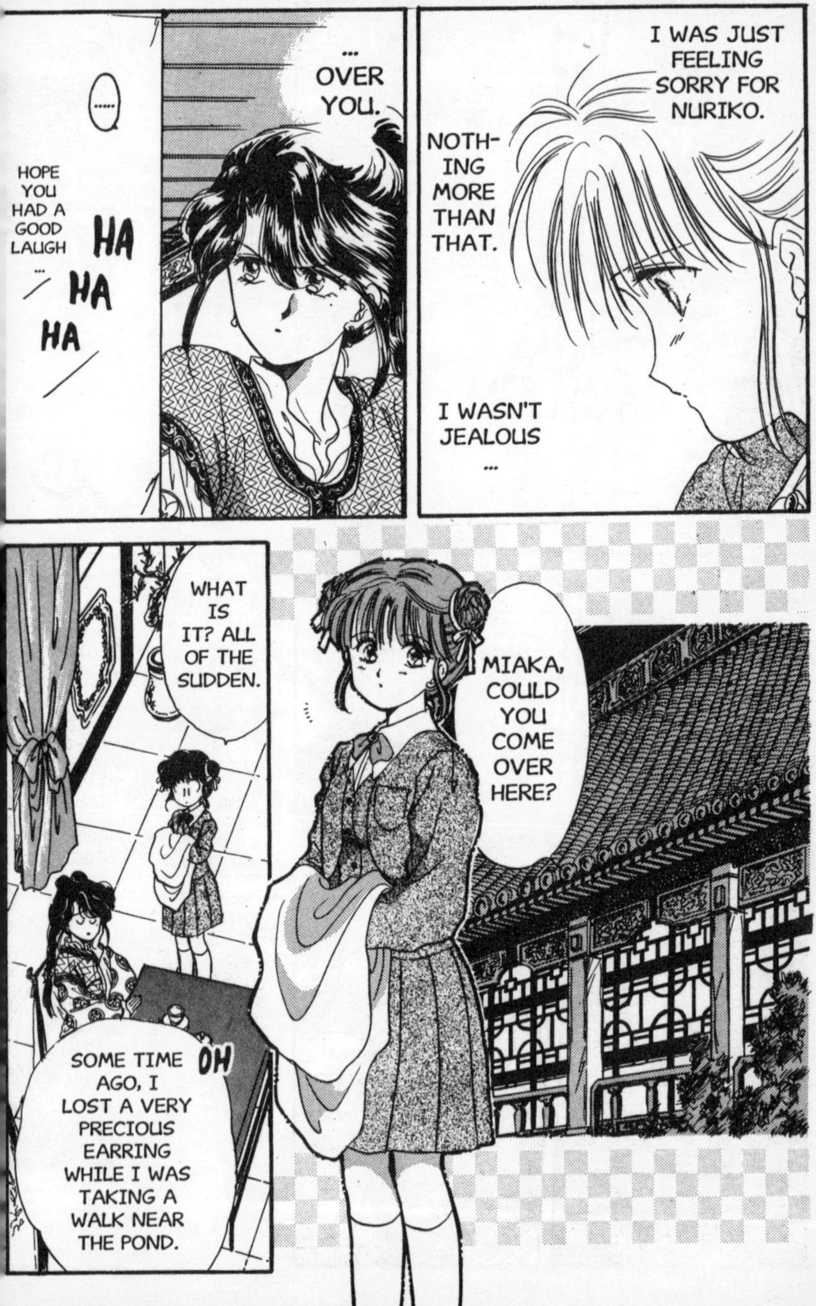
I WAS JUST FEELING SORRY FOR NURIKO.
NOTH-ING MORE THAN THAT.
I WASN'T JEALOUS ...
... OVER YOU.
......
HOPE YOU HAD A GOOD LAUGH ...
HA HA HA
MIAKA, COULD YOU COME OVER HERE?
WHAT IS IT? ALL OF THE SUDDEN.
OH
SOME TIME AGO, I LOST A VERY PRECIOUS EARRING WHILE I WAS TAKING A WALK NEAR THE POND.

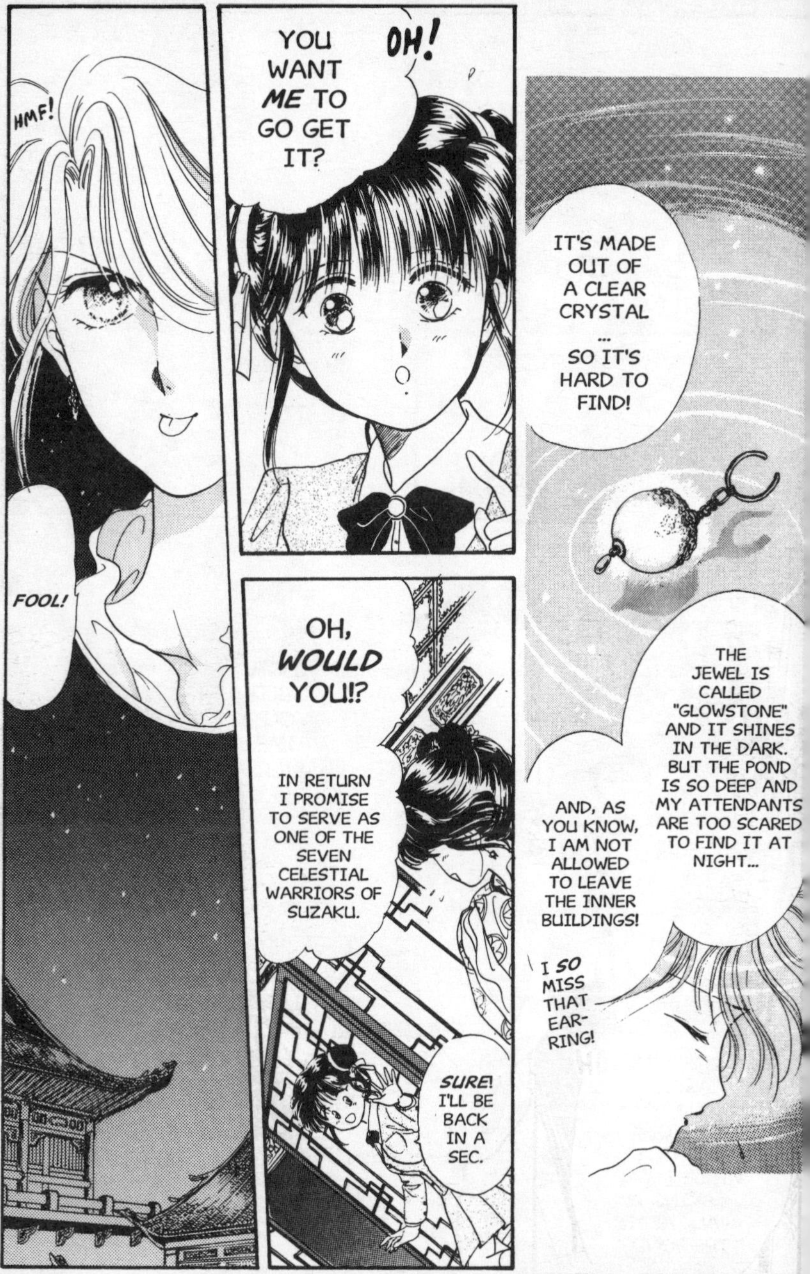
THE JEWEL IS CALLED "GLOWSTONE" AND IT SHINES IN THE DARK. BUT THE POND IS SO DEEP AND MY ATTENDANTS ARE TOO SCARED TO FIND IT AT NIGHT...
AND, AS YOU KNOW, I AM NOT ALLOWED TO LEAVE THE INNER BUILDINGS!
I SO MISS THAT EAR-RING!
IT'S MADE OUT OF A CLEAR CRYSTAL ... SO IT'S HARD TO FIND!
YOU WANT ME TO GO GET IT?
OH!
OH, WOULD YOU!?
IN RETURN I PROMISE TO SERVE AS ONE OF THE SEVEN CELESTIAL WARRIORS OF SUZAKU.
SURE! I'LL BE BACK IN A SEC.
HMF!
FOOL!

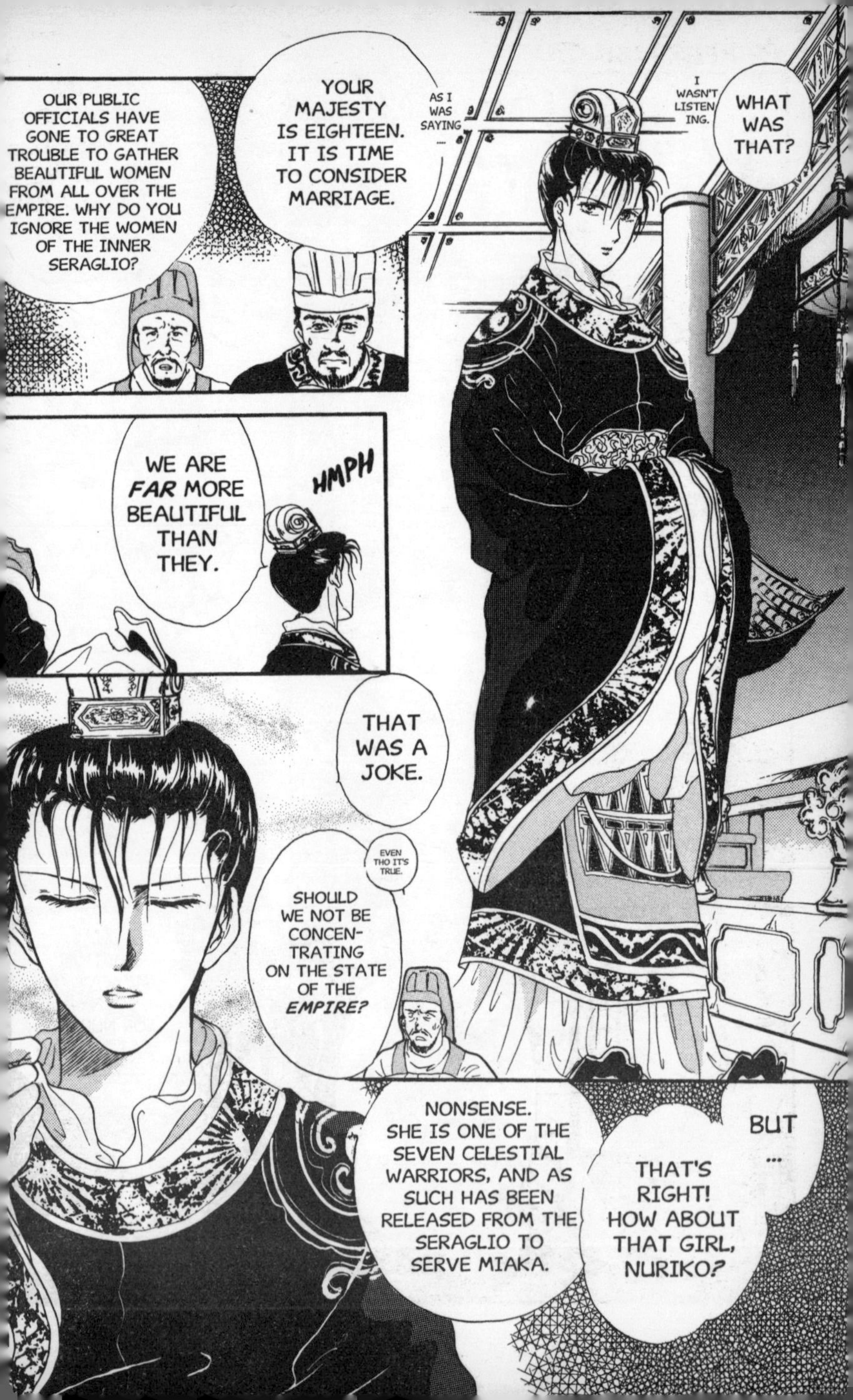
OUR PUBLIC OFFICIALS HAVE GONE TO GREAT TROUBLE TO GATHER BEAUTIFUL WOMEN FROM ALL OVER THE EMPIRE. WHY DO YOU IGNORE THE WOMEN OF THE INNER SERAGLIO?
WHAT WAS THAT?
I WASN'T LISTEN ING.
YOUR MAJESTY IS EIGHTEEN. IT IS TIME TO CONSIDER MARRIAGE.
AS I WAS SAYING ...
WE ARE *FAR* MORE BEAUTIFUL THAN THEY.
HMPH
THAT WAS A JOKE.
EVEN THO IT'S TRUE.
SHOULD WE NOT BE CONCEN-TRATING ON THE STATE OF THE *EMPIRE?*
BUT ...
THAT'S RIGHT! HOW ABOUT THAT GIRL, NURIKO?
NONSENSE. SHE IS ONE OF THE SEVEN CELESTIAL WARRIORS, AND AS SUCH HAS BEEN RELEASED FROM THE SERAGLIO TO SERVE MIAKA.

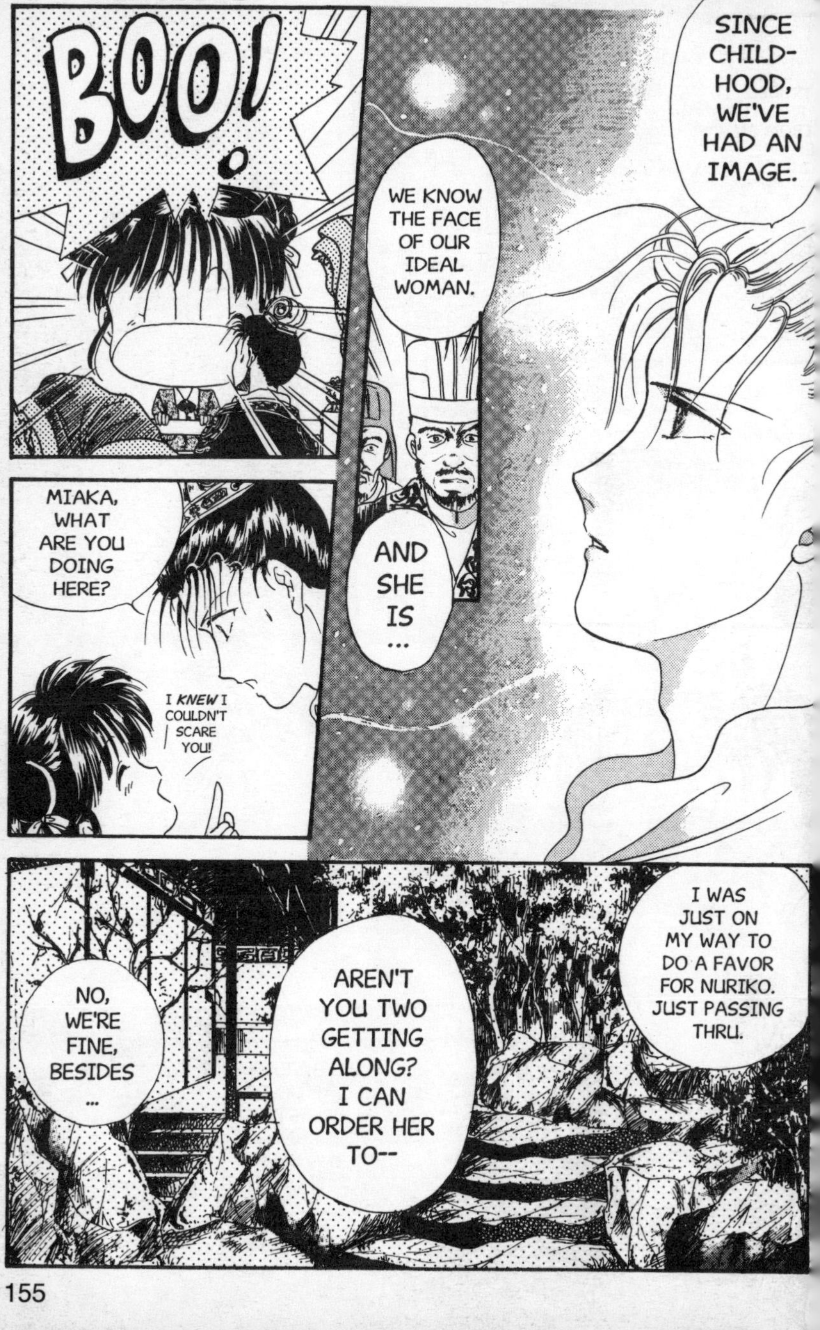
SINCE CHILDHOOD, WE'VE HAD AN IMAGE.
WE KNOW THE FACE OF OUR IDEAL WOMAN.
AND SHE IS ...
BOO!
MIAKA, WHAT ARE YOU DOING HERE?
I *KNEW* I COULDN'T SCARE YOU!
I WAS JUST ON MY WAY TO DO A FAVOR FOR NURIKO. JUST PASSING THRU.
AREN'T YOU TWO GETTING ALONG? I CAN ORDER HER TO--
NO, WE'RE FINE, BESIDES ...

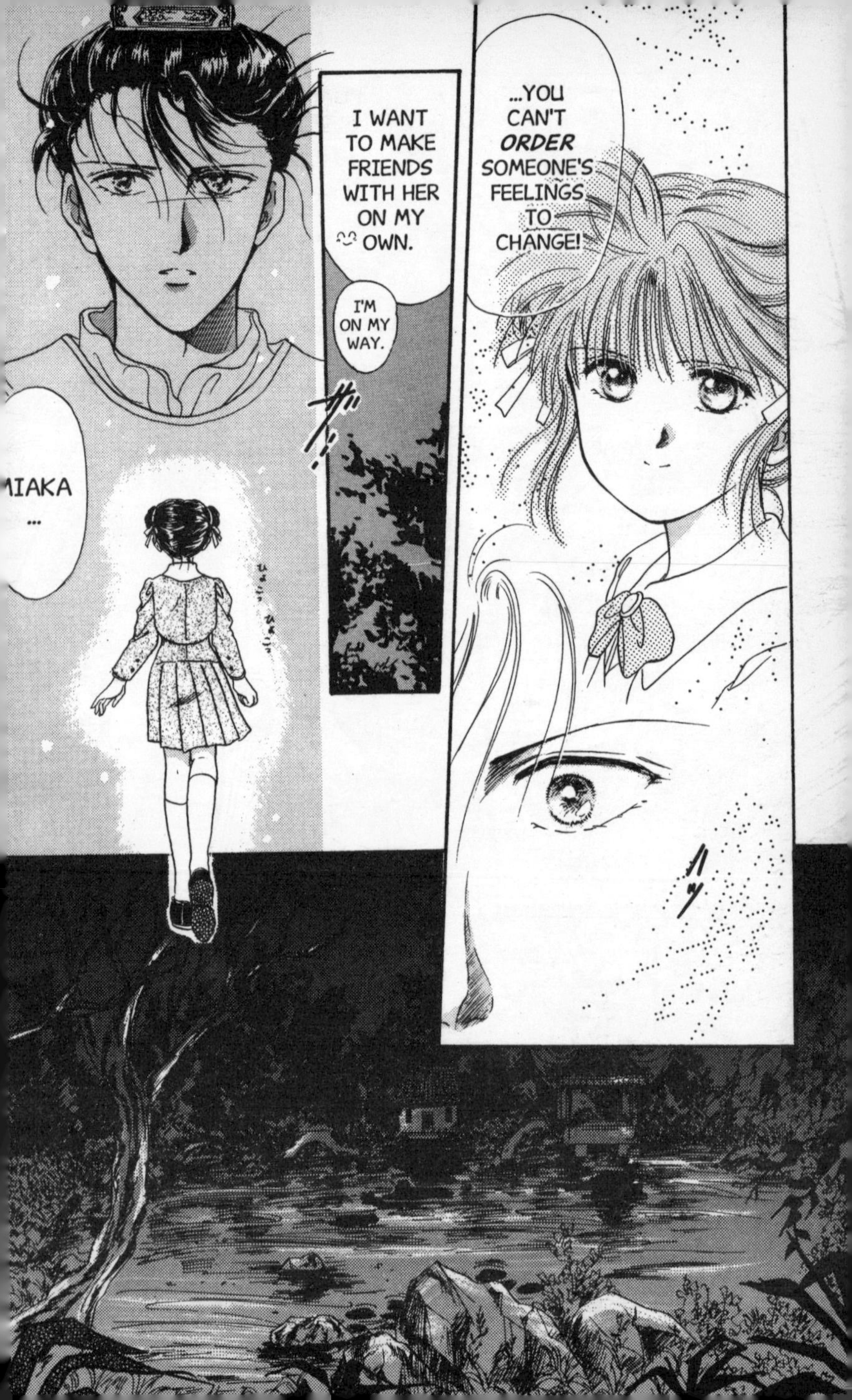
...YOU CAN'T ORDER SOMEONE'S FEELINGS TO CHANGE!
I WANT TO MAKE FRIENDS WITH HER ON MY OWN.
I'M ON MY WAY.
MIAKA ...

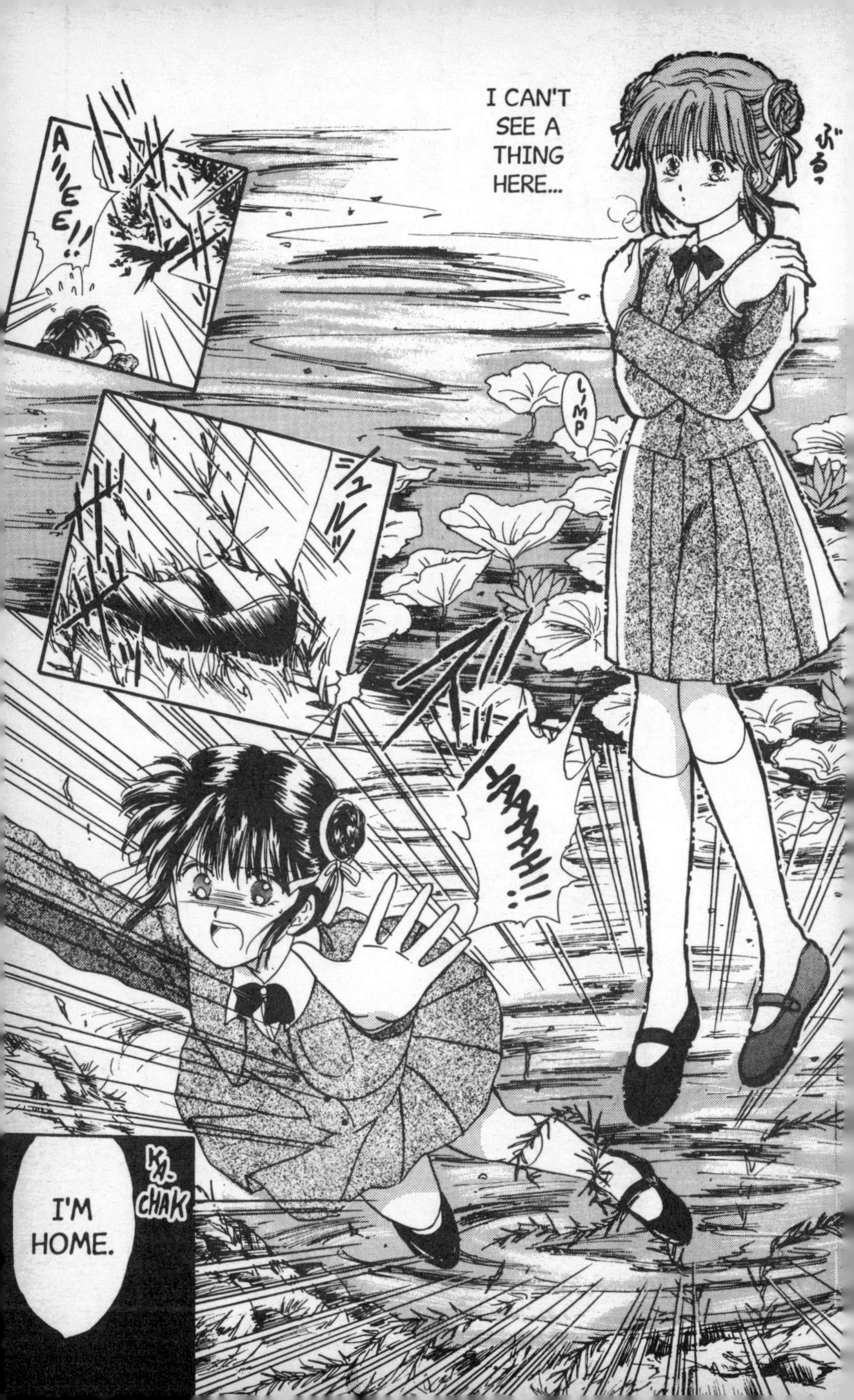

ぶるっ
I CAN'T SEE A THING HERE...
LIMP
AEE!!
シュルッ
YAAAAH!!!
KA-CHAK
I'M HOME.

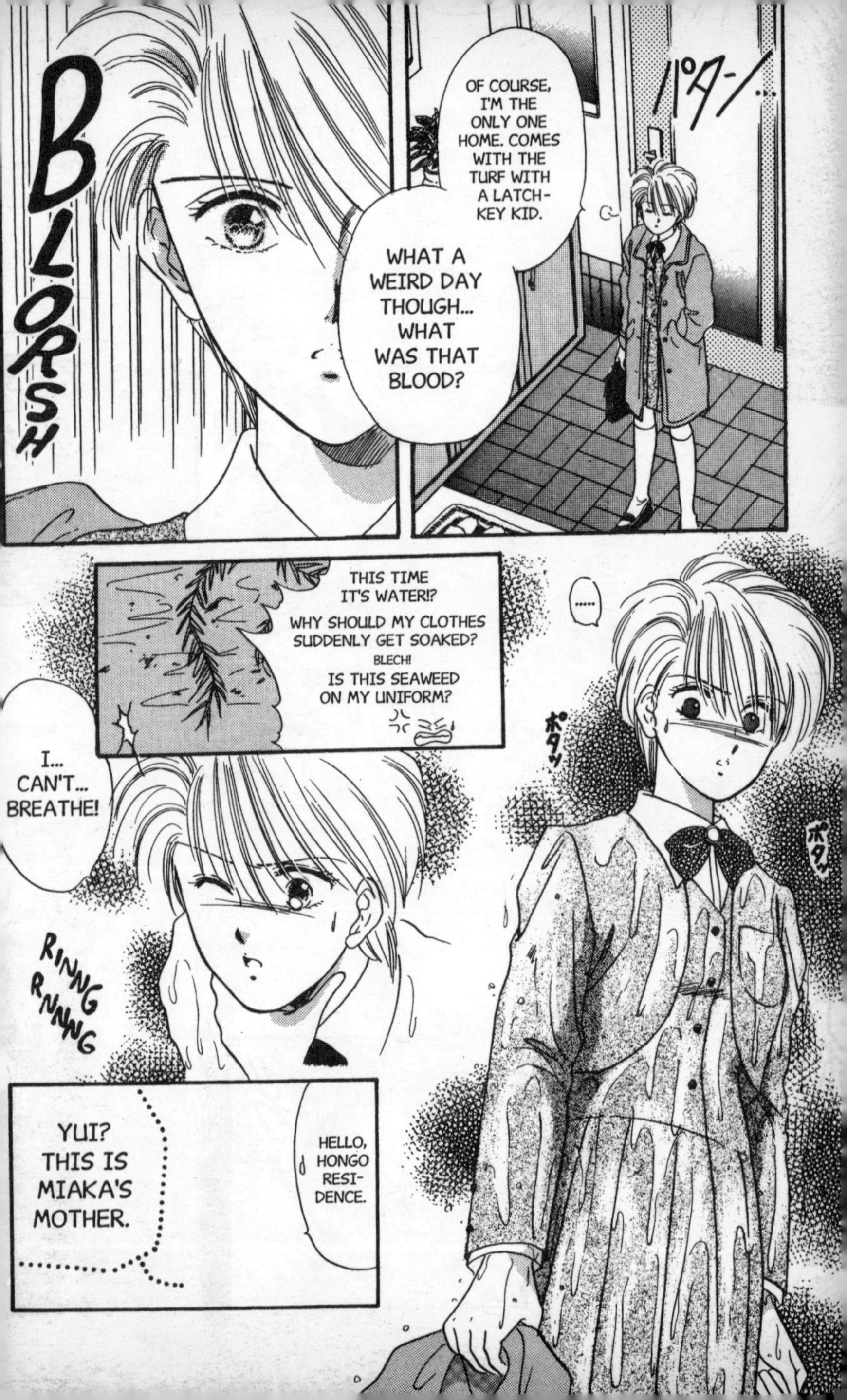
パターン…
OF COURSE, I'M THE ONLY ONE HOME. COMES WITH THE TURF WITH A LATCH-KEY KID.
WHAT A WEIRD DAY THOUGH... WHAT WAS THAT BLOOD?
BLORSH
......
THIS TIME IT'S WATER!?
WHY SHOULD MY CLOTHES SUDDENLY GET SOAKED?
BLECH!
IS THIS SEAWEED ON MY UNIFORM?
I... CAN'T... BREATHE!
RINNG RNNNG
HELLO, HONGO RESI-DENCE.
YUI? THIS IS MIAKA'S MOTHER.

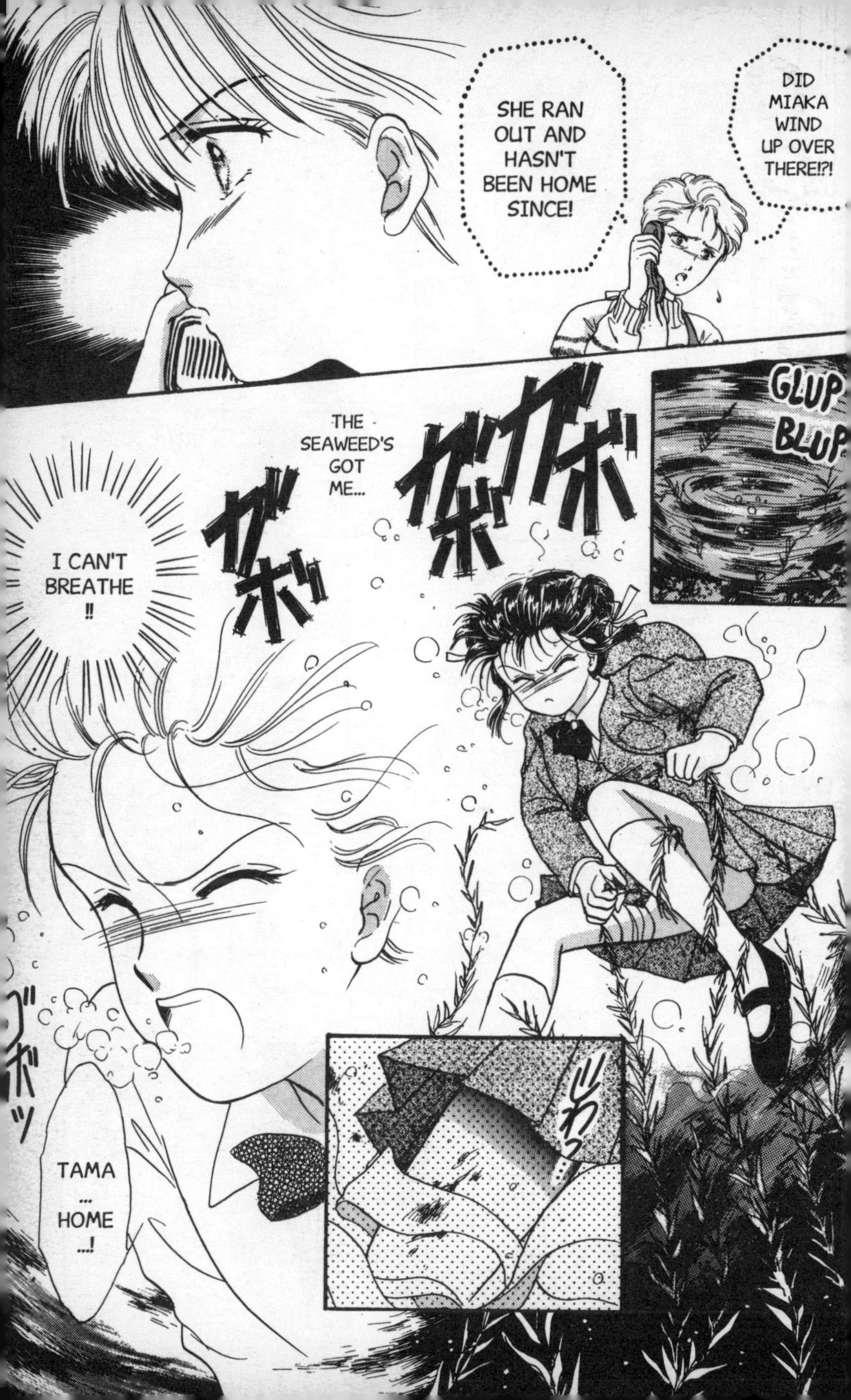

DID MIAKA WIND UP OVER THERE!?!
SHE RAN OUT AND HASN'T BEEN HOME SINCE!
GLUP BLUP
ガボガボ
THE SEAWEED'S GOT ME...
ガボッ
I CAN'T BREATHE!!
じわっ
ゴボッ
TAMA ... HOME ...!

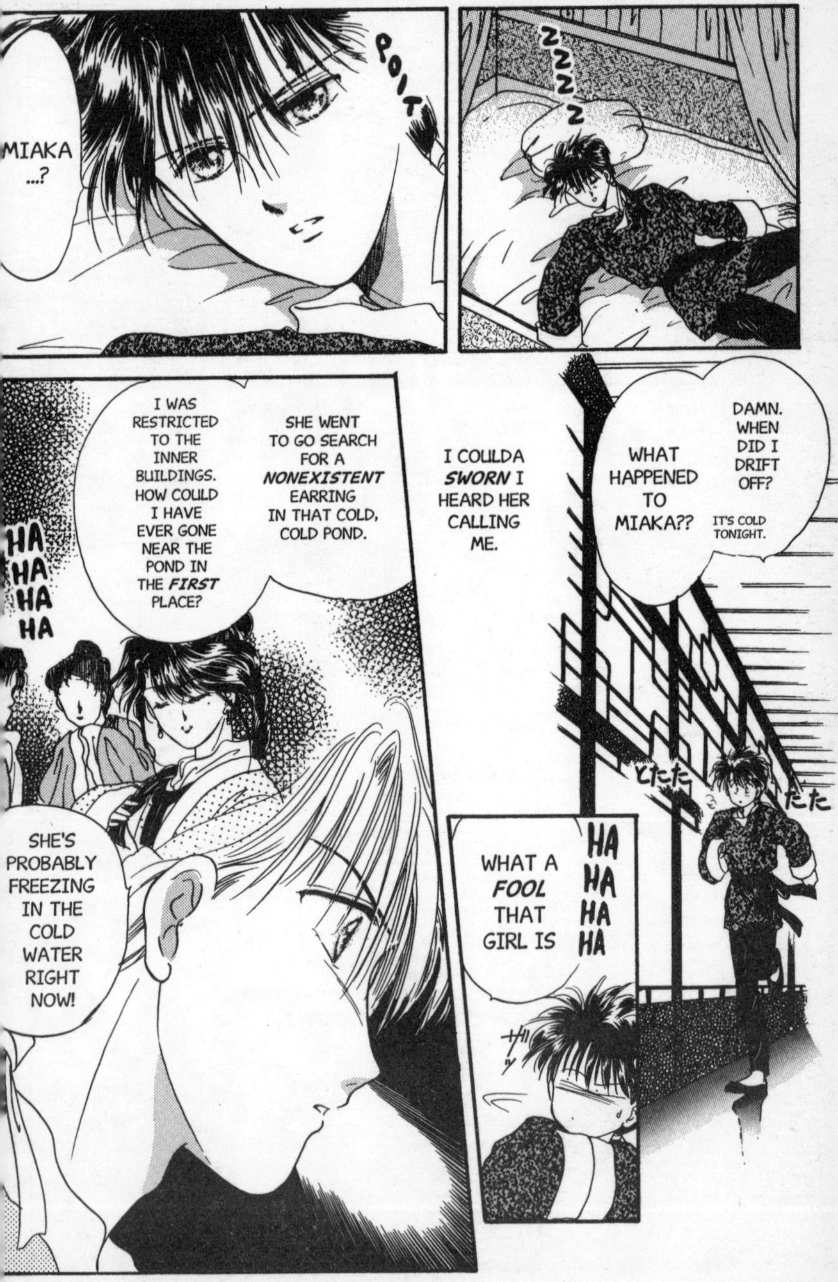
ZZZZ
POIT
MIAKA ...?
DAMN. WHEN DID I DRIFT OFF?
IT'S COLD TONIGHT.
WHAT HAPPENED TO MIAKA??
I COULDA SWORN I HEARD HER CALLING ME.
たた
とたた
SHE WENT TO GO SEARCH FOR A NONEXISTENT EARRING IN THAT COLD, COLD POND.
I WAS RESTRICTED TO THE INNER BUILDINGS. HOW COULD I HAVE EVER GONE NEAR THE POND IN THE FIRST PLACE?
HA HA HA HA
SHE'S PROBABLY FREEZING IN THE COLD WATER RIGHT NOW!
HA HA HA HA
WHAT A FOOL THAT GIRL IS

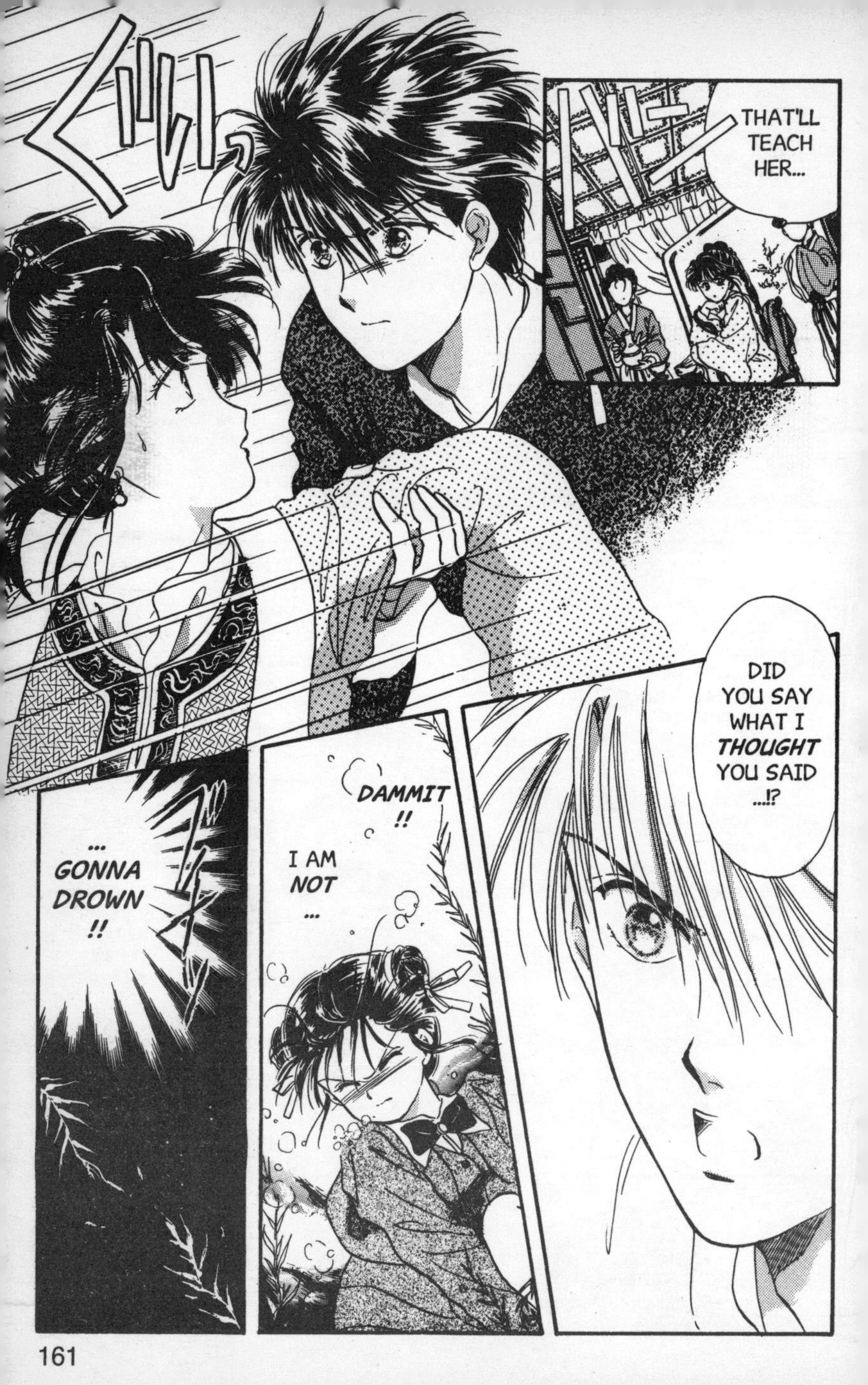
THAT'LL TEACH HER...
DID YOU SAY WHAT I *THOUGHT* YOU SAID ...!?
DAMMIT !!
I AM *NOT* ...
... GONNA DROWN !!

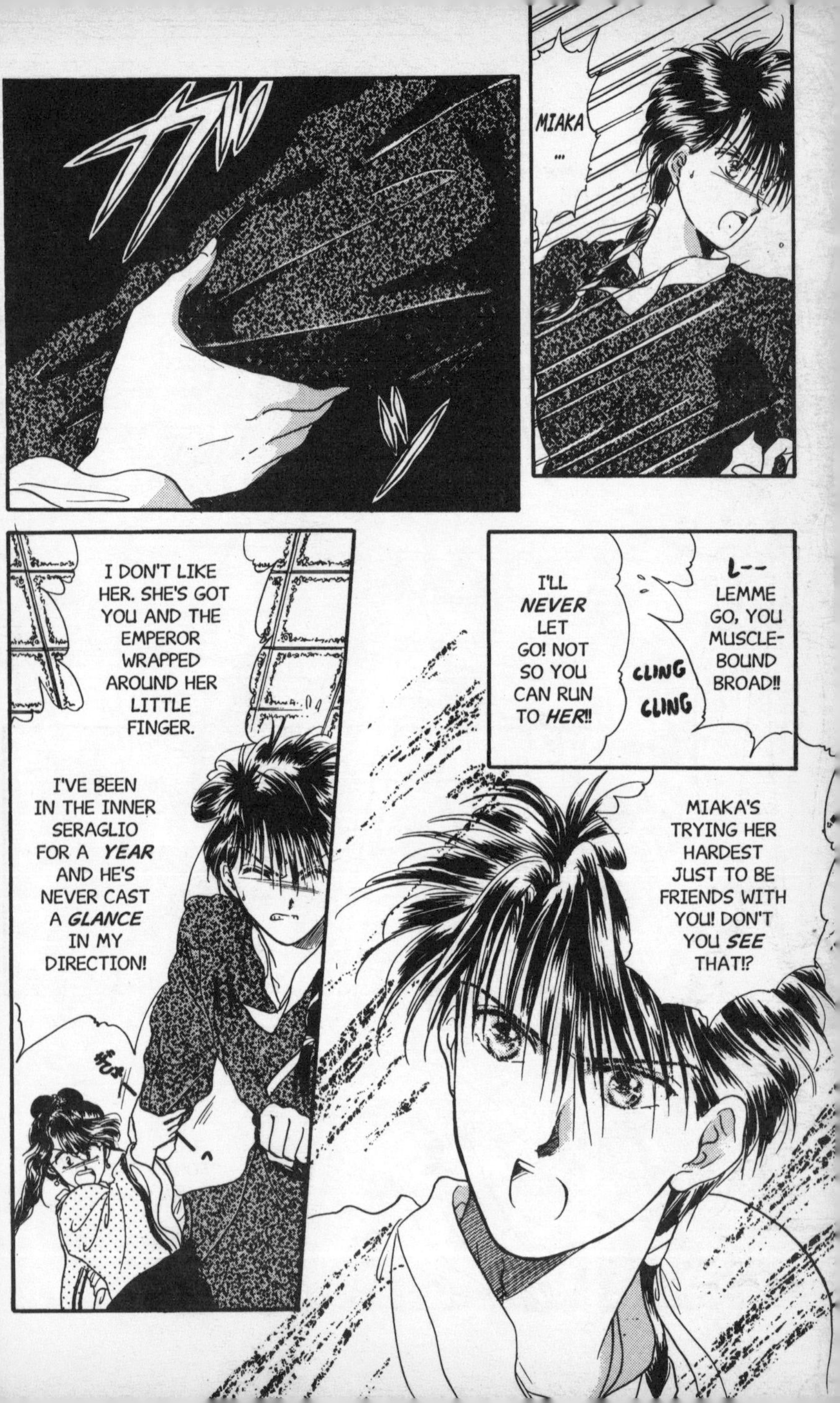

MIAKA ...
L-- LEMME GO, YOU MUSCLE-BOUND BROAD!!
CLING
CLING
I'LL *NEVER* LET GO! NOT SO YOU CAN RUN TO *HER*!!
I DON'T LIKE HER. SHE'S GOT YOU AND THE EMPEROR WRAPPED AROUND HER LITTLE FINGER.
I'VE BEEN IN THE INNER SERAGLIO FOR A *YEAR* AND HE'S NEVER CAST A *GLANCE* IN MY DIRECTION!
MIAKA'S TRYING HER HARDEST JUST TO BE FRIENDS WITH YOU! DON'T YOU *SEE* THAT!?

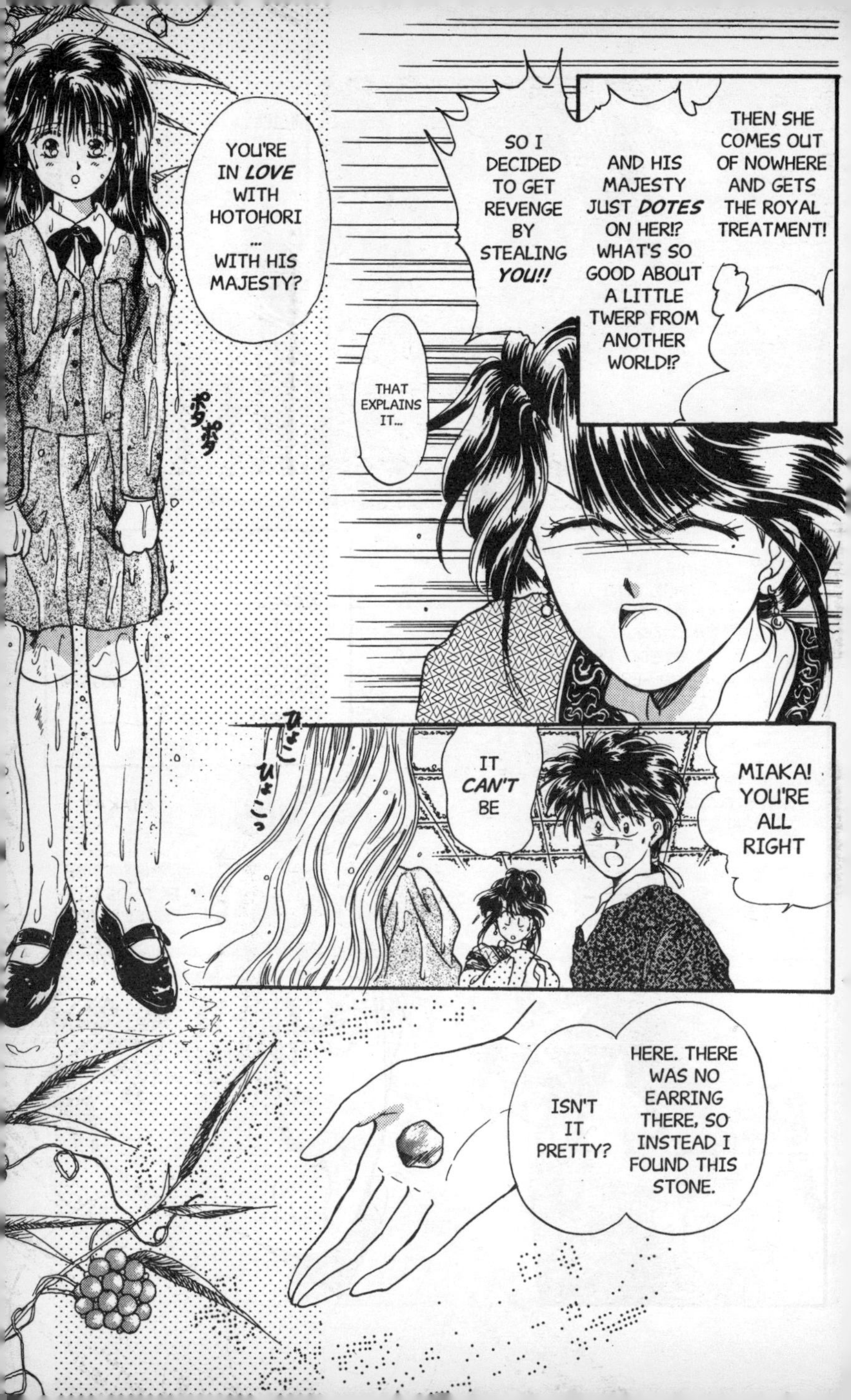

THEN SHE COMES OUT OF NOWHERE AND GETS THE ROYAL TREATMENT!
AND HIS MAJESTY JUST *DOTES* ON HER!? WHAT'S SO GOOD ABOUT A LITTLE TWERP FROM ANOTHER WORLD!?
SO I DECIDED TO GET REVENGE BY STEALING *YOU!!*
THAT EXPLAINS IT...
YOU'RE IN *LOVE* WITH HOTOHORI ... WITH HIS MAJESTY?
MIAKA! YOU'RE ALL RIGHT
IT *CAN'T* BE
HERE. THERE WAS NO EARRING THERE, SO INSTEAD I FOUND THIS STONE.
ISN'T IT PRETTY?

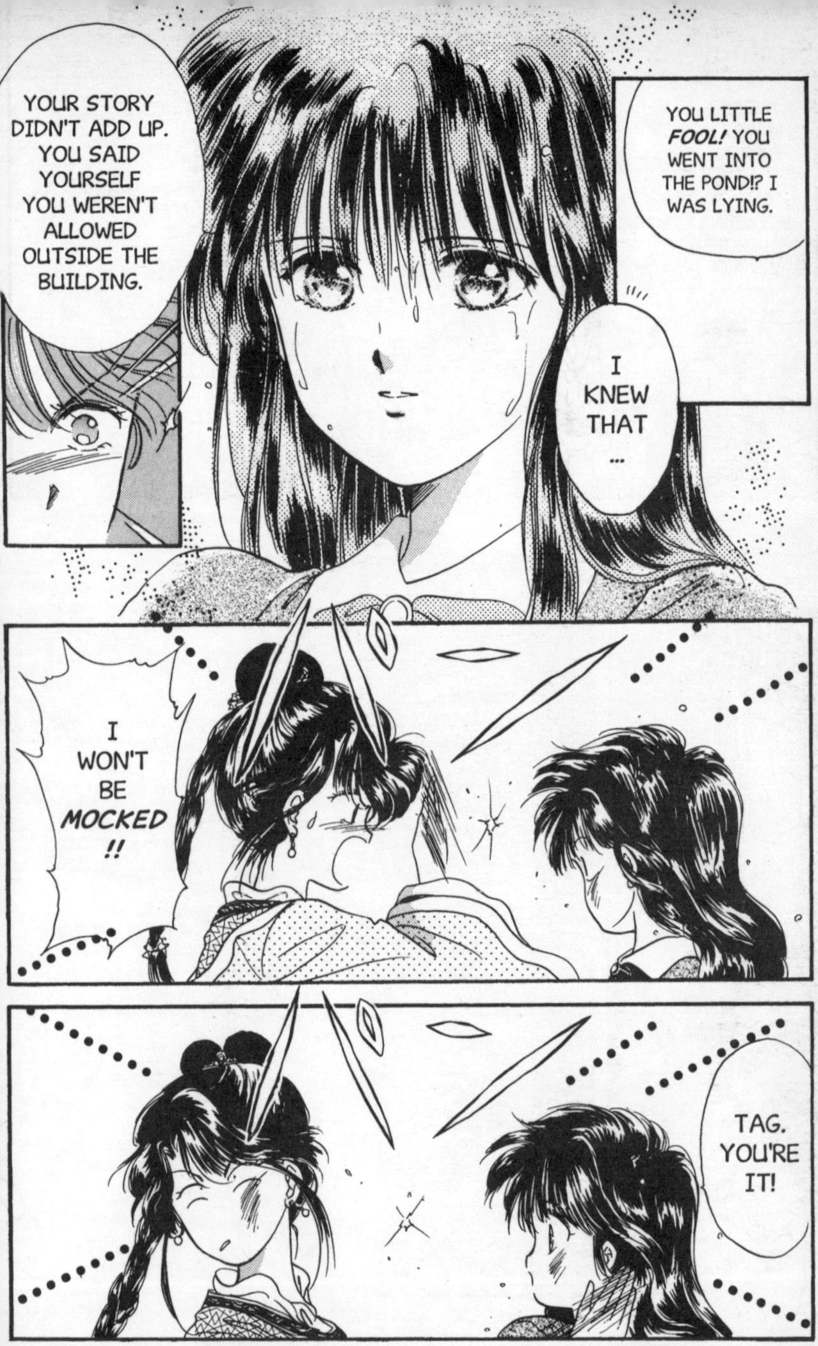
YOU LITTLE *FOOL!* YOU WENT INTO THE POND!? I WAS LYING.
I KNEW THAT ...
YOUR STORY DIDN'T ADD UP. YOU SAID YOURSELF YOU WEREN'T ALLOWED OUTSIDE THE BUILDING.
I WON'T BE *MOCKED* !!
TAG. YOU'RE IT!

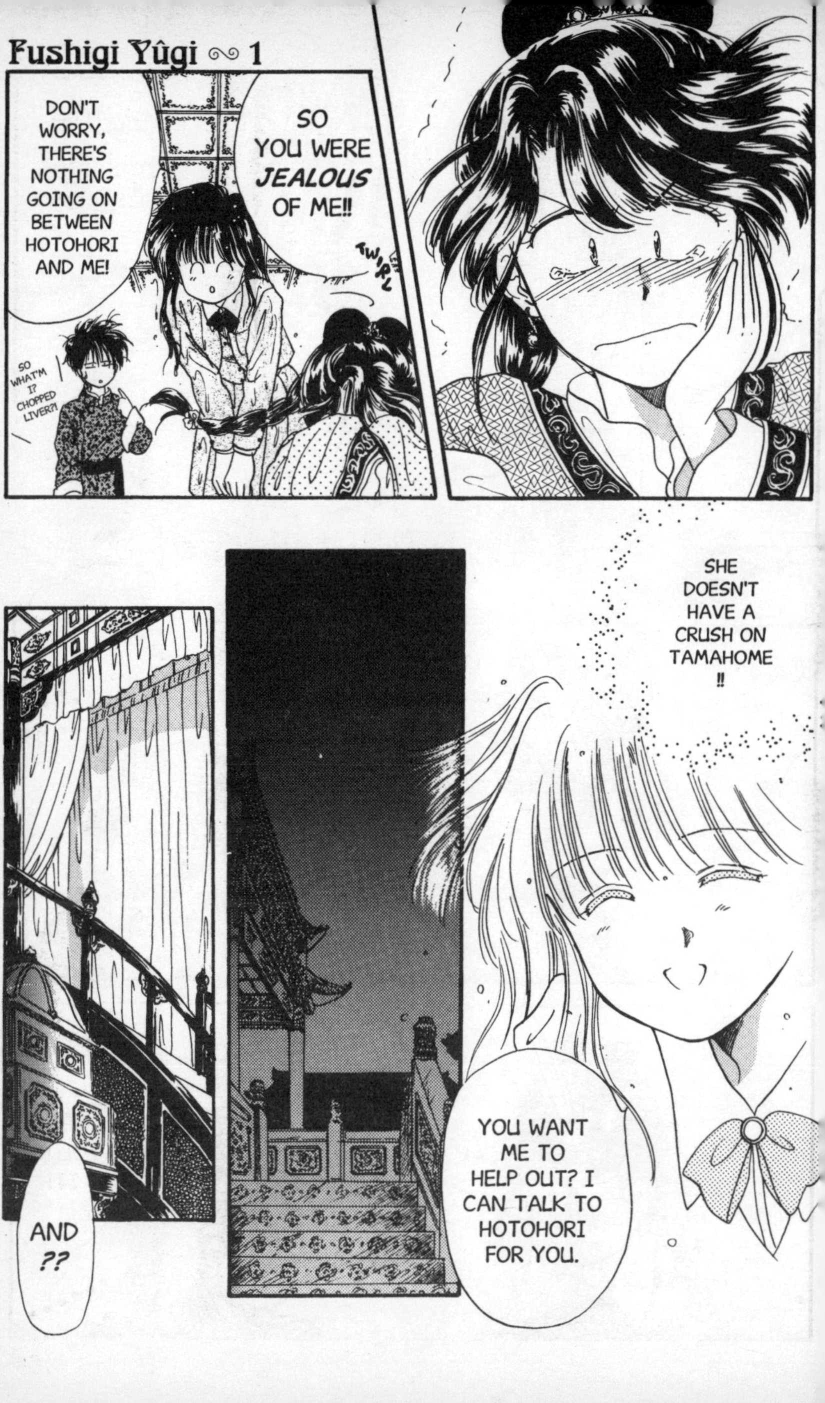
SO YOU WERE JEALOUS OF ME!!
DON'T WORRY, THERE'S NOTHING GOING ON BETWEEN HOTOHORI AND ME!
TWIRL
SO WHAT'M I? CHOPPED LIVER?!
SHE DOESN'T HAVE A CRUSH ON TAMAHOME !!
YOU WANT ME TO HELP OUT? I CAN TALK TO HOTOHORI FOR YOU.
AND ??

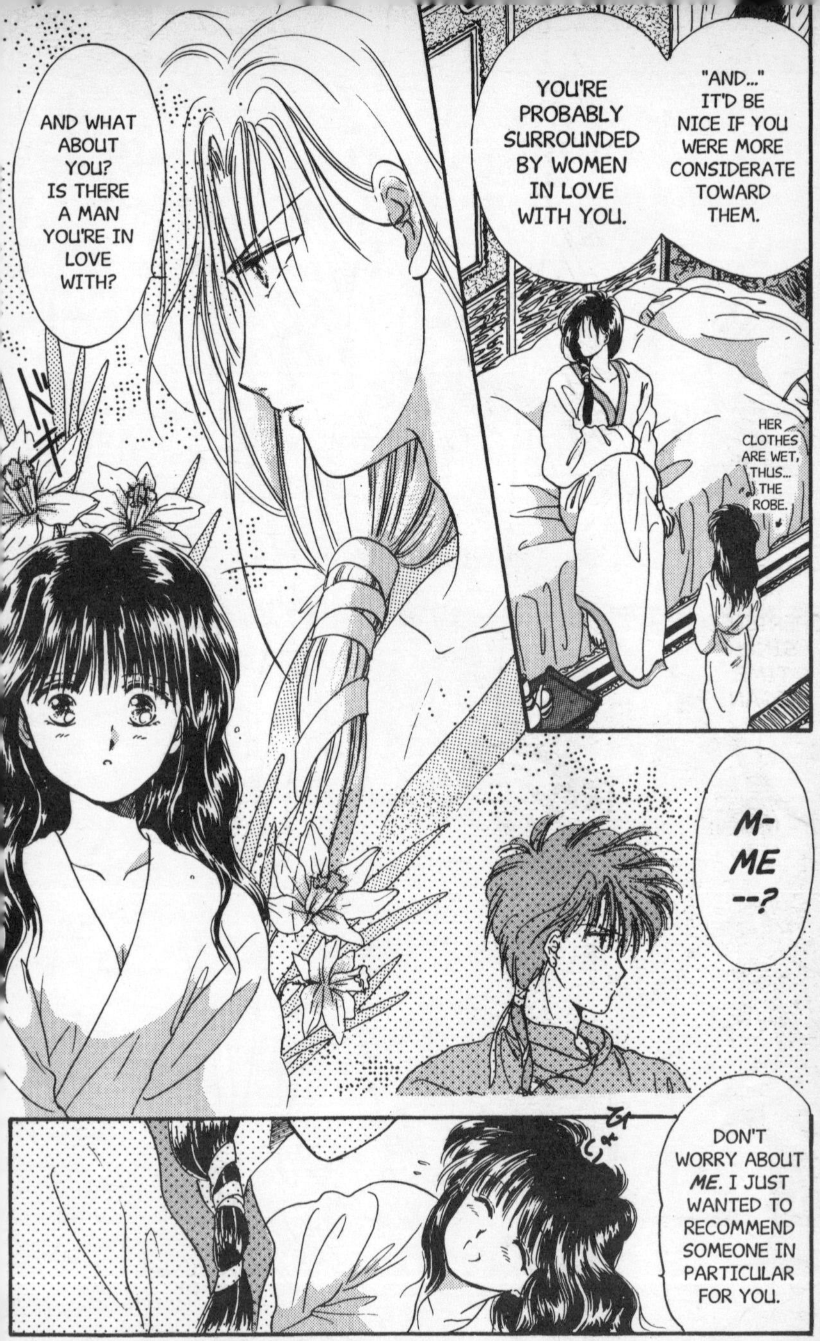

YOU'RE PROBABLY SURROUNDED BY WOMEN IN LOVE WITH YOU.
"AND..." IT'D BE NICE IF YOU WERE MORE CONSIDERATE TOWARD THEM.
HER CLOTHES ARE WET, THUS... THE ROBE.
AND WHAT ABOUT YOU? IS THERE A MAN YOU'RE IN LOVE WITH?
M- ME --?
ドキ
DON'T WORRY ABOUT *ME*. I JUST WANTED TO RECOMMEND SOMEONE IN PARTICULAR FOR YOU.

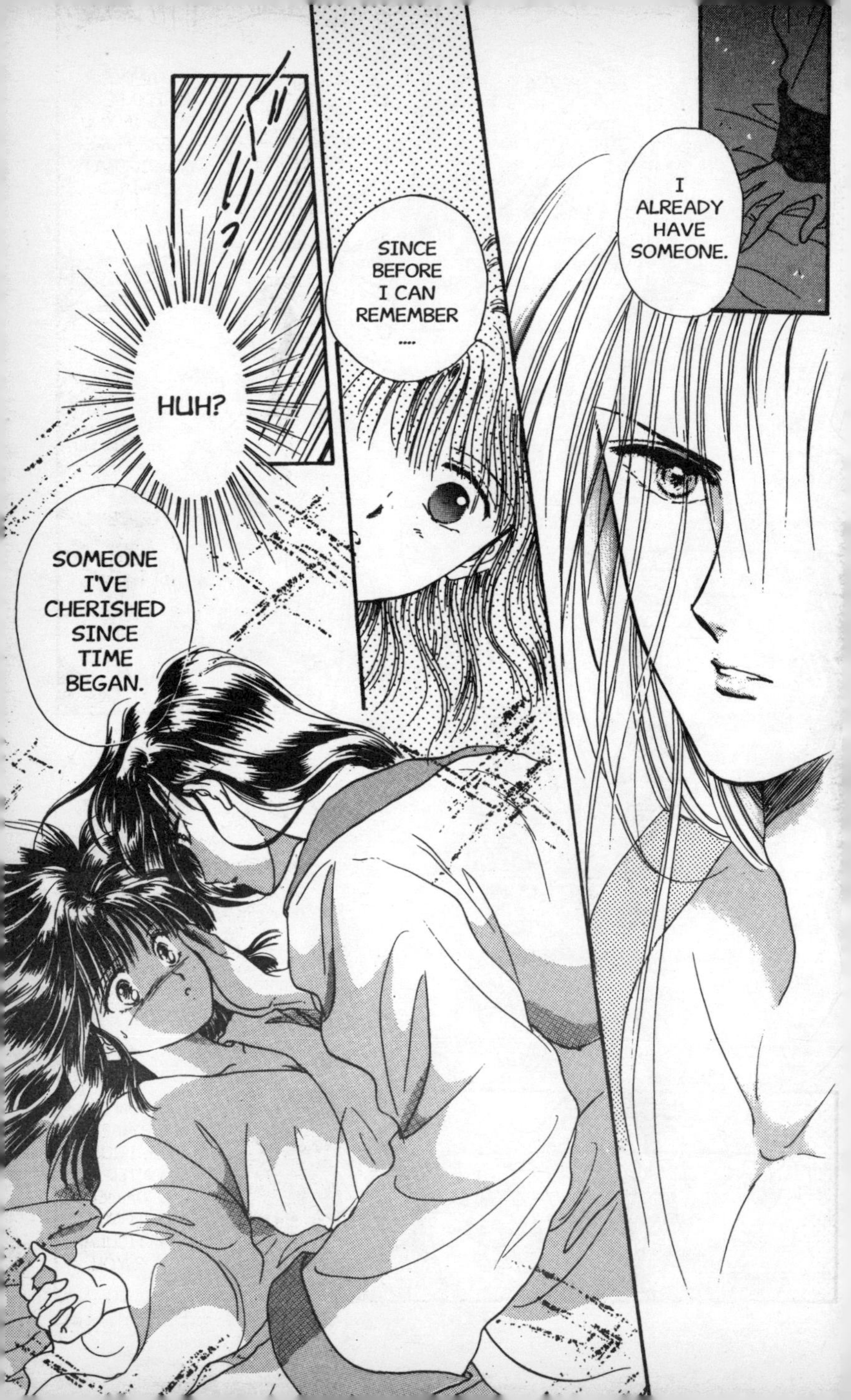

I ALREADY HAVE SOMEONE.
SINCE BEFORE I CAN REMEMBER ....
SOMEONE I'VE CHERISHED SINCE TIME BEGAN.
HUH?

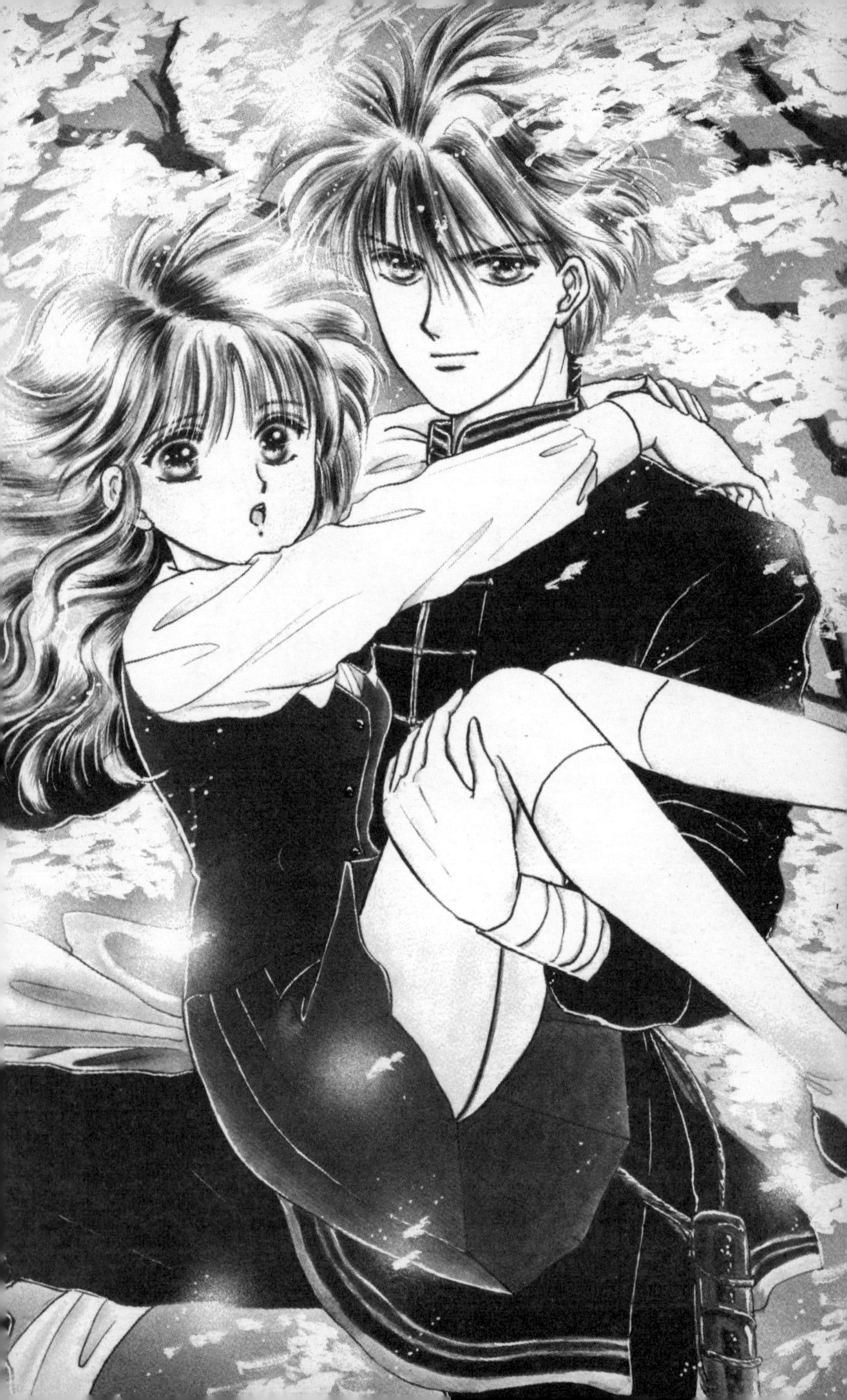

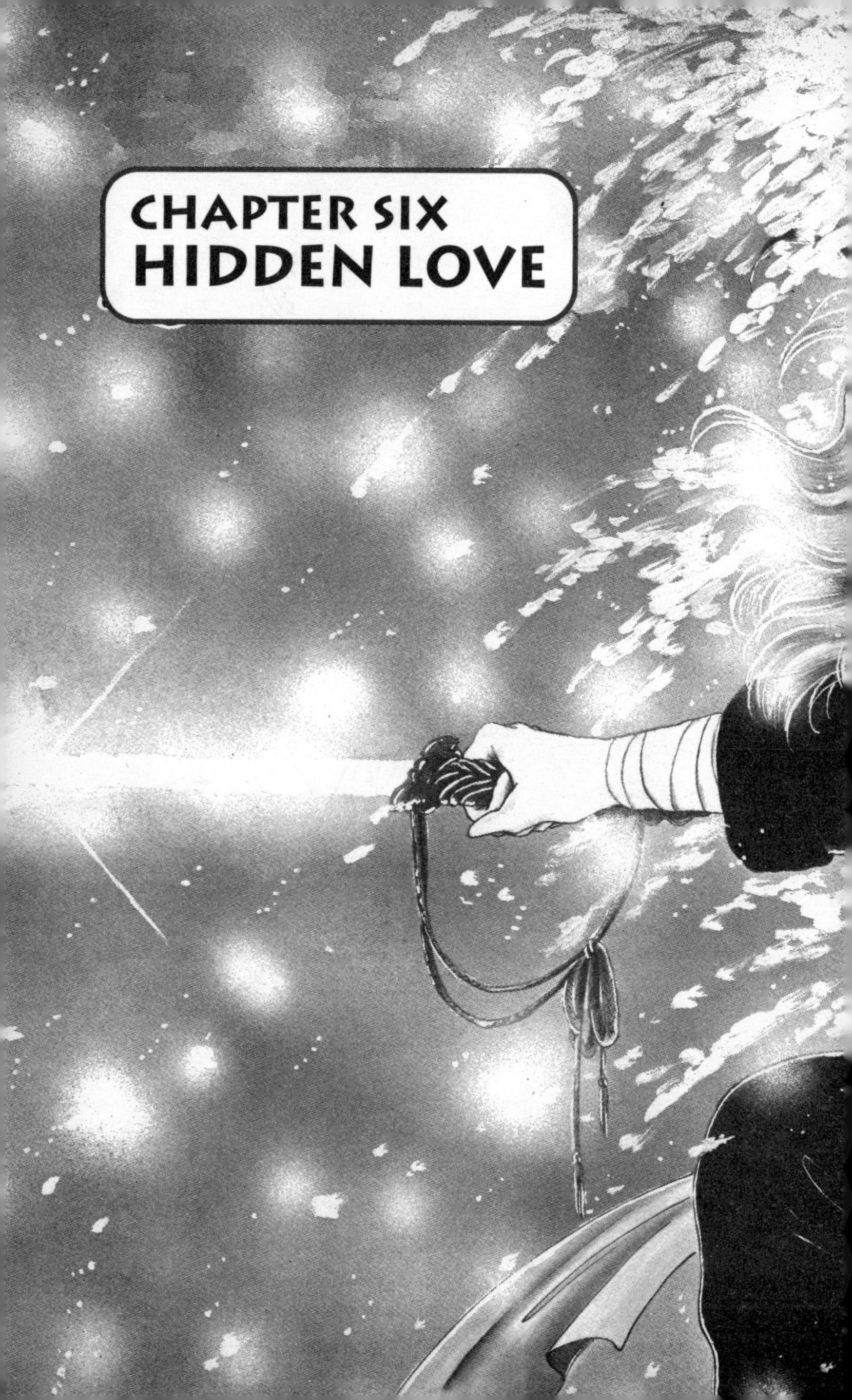
CHAPTER SIX
HIDDEN LOVE

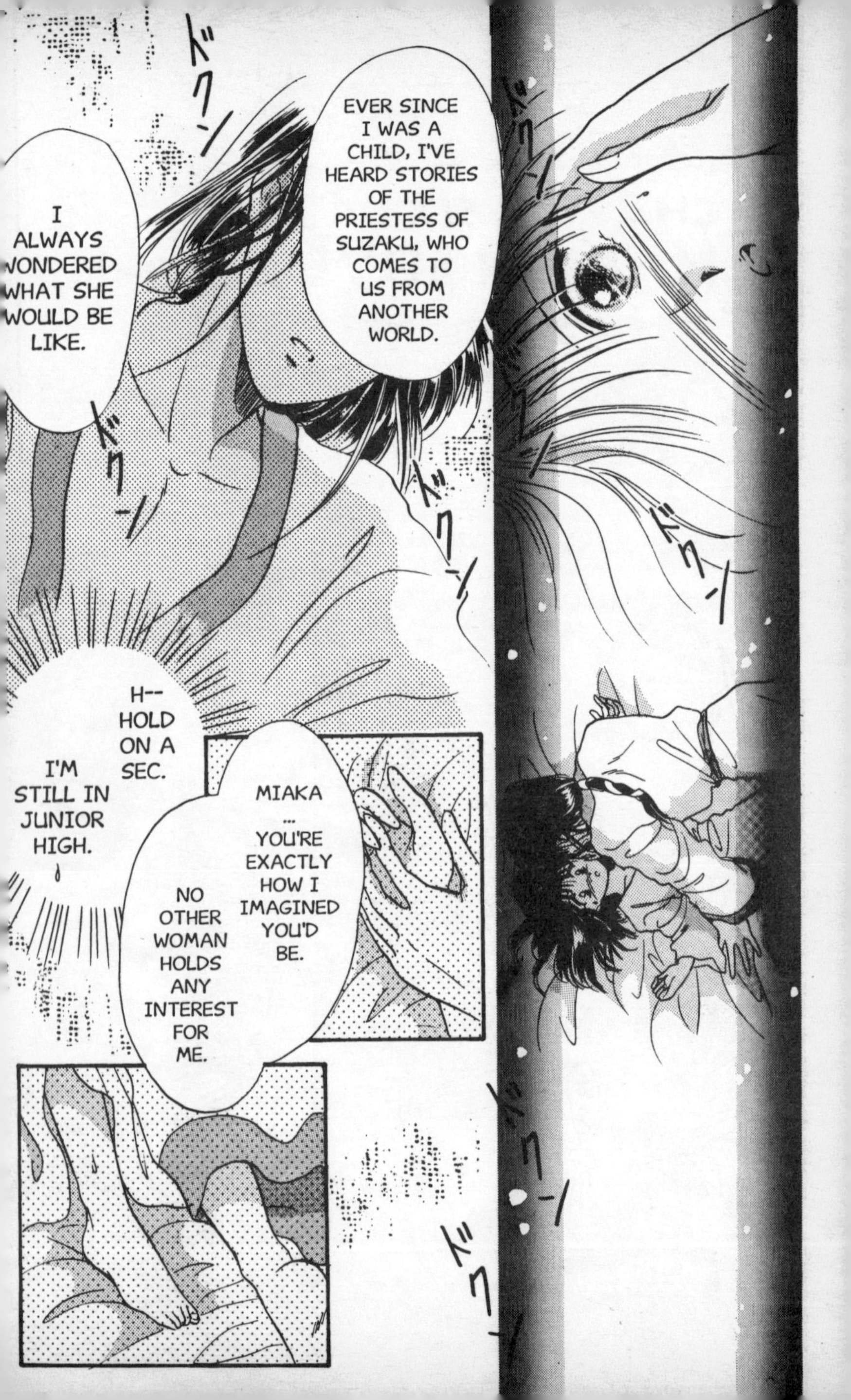
EVER SINCE I WAS A CHILD, I'VE HEARD STORIES OF THE PRIESTESS OF SUZAKU, WHO COMES TO US FROM ANOTHER WORLD.
I ALWAYS WONDERED WHAT SHE WOULD BE LIKE.
MIAKA ... YOU'RE EXACTLY HOW I IMAGINED YOU'D BE.
NO OTHER WOMAN HOLDS ANY INTEREST FOR ME.
H-- HOLD ON A SEC.
I'M STILL IN JUNIOR HIGH.

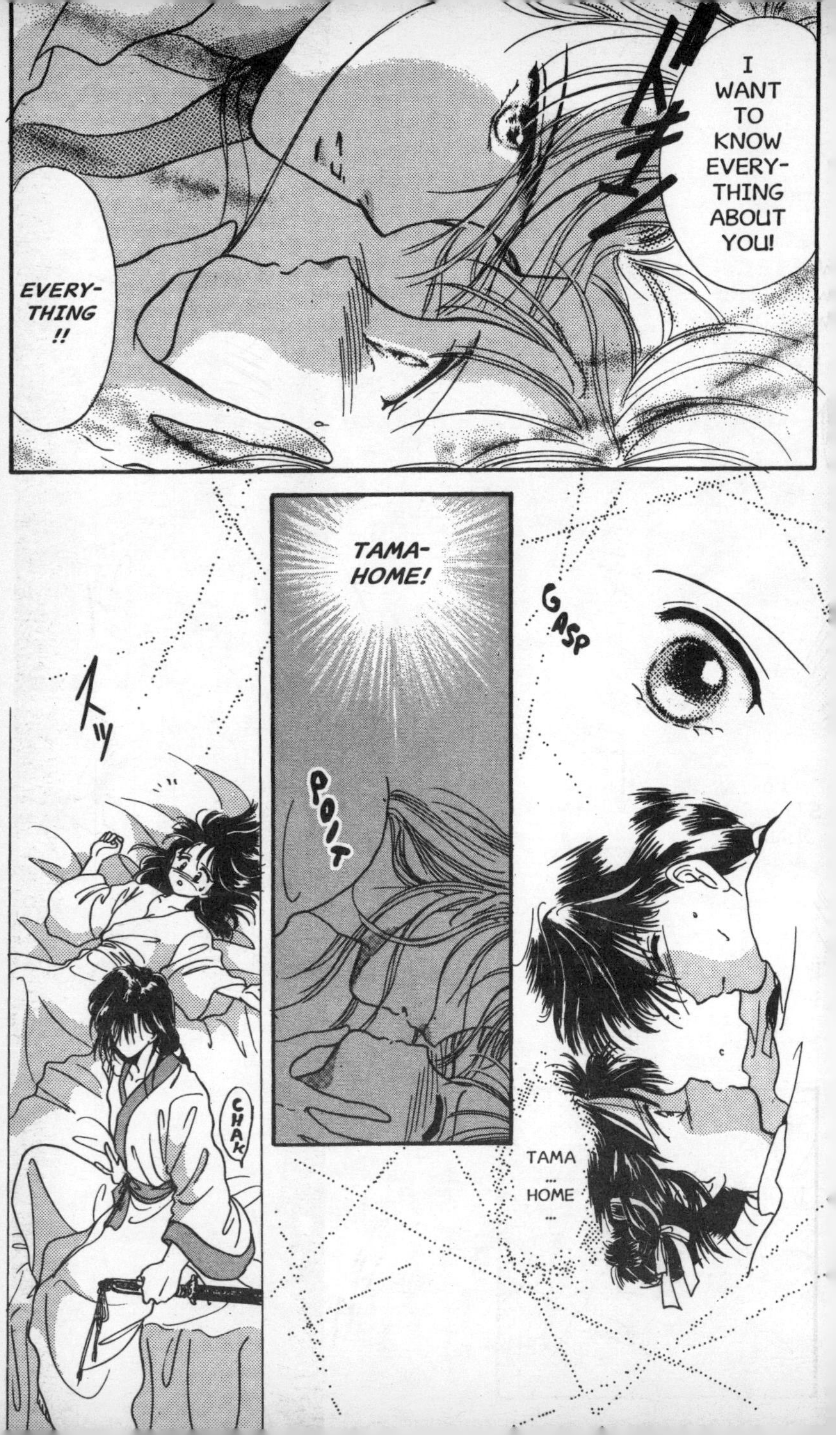
I WANT TO KNOW EVERYTHING ABOUT YOU!
EVERYTHING!!
TAMA-HOME!
GASP
POIT
TAMA... HOME...
CHAK

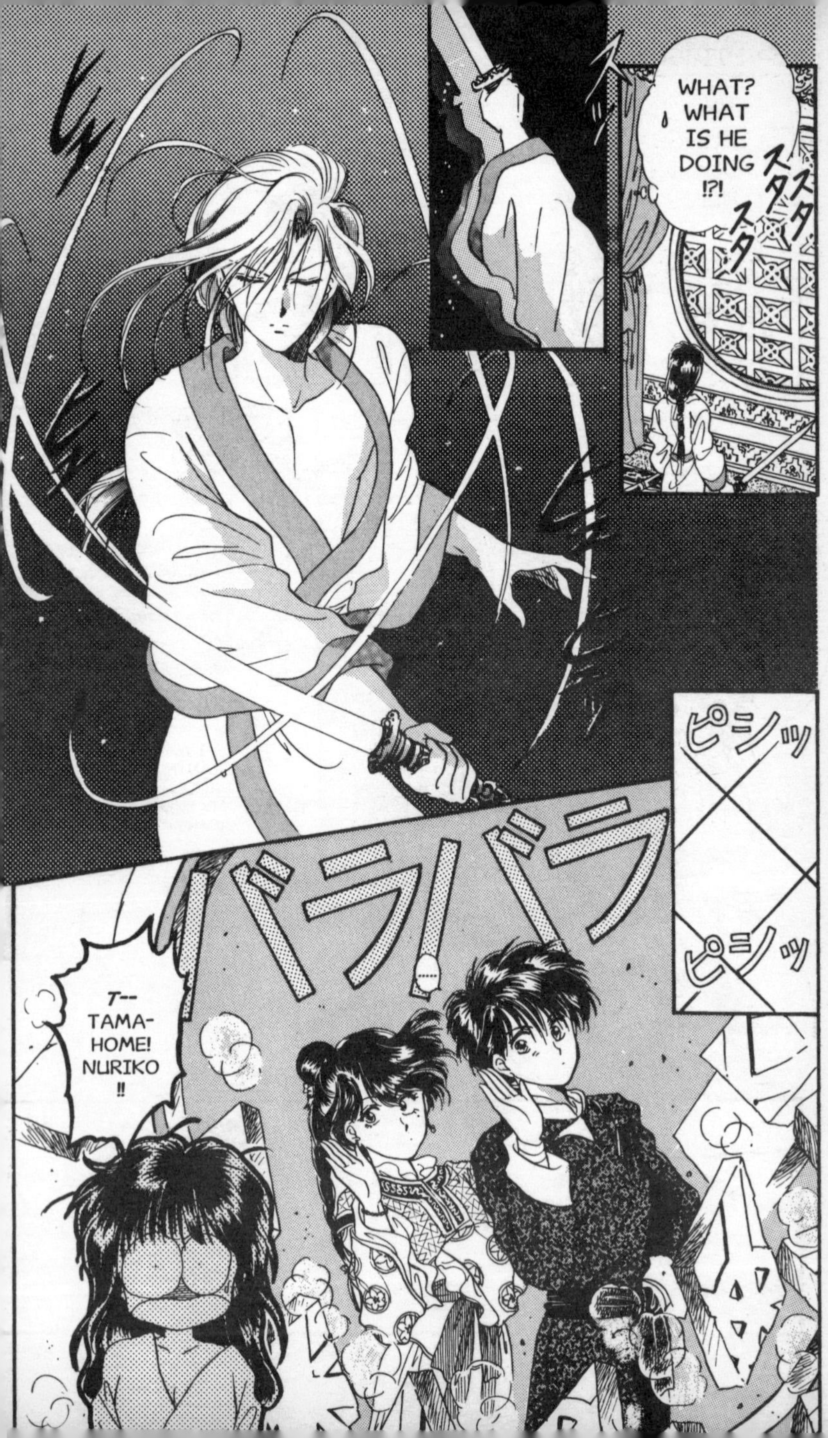

WHAT? WHAT IS HE DOING !?!
スタスタスタ
ピシッ
ピシッ
バラバラ
......
T-- TAMA-HOME! NURIKO !!

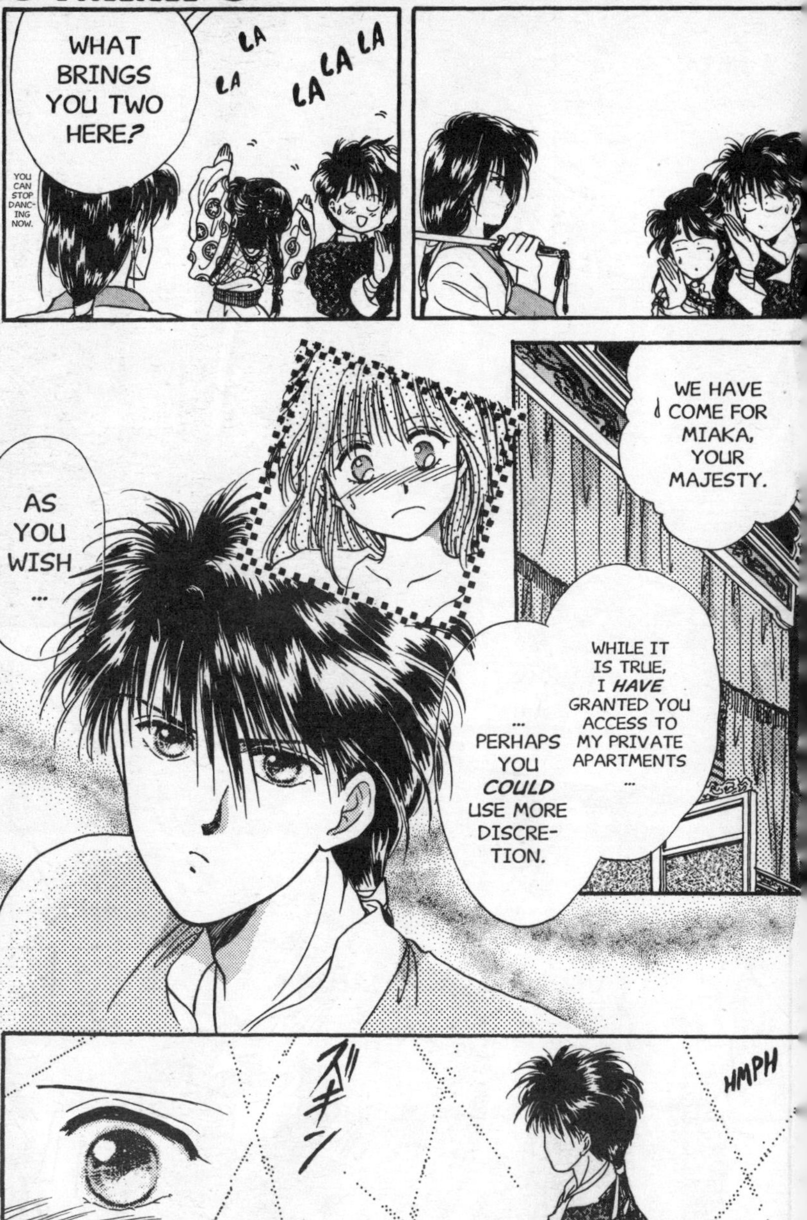
WHAT BRINGS YOU TWO HERE?
LA LA LA LA LA
YOU CAN STOP DANCING NOW.
WE HAVE COME FOR MIAKA, YOUR MAJESTY.
WHILE IT IS TRUE, I HAVE GRANTED YOU ACCESS TO MY PRIVATE APARTMENTS...
...PERHAPS YOU COULD USE MORE DISCRETION.
AS YOU WISH...
HMPH

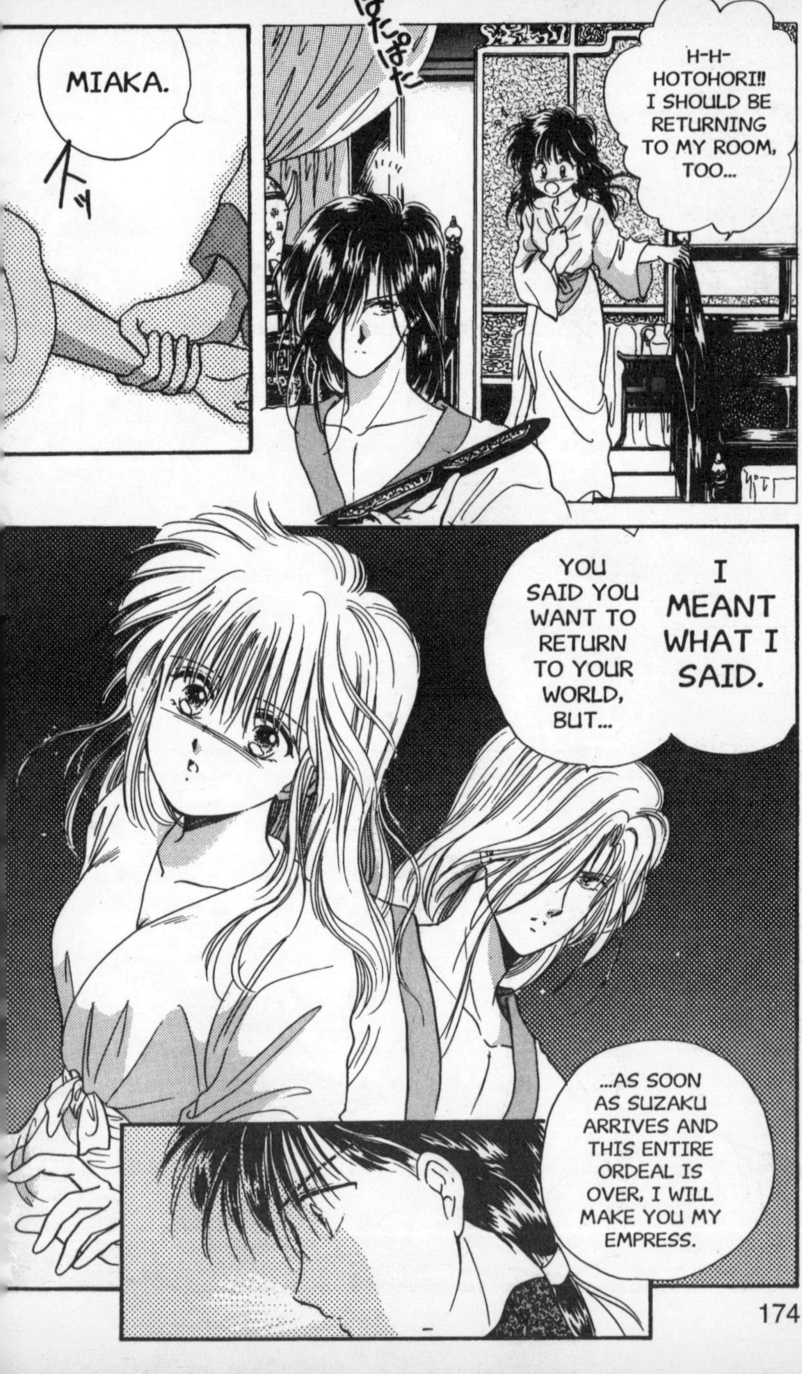

ぱたぱた
H-H-HOTOHORI!! I SHOULD BE RETURNING TO MY ROOM, TOO...
MIAKA.
トッ
YOU SAID YOU WANT TO RETURN TO YOUR WORLD, BUT...
I MEANT WHAT I SAID.
...AS SOON AS SUZAKU ARRIVES AND THIS ENTIRE ORDEAL IS OVER, I WILL MAKE YOU MY EMPRESS.

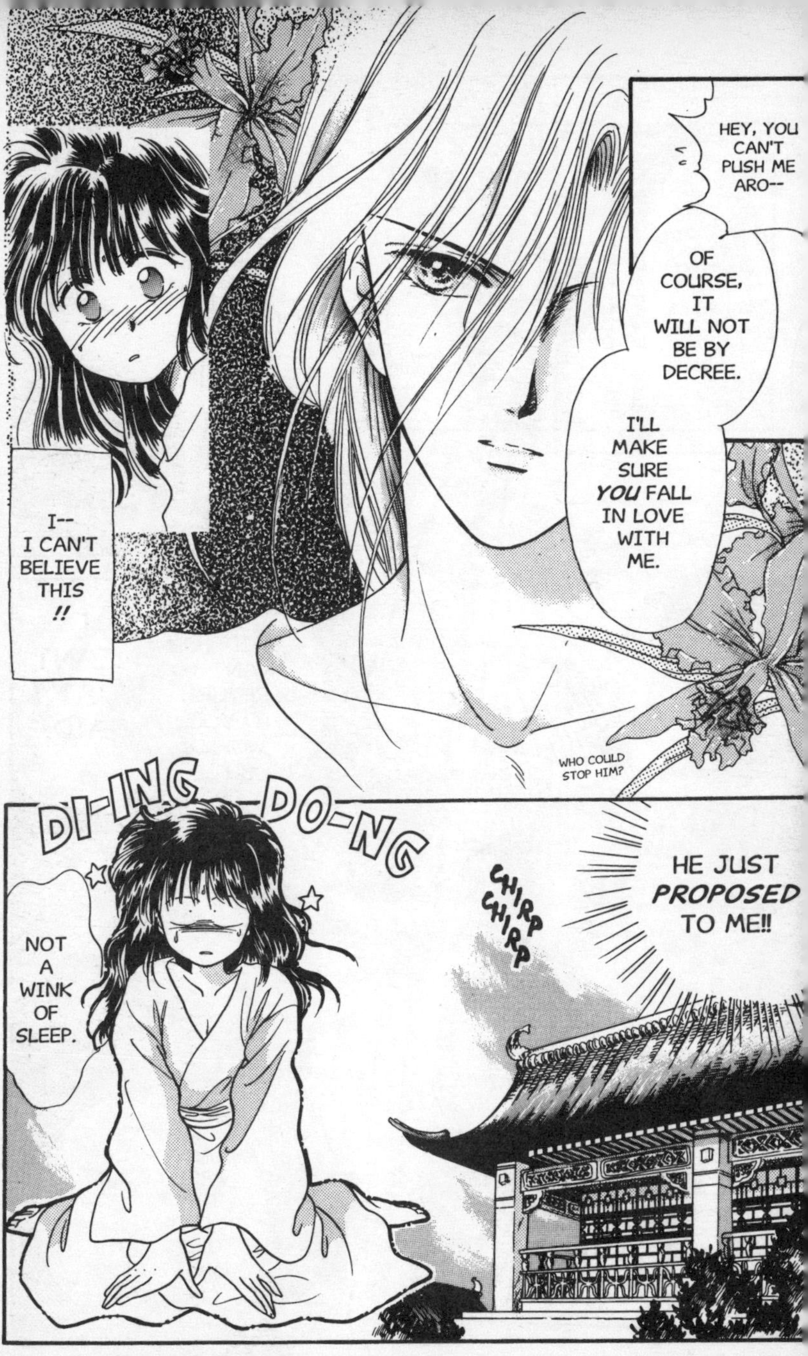
HEY, YOU CAN'T PUSH ME ARO--
OF COURSE, IT WILL NOT BE BY DECREE.
I'LL MAKE SURE YOU FALL IN LOVE WITH ME.
I-- I CAN'T BELIEVE THIS !!
WHO COULD STOP HIM?
HE JUST PROPOSED TO ME!!
CHIRP CHIRP
DI-ING DO-NG
NOT A WINK OF SLEEP.

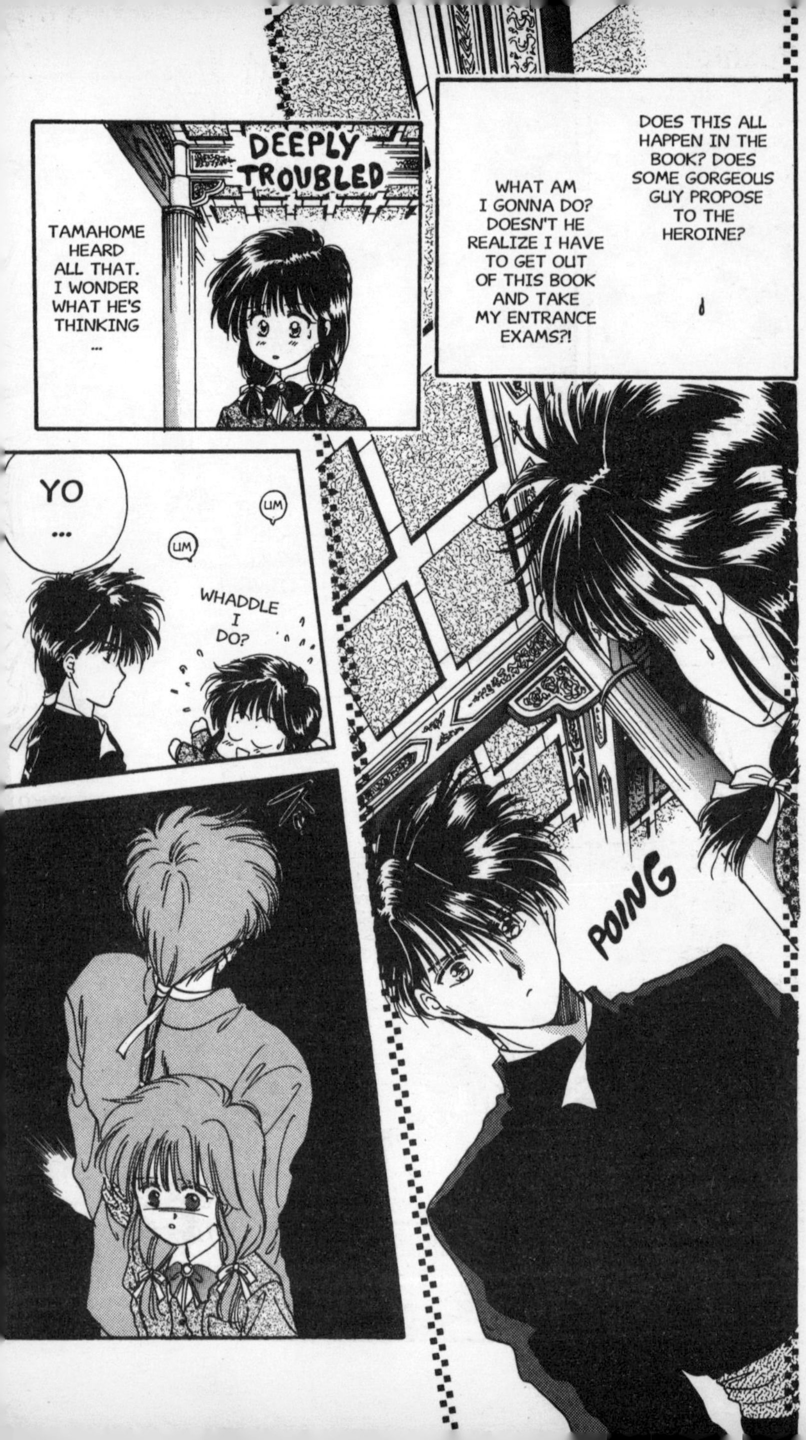
DEEPLY TROUBLED
TAMAHOME HEARD ALL THAT. I WONDER WHAT HE'S THINKING ...
WHAT AM I GONNA DO? DOESN'T HE REALIZE I HAVE TO GET OUT OF THIS BOOK AND TAKE MY ENTRANCE EXAMS?!
DOES THIS ALL HAPPEN IN THE BOOK? DOES SOME GORGEOUS GUY PROPOSE TO THE HEROINE?
YO ...
UM
UM
WHADDLE I DO?
POING

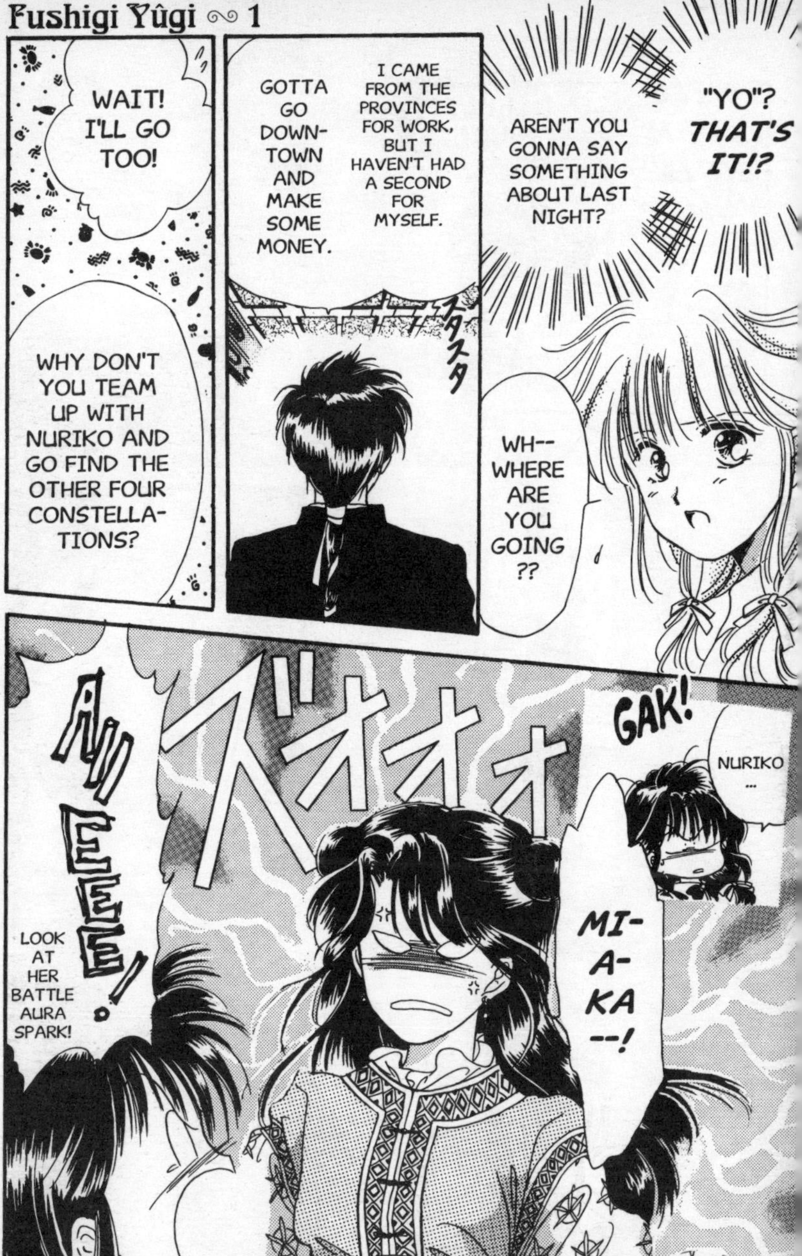
"YO"? THAT'S IT!?
AREN'T YOU GONNA SAY SOMETHING ABOUT LAST NIGHT?
WH-- WHERE ARE YOU GOING ??
I CAME FROM THE PROVINCES FOR WORK, BUT I HAVEN'T HAD A SECOND FOR MYSELF.
GOTTA GO DOWNTOWN AND MAKE SOME MONEY.
スタスタ
WAIT! I'LL GO TOO!
WHY DON'T YOU TEAM UP WITH NURIKO AND GO FIND THE OTHER FOUR CONSTELLATIONS?
GAK!
NURIKO ...
MI-A-KA--!
ズオオオ
AIIEEEE!
LOOK AT HER BATTLE AURA SPARK!

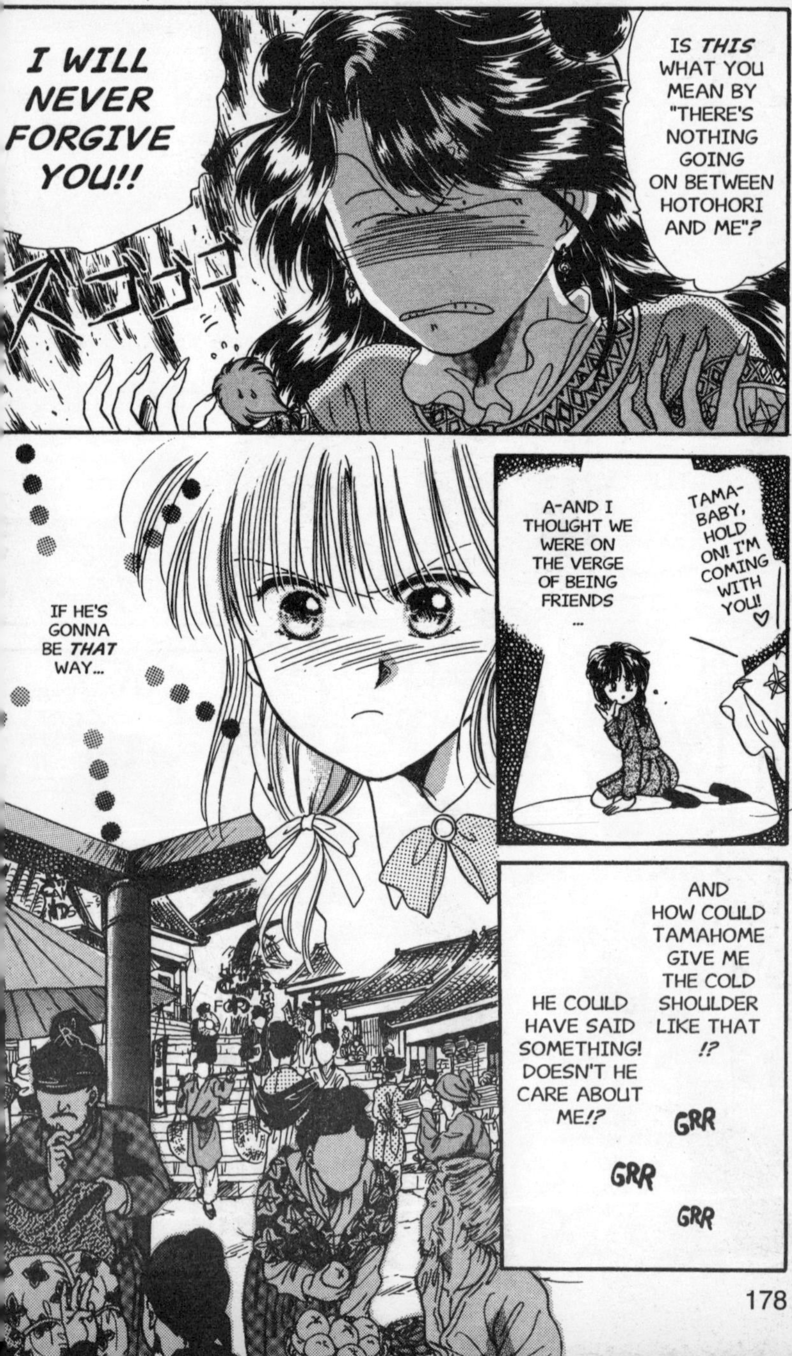
IS THIS WHAT YOU MEAN BY "THERE'S NOTHING GOING ON BETWEEN HOTOHORI AND ME"?
I WILL NEVER FORGIVE YOU!!
TAMA-BABY, HOLD ON! I'M COMING WITH YOU! ♡
A-AND I THOUGHT WE WERE ON THE VERGE OF BEING FRIENDS ...
IF HE'S GONNA BE THAT WAY...
AND HOW COULD TAMAHOME GIVE ME THE COLD SHOULDER LIKE THAT !?
HE COULD HAVE SAID SOMETHING! DOESN'T HE CARE ABOUT ME!?
GRR
GRR
GRR

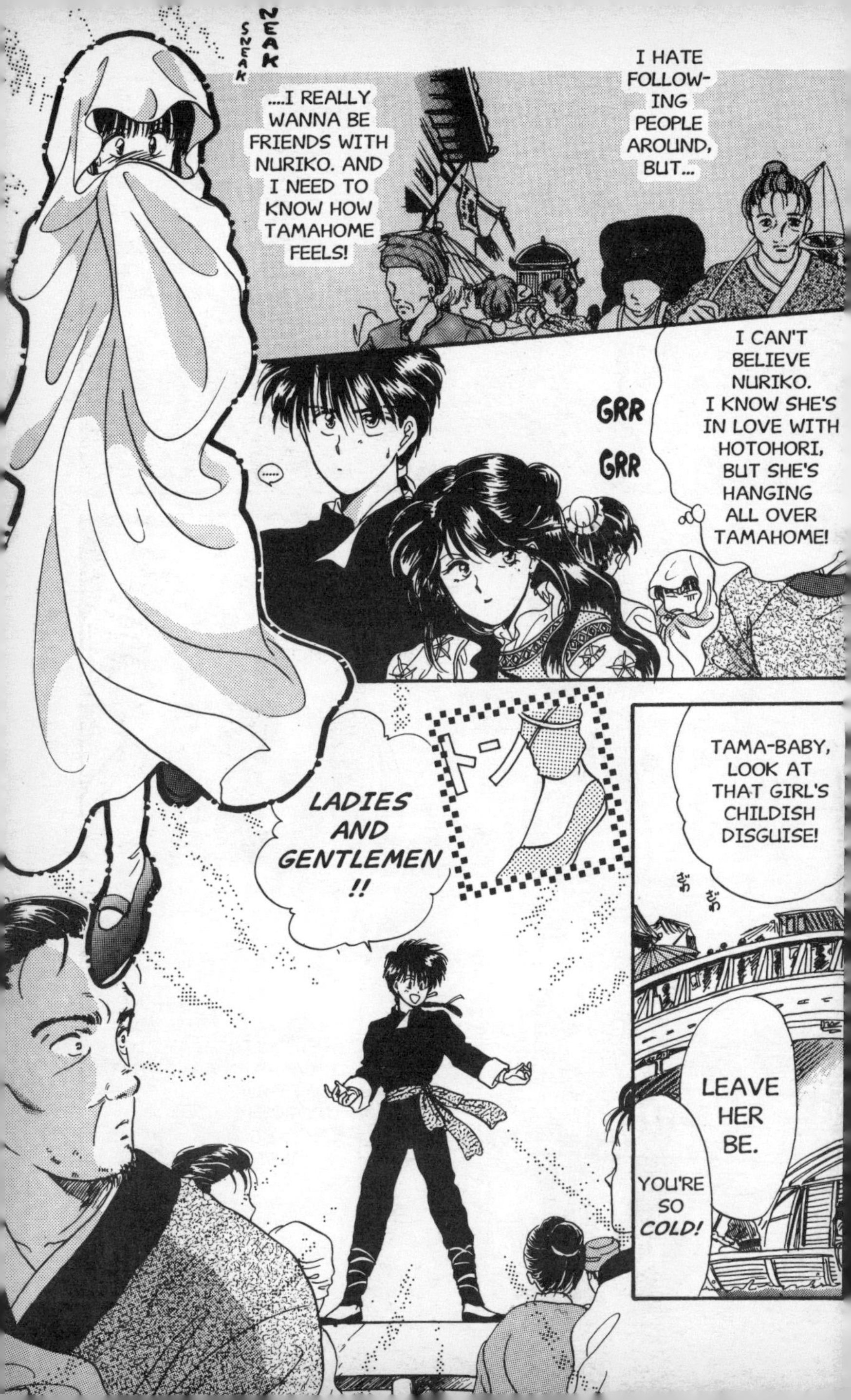
SNEAK SNEAK
I HATE FOLLOW-ING PEOPLE AROUND, BUT...
....I REALLY WANNA BE FRIENDS WITH NURIKO. AND I NEED TO KNOW HOW TAMAHOME FEELS!
I CAN'T BELIEVE NURIKO. I KNOW SHE'S IN LOVE WITH HOTOHORI, BUT SHE'S HANGING ALL OVER TAMAHOME!
GRR
GRR
......
TAMA-BABY, LOOK AT THAT GIRL'S CHILDISH DISGUISE!
ざわ ざわ
LEAVE HER BE.
YOU'RE SO COLD!
LADIES AND GENTLEMEN !!

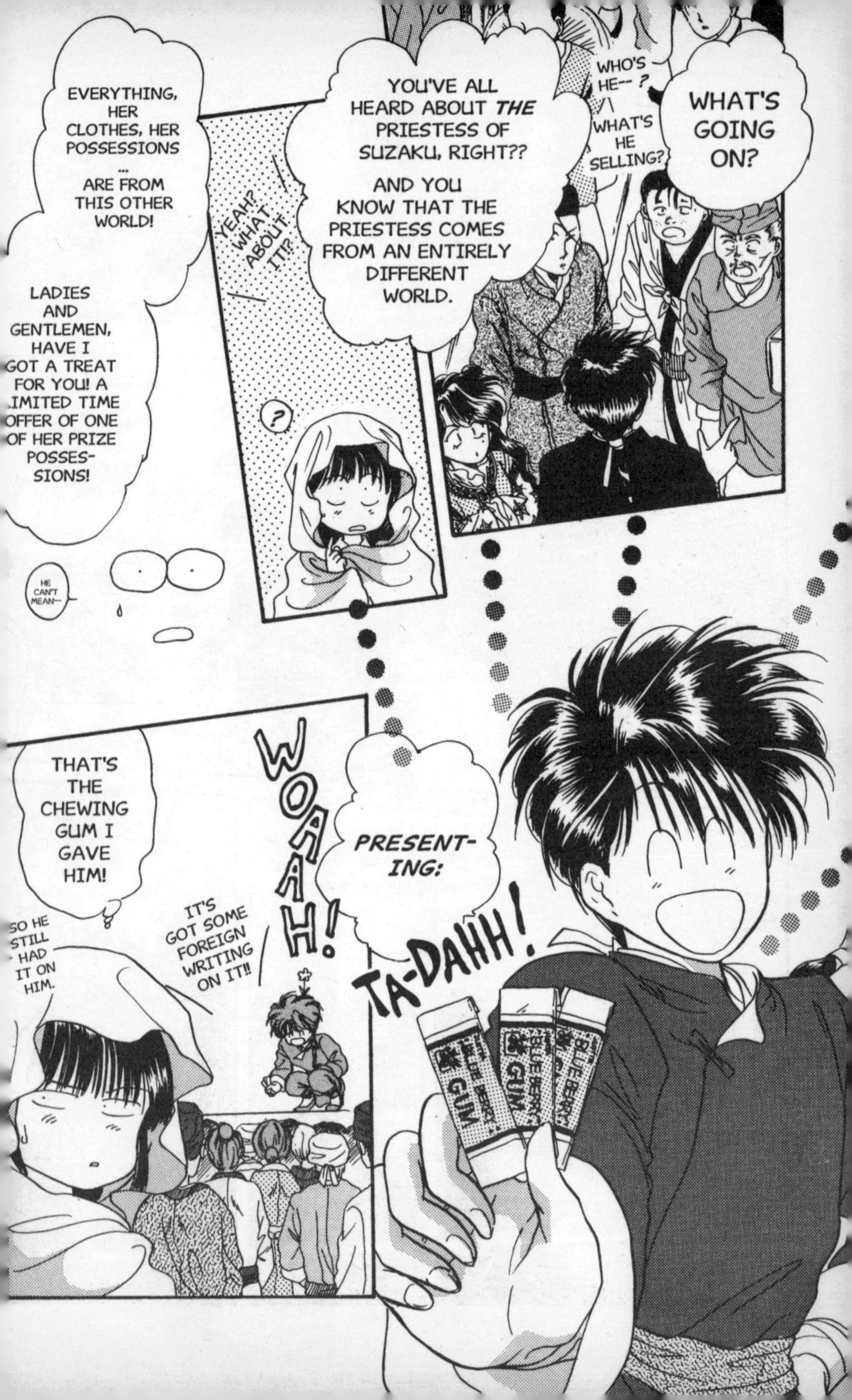
WHAT'S GOING ON?
WHO'S HE-- ? / WHAT'S HE SELLING?
YOU'VE ALL HEARD ABOUT THE PRIESTESS OF SUZAKU, RIGHT??
AND YOU KNOW THAT THE PRIESTESS COMES FROM AN ENTIRELY DIFFERENT WORLD.
YEAH? WHAT ABOUT IT!?
EVERYTHING, HER CLOTHES, HER POSSESSIONS ... ARE FROM THIS OTHER WORLD!
?
LADIES AND GENTLEMEN, HAVE I GOT A TREAT FOR YOU! A LIMITED TIME OFFER OF ONE OF HER PRIZE POSSES-SIONS!
HE CAN'T MEAN--
PRESENT-ING:
TA-DAHH!
WOAAAH!
BLUE BERRY GUM
IT'S GOT SOME FOREIGN WRITING ON IT!!
THAT'S THE CHEWING GUM I GAVE HIM!
SO HE STILL HAD IT ON HIM.

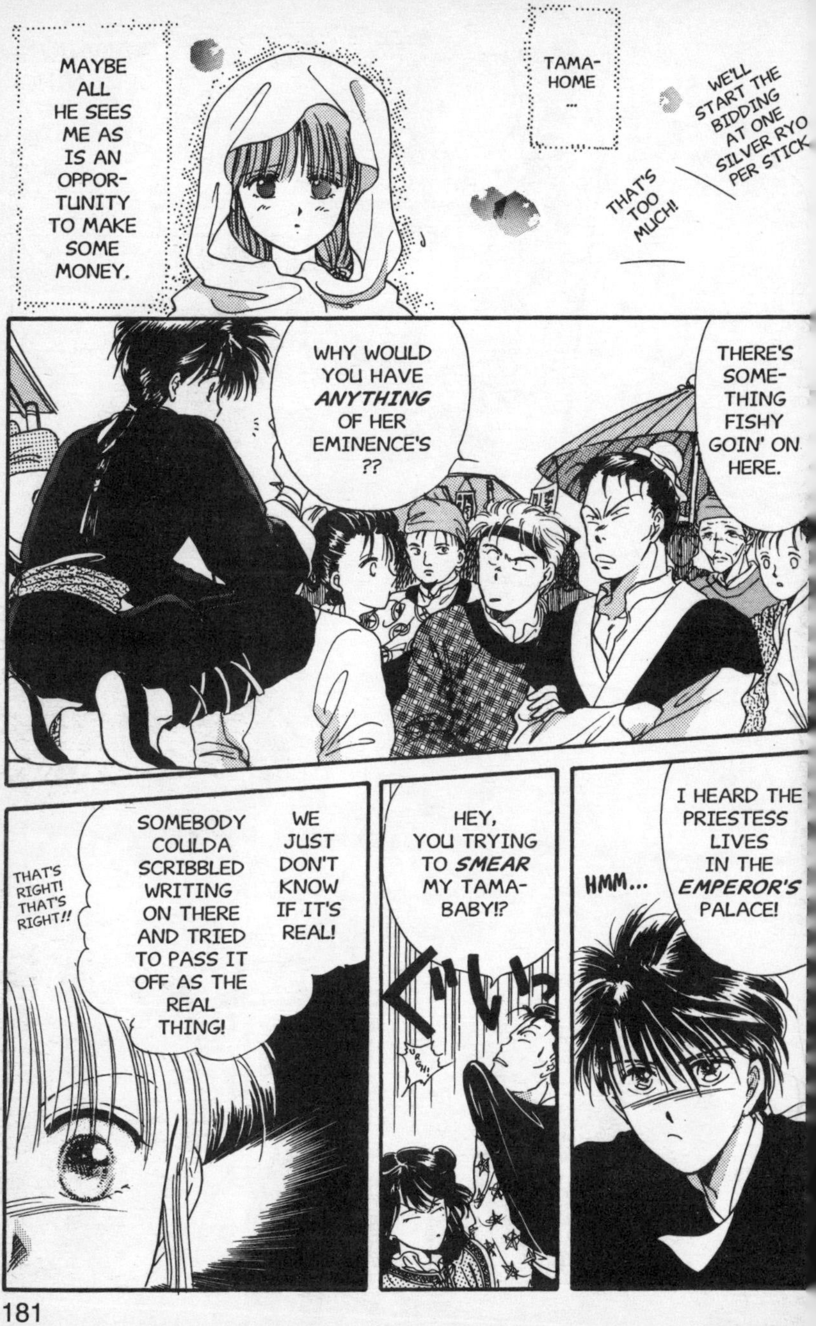
TAMA-HOME ...
WE'LL START THE BIDDING AT ONE SILVER RYO PER STICK
THAT'S TOO MUCH!
MAYBE ALL HE SEES ME AS IS AN OPPORTUNITY TO MAKE SOME MONEY.
THERE'S SOMETHING FISHY GOIN' ON HERE.
WHY WOULD YOU HAVE *ANYTHING* OF HER EMINENCE'S ??
I HEARD THE PRIESTESS LIVES IN THE *EMPEROR'S* PALACE!
HMM...
HEY, YOU TRYING TO *SMEAR* MY TAMA-BABY!?
ぐいっ
URGH!
WE JUST DON'T KNOW IF IT'S REAL!
SOMEBODY COULDA SCRIBBLED WRITING ON THERE AND TRIED TO PASS IT OFF AS THE REAL THING!
THAT'S RIGHT! THAT'S RIGHT!!

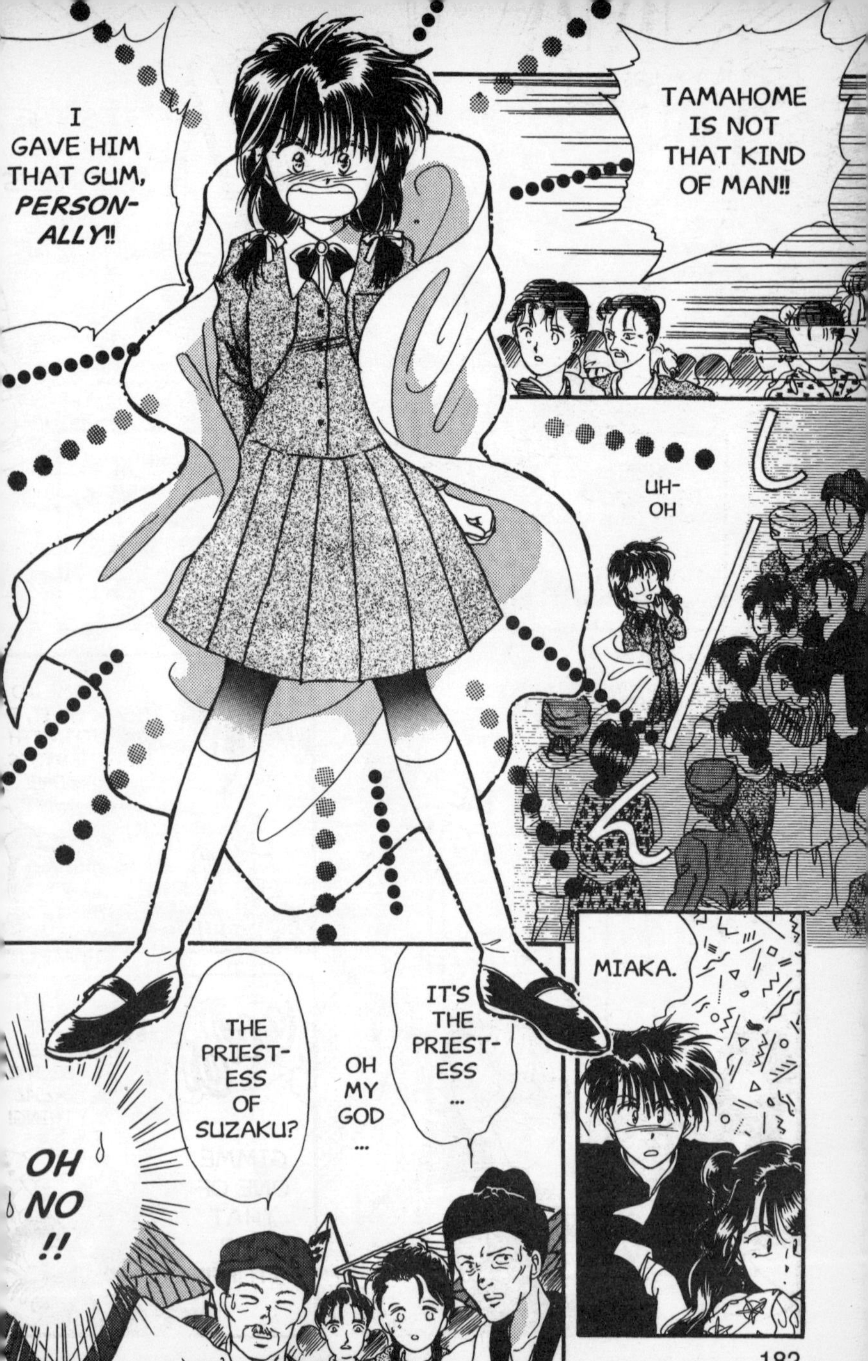
TAMAHOME IS NOT THAT KIND OF MAN!!
I GAVE HIM THAT GUM, *PERSON-ALLY*!!
UH-OH
MIAKA.
IT'S THE PRIEST-ESS ...
OH MY GOD ...
THE PRIEST-ESS OF SUZAKU?
OH NO !!

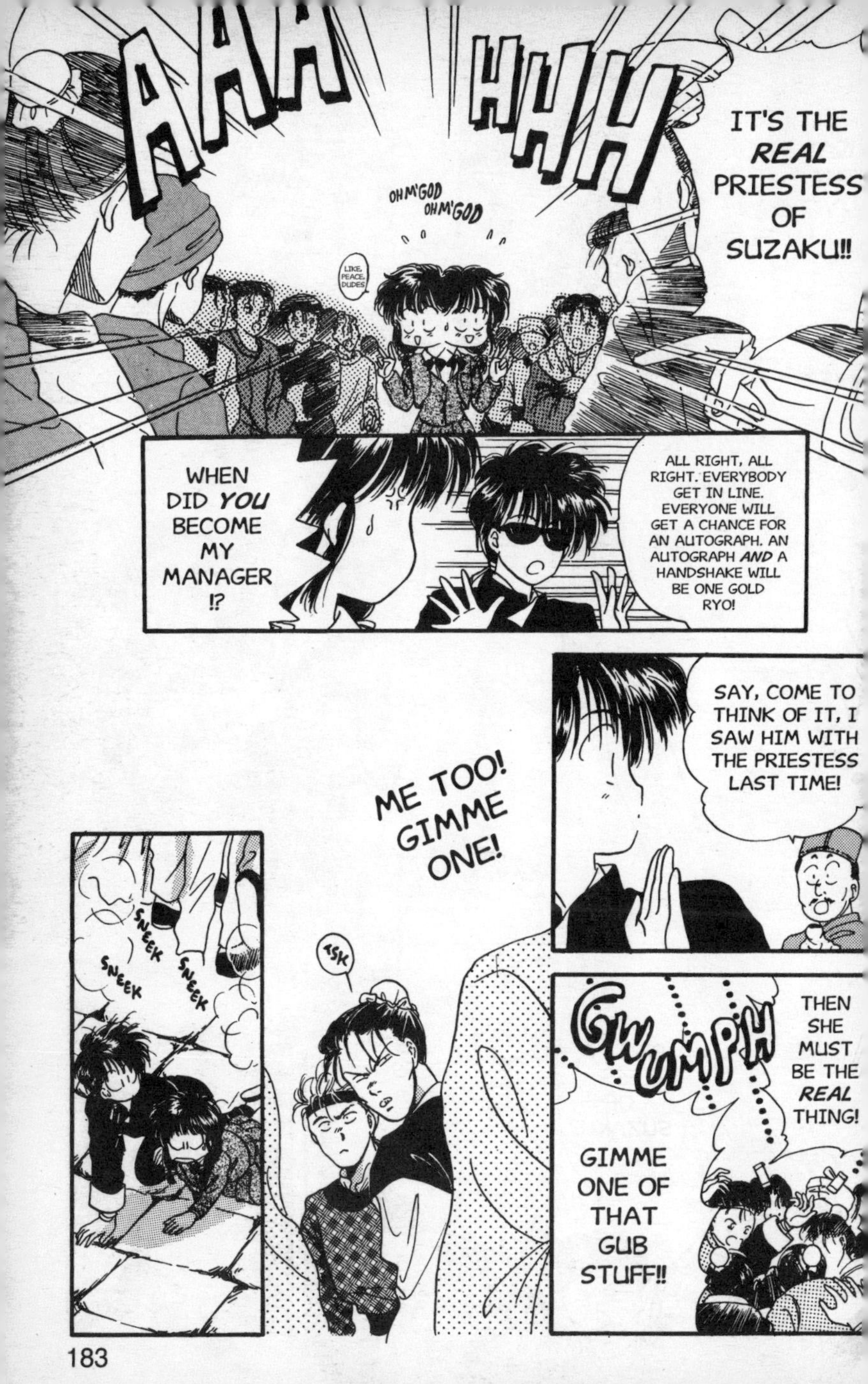
AAAHHH
IT'S THE REAL PRIESTESS OF SUZAKU!!
OHM'GOD OHM'GOD
LIKE, PEACE, DUDES
ALL RIGHT, ALL RIGHT. EVERYBODY GET IN LINE. EVERYONE WILL GET A CHANCE FOR AN AUTOGRAPH. AN AUTOGRAPH AND A HANDSHAKE WILL BE ONE GOLD RYO!
WHEN DID YOU BECOME MY MANAGER!?
SAY, COME TO THINK OF IT, I SAW HIM WITH THE PRIESTESS LAST TIME!
ME TOO! GIMME ONE!
GWUMPH
THEN SHE MUST BE THE REAL THING!
GIMME ONE OF THAT GUB STUFF!!
SNEEK SNEEK
SNEEK
ASK

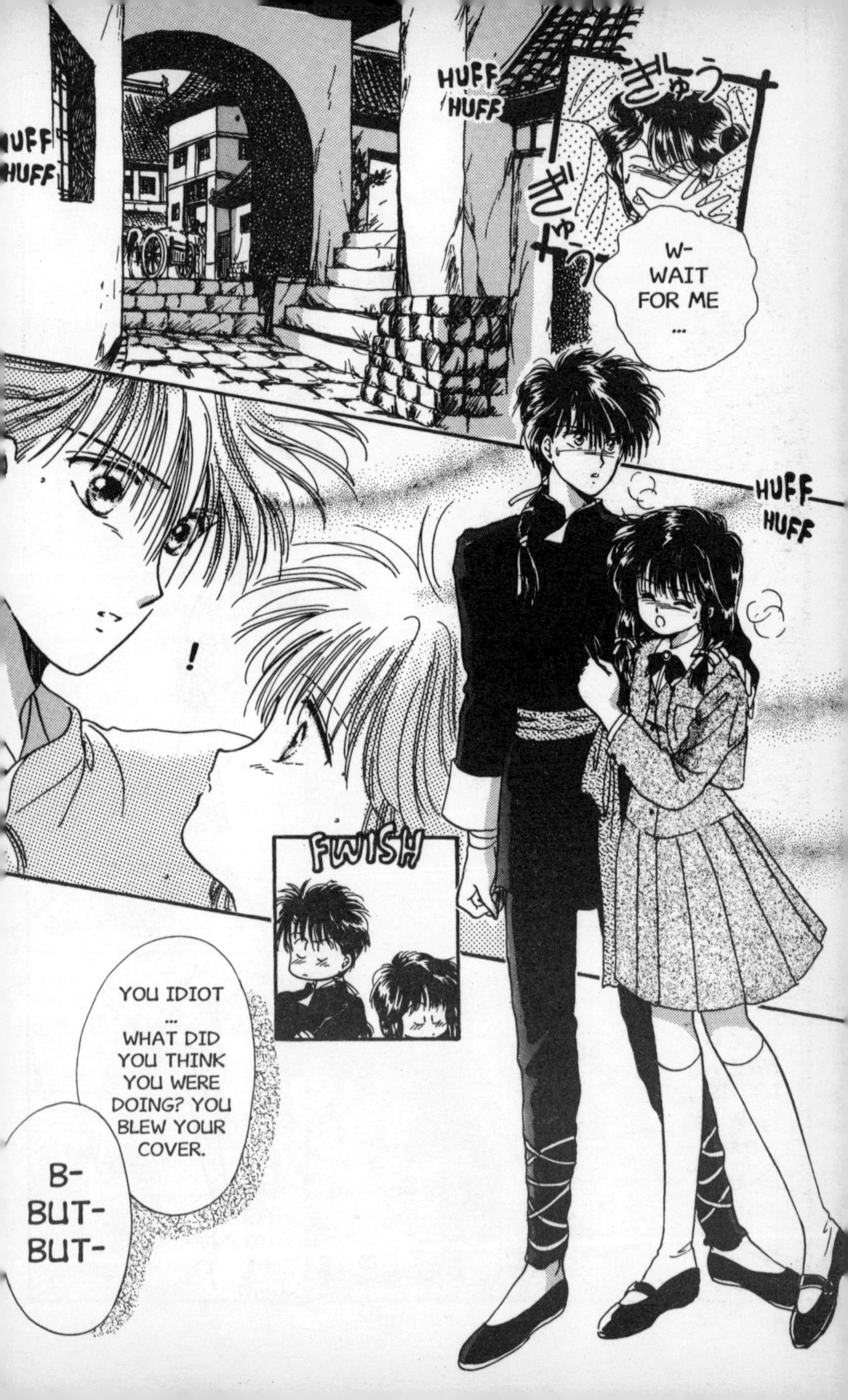

きゅう
ぎゅう
HUFF HUFF
W- WAIT FOR ME ...
HUFF HUFF
HUFF HUFF
!
FWISH
YOU IDIOT ... WHAT DID YOU THINK YOU WERE DOING? YOU BLEW YOUR COVER.
B- BUT- BUT-

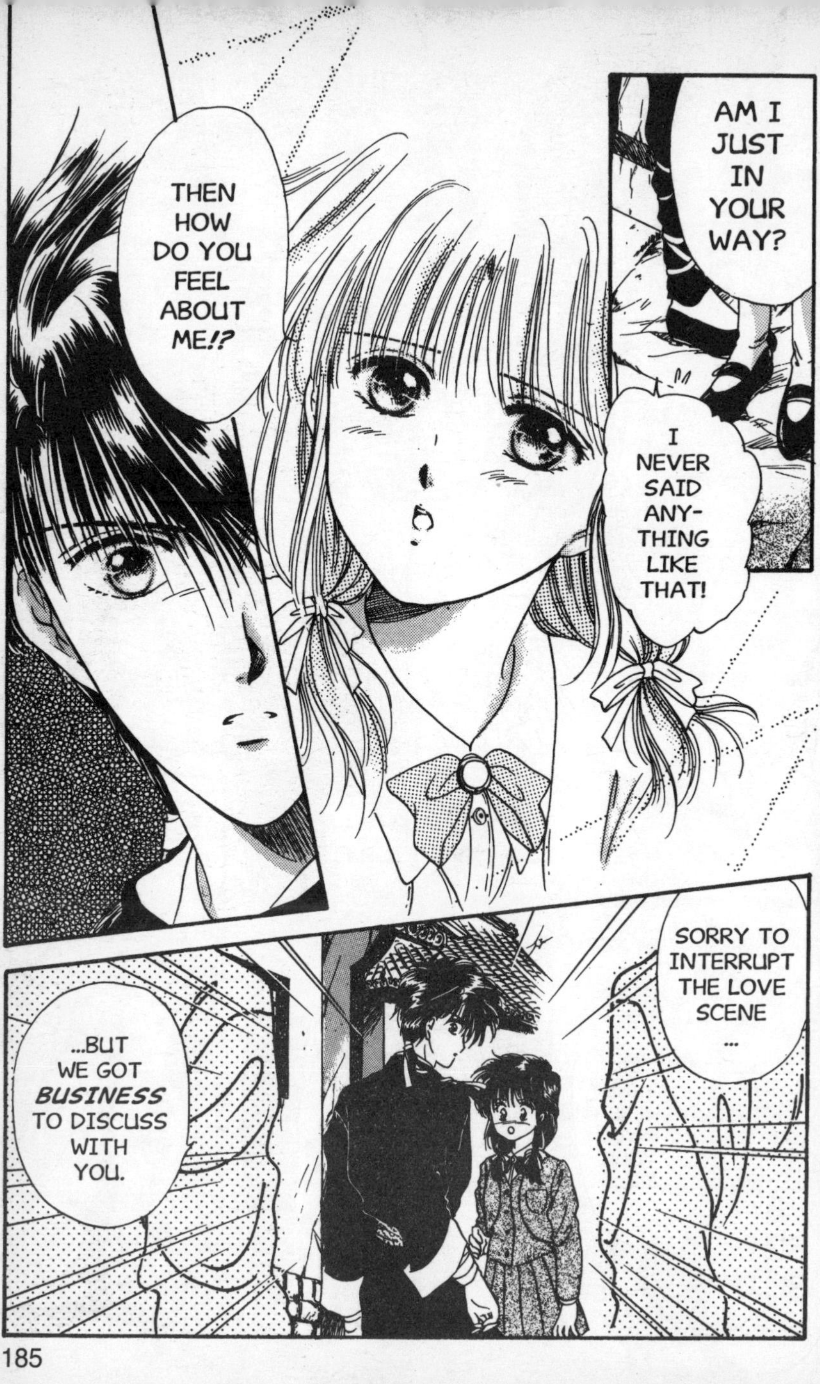
AM I JUST IN YOUR WAY?
I NEVER SAID ANY-THING LIKE THAT!
THEN HOW DO YOU FEEL ABOUT ME!?
SORRY TO INTERRUPT THE LOVE SCENE ...
...BUT WE GOT *BUSINESS* TO DISCUSS WITH YOU.

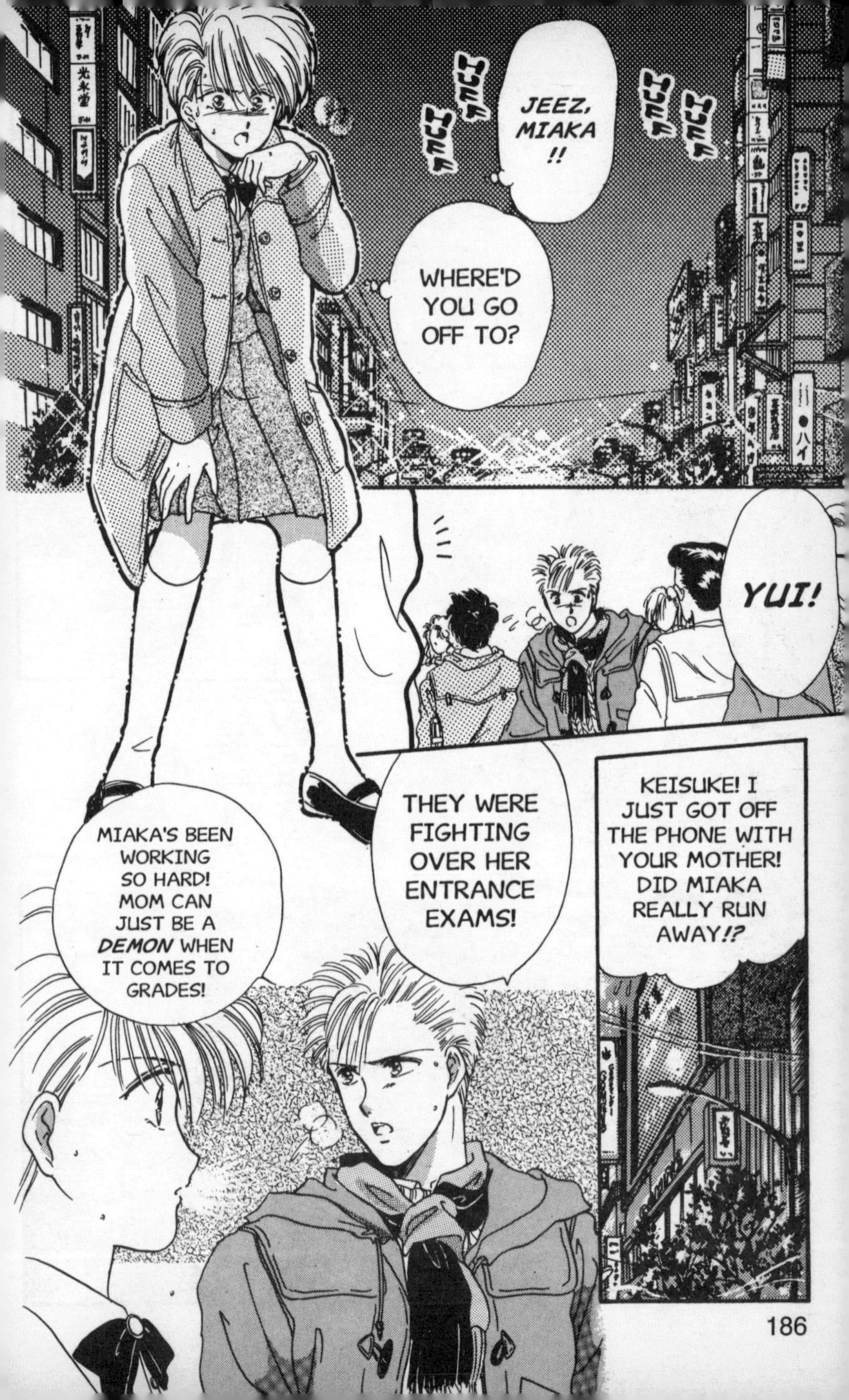
JEEZ, MIAKA !!
HUFF HUFF
HUFF HUFF
WHERE'D YOU GO OFF TO?
YUI!
KEISUKE! I JUST GOT OFF THE PHONE WITH YOUR MOTHER! DID MIAKA REALLY RUN AWAY!?
THEY WERE FIGHTING OVER HER ENTRANCE EXAMS!
MIAKA'S BEEN WORKING SO HARD! MOM CAN JUST BE A *DEMON* WHEN IT COMES TO GRADES!

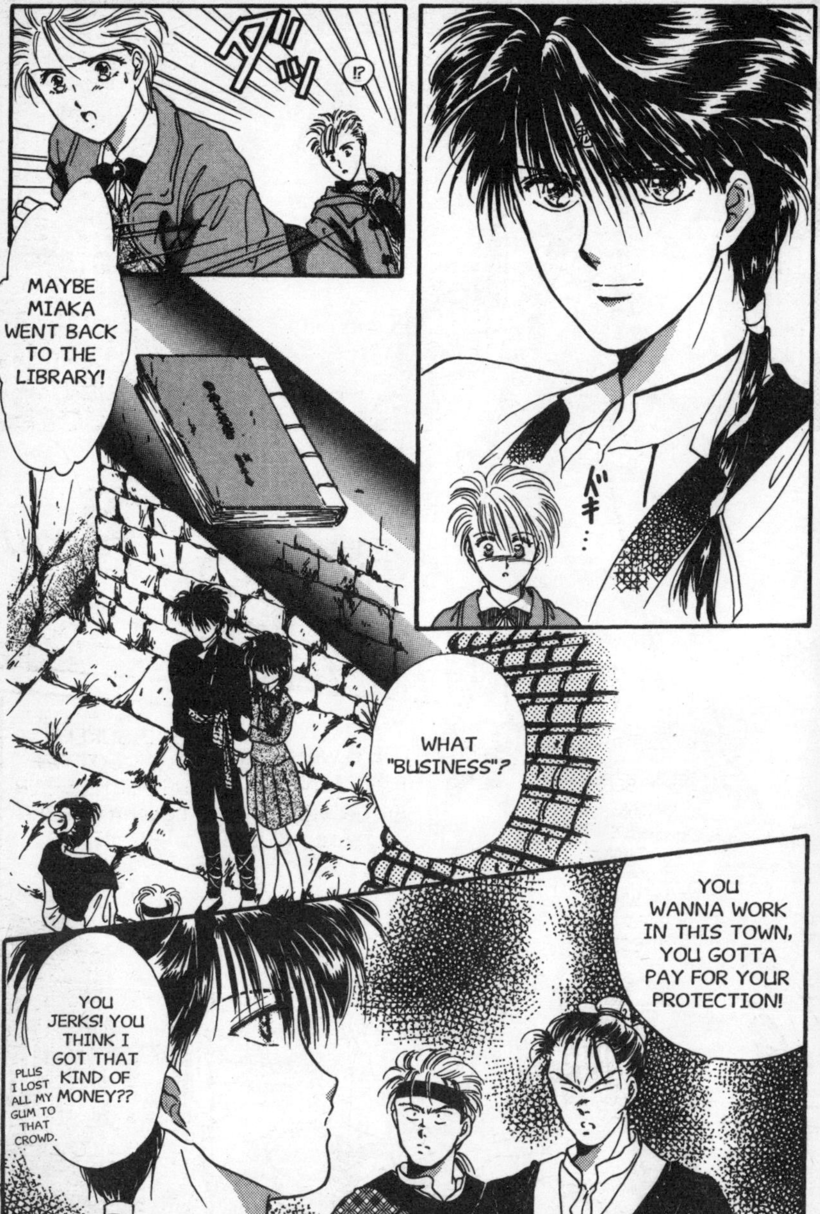

ダッ
!?
MAYBE MIAKA WENT BACK TO THE LIBRARY!
ドキ…
WHAT "BUSINESS"?
YOU WANNA WORK IN THIS TOWN, YOU GOTTA PAY FOR YOUR PROTECTION!
YOU JERKS! YOU THINK I GOT THAT KIND OF MONEY??
PLUS I LOST ALL MY GUM TO THAT CROWD.

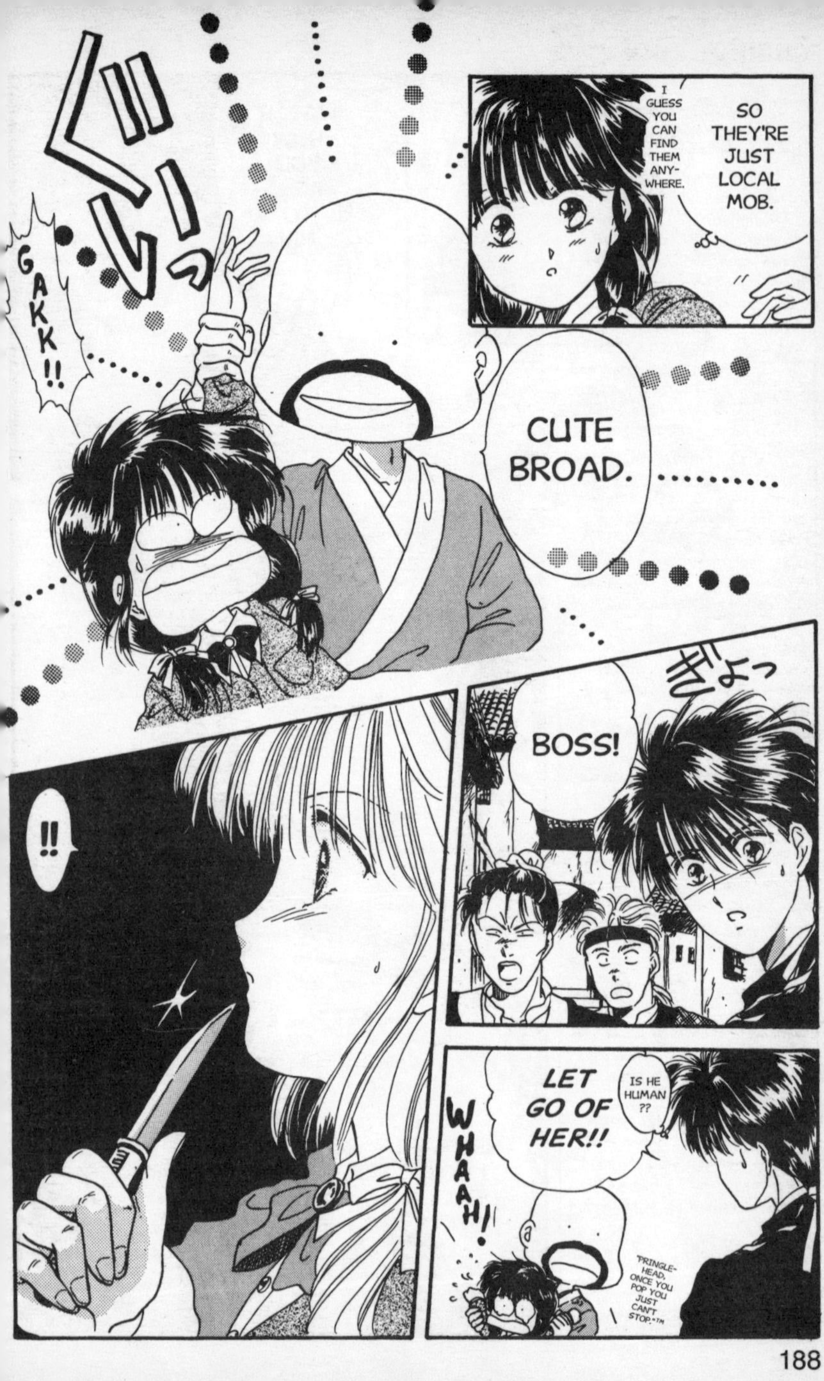
SO THEY'RE JUST LOCAL MOB.
I GUESS YOU CAN FIND THEM ANY-WHERE.
ぐいっ
GAKK!!
CUTE BROAD.
ぎょっ
BOSS!
LET GO OF HER!!
IS HE HUMAN??
WHAAH!
"PRINGLE-HEAD, ONCE YOU POP YOU JUST CAN'T STOP."TM
!!

Oops, my handwriting's getting sloppy again. Now here's something that caught me by surprise! I never thought you guys would like Tamahome with long hair!! When Tamahome's hair was trimmed shorter in this episode, the complaints came rushing in! I thought you'd prefer short hair, but boy was I wrong!! Tama's action scenes are hard to draw with his long hair. Don't worry, I'll never cut Hotohori's hair (My assistants and I call him "Ho-ri"). Apparently, the fans are divided between the Tamahome faction and Hotohori faction. I would never have believed your average junior high (and elementary) school student would be into Hotohori. Surprise! Which one will Miaka choose? I really can't portray a girl who can't decide on the guy she's in love with. I like a girl who's got her mind set on one guy. ♥♥ To say you like both guys equally only means that you aren't really in love with either of them. Although she herself might not even be aware of it. Well, let's not be too judgmental here.

I know I've said that I don't want any official fan club, but there are still people who want to join! Hmm, some people insisted on forming their own club and asked me how to let the entire country know about it. I got an idea! I'll print your address right here so everybody can see it! What do you think??

TA-DAHH.

Just kidding. You'd be so flooded with applications that you'd have a heart attack! (I'm not really that popular, though). Anyway, for your sake I won't mention it. Now, I heard there're people making their own Fushigi Yûgi dojinshi manga. That's okay, but be sure you send them to me too, okay? I'll be waiting to see them.♥

Until we meet again.

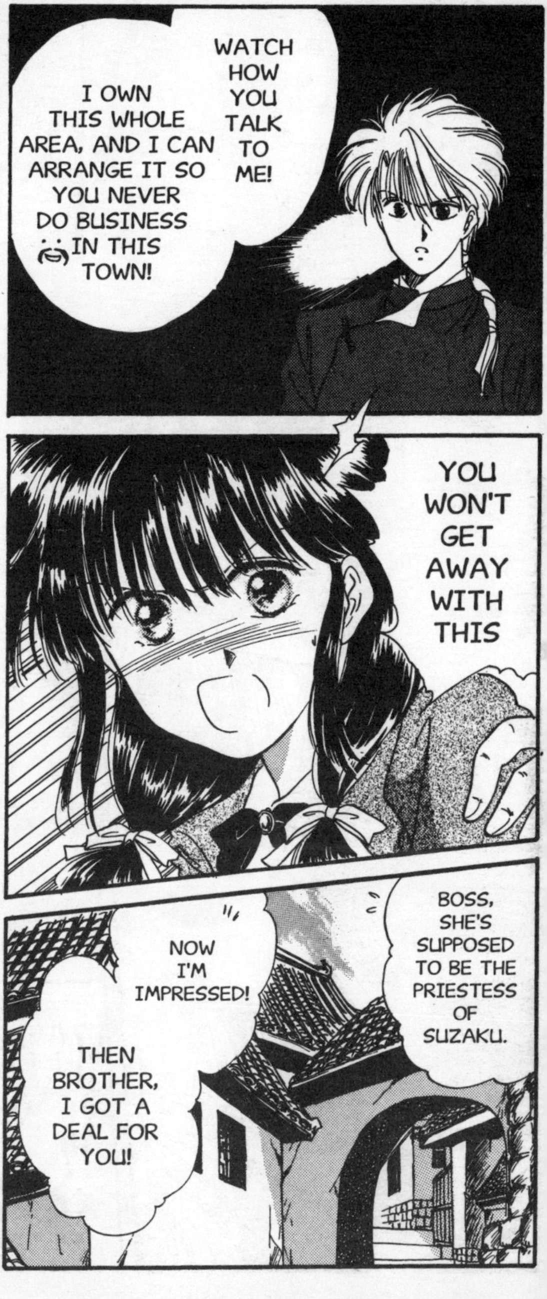
WATCH HOW YOU TALK TO ME!
I OWN THIS WHOLE AREA, AND I CAN ARRANGE IT SO YOU NEVER DO BUSINESS IN THIS TOWN!
YOU WON'T GET AWAY WITH THIS
BOSS, SHE'S SUPPOSED TO BE THE PRIESTESS OF SUZAKU.
NOW I'M IMPRESSED!
THEN BROTHER, I GOT A DEAL FOR YOU!

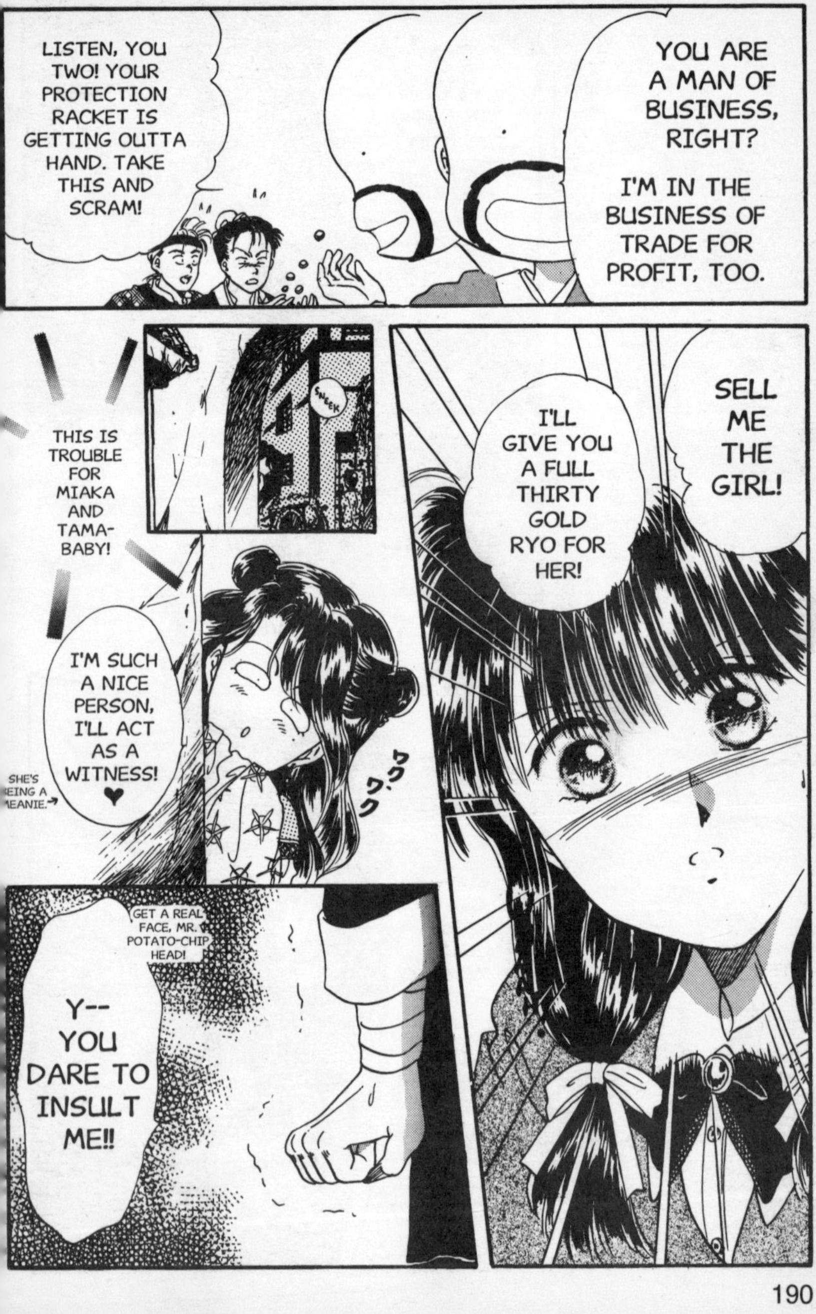
YOU ARE A MAN OF BUSINESS, RIGHT?
I'M IN THE BUSINESS OF TRADE FOR PROFIT, TOO.
LISTEN, YOU TWO! YOUR PROTECTION RACKET IS GETTING OUTTA HAND. TAKE THIS AND SCRAM!
SELL ME THE GIRL!
I'LL GIVE YOU A FULL THIRTY GOLD RYO FOR HER!
SNEEK
THIS IS TROUBLE FOR MIAKA AND TAMA-BABY!
I'M SUCH A NICE PERSON, I'LL ACT AS A WITNESS! ♥
SHE'S BEING A MEANIE.
Y-- YOU DARE TO INSULT ME!!
GET A REAL FACE, MR. POTATO-CHIP HEAD!

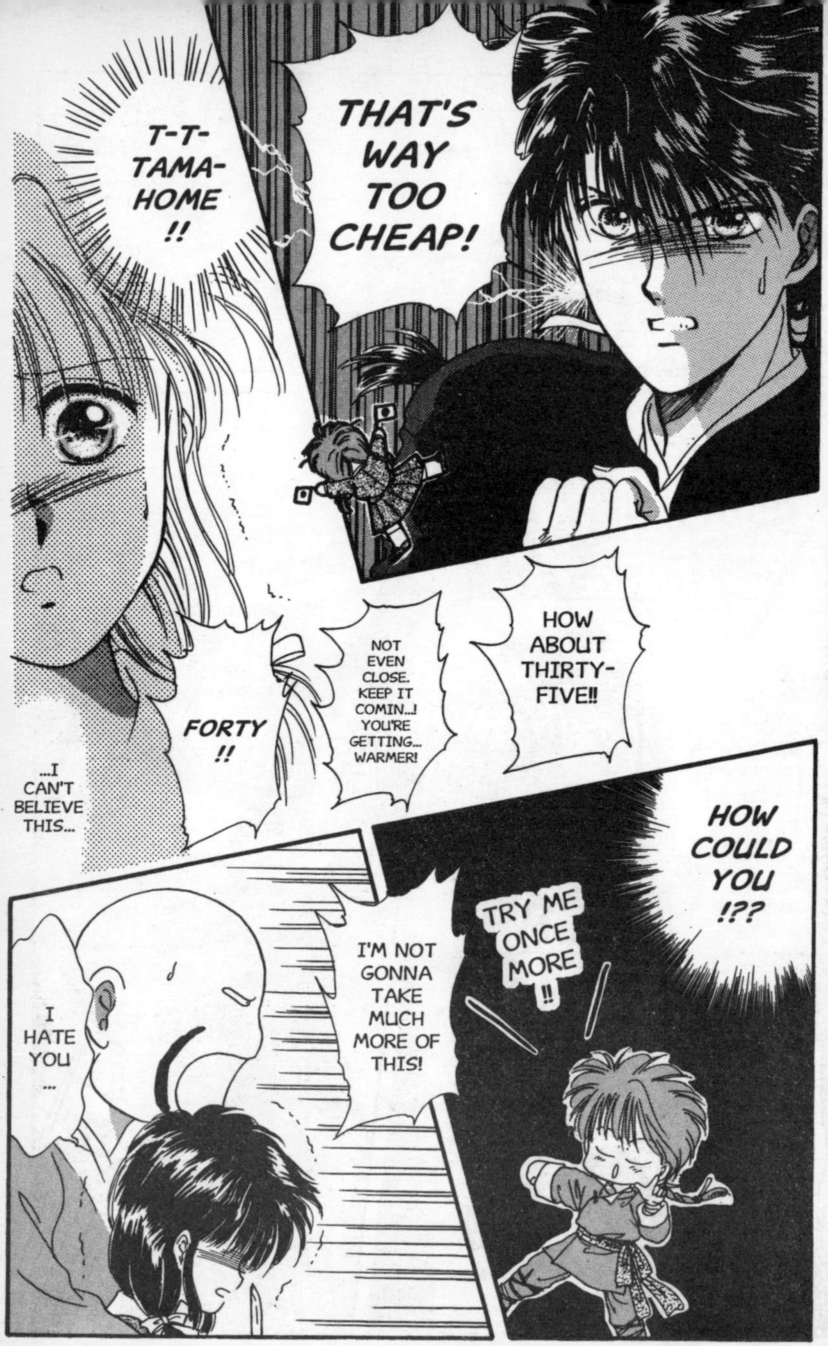
THAT'S WAY TOO CHEAP!
T-T-TAMA-HOME !!
HOW ABOUT THIRTY-FIVE!!
NOT EVEN CLOSE. KEEP IT COMIN...! YOU'RE GETTING... WARMER!
FORTY !!
...I CAN'T BELIEVE THIS...
HOW COULD YOU !??
TRY ME ONCE MORE !!
I'M NOT GONNA TAKE MUCH MORE OF THIS!
I HATE YOU ...

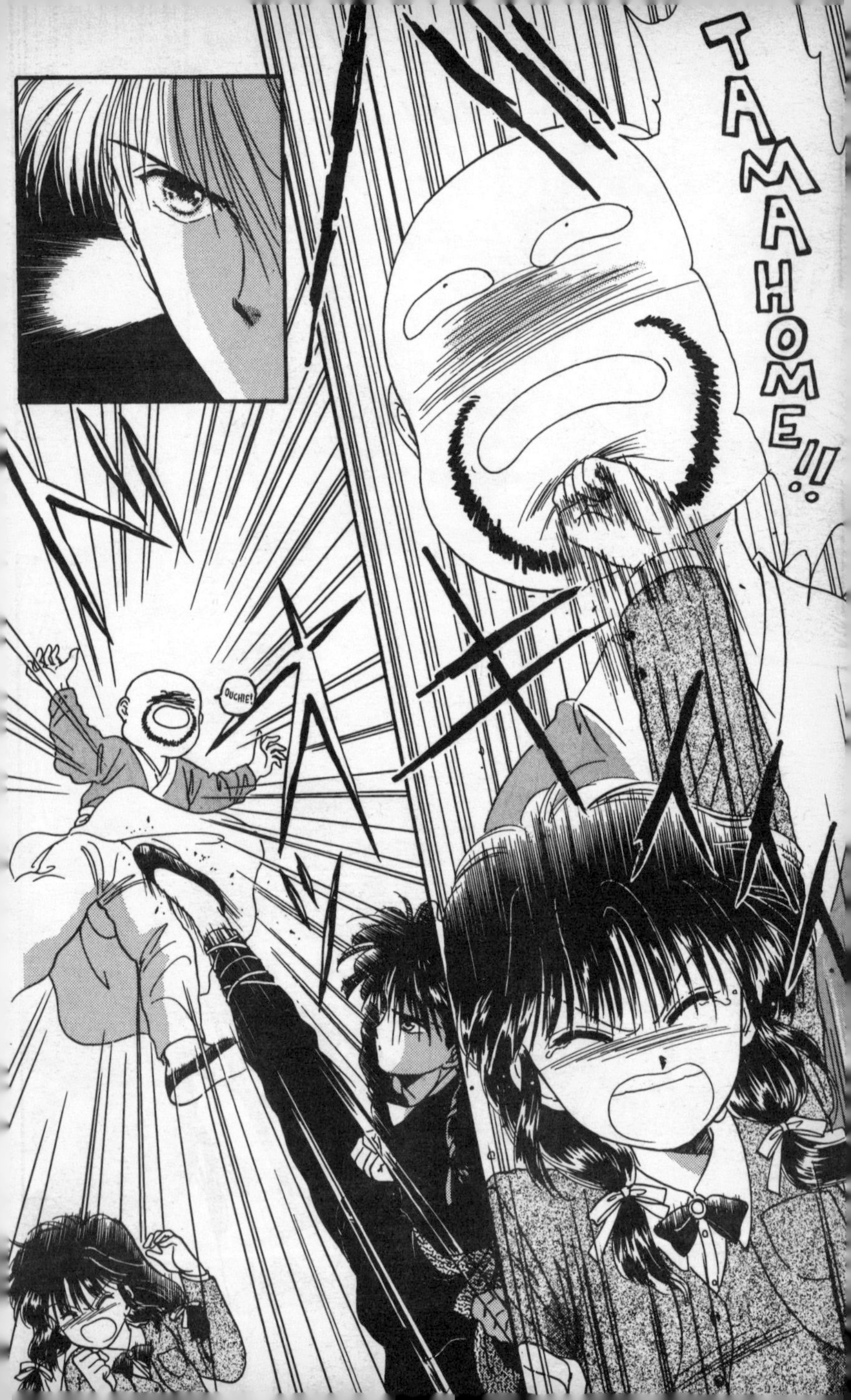
TAMAHOME!!
OUCHIE!

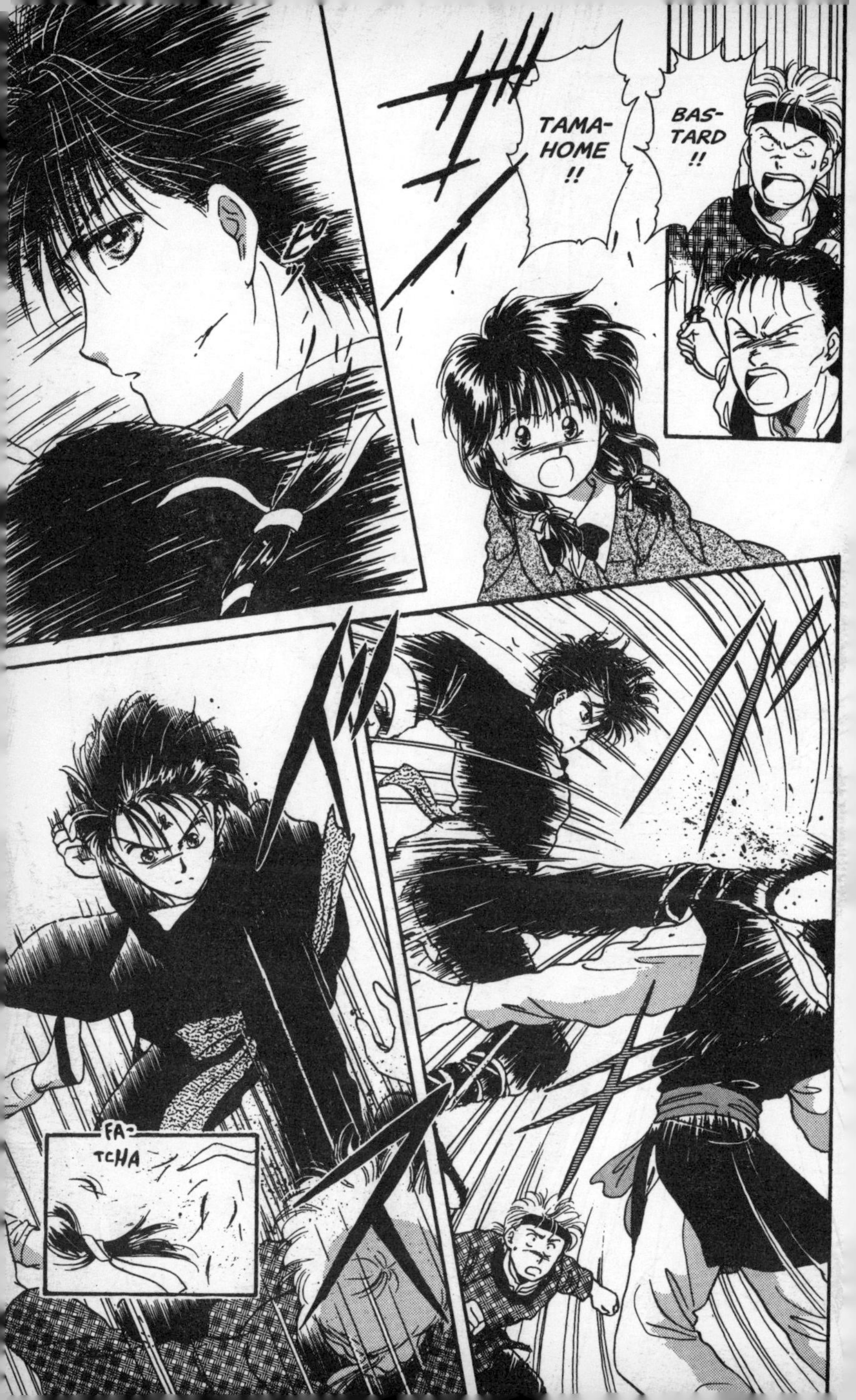
BAS-
TARD
!!
TAMA-
HOME
!!
FA-
TCHA

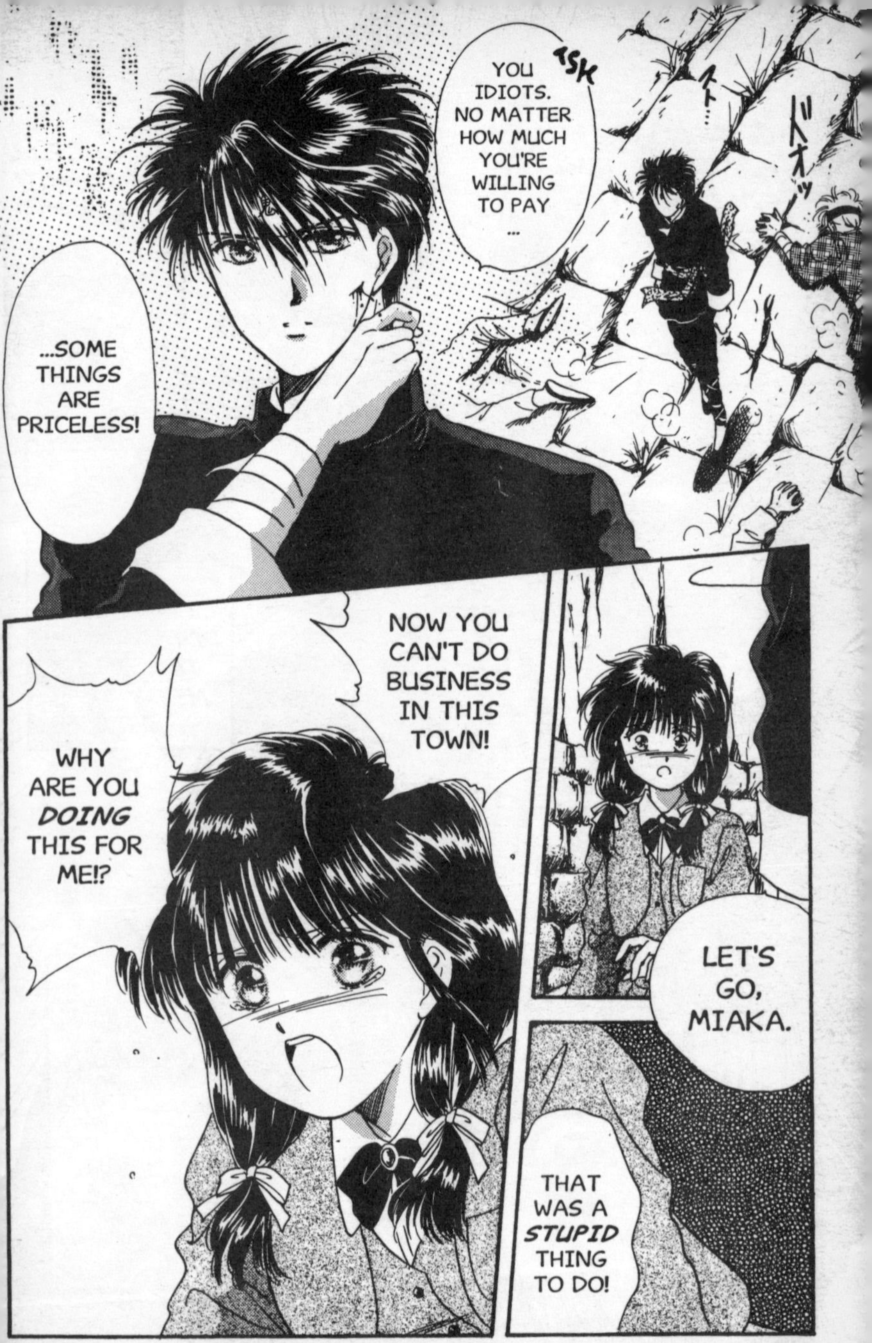
TSK
YOU IDIOTS. NO MATTER HOW MUCH YOU'RE WILLING TO PAY ...
...SOME THINGS ARE PRICELESS!
NOW YOU CAN'T DO BUSINESS IN THIS TOWN!
LET'S GO, MIAKA.
THAT WAS A *STUPID* THING TO DO!
WHY ARE YOU *DOING* THIS FOR ME!?

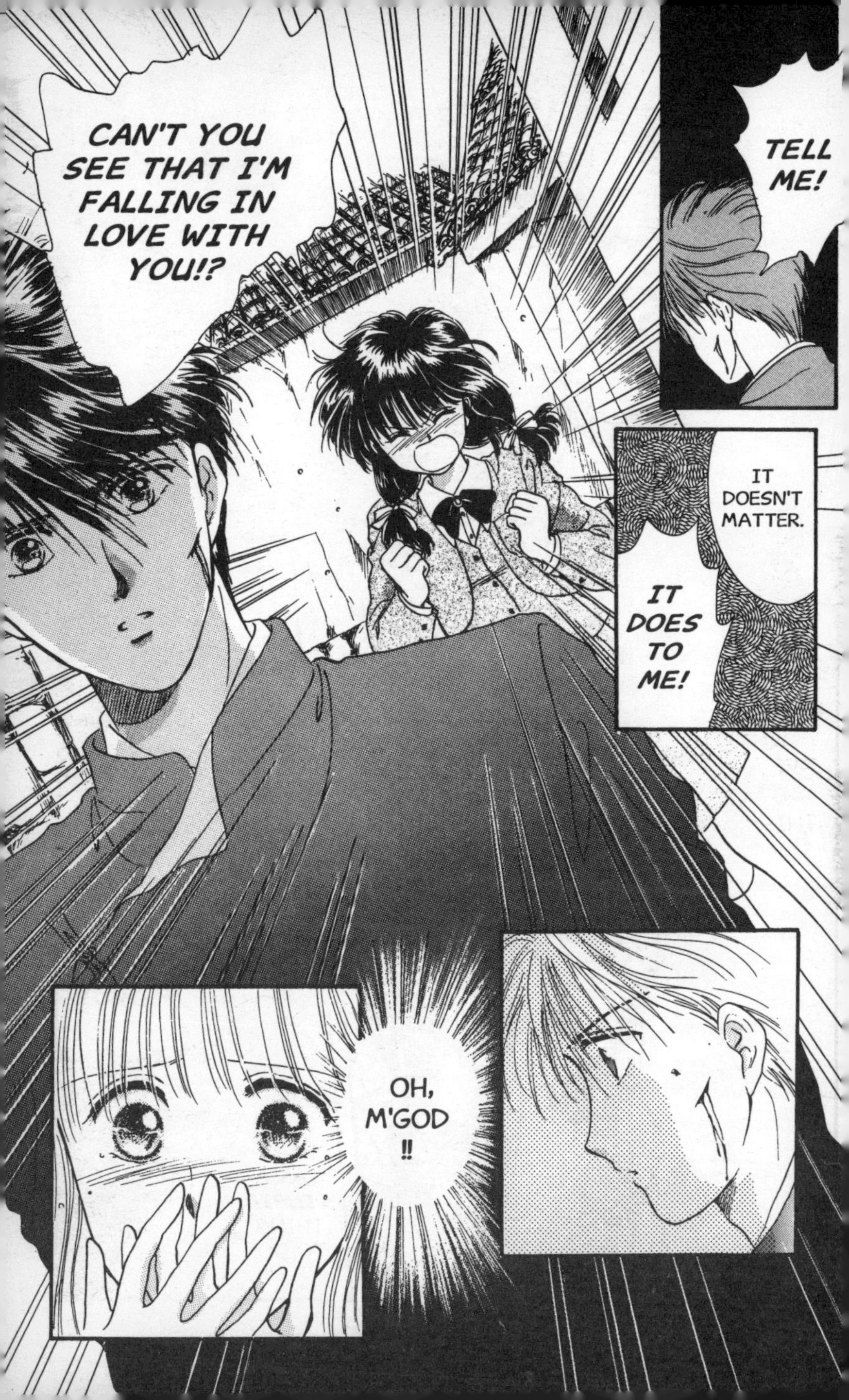
TELL ME!
CAN'T YOU SEE THAT I'M FALLING IN LOVE WITH YOU!?
IT DOESN'T MATTER.
IT DOES TO ME!
OH, M'GOD !!

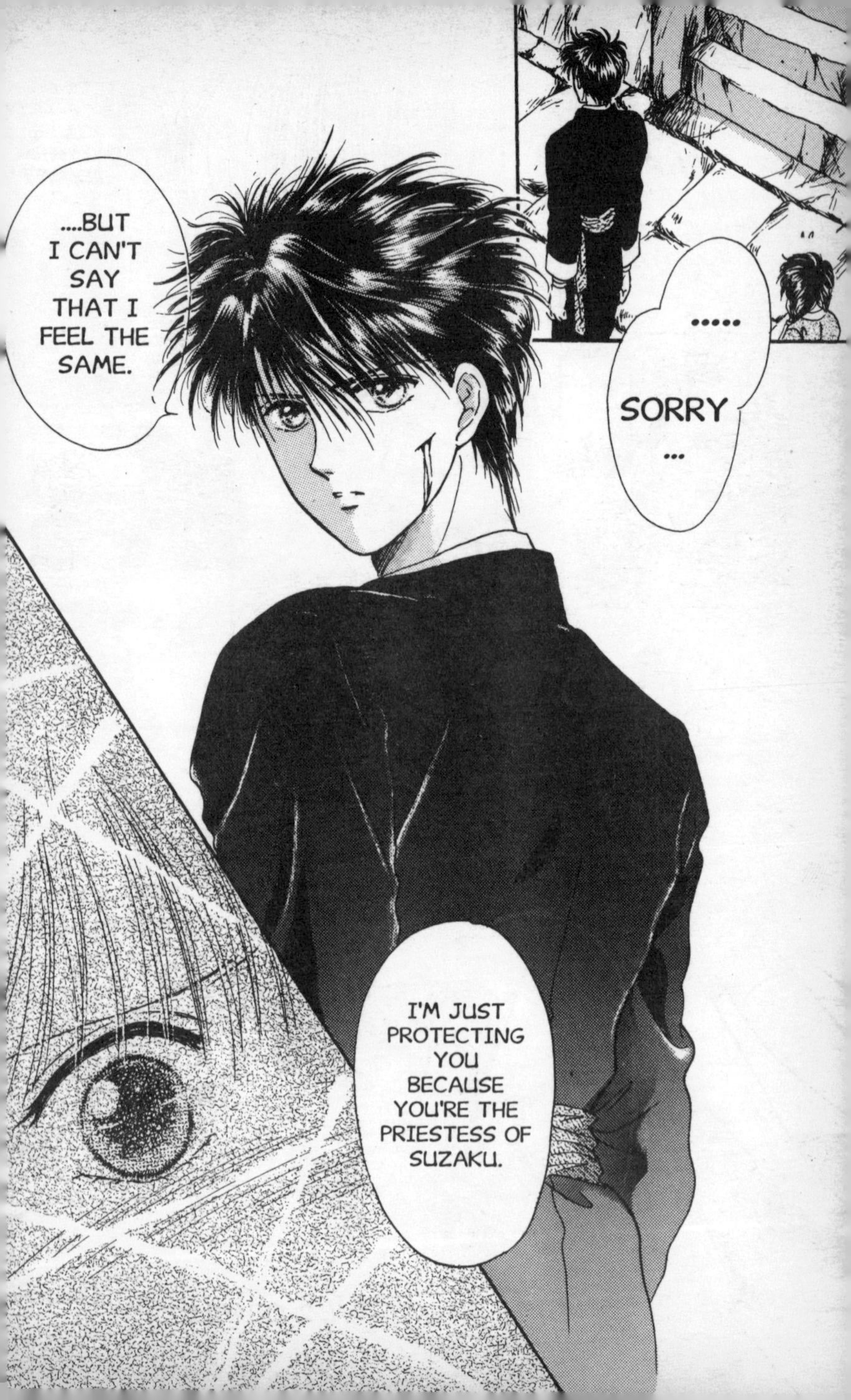
...... SORRY ...
....BUT I CAN'T SAY THAT I FEEL THE SAME.
I'M JUST PROTECTING YOU BECAUSE YOU'RE THE PRIESTESS OF SUZAKU.

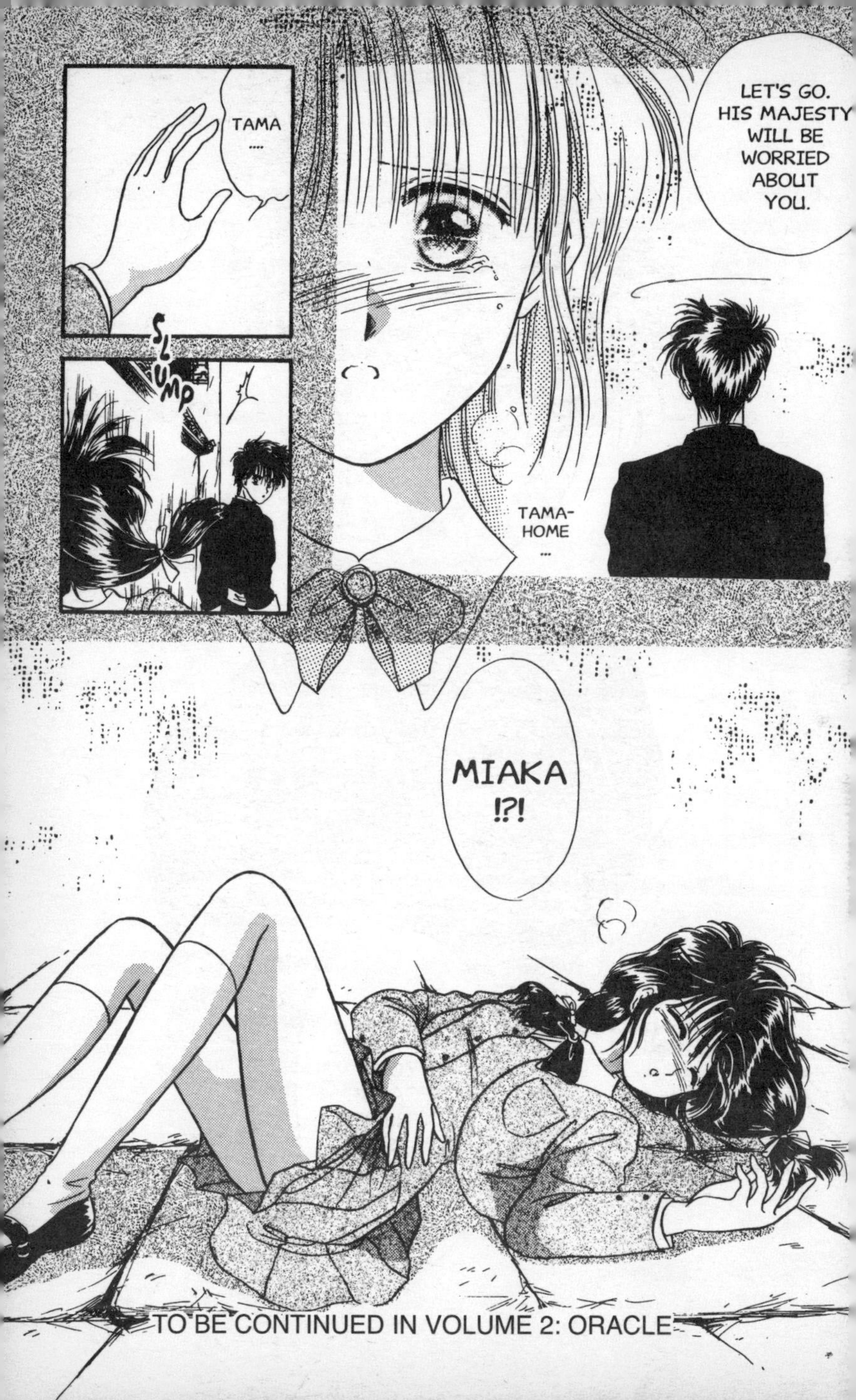
LET'S GO. HIS MAJESTY WILL BE WORRIED ABOUT YOU.
TAMA-HOME ...
TAMA ....
SLUMP
MIAKA !?!

TO BE CONTINUED IN VOLUME 2: ORACLE

The Fushigi Yûgi Guide to Sound Effects

Most of the sound effects in *FUSHIGI YÛGI* are the way Yuu Watase created them, in their original Japanese.

We created this glossary for a page-by-page, panel-by-panel explanation of the action and background noises. By using this guide, you may even learn some Japanese.

The glossary lists the page number then panel. For example, 1.1 would indicate page 1, panel 1.

27.6	FX: ZUZU [earth shaking]
28.1	FX: GULAAAA [tree leaning over]
	FX: MEKI MEKI [tree breaking]
28.2	FX: SHIN [silence]
29.1	FX: BATAN [door slamming open]
31.1	FX: BESHI [slam]
34.2	FX: GILI [gripping hard]
35.2	FX: PAAA [car horn beeping]
36.2	FX: DOKUN DOKUN DOKUN DOKUN DOKUN [ba-dump ba-dump ba-dump ba-dump ba-dump]
	FX: DA [dashing off]
37.1	FX: KON KON [tap tap]
37.3	FX: PATAN [click]
38.1	FX: GUI [yank]
40.1	FX: PAN [smack]
41.3	FX: DON [shove]
42.1	FX: BATAAN [slam]
	FX: ZUZUZU [sliding down wall]
43.3	FX: KYOLO KYOLO [glance glance]
43.4	FX: KII [creak]
43.5	FX: PATAN [door closing softly]
44.2	FX: PETA [plop]
45.2-3	FX: DOKUN DOKUN DOKUN DOKUN DOKUN [ba-dump ba-dump ba-dump ba-dump ba-dump]
46.1	FX: KA [flash of light]
46.3	FX: PINPON PINPON [bell chiming]
	FX: SAWA SAWA [people filing out]
47.1	FX: PALA PALA [flip flip]

CHAPTER ONE:
THE YOUNG LADY OF LEGENDS

10.3	FX: SU [bowl disappearing]
10.4	FX: SU [bowl disappearing]
11.1	FX: GATAN [desk bumping floor]
12.2	FX: DOKA DOKA [whack whack]
12.3	FX: PITA [stopping in place]
13.2	FX: PAPAAA BUOOO [car horns beeping]
13.3	FX: PAAA [car horn beeping]
15.3	FX: KALI KALI [scribble scribble]
16.3	FX: KOLO KOLO KOLO [roll roll roll]
16.4	FX: GII [creak]
17.5	FX: PALA PALA [flip flip]
19.1	FX: DOKA [whack]
19.3	FX: ZUZU [earth quaking]
	FX: ZUZUZUZU [bookshelves and earth shaking]
19.4	FX: BASA BASA BASA [books falling]
20-1.1	FX: BASA [book falling]
20-1.3	FX: BYOOOOOO [wind blowing]
22.1	FX: ELBO [whack]
22.2	FX: APPA [uppercut]
23.3	FX: KULULUN [twirl]
24.1	FX: DON [whump]
	FX: GOHO [coughing]
24.2	FX: DOSA [thud]
	FX: GEHO GEHO [coughing]
24.3	FX: BASHI [smack]
25.1	FX: GILI [gripping hard]
26.1	FX: BAKI [crack]
26.3	FX: FUWA [hair being lightly blown by a breeze]
26.4	FX: FUKI FUKI [wipe wipe]

64.1 FX: TOSA [whump]
64.2 FX: PASHI PASHI [flipping rock in palm]

65.1 FX: SUTO [landing lightly]
65.3 FX: GYU [squeeze]

66.2 FX: PON [pat]
66.3 FX: PA [quickly letting go]
66.5 FX: SUTA SUTA [stomp stomp]
66.6 FX: BITAN [thud]

67.2 FX: SUTA SUTA SUTA [stomp stomp stomp]
FX: TATA [scamper]

69.1 FX: DA [dash]
FX: BUTTOBI [boing]
69.4 FX: TATATA [running]

70.1 FX: GALA GALA [roll roll]
FX: TATA [walking]

71.1 FX: SHU SHU [small objects being thrown fast]
71.2 FX: BON BON [smoke bombs going off]
71.3 FX: BA [whisking away]
71.4 FX: HIHIIIN [horse whinny]
FX: GEHE GAHA [coughing]
FX: SUTA [landing on the ground]
FX: ZAWA ZAWA [crowd talking]

73.3 FX: POU [glow]
73.4 FX: GEHEGEHE GOHOGOHO [hacking, coughing]

74-5.1 FX: KAAAAAAAA [light emanating]
FX: SUU [becoming transparent]
74-5.2 FX: SUU [becoming transparent]
74-5.4 FX: WAAAAAAH [crowd shouting]
FX: KYAAAAA [woman screaming]

76.1 FX: SUUU [appearing]
76.2 FX: SUUU [appearing]
76.4 FX: HISHI [grasping tightly]
76.5 FX: SHIN [silence]

77.5 FX: JAKI [spears being pointed]

CHAPTER THREE:
THE PRIESTESS OF SUZAKU

80.1 FX: GYU [squeeze]
80.3 FX: ZAZA [backing away quickly]

82.3 FX: ZUKIN [stab at heart]
82.5 FX: PEN [slap]

84.2 FX: KASA [putting hand in skirt pocket]

85.4 FX: GASHI [grasp]

CHAPTER TWO:
THE BOY WITH THE DEMON STAR

49.3 FX: SHIN [silence]
49.4 FX: GALA GALA GALA GALA [clip clop clip clop]
49.5 FX: GABA [whoosh]

50.1 FX: GALA GALA GALA GALA [clip clop clip clop]
50.3 FX: ORO ORO [fluster fluster]

51.1 FX: GALA GALA GALA GALA [clip clop clip clop]
51.3 FX: GALA GALA [clop clop]
FX: TON [feet hitting ground]

52.3 FX: ZOLO ZOLO [shuffle shuffle]

53.4 FX: JIRO JIRO [stare stare]

54.1 FX: GUKYULULULU [growling stomach]
54.3 FX: DAAAA [drooling profusely]
54.4 FX: CHALIN [money clinking]

55.1-4 FX: TA TA TA TA TA TA TA [skipping lightly]

56.1 FX: WAAA WAAA [crowd yelling, cheering]
56.2 FX: TEKU TEKU [walking dispiritedly]
56.3 FX: PON [tap]

57.5 FX: ZAWA ZAWA ZAWA [laughing, talking]

58.1 FX: PIKU [ping]
58.2 FX: POLI POLI [crunch crunch]
58.4 FX: SA [swish]
58.5 FX: NIKO [grin]

59.1 FX: SUTA SUTA SUTA SUTA [stomp stomp stomp stomp]
59.3 FX: PIKA [stop]

60.3 FX: PILA [flip]
60.4 FX: PAN [whack]
60.5 FX: JILI JILI [scratch scratch]

61.2 FX: BA [rolling up sleeve]
61.4 FX: DOKOO [whack]

62.1 FX: DOSHEE [shriek]
62.2 FX: DON [thwack]
62.3 FX: DOKA DOKA DOKA [kick kick kick]
62.4 FX: YORO [wobble]
FX: Asia Kong is a pro wrestler in Japan.

63.1 FX: DOTA [thud]
63.2 FX: DAN [wham]
63.3 FX: BATA BATA [struggle struggle]
63.4 FX: SHU [swish]
63.5 FX: BISHI [smack]

114.2   FX: KYU [cuddle]

117.1   FX: SU [pulling shirt aside]

119.5   FX: POKI POKO [cracking knuckles]

120.1   FX: SU [getting into fighting position]
120.3   FX: DOKA GA BISHI [hitting, kicking]

121.1   FX: PITA [stopping suddenly]

123.5   FX: PIKU PIKU [twitch twitch]

124.1   FX: WANA WANA [tremble tremble]
124.2   FX: DON [very angry]
124.3   FX: BUN [punching]
        FX: HYOI [jumping out of the way]
124.4   FX: BAKI [breaking off]
        FX: SUTATATATA [scurry]
        FX: MEKI MEKI MEKI [crack crack crack]
124.5   FX: HAA HAA [pant, gasp]

125.1   FX: DON DOON [objects hitting columns]
125.2   FX: MEKI MEKI [crack crack]

126.2   FX: GALA GALA [crumble crumble]
126.4   FX: ZUDOON [structure imploding]
126.5   FX: PI PI [cha-ching]

127.4   FX: JIWA [blood soaking through skirt]

128.1   FX: ZUKIN [ouch]
128.4   FX: ZAWA ZAWA [murmur murmur]

129.3   FX: GIGIG [column pressing down]

130.2   FX: DOKUN [ba-dump]
130.3   FX: MIKI MIKI MIKI [crack crack crack]

131.3   FX: ZU [massive pressure]
131.4   FX: SU [moving quickly]

132.1   FX: GAKON [moving column]
        FX: HYOI [lifting]
132.2   FX: DOON [thud]
132.3   FX: PON PON PON [toss toss toss]
132.4   FX: GAKON [moving column]

134.2   FX: HELON [faint]
134.4   FX: NI [grin]

136.1   FX: NIKO [grin]

137.1   FX: SUI [whoosh]

CHAPTER FIVE: DANGEROUS LOVE

140.3   FX: BATAN [slam]

85.5   FX: GIII [creak]

86.1   FX: DOKI DOKI DOKI DOKI [ba-dump ba-dump ba-dump ba-dump]

87.4   FX: FULA FULA [stagger stagger]
87.5   FX: KULU [turn]

88.1   FX: SHIIIN [silence]
88.2   FX: FULA FULA [stagger stagger]

90.1   FX: GAAAAAAN [despair]

91.1   FX: NIKO [smile]
        FX: NIKO[smile]
91.3   FX: SUTA SUTA SUTA [stomp stomp stomp]
        FX: SUTO [landing lightly]
91.4   FX: NIKKORI [grin]

93.1   FX: HA [gasp]

94.3   FX: SALA [twinkle]
        FX: DOKI [ba-dump]

95.1   FX: HA [gasp]
95.4   FX: GA [whack]
95.5   FX: ZA [rushing out of bushes]

96.3   FX: GA [grab]
96.4   FX: DOGA [thwack]
96.5   FX: DOSA [konk]

97.1   FX: SU [symbol appearing on forehead]

98.1   FX: ZAZA [soldiers saluting]

101.5   FX: DOKUN DOKUN DOKUN DOKUN [ba-dump ba-dump ba-dump ba-dump]

103.3   FX: ZAWA [murmuring]

104.2   FX: ZA [bowing]

106.2   FX: KACHA KACHA [jiggling doorknob]
        FX: KOTSU KOTSU [shuffle shuffle]
106.5   FX: PALA PALA [flip flip]

107.2   FX: PATAN [whud]
107.4   FX: HETA [slump]

CHAPTER FOUR: THE SEVEN CONSTELLATIONS OF SUZAKU

109.1   FX: PAPAAA [car horns beeping]
109.2   FX: HA HA [huff huff]
109.3   FX: TATA [running]

112.4   FX: KON [thonk]

164.5 FX: PAN [smack]

166.2 FX: DOKI [ba-dump]
166.3 FX: HYOI [lowering head]

167.4 FX: GUI [tug]

CHAPTER SIX: HIDDEN LOVE

170.1-2 FX: DOKUN DOKUN DOKUN DOKUN
DOKUN DOKUN DOKUN DOKUN
[ba-dump ba-dump ba-dump ba-dump
ba-dump ba-dump ba-dump ba-dump]

171.1 FX: DOKIN [ba-dump]
171.4 FX: SU [moving quickly and quietly]

172.1 FX: SUTA SUTA SUTA [walking briskly]
172.2 FX: SU [drawing sword]
172.3 FX: HYU HYU HYU HYU [slice slice slice slice]
172.4 FX: PISHI PISHI [crack crack]
172.5 FX: BALA BALA [crumble]

173.6 FX: SUI [pang]

174.1 FX: PATA PATA [pitter patter]
174.2 FX: SU [grab]

176.4 FX: SU [walking by]

177.2 FX: SUTA SUTA [stomp stomp]
177.5 FX: ZUOOOOO [anger]

178.1 FX: ZUGOGOGOGO [anger]

179.4 FX: TON [stepping onto platform]

181.4 FX: GUI [whack]

182.2 FX: SHIIIIIN [silence]

184.1 FX: GYU GYU [squash squish]

187.1 FX: DOKI [ba-dump]
187.2 FX: DA [running]

188.2 FX: GUI [grab]
188.3 FX: GYO [shock]

192.1 FX: BAKI [thwack]
192.3 FX: DO [kick]

193.2 FX: ZAN [moving quickly]
193.3 FX: PI [snip]
193.4 FX: BAKI [thwack]
193.5 FX: DOSU [whud]

194.1 FX: SUTO [landing lightly on feet]

141.1 FX: JAAA [running water]
FX: GOSHI GOSHI [scrub scrub]
141.2-3 FX: SU [stain vanishing]

142.2 FX: ZUKI [ouch]
142.5 FX: DOTATATA [stomp]

143.1 FX: BAM [slam]
143.3 FX: SHULULU [sash being flung]

144.2 FX: BATAN [slam]
FX: HOHOHOHO [ha ha ha ha]

146.1 FX: HYOI [lifting hair]
146.2 FX: BISHA [splash]
146.6 FX: GAN [gonk]

148.1 FX: GAN [gonk]
148.2 FX: GYUU GYULULUUU [stomach growling]

150.2 FX: GUI [yank]
150.4 FX: DOKIN [ba-dump]

151.3 FX: JI [stare]
151.4 FX: PUPU [heh heh]

156.2 FX: ZA [wind rustling through trees]
156.3 FX: HYOKO HYOKO [limp limp]

157.1 FX: BULU [shiver]
FX: HYOKO [limp]
157.2 FX: BASA BASA [birds flapping wings]
157.3 FX: SHULU [tendril whipping out]
FX: ZAZA [drag]
157.4 FX: ZU [yank]

158.1 FX: PATAN [door closing quietly]
158.2 FX: BISHU [splash]
158.3 FX: POTA POTA [drip drip]

159.3 FX: GABO GABO GABO [gurgling underwater]
FX: GOBO [coughing underwater]
159.4 FX: JIWA [bandages loosening]

160.3 FX: TOTATATA [running]
160.4 FX: ZA [turn]

161.1 FX: BAN [wham]
161.2 FX: GUI [yank]
161.5 FX: BUCHI [snap]

162.2 FX: GA [grab]
162.5 FX: GYUU [clutch]

163.2 FX: POTA POTA [drip drip]
163.3 FX: HYOKO HYOKO [hobble hobble]

164.4 FX: PAN [smack]

ALSO AVAILABLE FROM GOLLANCZ MANGA

Miaka Yûki is an ordinary junior-high-school student who is transported into the world of a book, THE UNIVERSE OF THE FOUR GODS.

Exhausted by her adventures, she must go back to the real world, but the only one who can send her is the mysterious Oracle of Suzaku, Tai Yi-Jun.

find out more at www.orionbooks.co.uk

COMING SOON FROM GOLLANCZ MANGA

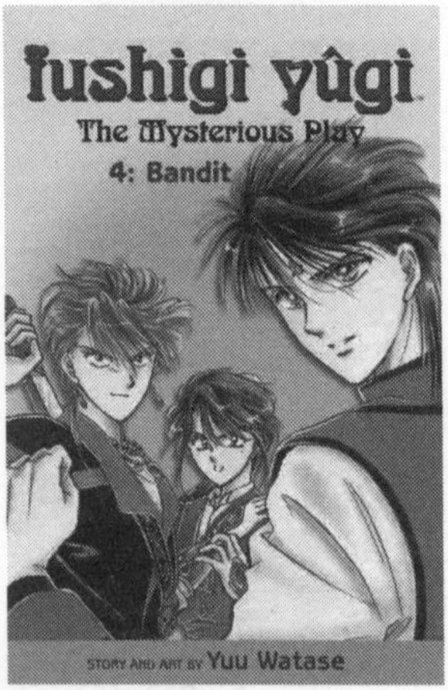
fushigi yûgi
The Mysterious Play
4: Bandit
STORY AND ART BY Yuu Watase

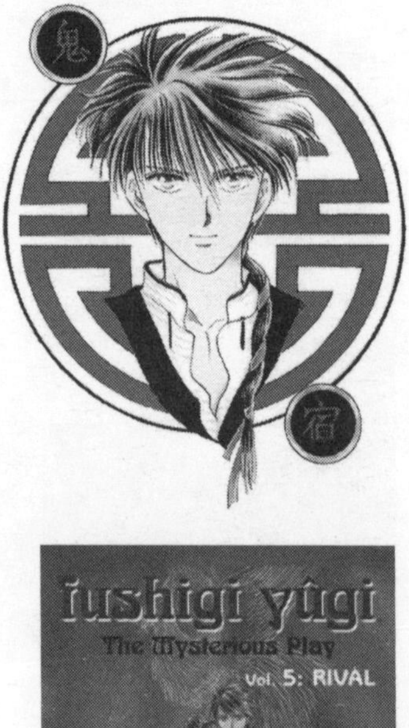

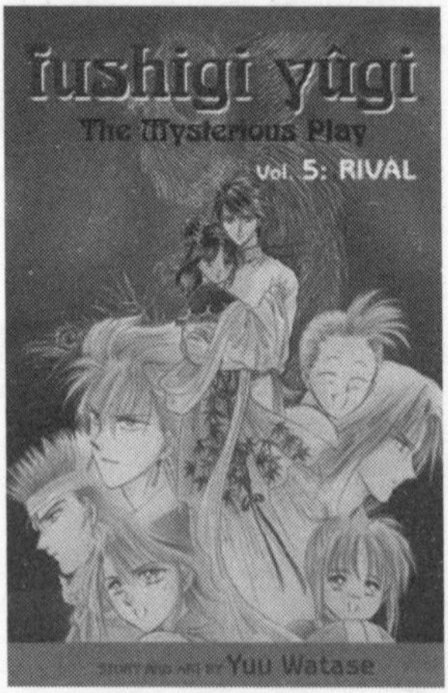
fushigi yûgi
The Mysterious Play
Vol. 5: RIVAL
STORY AND ART BY Yuu Watase

The magical country of Hong-Nan is in Miaka's hands, and to save it – and her true love, Tamahome – she must face bitter rivals, vicious enemies, and even death itself . . .

GOLLANCZ MANGA

find out more at www.orionbooks.co.uk

COMPLETE OUR SURVEY AND
LET US KNOW WHAT YOU THINK!

❑ Please do NOT send me information about Gollancz Manga, or other Orion title, products, news and events, special offers or other information

Name: _____

Address: _____

Town: _____ County: _____ Postcode: _____

❑ Male ❑ Female   Date of Birth (dd/mm/yyyy): ___ / ___ / _____
                   (under 13? Parental consent required)

What race/ethnicity do you consider yourself? (please check one)

❑ Asian   ❑ Black   ❑ Hispanic

❑ White/Caucasian   ❑ Other: _____

Which Gollancz Manga title did you purchase?
❑ Case Closed Vol 1   ❑ Case Closed Vol 2   ❑ Dragon Ball Vol 1
❑ Dragon Ball Vol 2   ❑ Fushigi Yûgi Vol 1   ❑ Fushigi Yûgi Vol 2
❑ Yu-Gi-Oh! Vol 1   ❑ Yu-Gi-Oh! Vol 2

What other Gollancz Manga do you own?
❑ Case Closed Vol 1   ❑ Case Closed Vol 2   ❑ Dragon Ball Vol 1
❑ Dragon Ball Vol 2   ❑ Fushigi Yûgi Vol 1   ❑ Fushigi Yûgi Vol 2
❑ Yu-Gi-Oh! Vol 1   ❑ Yu-Gi-Oh! Vol 2

How many anime and/or manga titles have you purchased in the last year?
How many were Gollancz Manga titles?

Anime	Manga	GM
❑ None	❑ None	❑ None
❑ 1-4	❑ 1-4	❑ 1-4
❑ 5-10	❑ 5-10	❑ 5-10
❑ 11+	❑ 11+	❑ 11+

Reason for purchase: (check all that apply)

- ❑ Special Offer ❑ Favourite title ❑ Gift
- ❑ In store promotion If so please indicate which store: ______________________
- ❑ Recommendation ❑ Other ______________________

Where did you make your purchase?

- ❑ Bookshop ❑ Comic Shop ❑ Music Store
- ❑ Newsagent ❑ Video Game Store ❑ Supermarket
- ❑ Other: ____________ ❑ Online: ______________________

What kind of manga would you like to read?

- ❑ Adventure ❑ Comic Strip ❑ Fantasy
- ❑ Fighting ❑ Horror ❑ Mystery
- ❑ Romance ❑ Science Fiction ❑ Sports
- ❑ Other: ______________________

Which do you prefer?

- ❑ Sound effects in English
- ❑ Sound effects in Japanese with English captions
- ❑ Sound effects in Japanese only with a glossary at the back

Want to find out more about Manga?

Look us up at www.orionbooks.co.uk, or www.viz.com

THANK YOU!

Please send the completed form to:

Manga Survey
Orion Books
Orion House
5 Upper St Martin's Lane
London, WC2H 9EA

All information provided will be used for internal purposes only.
We promise not to sell or otherwise divulge your details.

NO PURCHASE NECESSARY. Requests not in compliance with all terms of this form will not be acknowledged or returned. All submissions are subject to verification and become property of Gollancz Manga.